WITHDRAWN

LINGUISTIC EVOLUTION THROUGH LANGUAGE ACQUISITION

This is a new and groundbreaking study of how children acquire language and how this affects language change over the generations.

Written by an international team of experts, the volume proceeds from the basis that we should address not only the language faculty *per se* within the framework of evolutionary theory, but also the origins and subsequent development of languages themselves; languages evolve via cultural rather than biological transmission on a historical rather than genetic timescale. The book is distinctive in utilizing computational simulation and modeling to help ensure that the theories constructed are complete and precise.

Drawing on a wide range of examples, the book covers the why and how of specific syntactic universals, the nature of syntactic change, the language-learning mechanisms needed to acquire an existing linguistic system accurately and to impose further structure on an emerging system, and the evolution of language(s) in relation to this learning mechanism.

TED BRISCOE is Lecturer in the Computer Laboratory at the University of Cambridge. His research interests include computational and theoretical linguistics, and automated speech and language processing. He has published around fifty research articles.

LINGUISTIC EVOLUTION THROUGH LANGUAGE ACQUISITION

EDITED BY

TED BRISCOE

University of Cambridge

PUBLISHED BY THE PRESS SYNDICATE OF THE UNIVERSITY OF CAMBRIDGE
The Pitt Building, Trumpington Street, Cambridge, United Kingdom

CAMBRIDGE UNIVERSITY PRESS
The Edinburgh Building, Cambridge CB2 2RU, UK
40 West 20th Street, New York, NY 10011-4211, USA
477 Williamstown Road, Port Melbounre, VIC 3207, Australia
Ruiz de Alarcón 13, 28014 Madrid, Spain
Dock House, The Waterfront, Cape Town 8001, South Africa

http://www.cambridge.org

First published 2002

Printed in the United Kingdom at the University Press, Cambridge

Typeface Baskerville 11 / 12.5 pt   *System* LaTeX 2$_\varepsilon$ [TB]

A catalogue record for this book is available from the British Library

ISBN 0 521 66299 0 hardback

Contents

v

Contributors

JOHN BATALI Department of Cognitive Science, University of California at San Diego

TED BRISCOE Natural Language and Information Processing Group, Computer Laboratory, University of Cambridge

JAMES R. HURFORD Department of Linguistics, University of Edinburgh

SIMON KIRBY Department of Linguistics, University of Edinburgh

PARTHA NIYOGI Department of Computer Science, University of Chicago

MICHAEL OLIPHANT Department of Linguistics, University of Edinburgh

LUC STEELS SONY Computer Science Laboratory, Paris

WILLIAM J. TURKEL Department of Brain and Cognitive Sciences, MIT

ROBERT WORDEN Charteris Consultants, London

1

Introduction

Ted Briscoe
Natural Language and Information
Processing Group, Computer Laboratory,
University of Cambridge

1.1 Linguistic theory and evolutionary theory

Taking an evolutionary perspective on the origins and development of human language, and on linguistic variation and change, is becoming more and more common, as the papers in Hurford *et al.*(1998) attest. The term 'evolution' now crops up regularly in work emerging from the broadly generative tradition in linguistic theory (e.g. Jackendoff, 1997; Steedman, 2000). The latter development is probably a more or less direct consequence of several influential attempts to reconcile Chomskyan nativism with evolutionary theory, primarily in terms of a gradualist and adaptionist account of the origins and development of the language faculty (e.g. Hurford, 1989; Newmeyer, 1991; Pinker and Bloom, 1990). However, most of the contributions to this book owe more to the complementary but very different insight (e.g. Hurford, 1987, 1999) that not only the language faculty *per se*, but also the origins and subsequent development of *languages themselves* can be fruitfully addressed within the framework of evolutionary theory. Under this view, languages are evolving, not metaphorically but literally, via cultural rather than biological transmission on a historical rather than genetic timescale. This represents a very distinct and quite narrow theme within the broader program of integrating linguistic theory and evolutionary theory, and it is this theme which is primarily addressed by the contributors to this volume.

Evolutionary ideas have had a rather checkered history within linguistic theory despite their close mutual influence in the nineteenth century. McMahon (1994:ch12) provides a brief account of this history and also discusses linguistic work influenced by evolutionary theory during the fifties and sixties. However, the insight that languages *per se* can be studied as (culturally) evolving systems, post the modern synthesis in biology and post mathematical and computational work on dynamical systems, does not seem to have reemerged until the eighties when Lindblom (1986) in phonology, Keller (1984, (1994)) in historical linguistics, and Hurford (1987) in syntactic theory independently articulated this view (using somewhat different terminology). The idea is an instance of the 'universal Darwinist' claim (Dawkins, 1983; Dennett, 1995:343f) that the methodology of evolutionary theory is applicable whenever any dynamical system exhibits (random) variation, selection amongst variants, and thus differential inheritance. In the nineties, this perspective on languages has been espoused enthusiastically and persuasively by non-linguists (e.g. Cziko, 1995; Deacon, 1997). However, it has not had significant impact in mainstream linguistic theory as yet, perhaps partly because work has only recently begun to address questions seen as central to (generative) linguistic theory.

The contributions to this volume are less concerned with questions of linguistic origins or the development of a broad evolutionary account of human language, than with why and how specific syntactic universals evolved (Kirby, Batali, Briscoe), why homonymy and synonymy are present and maintained in vocabulary systems (Steels and Kaplan), the nature of (E-) language syntactic change (Niyogi, Briscoe), the kind of language learning mechanism required to not only acquire an existing linguistic system accurately but also impose further structure on an emerging system (Oliphant, Kirby, Worden), and the (co)evolution of language(s) and this learning mechanism (Turkel, Briscoe). A second and equally important way in which the contributions here represent a tightly circumscribed theme within evolutionary linguistic work is that all utilize a methodology of computational implementation and simulation of (more or less explicit) formal models. For this reason too, there is a close connection with formal generative linguistic theory. Mathematical modeling and/or computational simulation help ensure that theories constructed are complete and precise, and also help with their evaluation by making the assumptions on which they rest fully explicit. This is particularly critical in the context of largely speculative accounts of the prehistoric development of human languages, as without such a methodology there is little to constrain such speculation.

The rest of this introduction describes the key ideas and techniques which underlie the contributions to this book, and, more broadly, the evolutionary approach to linguistic variation, change and development, relating them to current linguistic theory and discussing critical methodological issues. The contribution by Hurford contains a thorough and insightful analysis and comparison of five different computational models of linguistic evolution, two of which are described here (Batali, Kirby), as well as developing a more general framework for such comparisons that could, in principle, be applied to all the work presented here. Therefore, I limit myself here to additional, I hope complementary, remarks and refer the reader to Hurford's contribution for a much more detailed exposition of the general structure of many of the models.

1.2 The formal framework

1.2.1 Generative linguistics

Chomsky (1965) defined grammatical competence in terms of the language of (i.e. stringset generated by) an ideal speaker-hearer at a single instant in time, abstracting away from working memory limitations, errors of performance, and so forth. The generative research program has been very successful, but, one legacy of the idealization to a single speaker at a single instant has been the relative sidelining of language variation, change and development. More recently, Chomsky (1986) has argued that generative linguistics can offer a precise characterization of I-language, the internalized language or grammar of an individual speaker, but has little to say about E-language, 'external' language, which is an epiphenomenon of the I-languages of the individual speakers who comprise a speech community.

Consequently, the study of language change within the generative tradition has largely focused on 'I-language change'; that is, the differences between I-languages or their corresponding grammars internalized by child language learners across generations. And within I-language change on the (parametric) properties of internalized grammars (e.g. Lightfoot, 1979, 1999). The generative approach to language change treats (major) grammatical change as a consequence of children acquiring different grammars from those predominant amongst the adults in the population, perhaps as a consequence of variation in the internalized grammars of these adults. However, theories of language variation, change and development will (minimally) require an account of how the E-language(s) of an adult population can be defined in terms of the aggregate output of these (changing) individuals.

1.2.2 Language agents

A language agent is a idealized model of just what is essential to understanding an individual's linguistic behavior. I use the term 'agent', in common with several contributors to this volume and with (one) current usage in computer science and artificial intelligence, to emphasize that agents are artificial, autonomous, rational and volitional, and that agents are embedded in a decentralized, distributed system, i.e. a speech community.

A language agent must minimally be able to learn, produce and interpret a language, usually defined as a well-formed set of strings with an associated representation of meaning, by acquiring and using linguistic knowledge according to precisely specified procedures. Beyond this, the models of language agents deployed by the contributors differ substantially, depending on theoretical orientation and the precise questions being addressed. Oliphant, and Steels and Kaplan define linguistic knowledge entirely in terms of word–meaning associations in a lexicon, reflecting their focus on the acquisition of vocabulary. Niyogi, Turkel and Briscoe focus on the acquisition of parametrically-defined generative grammars and thus define linguistic knowledge primarily in terms of (sets of) parameter settings. Batali, Kirby and Worden all develop broadly lexicalist models of linguistic knowledge, in which the acquisition of lexical and grammatical knowledge is closely integrated.

All the models provide some account of the acquisition, comprehension and production of (I-) language. Again the details vary considerably depending on the theoretical orientation and questions being addressed. For example Niyogi and Turkel largely assume very idealized, simple accounts of parameter setting in order to focus on the dynamics of E-language change and the genetic assimilation of grammatical information, respectively. The other contributors concentrate on specifying acquisition procedures in some detail, since properties of the acquisition procedure are at the heart of linguistic inheritance and selection. As acquisition is closely bound up with comprehension, most of these contributors also develop detailed accounts of aspects of the comprehension, or at least parsing, of linguistic input. However, none really provide a detailed account of language production, beyond the minimal assumption that linguistic utterances are generated randomly from a usually uniform distribution over the strings licensed by an agent's grammar and/or lexicon.

Additionally, language agents can have further properties, such as the ability to invent elements of language, the ability to reproduce further language agents, an age determining the learning period and/or their 'death', and so forth. For example, the contributors on the development of language or emergence of new traits, often endow their language agents with the ability to 'invent' language in the form of new utterance–meaning pairs, where the utterance can either be essentially an unanalysed atom ('word') or a string with grammatical structure ('sentence'). Invention is again modeled very minimally as a (rare) random process within a predefined space of possibilities, and is one method of providing the variation essential to an evolutionary model of linguistic change and/or development.

1.2.3 Languages as dynamical systems

E-languages are the aggregate output of a population of language users. Such a population constitutes a speech community if the internalized grammars of the users are 'close' enough to support mutual comprehension most of the time. Membership of the population/speech community changes over time as people are born, die or migrate.

Perhaps the simplest model which approximates this scenario is one in which the population initially consists of a fixed number of 'adult' language agents with predefined internalized grammars, and their output constitutes the data from which the next generation of 'child' language learning agents acquires new internalized grammars. Once the learning agents have acquired grammars, this new generation replaces the previous one and becomes the adult generation defining the input for the next generation of learners, and so on. We can define a dynamical model of this form quite straightforwardly. A dynamical system is just a system which changes over time. We represent it by a sequence of states where each state encodes the system properties at each time step and an update rule defines how state s^{t+1} can be derived from state s^t:

$$s^{t+1} = Update(s^t)$$

Time steps in this model correspond to successive non-overlapping generations in the population. Minimally, states must represent the E-language(s) of the current generation of language agents, defining the input for the next generation of learners. The *Update* rule must specify how the internalized grammars of the learners are derived from the E-language input.

Niyogi and Berwick (1997) develop a deterministic version of this model in which each state is defined by a probability distribution over triggers, a finite subset of unembedded sentences from each language defined by each internalized grammar present in the population. The deterministic update rule defines a new probability distribution on triggers by calculating the proportions of the population which will acquire the internalized grammars exemplified in the input data. In this volume, Niyogi describes this model in detail and develops it by exploring the predictions of deterministic update rules which assume that different learners will receive different input depending on their parents or on their geographical location. Niyogi shows how this model makes predictions about the direction and timecourse of E-language change dependent on the learning algorithm and the precise form of the update rule. Throughout, E-language change is modeled as a consequence of a number of 'instantaneous' I-language changes across generations, in common with standard generative assumptions about major grammatical change. However, the population-level modeling demonstrates that the consequent predictions about the trajectory and direction of change are often surprising, very varied, and always sufficiently complex that mathematical modeling and/or computational simulation are essential tools in deriving them.

Niyogi's use of deterministic update rules assumes that random individual differences in the learners' input are an insignificant factor in language change. In his model, learners are exposed to a finite number of triggers randomly drawn according to a probability distribution defined by the current adult population. Sampling variation may well mean that learners will or will not see triggers exemplifying particular internalized grammars present in the adult population. If the number of triggers sampled and/or the size of the population is large, then this variation is likely to be insignificant in defining the overall trajectory and timecourse of E-language change. Therefore, Niyogi models the behavior of an *average* learner in the population. In the limit, the behavior of the overall model will be identical to one in which the behavior of individuals is modeled directly but the population is infinite. The great advantage of this approach is that it is possible to analytically derive fixed points of the resulting dynamical models, and thus prove that certain qualitative results are guaranteed given the model assumptions.

The models utilized by the other contributors are all stochastic in the sense that they model the behavior of individual agents directly and deploy stochastic or random agent interactions. Therefore, there may be sampling variation in learner input. Time steps of the resulting dynamical models are defined in a more fine-grained way in terms of individual agent interactions or sets of such interactions. For example, Batali, Kirby, Oliphant, and Steels and Kaplan all take individual linguistic interactions as the basic time step, so the update rule in their simulations is defined (implicitly) in terms of the effect on E-language of any change in the linguistic knowledge of two interacting agents. In these and most of the other models, language acquisition is no longer viewed as an 'instantaneous' event. Rather agents interact according to their (partial) knowledge of the E-language(s) exemplified in the environment and continue to update this knowledge for some subset of the total interactions allotted to them. Turkel uses a standard (stochastic) genetic algorithm architecture with fitness-based generational replacement of agents so that time steps in his system correspond to non-overlapping generations. However, the fitness of each agent is computed individually based on 10 learning trials between it and another randomly chosen agent in the current population. Briscoe defines time steps in terms of interaction cycles consisting of a set number of interactions proportional to the current population size. Agents interact randomly and a proportion of interactions will involve learners. Once a stochastic model of this type is adopted it is also easy to introduce overlapping generations in which learners as well as adults may contribute utterances to E-language. The stochastic approach provides greater flexibility and potential realism but relies even more heavily on computational simulation, as analytic mathematical techniques are only easily applicable to the simplest such systems. For this reason, it is important that the results of simulation runs are shown to be statistically reliable and that the stochastic factors in the simulation are not dominating its behavior.

Interestingly, though Kirby derives his results via a stochastic simulation of a single speaker providing finite input to a single learner, the critical time steps of his model are generation changes, in which the learner becomes the new adult speaker, and a new learner is introduced. Therefore, it would appear that the analytic model developed by Niyogi and Berwick could, in principle, be applied to Kirby's simulation. The effect of such an application would be to factor out sampling variation in learner input. It should then be possible to prove that the qualitative results observed are guaranteed in any run of such a simulation. Indeed, what we might expect is that, over the predefined meaning space, a single *optimal* grammar, relative to the subsumption based grammar compression algorithm employed, is the sole fixed point of the dynamical system.

1.2.4 Languages as adaptive systems

Niyogi and Berwick (1997) argue that their model of E-language does not need or utilize a notion of linguistic selection between linguistic variants. However, the specific learning algorithm they utilize is selective, in the sense that it is parametric. They examine, in detail, the predictions made by the Trigger Learning Algorithm (TLA, Gibson and Wexler, 1994) embedded in their dynamical model. The TLA is a parameter setting algorithm based on the principles and parameters account of grammatical acquisition (Chomsky, 1981). The TLA selects one grammar from the finite space of possible grammars defined by the settings of a finite number of finite valued parameters. Thus, when faced with variation exemplifying conflicting parameter settings in the input, the TLA selects between the variants by assigning all parameters a unique value. So, selection between variants is a direct consequence of the learning procedure.

It is possible to imagine a learning procedure which when faced with variation simply incorporated all variants into the grammatical system acquired. Briscoe (2000a) describes one such algorithm in some detail. In order to claim that no selection between linguistic variants is happening in dynamical models of the type introduced in the previous section, we would need to demonstrate that the specific learning procedure being deployed by agents in the system was not itself selective in this sense. However, such a learning procedure seems implausible as a model of human language learning because it predicts that the dynamic of language change would always involve integration of variation and construction of larger and larger 'covering' grammars of learner input. Loss of constructions, competition between variants, and the very existence of different grammatical systems would all be problematic under such an account.

Once we adopt an account of language learning which is at least partially selective, then it is more accurate to characterize linguistic dynamical systems as *adaptive* systems; that is, as dynamical systems which have evolved in response to environmental pressure. In this case, to be learnable with respect to the learning algorithm deployed by child language learners (whatever this is). The nature of the pressure depends on properties of the learning procedure and need not be 'functional' in the conventional linguistic sense. For example, the TLA selects between variants by either selecting the parameter setting dictated by the last unambiguous trigger (with respect to the relevant parameter) in the input before the end of the learning period or by making an unbiased random guess. Therefore, the relative frequency with which variants are exemplified in learner input is the main determinant of which variants are culturally transmitted through successive generations of language learning agents. However, most of the learning procedures developed by other contributors exhibit various kinds of inductive bias which interact with the relative frequency of variant input to create additional pressures on learnability.

It is striking that with the exception of Turkel's quite idealized account of learning (which is not intended as a serious model of parameter setting), the other contributors all develop learning algorithms which, unlike the TLA, incorporate Ockham's Razor in some form; that is, a broad preference for the *smallest* grammar and/or lexicon ('compatible' with the input). In addition, most of the models remain selective, in the sense defined above with respect to the TLA, in that they bias learning towards acquisition of *unambiguous* word-meaning associations and/or syntactic means of realizing non-atomic meaning representations. Indeed the latter bias is a direct consequence of the former, as alternative encodings of the mapping from meaning to form result in larger descriptions. All the models impose hard constraints in the form of representational assumptions about the kind of grammars and/or lexicons which can be acquired; that is, assumptions about the form of universal grammar. It is in terms of such representational assumptions which incorporate hard inviolable constraints on what can be learnt that the soft, violable constraints or inductive bias in favour of small unambiguous mappings can be stated. As these representational assumptions vary a good deal between the contributions, the precise effect of the bias will also vary. Nevertheless, very broadly, Ockham's Razor creates an additional selection pressure for regularity in linguistic systems, over and above the requirement for frequent enough exemplification in learner input.

One might argue that the incorporation of such inductive biases into these models is no more than a method of ensuring that the simulations deliver the desired results. However, Ockham's Razor has been a central tenet of learning theory for centuries, and in the theory of informational complexity has been formally proved to provide a universally accurate prior or inductive bias over a universal representation language (Rissanen, 1989). In the framework of Bayesian learning, the minimum description length principle, over a given representation language or class of grammars/models, provides a concrete, practical instantiation of Ockham's Razor, which has been used to develop learnability proofs for non-finite classes of grammar (e.g. Muggleton, 1996) and to develop theoretical and computational models of lexical and grammatical acquisition (e.g. Brent and Cartwright, 1996; de Marcken, 1996; Rissanen and Ristad, 1994; Osborne and Briscoe, 1997). Therefore, the learning procedures developed here, which incorporate this principle in some form, are not in any way unusual, controversial or surprising. Indeed, inductive bias has been argued to be essential to successful learning (Mitchell, 1990, 1997), this insight is central to the Bayesian framework, and within the space of possible inductive biases, Ockham's Razor remains the single most powerful and general principle, which under the idealized conditions of a universal representation language has been shown to subsume all other forms of bias (e.g. Rissanen, 1989).

Kirby (this volume, 1998, 2000) extends this insight in several ways arguing that the bias for smaller grammars is tantamount to the assumption that learners generalize from data and will, therefore, be a component of any language learning procedure. He argues that the syntactic systems which emerge in his simulations would emerge given many other possible learning procedures. Oliphant, in the context of word learning, similarly argues that the only kind of learning procedure which will *impose* order on random, inconsistent vocabulary systems is one which prefers unambiguous word-meaning mappings. However, as we have seen above, at root this follows from Ockham's Razor, since this is equivalent to saying that a learner prefers to retain the smallest number of word–meaning associations.

The picture which emerges then, is that languages have adapted to the human language learning procedure, in the sense that this procedure incorporates inductive bias – itself virtually definitional of the concept of learning. Inductive bias creates linguistic selection for more learnable linguistic variants relative to this bias and thus as languages are culturally transmitted from generation to generation via successive child language learners, linguistic systems will evolve that fit, or are adapted to, these biases. However, this picture cannot be the whole truth, for if it were we would predict that all languages should eventually converge to a single optimal system, that change should always be unidirectional, and that variation should decrease and eventually disappear, at least with respect to these biases. However, this is not a realistic picture, variation is maintained and increases in some social contexts (e.g. Nettle, 1999), and unidirectional change in the form of 'grammaticalization' is at best a tendency (e.g. Newmeyer, 1998).

1.2.5 Languages as complex adaptive systems

Evolution is *not* a process of steady improvement along a single trajectory leading to a single optimal solution. Sewall Wright (1931) introduced into evolutionary theory the idea of adaptive or fitness landscapes with multiple local optima or peaks, and this idea has been considerably refined since (e.g. Kauffman, 1993:33f). The modern picture of (co)evolution is of a process of local search or hill climbing towards a local optimum or peak in a fitness landscape which itself inevitably changes. Conflicting selection pressures will cause the fitness landscape to contain many locally optimal solutions, and thus the evolutionary pathways will be more complex and the space of near optimal solutions more varied (Kauffman, 1993:44f). A simple and well-attested example of conflicting selection pressures from biology is the case of 'runaway' sexual selection for a non-functional marker such as the peacock's tail, counterbalanced by natural selection for efficient movement (e.g. Dawkins, 1989:158f). Adaptive systems which change on the basis of interactions between conflicting selection pressures in unpredictable ways, involving positive or negative feedback, with no centralized control are increasingly termed *complex* adaptive systems (e.g Kauffman, 1993).

The idea that there are competing motivations or conflicting pressures deriving from the exigencies of production, comprehension and acquisition has been developed by linguists working from many different perspectives (e.g. Langacker, 1977; Fodor, 1981; Croft, 1990:192f). However, in linguistics little progress has been made in quantifying these pressures or exploring their interaction (Newmeyer, 1998). Computational simulation and mathematical analysis of E-languages, modeled as dynamical systems adapting to such conflicting pressures, provides a powerful new methodology for deriving precise, quantitative and qualitative predictions from the interaction of such conflicting pressures. For example, one perhaps better understood pressure on the evolution of grammatical systems derives from parsability (e.g. Gibson, 1998; Hawkins, 1994; Miller and Chomsky, 1963; Rambow and Joshi, 1994).

A number of metrics of the relative parsability of different constructions have been proposed, both as accounts of the relative psychological complexity of sentence processing and of the relative prevalence of different construction types in attested languages. A metric of this type can be incorporated into an evolutionary linguistic model in a number of ways. Kirby (1999) argues, for example, that parsability equates to learnability, as input must be parsed before it can be used by a learner to acquire a grammar. By contrast, Hawkins (1994:83f) argues that parsability may influence production so that more parsable variants will be used more frequently than less parsable ones (within the space of possibilities defined by a given grammar), and presents evidence concerning the relative frequency of constructions from several languages in support of this position. This would entail that less parsable constructions would be less frequent in learner input, in any case. Briscoe (2000b) reports experiments, using the same simulation model described in this volume, which show that either approach alone or in tandem can, in principle, account for adaptation towards more parsable typological variants.

It is also likely that production pressures, for example for economy of expression, also play a significant role. In general, these have not been quantified to the same extent, at least in work on syntax. However, there are already some interesting computational models. Kirby (2000), for example, extends the simulation and model described in this volume to include a speaker bias towards minimal encoding of meaning representations. Once this is done the grammars in the simulations no longer evolve so inexorably towards optimally regular encoding of the meaning–form mapping, but unstable irregular and less compositional, but nevertheless short mappings repeatedly emerge. If the further assumption is made, that meanings are expressed according to a highly-skewed 'Zipfian' distribution, then irregular, minimal encodings of very frequent meanings emerge and persist stably across generations.

Once we recognise that there are conflicting selection pressures, it is easier to see why language change does not move inexorably (and unidirectionally) towards a unique global optimum. No such optimum may exist, and in any case, change will alway be relative to and local with respect to the current 'position' in the current adaptive landscape. For instance, a canonical SOV grammar might evolve increasingly frequent extraposition because SOV clauses with long or 'heavy' object phrases are relatively unparsable (e.g. Hawkins, 1994:196f). However, SVO grammars will be less likely to do so since long object phrases will mostly occur postverbally anyway and will not create analogous parsing problems. Once such a change has spread, it may in turn create further parsability (or expressiveness or learnability) issues, altering the adaptive landscape; for example, by creating greater structural ambiguity, resulting perhaps in evolution of obligatory extraposition. (It is this locality or blindness in the search for good solutions that makes the evolutionary process more like tinkering than engineering.) In the framework advocated here, we can recognize that such historical pathways can be stereotypical responses to similar pressures arising in unrelated languages, in much the same way that eyes and wings have evolved independently in different lineages many times, without the need to posit a substantive theory of such changes or to see them as deterministic.

1.2.6 Genetic assimilation

So far we have implicitly assumed that the learning procedure and wider language faculty is universal and invariant across the human species. Most of the contributors to this volume focus exclusively on the effects of a universally shared and preadapted (language) learning procedure on the evolution of language itself. Nevertheless, without the assumption of a shared and effective learning procedure across all agents in the population, it would not be possible to demonstrate the emergence and development of consistent and coherent communication systems. For example, Sharpe (1997) demonstrates that vocabulary systems of the type investigated by Oliphant and Steels and Kaplan only emerge under the assumption that all the agents are deploying the same learning algorithm incorporating the same or very similar inductive biases.

The evolution by natural selection of the human (language) learning procedure, and of other elements of the language faculty such as the human parsing and generation mechanisms, has been addressed in a number of recent papers (Pinker and Bloom, 1990; Newmeyer, 1991), and genetic assimilation (e.g. Waddington, 1942), or the so-called Baldwin Effect (Baldwin, 1896), in which changes in a species' behavior (the advent of language) create new selection pressures (the need to learn language efficiently) has been proposed as a plausible evolutionary mechanism through which a language faculty could have gradually evolved. However, this view is certainly controversial; others have proposed saltationist or single step scenarios (e.g. Bickerton, 1998) or argued that preadapted general-purpose learning mechanisms suffice to account for language emergence and subsequent acquisition (e.g. Steels, 1998; Deacon, 1997; Worden, this volume).

The evolutionary perspective on language development and change described above, and the commitment to develop an evolutionarily plausible account of the emergence and subsequent evolution of any putative language faculty, certainly provide new ways of addressing this central issue in Chomskyan linguistic theory. Firstly, under either a gradualist or saltationist account, the presence of (proto)language(s) in the environment is an essential assumption to provide the necessary selection pressure to ensure that a newly emerged faculty persists; if the ability to learn language reliably does not enhance fitness then there would be no selection pressure to maintain such a faculty, and fitness can only be enhanced by it if there is an existing communicative system (e.g. Kirby, 1998). Secondly, if (proto)language precedes the language faculty, then (proto)language must be learnable via general-purpose learning mechanisms. Thirdly, as the historical evolution of languages will be orders of magnitude faster than the genetic evolution of such a faculty, it is quite plausible that languages simply evolved to fit these general-purpose learning mechanisms before these mechanisms themselves had time to adapt to language. As Deacon (1997:109) memorably puts it: "Languages have had to adapt to children's spontaneous assumptions about communication, learning, social interaction, and even symbolic reference, because children are the only game in town... languages need children more than children need languages." On the other hand, if the language faculty has evolved significantly subsequent to its emergence, then it is of little consequence whether it emerged gradually or by saltation. As Ridley (1990) points out, evolutionary theory tells us more about the maintenance and refinement of traits than their emergence, and the selection pressures subsequent to emergence would be the same given either a saltationist or gradualist account. Fourthly, Pinker and Bloom (1990) and others assume that linguistic universals provide evidence for a language faculty, but if languages evolve to adapt to the inductive bias in the human learning procedure, then linguistic universals need not be genetically-encoded constraints, but instead may just be a consequence of convergent evolution towards more learnable grammatical systems. Again to quote Deacon (1997:116) "universal[s]... emerged spontaneously and independently in each evolving language, in response to universal biases in the selection processes affecting language transmission. They are *convergent* features of language evolution in the same way that the dorsal fins of sharks, ichthyosaurs, and dolphins are independent convergent adaptations of aquatic species."

Worden develops this evolutionary argument against the language faculty, describing a unification-based model of language processing and acquisition and suggesting that a general Bayesian learning algorithm can be used to learn lexical entries in such a model. But the degree to which this is an argument against the existence of or need for a language faculty depends on exactly how domain-independent the unification-based representation language in which linguistic knowledge is couched. Though the representation language is partly encoding conceptual information it is also encoding facts about morphosyntactic realization of meaning (i.e. grammar). Within the context of this more detailed model, Worden is able to make the argument about differential selection pressures on languages and the language faculty and the relative speed of evolution more precise, and tentatively concludes that there would be little pressure for natural as opposed to linguistic selection in line with Deacon's (1997) position.

Turkel, by contrast, simulates evolution of a principles and parameters model of the language faculty and argues that the emergence of a community of speakers endowed with such a faculty, without invoking genetic assimilation, is implausible. The probability of compatible language faculties emerging *de nihilo* in two or more individuals via natural selection is astronomically low. Yet for such a trait to be maintained it must be shared by members of a speech community in order to confer any benefit in fitness. Genetic assimilation provides a mechanism by which a (proto)language using population can gradually converge on a shared language faculty, because individuals able to learn the existing (proto)language slightly more effectively will be selected for over successive generations. Briscoe takes a similar position, presenting a model which integrates Bayesian learning with a principles and parameters account of language acquisition, and arguing that this faculty would be refined by genetic assimilation even in the face of very rapid language change (or 'coevolution').

1.3 Methodological issues

The use of computational simulation and/or mathematical modeling to derive predictions from dynamical models is a vital tool for the exploration of evolutionary accounts of language variation, change and development, and of the development of the language faculty. The behavior of even simple dynamical systems is notoriously complex and often unintuitive, therefore models or theories based entirely on verbal reasoning run a serious danger of being incomplete or not making the predictions assumed. Simulation and modeling force the theorist to be precise enough to specify a complete model and to look at its actual rather than assumed predictions. This places powerful constraints on the development of evolutionary models since it often becomes clear in the process of creating them that some of the assumptions required to make the model 'work' are unrealistic, or that apparently realistic assumptions simply do not yield plausible predictions. However, the mere existence of a 'successful' simulation or mathematical model does not guarantee either the correctness of the assumptions leading to its predictions or of the evolutionary pathway to these predictions.

Evolution is an irreducibly historical process which can be, and often is, affected by accidents, such as population extinctions or bottlenecks, which are beyond the purvue of any rational reconstruction (i.e. model) of an evolutionary process. Since the precise prehistoric pathways that were followed during the emergence and initial development of human language are unknowable, this places a fundamental limit on what we can learn from simulations which (exclusively) address such questions. At the very best such argumentation is irreducibly probabilistic. On the other hand, work in the same framework which addresses historically attested language changes and associated demographic upheavals, such as those occurring during language genesis, is less susceptible to this problem.

A simulation or mathematical model rests on a set of hopefully explicit assumptions just as an argument rests on premises. Often it is not possible to reliably assess the truth of these assumptions or their causal relevance in a prehistoric setting. Thus the predictions made by the model are only as strong as the assumptions behind it. The advantage of models is that *all and only* the critical assumptions required to derive a specific conclusion should be manifest if a good methodology is adopted. The use of computational simulation greatly facilitates the testing of many parameterized variants of a model to explore exactly what is critical. However, it is also important that the initial model adopted abstracts away from as many contingent specific details as possible in order to achieve greatest generality and to derive results from the weakest set of assumptions possible. Ultimately, this is a matter of judgement and experience in the development of such models – there is no 'logic of discovery' – but without such abstraction even computational simulation and exploration of such models will become rapidly intractable.

One example of both the benefits and limits of the methodology is provided by the issue of genetic assimilation of linguistic constraints into the language faculty (discussed in the previous section). Deacon (1997:322f) argues quite persuasively that language change would have been too rapid to create the constant selection pressure on successive generations of language users required for genetic assimilation. However, one simulation in which both language change and genetic assimilation are modeled demonstrates that genetic assimilation still occurs even when language changes are happening as fast as is compatible with maintenance of a speech community (Briscoe, 2000b). The key implicit assumption in Deacon's argument is that the hypothesis space of possible grammars defining the environment for adaptation is sufficiently small that most grammars will be sampled in the time required for genetic assimilation to go to fixation in a population of language users. The model makes clear that if this hypothesis space is large enough then significant portions of it are unlikely to be sampled during this time, so there is constant pressure to assimilate constraints that rule out or disprefer the unsampled grammars. On the other hand, this demonstration, though it undermines Deacon's specific argument, does not guarantee that genetic assimilation of such constraints into the language faculty did, in fact, occur. The model, in conjunction with related work on genetic assimilation (Mayley, 1996) also makes it clear that one critical assumption is that there is correlation between the neural mechanisms underlying language learning and the genetic specification of these mechanisms which will enable the 'transfer' of such constraints to the genetic level. We simply do not know, given our current understanding of both the genetic code and relevant neural mechanisms, whether or to what degree this is the case.

In addition to these general points, there are more specific methodological issues contingent on the type of model adopted. Deterministic models based on analytic techniques, such as that of Niyogi, are methodologically stronger in the sense that predictions derived from them are guaranteed to hold of any specific experimental realization of such models. However, analytic techniques are hard to apply to all but the simplest models. Computational simulation – that is, the running of specific experiments with a model – can be used as an alternative to mathematical analysis. However, the behavior of such simulation runs needs to be considered carefully before conclusions are drawn. If the simulation is stochastic in any way, as most of those presented in this volume are, then we need to be sure that predictions are reliable in the sense that they represent high probability or typical results of such simulations. One basic technique for achieving this is to examine the results from multiple identically-parameterized runs. However, if the qualitative behavior of the model over multiple runs is not absolutely clearcut, then statistical analysis of results may also be required. The advantage of computational simulation is that more realistic models can be explored rapidly in which, for example, there are no fixed points or deterministic attractors in the underlying dynamical system (i.e. no endpoint to evolution). Nevertheless, as this work grows in sophistication, careful statistical analysis of the underlying models will become increasingly important, as is the norm, for example, in population genetics (e.g. Maynard Smith, 1998).

It is sometimes suggested that simulations are too dangerous: "I have resisted the temptation to utilize computer simulations, mostly for reasons of clarity (in my own head – and perhaps also the reader's). Simulations, if they are to be more than mere animations of an idea, have hard-to-appreciate critical assumptions." (Calvin, 1996:8). Behind such sentiments lurks the feeling that simulations are 'doomed to succeed' because it is always possible to build one in which the desired result is achieved. I hope this introduction and the contributions to this volume will convince the reader that, though simulation without methodological discipline is a dangerous tool, methodologically rigorous simulation is a critical and indispensable one in the development of evolutionary dynamical models of language.

1.4 What next?

Though the contributors to this book approach the question of the role of language acquisition in linguistic evolution from a wide variety of theoretical perspectives and develop superficially very different models, there is a deep underlying unity to them all in the realization of the centrality of acquisition to insightful accounts of language emergence, development, variation and change. I hope the reader will recognize this unity and agree with me that this work makes a powerful case for the evolutionary perspective on language. Nevertheless, it should also be clear that much work remains to be done. Methodologically, we have a long way to go in assimilating and evaluating techniques from fields such as population genetics, in which a powerful set of mathematical techniques for studying dynamical systems has been developed. Substantively, we have only begun to scratch the surface of critical issues, such as that of conflicting selection pressures or competing motivations in linguistic evolution, which will take us well beyond the realm of simple models/simulations with fixed points to ones with very complex and dynamic adaptive landscapes. Despite this, I hope the reader will also agree with me that the study of E-languages as complex adaptive systems is a potentially very productive research programme which can be tackled in a methodologically sound way.

References

Baldwin, J. M. (1896). 'A new factor in evolution', *American Naturalist, vol.30*, 441–451.

Bickerton, D. (1998). 'Catastrophic evolution: the case for a single step from protolanguage to full human language' in Hurford, J., Studdert-Kennedy, M. and Knight, C. (eds.), *Approaches to the Evolution of Language*, Cambridge University Press, Cambridge, pp. 341–358.

Brent, M. and Cartwright, T. (1996). 'Distributional regularity and phonotactic constraints are useful for segmentation', *Cognition, vol.61*, 93–125.

Briscoe, E. J. (2000a). 'Evolutionary perspectives on diachronic syntax' in Pintzuk, Susan, Tsoulas, George, and Warner, Anthony (eds.), *Diachronic Syntax: Models and Mechanisms*, Oxford: Oxford University Press, pp. 75–108.

Briscoe, E. J. (2000b). 'Grammatical acquisition: inductive bias and coevolution of language and the language acquisition device', *Language, vol.76.2*, 245–296.

Calvin, W. (1996). *The Cerebral Code*, MIT Press, Cambridge, MA.

Chomsky, N. (1965). *Aspects of the Theory of Syntax*, MIT Press, Cambridge, MA.

Chomsky, N. (1981). *Government and Binding*, Foris, Dordrecht.

Chomsky, N. (1986). *Knowledge of Language: Its Nature, Origin and Use*, Praeger, New York.

Croft, W. (1990). *Typology and Universals*, Cambridge University Press, Cambridge.

Cziko, G. (1995). *Without Miracles: Universal Selection Theory and the Second Darwinian Revolution*, MIT Press, Cambridge, MA.

Dawkins, R. (1983). 'Universal Darwinism' in Bendall, D. S. (ed.), *Evolution: From Molecules to Men*, Cambridge University Press, Cambridge, pp. 403-425.

Dawkins, Richard (1989). *The Selfish Gene*, Oxford University Press, Oxford, 2nd edition.

de Marcken, C. (1996). 'Unsupervised language acquisition', Doctoral dissertation, MIT, EECS.

Deacon, T. (1997). *The Symbolic Species: Coevolution of Language and Brain,* MIT Press, Cambridge, MA.

Dennett, D. (1995). *Darwin's Dangerous Idea: Evolution and the Meanings of Life,* Simon and Schuster, New York.

Fodor, J. D. (1981). 'Does performance shape competence?', *Phil. Trans. Royal Society of London, vol.B295,* 285–295.

Gibson, E. (1998). 'Linguistic complexity: locality of syntactic dependencies', *Cognition, vol.68,* 1–76.

Gibson, E. and Wexler, K. (1994). 'Triggers', *Linguistic Inquiry, vol.25.3,* 407–454.

Hawkins, J. A. (1994). *A Performance Theory of Order and Constituency,* Cambridge University Press, Cambridge.

Hurford, Jim (1987). *Language and Number,* Blackwell, Oxford.

Hurford, J. (1989). 'Biological evolution of the Saussurean sign as a component of the language acquisition device', *Lingua, vol.77,* 187–222.

Hurford, J. (1999). 'The evolution of language and languages' in Dunbar, R., Knight, C., and Power, C. (eds.), *The Evolution of Culture,* Edinburgh University Press, Edinburgh, pp. 173–193.

Hurford, J., Studdert-Kennedy, M., and Knight, C. (1998). *Approaches to the Evolution of Language,* Cambridge University Press, Cambridge.

Kauffman, S. (1993). *The Origins of Order: Self-Organization and Selection in Evolution,* Oxford University Press, New York.

Keller, R. (1984 (1994)). *On Language Change: The Invisible Hand in Language* (English translation), Routledge, London.

Kirby, S. (1998). 'Fitness and the selective adaptation of language' in Hurford, J., Studdert-Kennedy, M., and Knight, C. (eds.), *Approaches to the Evolution of Language,* Cambridge University Press, Cambridge, pp. 359–383.

Kirby, S. (1999). *Function, Selection and Innateness: The Emergence of Language Universals,* Oxford University Press, Oxford.

Kirby, S. (2000, in press). 'Spontaneous evolution of linguistic structure: an iterated learning model of the emergence of regularity and irregularity', *IEEE Trans. on Evolutionary Computation, vol.8*

Jackendoff, R. (1997). *The Architecture of the Language Faculty,* MIT Press, Cambridge, MA.

Langacker, R. (1977). 'Syntactic reanalysis' in Li, C. (ed.), *Mechanisms of Syntactic Change,* University of Texas Press, Austin, pp. 57–139.

Lightfoot, D. (1979). *Principles of Diachronic Syntax,* Cambridge University Press, Cambridge.

Lightfoot, D. (1999). *The Development of Language: Acquisition, Change, and Evolution,* Blackwell, Oxford.

Lindblom, B. (1986). 'Phonetic universals in vowel systems' in Ohala, J. and Jaeger, J. J. (eds.), *Experimental Phonology,* Academic Press, Orlando, FL, pp. 13–44.

Mayley, G. (1996). 'Landscapes, learning costs and genetic assimilation' in Turney, Peter, Whitley, D., and Anderson, R. (eds.), *Evolution, Learning and Instinct: 100 Years of the Baldwin Effect,* MIT Press, Cambridge MA.

Maynard-Smith, J. (1998). *Evolutionary Genetics,* Oxford University Press, Oxford, 2nd edition.

McMahon, A. (1994). *Understanding Language Change,* Cambridge University Press, Cambridge.

Miller, G. A. and Chomsky, N. (1963). 'Finitary models of language users' in Luce, R. D., Bush, R. R. and Galanter, E. (eds.), *Handbook of Mathematical Psychology,* vol II, Wiley, New York, pp. 419–491.

Mitchell, Tom (1990). 'The need for biases in learning generalizations' in Shavlik, Jana and Dietterich, Tom (eds.), *Readings in Machine Learning,* Morgan Kaufmann, San Mateo, CA.

Mitchell, Tom (1997). *Machine Learning,* McGraw Hill, New York.

Muggleton, S. (1996). 'Learning from positive data', *Proceedings of the 6th Inductive Logic Programming Workshop,* Stockholm.

Nettle, Daniel (1999). *Linguistic Diversity,* Oxford University Press, Oxford.

Newmeyer, F. (1991). 'Functional explanation in linguistics and the origins of language', *Language and Communication, vol.11,* 3–28.

Newmeyer, F. (1998). *Language Form and Language Function,* MIT Press, Cambridge, MA.

Niyogi, P. and Berwick, R. (1997). 'A dynamical systems model of language change', *Linguistics and Philosophy, vol.17,*

Osborne, M. and Briscoe, E. J. (1997). 'Learning stochastic categorial grammars', *Proceedings of the ACL Comp. Nat. Lg. Learning (CoNLL97) Workshop,* Madrid, pp. 80–87.

Pinker, S. and Bloom, P. (1990). 'Natural language and natural selection', *Behavioral and Brain Sciences, vol.13,* 707–784.

Rambow, O. and Joshi, A. (1994). 'A processing model of free word order languages' in Clifton, C., Frazier, L., and Rayner, K. (eds.), *Perspectives on Sentence Processing,* Lawrence Erlbaum, Hillsdale, NJ., pp. 267–301.

Ridley, M. (1990). 'Reply to Pinker and Bloom', *Behavioral and Brain Sciences, vol.13,* 756.

Rissanen, J. (1989). *Stochastic Complexity in Statistical Inquiry,* World Scientific, Singapore.

Rissanen, J. and Ristad, E. (1994). 'Language acquisition in the MDL framework' in Ristad, E. (ed.), *Language Computations,* DIMACS Workshop, American Mathematics Association.

Sharpe, T. (1997). *Acquiring a shared vocabulary,* MPhil Dissertation, University of Cambridge.

Steedman, M. (2000). *The Syntactic Process,* MIT Press, Cambridge, MA.

Steels, L. (1998). 'Synthesizing the origins of language and meaning using co-evolution, self-organization and level formation' in Hurford, J., Studdert-Kennedy, M., and Knight, C. (eds.), *Approaches to the Evolution of Language,* Cambridge University Press, Cambridge, pp. 384–404.

Waddington, C. (1942). 'Canalization of development and the inheritance of acquired characters', *Nature, vol.150,* 563–565.

Worden, R. P. (1998). 'The evolution of language from social intelligence' in Hurford, J., Studdert-Kennedy, M., and Knight, C. (eds.), *Approaches to the Evolution of Language,* Cambridge University Press, Cambridge, pp. 148–168.

2

Learned systems of arbitrary reference: The foundation of human linguistic uniqueness

Michael Oliphant
Language Evolution and Computation
Research Unit, Department of Linguistics,
University of Edinburgh

2.1 Features of human language

To theorize about the evolution of human language is to theorize about how human communication differs from the communication systems used by other species, and what biological basis underlies these differences. The features of human language that I would suggest we need to account for are as follows:

- **Syntax:** Human language is compositional, conveying structured meanings through the use of structured forms.
- **Learning:** Human language is passed on from one generation to the next via cultural transmission.
- **Symbolic reference:** The mapping between basic lexical elements and their meanings is arbitrary and conventional.

In distinguishing human language from other forms of communication, the attention has largely been focused on the evolution of syntax (Bickerton, 1990; Pinker and Bloom, 1990; Newmeyer, 1991). This is unsurprising, as syntactic structure is certainly the most salient feature of human language. Because other species seem to have no means of combining simple signals with each other to form more complex meanings, the prime objective of most research on the evolution of language has been to explain how such an ability arose in humans.

In this chapter, I will instead focus on the other, perhaps more basic, features of human language that make it unique – learning and symbolic reference. While there are other forms of communication that are *learned*, and there are other forms of communication that are *symbolic*, I will argue that human language is the only existing system of com-

munication that is both learned *and* symbolic. Moving from a simple
(non-syntactic) innate system of communication to an equally simple
learned system is non-trivial. Making such a transition is particularly
difficult if the mapping between forms and meanings is an arbitrary
convention.

2.2 Signaling systems, innateness and symbolic reference

Because I am putting aside the issue of syntax, the systems of communication that I am concerned with are what Lewis (1969) termed
signaling systems – systems that map between unstructured signals and
unanalyzed meanings. I will refer to each bi-directional association between a signal and the meaning it denotes as a *sign*, after de Saussure (1959). In classifying a system of communication, I will ask two
questions about the signs that compose it. First, are the signs innate
or learned? An innate sign is an association that is specified genetically
and passed on from one generation to the next through reproduction.
A learned sign, on the other hand, is established experientially through
the use of some learning mechanism. Rather than being passed on
genetically, if a learned sign is to be perpetuated it must be culturally
transmitted from one generation to the next.

The second question that I want to ask is whether or not the signs are
symbolic. Peirce (1932) defines a symbol as "a sign which refers to the
Object that it denotes by virtue of a law, usually an association of general
ideas, which operates to cause the Symbol to be interpreted as referring
to that Object" (276). A symbol, then, is linked with its referent by
convention. Symbols are arbitrary, bearing no inherent relationship to
that which they denote. There is no sense, for example, in which the
word *dog* has any 'dogness' in it, in either its spoken or written form.
One might object that any particular individual's use of *dog* is in fact *not*
arbitrary – an individual's use of any particular word is determined by
the way that word is used in the language community. This objection
makes it clear that in stating that a sign is arbitrary, we must state
exactly what it is arbitrary with respect to. We can thus clarify the
definition of a symbol in the following way:

**A symbol is a sign that refers to the object that it denotes
in a way that is arbitrary with respect to the process of
conventionalization that established it.**

	Non-Symbolic	Symbolic
Innate	Threat displays Bee dance Facial expressions	Most alarm calls
Learned	Chimpanzee gestures Road signs	Human language

figure 2.1. Classifying communicative behavior with respect to innateness and symbolic reference.

In the case of learned signs, then, we would say that they are symbolic if they are arbitrary with respect to the relevant learning mechanism. A child's use of *dog* is symbolic because this use simply reflects the convention used by the language community. We can evaluate the signs used in innate animal communication systems in a similar way. Although it may seem strange to talk of innate symbols, it is completely consistent with the definition of what it is to be symbolic. In the case of innate communication, the process of conventionalization is natural selection. Animal signaling behavior, then, is symbolic if it is arbitrary with respect to the process of natural selection.

2.3 Classifying communicative behavior

The distinctions made in the previous section give us the means to classify systems of communication based on whether they are innate or learned, and whether they are symbolic or not.[1] Figure 2.1 shows the four possible combinations under this classification. In the following sections, I will look at each of these classes of communication in turn.

2.3.1 Innate non-symbolic systems

One way in which reference can be non-symbolic is for the sign to be what Peirce calls *iconic*. An icon refers by virtue of resemblance, such as the way a road sign indicates that a road is slippery by using wavy lines. In the realm of animal communication, iconic signaling often occurs in

---

[1] A similar analysis, though broken down based on different features, can be found in Burling (2000).

threat display behavior, where aggressive intent is conveyed by such actions as the lowering of antlers or the revealing of teeth. Another example of iconic communication is the dance done by honeybees to convey information about the information of food sources to other bees in the hive. The bee 'language', decoded by von Frisch (1974), is used by a bee that has discovered a source of food to inform others of its approximate angle and distance from the hive. A bee, upon returning to the hive, performs a tail-wagging dance in the shape of a figure-eight. The amount of time it takes the bee to traverse the straight, central portion of the dance indicates the distance to the food source, while the angle of this traversal gives the angle of the source using the position of the sun as a reference. The degree of vigorousness of the dances indicates the quality of food at the source.

Communicative behavior need not be iconic to be non-symbolic. Many animal signals derive from intentional movements through a process of ritualization (Tinbergen, 1952). Consider the problem faced by flocks of birds that take flight as a group. If one bird is preparing to fly, the others need to recognize this and prepare to fly as well. To accomplish this, selection can tune the behavior of the birds such that the preparatory motions of other birds trigger the initiating of flight. In Peirce's terms, this form of reference is *indexical* – the preparatory motions signal a bird's intent to take flight by virtue of being part of the same causal chain of events.

2.3.2 Innate symbolic systems

Humans are not the only species that have a symbolic system of communication. Many non-human animals have innate symbolic systems of communication – arbitrary systems of reference that have been tuned by natural selection. The process by which natural selection can tune such systems is well understood, both mathematically (Warneryd, 1993; Blume, Kim, and Sobel, 1993; Kim and Sobel, 1995; Skyrms 1996) and computationally (see for example Oliphant, 1997, Di Paolo, 1997, and Noble, 1998).

Perhaps the most commonly cited example of an innate system of arbitrary reference is the alarm call behavior of the vervet monkey (Strusaker, 1967; Seyfarth, Cheney, and Marler, 1980a; Seyfarth, Cheney, and Marler, 1980b). Vervets use a system of alarm calls that distinguishes the different kinds of danger posed by various species of their predators. When a vervet sees an eagle, it gives an alarm call that sounds like a cough. When a large cat such as a leopard is seen, a barking sound is made. When a vervet sees a snake, it utters a chuttering sound. Each of these alarm calls causes other vervets that hear them to engage in evasive behavior appropriate to the predator: in response to the eagle call, the monkeys look up or run into bushes, the calls given in response to large cats cause vervets to run into trees, and the snake call causes the monkeys stand up and look in the grass. That the monkeys are responding to the alarm calls, and not to the predators themselves is indicated by the results of playback studies. Seyfarth *et al.* (1980b) have shown that vervets make the appropriate response to recorded calls in the absence of an actual predator.

The vervet system is symbolic because there is no sense in which the acoustic properties of the alarm calls are intrinsically related to either the predators they correspond to, or the appropriate evasive behavior. In fact, it is difficult to imagine what an iconic alarm call would be like, unless it imitated some sound that the predator made.

While the vervet alarm call system involves a learned component, it is best thought of as an innate system of communication. Comparisons of recordings of spontaneous calls given by immature animals to alarm calls given by adults indicates that learning is relatively unimportant in determining the acoustic properties of calling behavior (Seyfarth and Cheney, 1986; Hauser, 1996). The set of alarm calls appears to be innately constrained. Vervets do, however, learn to fine-tune the use of alarm calls through experience. Seyfarth and Cheney (1986), in analyzing the use of the eagle alarm call, have found that it initially is used by infants and juveniles in response to perceptually similar non-predatory species such as vultures. Only later in life does it get narrowed to be a response to the eagles that prey on the vervets. While learning plays a role in tuning the specificity of an alarm call, it seems that the general danger categories such as "airborne eagle-like predator" are determined innately (Hauser, 1996). Because adult vervets generally ignore false-alarm calls by infants, it seems likely that these categories get narrowed through selective reinforcement; only in the case of a true predator will an infant's alarm call generate a response from others.

A schematic diagram of this view of the vervet call system is shown in figure 2.2. Solid lines represent associations that are innate, while dashed lines represent learned associations. The association between a given danger category (such as "airborne predator") and the correspond-

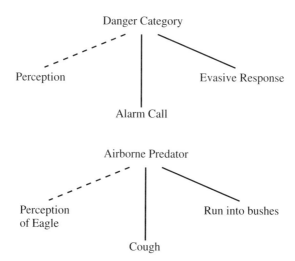

figure 2.2. Innate and learned components of the vervet alarm call system. The top diagram represents the system as a whole, while the diagram on the bottom shows the alarm call behavior in response to eagles. Solid lines represent innate associations, while dashed lines represent associations that are learned.

ing alarm call (a coughing sound) is innately specified. The association between a danger category and the precise nature of the perceptual stimulus that represents it is learned. The plasticity in the system involves perception, rather than communication. What is the reason for this plasticity? It may give some flexibility in the class of predators an alarm call can refer to. Perhaps more likely, however, is the possibility that the plasticity only exists because it isn't feasible to genetically encode the precise perceptual description of a predator.

2.3.3 Learned non-symbolic systems

Learned systems of communication are extremely rare. By far the more common case is for communication to involve an innate mapping between signal and meaning. One of the few cases where we do find evidence of learned communication is, perhaps unsurprisingly, in the apes. Chimpanzees use a wide variety of gestural signals to mediate social interaction, using them in situations such as play, care-giving, and aggressive and sexual interactions. At least some aspects of this gestural communication appear to be learned. Evidence that this is the case comes both from observation of the animals in their natural habitat (Goodall, 1986), and from observational studies of gesturing in captive chimpanzees placed in a physical and social setting designed to resemble that which exists in the wild (Tomasello, George, Kruger, Farrar, and Evans, 1985; Tomasello, Gust, and Frost, 1989; Tomasello, Call, Nagell, Olguin, and Carpenter, 1994). The communicative behavior shows variation across groups and individuals, and also changes ontogenetically, apparently adapting to the changing social environment as the animal grows from infant to adult (Tomasello, Gust, and Frost, 1989).

While the animals do seem to learn to use gestures, this communicative behavior is of a specific and limited kind. The gestures tend to be simple, ritualized shortcuts, where a component of a behavior is used as a signal for the entire sequence of action. An example is an infant touching its mother's arm as a nursing request. This signal is a ritualized version of an action that initially involved the infant moving its mother's arm to get access to the nipple (Tomasello, 1990). Tomasello (1996) calls this process *ontogenetic ritualization*. As the name suggests, this process can be seen as a learning equivalent of the ritualization of innate behaviors described in section 2.3.1.

Chimpanzee gestural communication, then, is indexical rather than symbolic, with the signal being related causally to the meaning it represents. Because of the derived nature of the signals that are used, the ritualization process limits what meanings can be referred to. Communication involving more arbitrary relationships between signal and meaning would be much more difficult to establish through such ritualization.

2.3.4 Learned symbolic systems

While, as the previous several sections have shown, there are a variety of non-human communication systems that are either learned or symbolic, human language seems to be the only system that is both. I would argue that this is true despite the results of a large number of studies demonstrating the ability of a variety of species to learn to use symbolic systems of communication (Hayes and Hayes, 1951; Gardener and Gardener, 1969; Premack, 1971; Herman, Richards, and Wolz, 1984; Pepperberg, 1987).

The key issue here is what it means to say that a system of communication is learned. In the cases cited above, the system was designed by the researchers and explicitly taught to the animals using a reinforcement-based training program. These studies do not constitute evidence that the species in question are capable of supporting a learned symbolic system of communication because there is no evidence that the system would perpetuate in a population of animals without human intervention.

Work done by Savage-Rumbaugh and colleagues with bonobo chimpanzees comes closer to providing such evidence. While training a mother chimpanzee in a traditional reinforcement-based communication task, they found that the animal's infant showed evidence of having learned the task. The fact that the infant was present, but not actively participating in the task, suggests that perhaps explicit reinforcement is not required (Savage-Rumbaugh, McDonald Sevcik, Hopkins, and Rubert, 1986). While this kind of study is exactly what is needed to refine our understanding of the differences (and similarities) between humans and other apes, it has not yet demonstrated learned symbolic communication among bonobos. Instead, it has shown that, under the right conditions, bonobos can learn a symbolic system of communication from humans. We still have no evidence that bonobos can use and maintain such a system over time, passing it from one generation to the next. The fact that we do not see such systems in the wild would seem to indicate there must be *some* difference between humans and other primates that accounts for this absence.[2]

2.4 Transmission of learned communication systems

If we accept that human language is the only existing system of learned symbolic communication, the next step is to come up with an explanation as to why this might be the case. What is it that makes a simple learned system more problematic than an equally simple innate system? One possible answer to this question lies in differences in how innate and learned systems are transmitted.

For a system of communication to persist in a population, it must be heritable from one generation to the next. In the case of an innate

---

[2] This assumes, of course, that we have an accurate picture of what the animals are doing in the wild. While it is possible that learned symbolic systems exist that we are unaware of, and we must be open to this possibility, it seems best to theorize based on what evidence we currently have available to us.

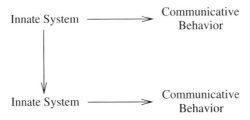

figure 2.3. Transmission of an innate communication system. The representation of the system is passed on genetically.

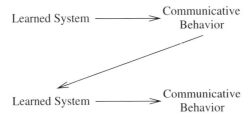

figure 2.4. Transmission of a learned communication system. The representation of the system cannot be passed on directly, but must be mediated by the production of and exposure to communicative behavior.

system, such heritability is well understood. If the innate system has been tuned by natural selection, it is simply transmitted genetically (see figure 2.3). In the case of learned communication, however, the system cannot be passed on directly from one individual to another. Instead, transmission must be mediated by the communicative behavior itself (see figure 2.4). The extent to which such transmission is possible will be determined by how difficult it is to learn a communication system by being exposed to its use by others.

In the next several sections, I will explore the computational problems involved in supporting a learned system of communication. This will be done with the aid of computational simulations and, where possible, mathematical analysis.

2.4.1 Evaluating a learning mechanism

There are many possible ways in which an individual can learn, using observations of the behavior of others to determine its own behavior. In evaluating a learning mechanism, I will require more of it than is generally demanded. A suitable learning mechanism must satisfy three requirements:

- **Acquisition:** A learning mechanism must be able to acquire a pre-existing optimal system of communication when it is introduced into a population that uses it.
- **Maintenance:** A learning mechanism must be able to maintain a preexisting optimal system of communication against reasonable levels of noise.
- **Construction:** A learning mechanism must improve a non-optimal system of communication in such a way that, as new individuals who use the learning mechanism are added to the population, the communicative accuracy of the population increases and eventually reaches an optimal state.

Thus, the present approach differs from traditional language learnability theory in that we are not only interested in how a new individual might acquire an existing system, but also how such systems are created in the first place and maintained over time. The problems of acquisition, construction and maintenance are seen as being intrinsically linked to one another.

2.4.2 Signaling systems and communicative accuracy

As was previously explained in section 2.2, because we are currently concerned with the basic requirements of learning *any* system of communication (be it syntactic or not) we will use signaling systems as our model of communication. In such a model, the basic unit of analysis is a *communicative interaction*, which consists of an exchange between two individuals: a *sender* and a *receiver*. The sender, given a meaning, produces a signal. The receiver is then given this signal and interprets it as a meaning. The communicative interaction is said to be successful if the meaning the receiver interprets the sender's signal as the same meaning the sender was given.

More formally, we can describe transmission and reception behavior as a pair of probability functions, s and r. $s(\mu, \sigma)$ represents the probability that a signal σ will be sent for a meaning μ by a transmitter, and $r(\sigma, \mu)$ represents the probability that a signal σ with be interpreted as meaning μ by a receiver. The send function s, then, gives a probabilistic mapping from meanings to signals, while the receive function r maps back from signals to meanings.

Using these probability functions, we can compute the expected probability that signals sent using send function s will be correctly interpreted by receive function r. This probability, which we will write as ca(s, r), will be called the *communicative accuracy* from s to r. If we assume that all meanings are equally likely to serve as the subject of a communicative interaction, then this value is the average probability that any given meaning will be correctly communicated:

$$\text{ca}(s, r) = \frac{1}{|M|} \sum_{\mu} \sum_{\sigma} s(\mu, \sigma)\, r(\sigma, \mu) \tag{2.1}$$

where $|M|$ is the number of meanings. The maximum value of ca(s, r) is $|S|/|M|$, giving a maximum communicative accuracy of 1.0 as long as there are at least as many signals available as there are meanings to be conveyed.

Figure 2.5 shows the behavior of an example population communicating about three meanings using three signals. The two tables give the average transmission and reception behavior of individuals in the population. Members of this population will, for example, always (with probability 1.0) send signal a in response to meaning 1, and will interpret signal b as meaning 2 with probability 0.4. Overall, the communicative accuracy of this population is 0.65, meaning that a communicative interaction can be expected to succeed 65% of the time.

A population will be said to communicate *optimally* if its communicative accuracy is 1.0 – the case when every individual communicates accurately with every other individual for every meaning. An example of an optimally communicating population is shown in figure 2.6.

2.4.3 The learning model

The model of learning I will use is similar to that used in Hurford, (1989) and Oliphant and Batali, (1997). I assume that the life of an individual proceeds in two stages: a learning stage and a behaving stage. During the learning stage, an individual observes the behavior of the other individuals in the population, and uses these observations to construct its

Transmission

s	*a*	*b*	*c*
1	1.0	0.0	0.0
2	0.0	0.6	0.4
3	0.0	0.4	0.6

Reception

a	*b*	*c*	*r*
1.0	0.0	0.0	*1*
0.0	0.4	0.6	*2*
0.0	0.6	0.4	*3*

figure 2.5. An example of a population's communication behavior for a system that uses three meanings (1, 2, 3) and three signals (a, b, c). The probability, $s(\mu, \sigma)$, that an individual in the population will transmit a given signal for a given meaning is shown in the upper table. The lower table gives the probability, $r(\sigma, \mu)$, that a given signal will be interpreted as a given meaning. The communicative accuracy for this population is 0.65.

Transmission

s	*a*	*b*	*c*
1	0.0	1.0	0.0
2	1.0	0.0	0.0
3	0.0	0.0	1.0

Reception

a	*b*	*c*	*r*
0.0	1.0	0.0	*1*
1.0	0.0	0.0	*2*
0.0	0.0	1.0	*3*

figure 2.6. A population that communicates optimally (a communicative accuracy of 1.0). Each meaning is expressed unambiguously with a single signal and the reception behavior of the population is such that all signals are correctly interpreted.

own communication system. After learning, this communication system remains fixed.[3] At no point during the learning stage does an individual use its forming communication system and modify it based on feedback regarding its success. This is in contrast with other models of learned communication where reinforcement is involved (Yanco and Stein, 1993; Hutchins and Hazelhurst, 1995; Steels, 1996; Murciano and

[3] There is one exception to this. When a member of the behaving population is used as a model for the learner, they are also trained on their own behavior.

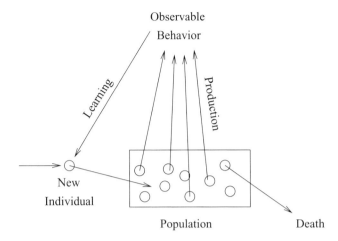

figure 2.7. The learning cycle. Old individuals are continually replaced by new ones in the population. New individuals learn from an observed sample of behavior produced by the existing population.

Millan, 1996). During the behaving stage, individuals interact with one another, providing the basis for the learning of new individuals.

The population is initially seeded with individuals with 'blank' communication systems (exactly what constitutes a 'blank' communication system will be explained in Section 2.4.3). At each time-step, or *round*, a new individual (also with a blank communication system) is introduced. Only during an individual's first round in the population are they in the learning stage. In subsequent rounds, they are treated as behaving members of the population. In addition, a randomly chosen individual is removed, keeping the population at a constant size. This occurs in a continuous cycle, as is shown in figure 2.7.

In the simulations I will present, learning takes place using simple networks operating within an associative learning framework. In this case, the association to be learned is between signals and meanings. The general network architecture can be seen in figure 2.8. A signal is represented on one layer of the network by activating a single unit. Meanings are represented in similar fashion on the other layer. Associations between signal and meaning are represented by the bidirectional weights that connect the units of the signal layer to the units of the meaning layer. More formally, the networks consist of a set of signal units, S, and a set of meaning units, M. Individual units will be referred to as S_i and M_j, with w_{ij} designating the weight connecting signal unit S_i and

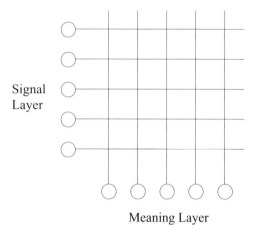

Signal
Layer

Meaning Layer

figure 2.8. The associative network model. Signals and meanings are each represented by a layer of units, with the interconnecting weights storing the association between them.

meaning unit M_j.

New networks begin with blank communication systems. This is done by setting all weights to zero, which produced random initial behavior through absence of any particular bias.[4] All learning is done based on observed samples of transmission behavior (an individual producing a signal for a given meaning). Because the bidirectional weights in the network impose an inherent link between transmission and reception behavior, observations of either behavior are sufficient. New individuals entering the population are exposed to three samples of signals produced in response to each meaning.[5] Each sample is taken from an independently chosen member of the behaving population. When an individual is used as a model for a learner, it is also trained on its own response. This is the only case where a member of the behaving population is

[4] Simulation runs were also carried out in which networks were initialized by setting each weight to a random value between 0 and 1. This change had no effect on the simulation results.

[5] The number of samples required in order for a population to converge on a single, common communication system depends on the number of signals and meanings and the population size. For small populations and small communication systems, a single exposure can be sufficient to result in convergence through drift. Any number of exposures greater than one will always results in convergence eventually – the higher the number of exposures, the more quickly convergence will result.

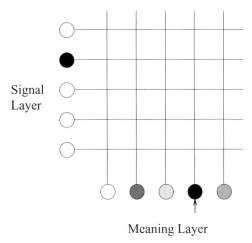

Signal
Layer

Meaning Layer

figure 2.9. Winner-take-all recall. A particular signal is being interpreted by the network. The resulting meaning is the mostly highly activated unit, as indicated by the arrow.

trained. It is necessary to ensure consistency in cases where the network has no bias in the current situation (something that happens very often in the early rounds, where the population consists almost entirely of the initial, unbiased networks used to begin the simulation).

While the learning rule that modifies the weights in response to the presentation of signal/meaning pairs will vary depending on the type of network, all of the simulations presented use a winner-take-all output strategy. Given a particular input pattern, the most highly active output unit is set to be active, while the other units are turned off. Thus, to use the network to interpret a particular signal, the unit corresponding to the signal is activated (set to 1.0), and the output unit, with the largest net input:

$$a_j = \sum_i S_i w_{ij} \qquad (2.2)$$

is the winner. This procedure is diagrammed in figure 2.9. Recall operates in a corresponding way for transmission behavior.

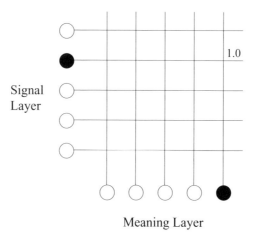

figure 2.10. Training in a Willshaw network. A weight is set to 1 if the input and output units it connects are both active.

2.4.4 *Willshaw networks*

Perhaps the most basic kind of associative networks are Willshaw networks, designed to associate pairs of sparse binary patterns (Willshaw, Buneman, and Longuet-Higgins, 1969; Willshaw, 1971). The learning rule used by these networks simply sets a weight, w_{ij}, to 1 if both S_i and M_j are activated for a given pair of input and output patterns. This learning rule is diagrammed in figure 2.10.

Used as the learning/production mechanism for a population of individuals in an observational learning simulation as outlined in Section 2.4.3, Willshaw networks are capable of learning an existing communication system. If the initial population is seeded with individuals that are communicating successfully, the communication system will be accurately learned by new individuals as long as they are given sufficient exposure (at least one observation of a signal being sent for each meaning is required). This is unsurprising, as the data set that the networks need to learn is of the simplest possible form. The sets of vectors representing both the signals and the meanings are orthogonal, resulting in no inter-correlations and a very easy learning task.

If, however, a modest amount of noise is introduced into the system, performance degrades over time. Figure 2.11 shows how communicative accuracy quickly drops to chance levels if a learner is prone to misobserve a signal/meaning pair 5% of the time. This occurs because there is no

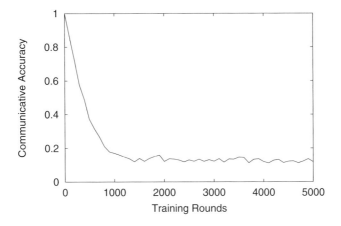

figure 2.11. Failure of the Willshaw network to maintain a communication system under noisy conditions. The simulation is initially seeded with an optimally communicating population. Given a 5% chance of misobservation, a perfect communication system degrades to chance performance. Ten signals and ten meanings are used. Results are averaged over ten simulation runs. All simulations involve populations of 100 individuals, unless otherwise specified.

way for a Willshaw network to represent one of two existing associations as being stronger than another. The network is unable to distinguish a low level of noise from the stronger, true behavior of the population. The effects of noise accumulate over time, resulting in an eventual destruction of the previously optimal communication system given even the smallest amount of noise.

For similar reasons, Willshaw networks are unable to improve the communicative accuracy of a population that is initially communicating randomly, even given a noise-free environment. Performance remains at chance levels, as can be seen in figure 2.12.

2.4.5 Cumulative-Association networks

To correct the problem that Willshaw networks have in discriminating different levels of association, one can simply increment a weight when an association is perceived, rather than just setting the weight to 1. The weight update rule for such a network, which I will call a *Cumulative-Association* network, is as follows:

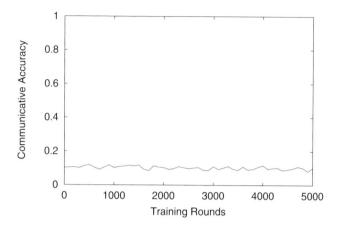

figure 2.12. Failure of the Willshaw network to construct a communication system. Beginning with a population of blank networks, the Willshaw learning rule is unable to improve communicative success. Ten signals and ten meanings are used. Results are averaged over ten simulation runs.

$$\Delta w_{ij} = \begin{cases} 1 \text{ if } S_i = 1 \text{ and } M_j = 1; \\ 0 \text{ otherwise}; \end{cases} \tag{2.3}$$

This new learning rule is able to maintain a communication system against reasonable rates of noise (where the noise does not drown out the signal). It also improves the communicative accuracy of an initially random population of networks, as can be seen in solid line of the graph shown in figure 2.13.

The Cumulative-Association learning rule does not, however, result in a population that communicates optimally. Given any random initial tendency to use a particular signal for a particular meaning, this tendency will be exaggerated in the population until that signal is used conventionally. This exaggeration occurs because each individual does not base its behavior on the actual distribution it observes, but rather the mode of that distribution. The learning rule fails to produce optimal communication because it has no pressure to avoid ambiguously using the same signal for multiple meanings. There is nothing to prevent the signal of choice being the same for more than one meaning, however. An example of the kind of sub-optimal system that results is shown in figure 2.14.

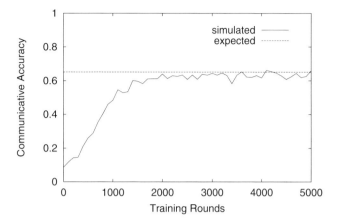

figure 2.13. Performance of the Cumulative-Association network, and the expected value based on Equation 2.4. Performance is better than chance, but the Cumulative-Association learning rule fails to reliably produce an optimal system from random initial conditions. Ten signals and ten meanings are used. Results are averaged over ten simulation runs.

Transmission

	a	b	c
1	1.0	0.0	0.0
2	0.0	1.0	0.0
3	0.0	1.0	0.0

a	b	c	
1.0	0.0	0.0	*1*
0.0	0.5	0.0	*2*
0.0	0.5	0.0	*3*

Reception

figure 2.14. An example of the communicative behavior converged upon by a population of Cumulative-Association networks for a system of three signals and three meanings. While meaning 1 is uniquely conveyed by signal a, signal b is used for both meanings 2 and 3, while signal c is not used at all. Individuals in this population will communicate successfully with each other two times out of three.

The expected performance of the Cumulative-Association learning rule can be mathematically predicted. Because biases in the random communication behavior of the initial population will simply be exaggerated over time, this effectively results in the population using a randomly selected signal for each meaning. The expected number of unique signals resulting from randomly choosing from s signals to represent m meanings is simply the expected number of unique items obtained from selecting m times from s items with replacement. This value can be calculated as follows:

$$n_u = s(1 - (1 - (1/s))^m) \qquad (2.4)$$

This allows for accurate communication about n_u of the m meanings, resulting in an expected communicative accuracy of n_u/m. This expected value is plotted with the simulated results in figure 2.13. The simulation results conform very closely to the level of accuracy that is predicted.

2.4.6 Hebbian networks

It turns out that a very simple way to provide a tendency to use a unique signal for every meaning in a network is the addition of lateral inhibition to the weight update rule. Adding lateral inhibition to the Cumulative-Association rule described in the previous section results in a form of Hebbian learning (Hebb, 1949). Inhibition is implemented by decreasing the strength of a connection between a signal unit and a meaning unit if one, but not both of them are active. This results in the following weight update rule:

$$\Delta w_{ij} = \begin{cases} 1 \text{ if } S_i = 1 \text{ and } M_j = 1; \\ 0 \text{ if } S_i = 0 \text{ and } M_j = 0; \\ -1 \text{ otherwise}; \end{cases} \qquad (2.5)$$

This new update rule is diagrammed in figure 2.15.

It is important to note that this update rule does not increase the weights if both units are not firing, as is done in the most common formulation of the Hebbian learning rule.[6] This modification results in better performance, and is in fact more compatible with the original hypothesis of Hebb (1949). It is also important that the networks use binary units rather than the signed $(+1,-1)$ units that are used for mathematical convenience in the most standard formulation of Hebbian

---

[6] A learning rule similar to the one used here was used by Billard and Dautenhahn (1997) to coordinate the activity of two robotic agents – one the teacher and one the learner – engaged in a simple following task.

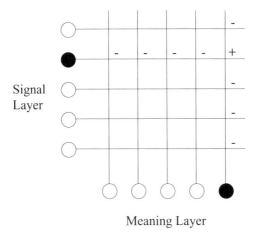

Signal
Layer

Meaning Layer

figure 2.15. Training in a Hebbian network. A weight is increased if the input and output units it connects are both active. The weight is decreased if one, but not both of the units are active.

networks. Aside from the resulting problems in making analogies with real neural activity, using signed units in a task where patterns are sparse creates a great deal of spurious correlation. Two different patterns, each with one unit active, will be correlated in all but two of their units. This makes the task of the network unnecessarily difficult, and use of signed units results in very poor performance.

The performance of populations of networks using this formulation of the Hebbian learning rule as shown in (2.5) is presented in figure 2.16. The addition of lateral inhibition to the network learning rule results in the ability to produce an optimal communication system in a population that begins with random behavior. This ability to construct a communication system necessarily entails the ability to acquire and maintain an existing system. After a communicative accuracy of 1.0 is reached soon after round 1000, new individuals are accurately acquiring this optimal system. Maintenance against noise can essentially be thought of as continual reconstruction of the system each time it is degraded by noise. The Hebbian learning rule, then, satisfies all three of the requirements set out in Section 2.4.1, providing a possible mechanism for the use of a simple system of learned communication.

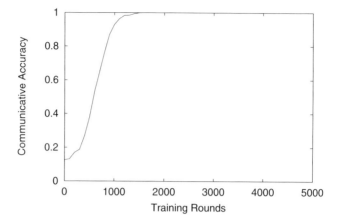

figure 2.16. Performance of the Hebbian network. Populations of Hebbian networks are able to construct optimal communication systems. Ten signals and meanings are used. Results are averaged over 10 simulation runs.

Scalability

The performance of the Hebbian network scales well for increased numbers of meanings. Figure 2.17 shows that, while the time it takes a population to converge on an optimal system increases with the number of meanings, optimal communication is nevertheless always achieved. The increase in convergence time is likely due to a lowered starting point – the chance level of communicative accuracy decreases as the number of meanings goes up.

It is important to be clear that the increase in time shown here is in terms of the number of rounds (replacements of an existing individual with a blank, new individual) it takes the population to reach an optimal state, not the amount of time that it takes each new individual to learn. Learning involves observing three communicative interactions based on the transmission of each meaning. Thus, as the number of meanings increase, so does the number of observed samples of behavior. This is a result of the number of observations required to get a representative sample of a larger system, and is not reflected by the number of rounds.

Time to convergence is also affected by the size of the population, as can be seen in figure 2.18. As the number of individuals in the population increases, so does the number of rounds required to reach an optimal state of communication. This increase seems to be linear in the size of

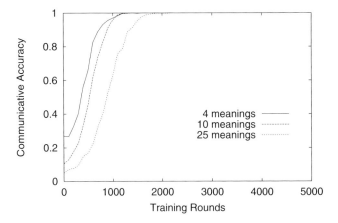

figure 2.17. Performance of the Hebbian network using varying numbers of signals and meanings. The number of signals and meanings is equal in each case. Results for each plot are averaged over ten simulation runs.

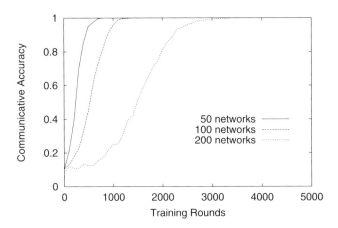

figure 2.18. Network populations of varying sizes establishing a conventional encoding for ten input patterns. All plots are averaged over ten simulation runs.

the population, and likely reflects the additional time to reach consensus in a larger population.

Multiple-unit meanings

Using Hebbian networks, it is also possible to deal with more complex meaning patterns than the ones used in the previous simulations. Instead of turning a single unit on in the vector to represent a particular meaning, a pattern across multiple units can be used. This allows the meanings to be structured according to some task-based metric. It also provides a way in which meanings can be more or less similar to each other as patterns can overlap, sharing some of the same units.

The addition of structure transforms the problem into a form of vector quantization (Kohonen, 1989). The difficulties that arise because of correlations between the new structured meanings can be avoided by adding a conscience mechanism to the winner-take-all output threshold, as is done in other vector quantization tasks (Grossberg, 1976; Bienenstock, Cooper, and Munro, 1982). Additional details about this type of network, and results demonstrating its performance can be found in Oliphant (in preparation).

2.4.7 Summary of simulation results

The simulations that I have presented demonstrate that associative-network learning is capable of supporting a learned system of communication in a population of individuals. This result is particularly significant in that the learning framework used involved no success-based reinforcement. Although I have shown plots of communicative success of the simulated populations, at no point are such measures used to provide learners with a reinforcement signal. The success of the Hebbian learning strategy indicates that, while an error signal might be used if one was available, reinforcement is not strictly required to learn to communicate.

Not just any learning mechanism is sufficient, however. Learning strategies that simply exaggerate initial random tendencies in the populations behavior will fail to reliably result in populations that communicate successfully. Instead, a learning mechanism must be such that it pushes the population's communicative behavior toward a state where each meaning is expressed unambiguously.[7] This is exactly what the Hebbian learning rule does.

---

[7] This assumes, of course, the absence of any context. If contextual information is available, communication can tolerate some level of ambiguity, as human language clearly demonstrates.

Hebbian learning is perhaps the most simple, biologically plausible learning mechanism known. Tuning simple associations based on correlations is what nervous systems are designed to do. This would seem to place the ability to utilize learned communication within the means of virtually any animal species. The fact that such a simple form of learning seems sufficient both to acquire an existing system of communication and to construct such a system in the first place raises a rather puzzling question. Why are learned communication systems so unique?

2.5 The problem of observing meaning

One possible answer to this question lies in one of the assumptions that is inherent in the model of learning that I have presented. I assume that a learner has access to the behavior of others in the form of signal/meaning pairs. While this is a useful initial course of action, making it possible to actually carry out the simulations, it is likely to be unjustified in general. In particular, it seems unrealistic for a learner to have easy access to the meanings that others are using their signals to convey. If a child is out for a walk with its mother, and hears *dog*, how is she to know that her mother is referring to the furry, brown creature wagging its tail, rather than the wagging tail itself, or even the fact that it is a sunny day?

The difficult aspects of observational learning might then have less to do with *learning* than they do with *observing*. While I have given an analysis of the computational requirements of the learning mechanism, it still remains an open question how learners extract the signal/meaning pairs that they are to associate. In particular, understanding the problem a learner faces in determining the meaning a signal is intended to convey is central, I think, to explaining the rarity of learned communication. In the case of innate communication, the problem does not exist, simply for the reason that learning is not required for the system to be transmitted from one generation to the next.

The difficulty of observing meaning also accounts for why learned *symbolic* communication is so rare. In an innate system, transmission of an arbitrary sign is no more difficult that transmitting an iconic one – such distinctions are unimportant to the process of biological reproduction. This is not the case with respect to the transmission of a learned system. Iconic or indexical signs refer by resemblance and causal relationship respectively. In both cases, the signal gives direct information about the meaning it refers to. In contrast, a symbol will, by definition, bear no discernible relationship to the meaning to which it refers – the association is purely conventional.

Learned symbolic systems of communication are rare, then, because it is in the case of symbolic reference that the problem of observing meaning is most difficult. Humans seem to be the only species that have managed to find a way to cope with this difficulty. Children are able to learn to use words because they are adept at determining their meaning from the context in which they appear. They seem to simplify the task of deciding what a word denotes through knowledge of the existence of taxonomic categories (Markman, 1989), awareness of the pragmatic context (Tomasello, 1995), and reading the intent of the speaker (Bloom, 1997). In addition, human adults seem, at least to some degree, to make the meaning of their utterances more salient to the child. When talking to young children, parents modify their speech along a number of dimensions, and this may aid the child in acquisition (Snow, 1977). Although the degree to which parents facilitate the language learning environment of their children is a matter of some controversy (see Ochs and Shieffelin (1995) for an opposing view), it is an area that should be considered when investigating the differences between humans and other primates.

2.6 Discussion

I have argued in this chapter that human language is the only existing system of learned symbolic communication. While other species use innate symbolic systems, or learned non-symbolic systems, cultural transmission of arbitrary reference seems to exist only in humans. This uniqueness can be explained by looking at how the problem of transmission is different in the case of learned communication, even if the communication system itself is no more complex. While innate systems can simply be transmitted genetically, learned systems must be acquired ontogenetically. Learned systems cannot be transmitted directly, but must instead involve acquisition of the behavior produced by others.

Although the simulation work has shown that very simple learning mechanisms are sufficient to support this process of acquisition, this has been based on the assumption that a learner has easy access to the meaning that a signal is intended to convey. Getting such access is likely to be a non-trivial process, particularly in the case of symbolic reference, where the signal and meaning are linked purely by convention. Given this, I propose that a key milestone in the evolution of language is the ability to transmit a learned symbolic system of communication from one generation to the next. It is only when this ability is in place that the stage is set for the development of linguistic complexity.

At this point, perhaps the addition of syntactic structure will require additional biological change. It is possible that the ability to communicate by combining sequences of signals requires cognitive skill that other animals do not have. It may be, however, that the the problem of transmitting a learned symbolic system is the primary factor limiting the evolution of language ability. Perhaps, the achievement of syntactic communication is an extension that is comparatively less difficult. That this might be true is supported by evidence that non-human animals can be trained to use syntactic forms (Greenfield and Savage-Rumbaugh, 1990), and computational work showing that syntactic structure can emerge on a cultural, rather than evolutionary time scale (Batali, 1997; Hutchins and Hazelhurst, 1997; Worden, 2000; and the chapters in this volume by Hurford, Kirby and Steels).

In either case, it is a mistake to take the existence of simple innate communication systems in other species to imply that the problem of the lexicon in language evolution is solved. To do so is to ignore the important distinction between innate and learned communication. The rarity of simple, learned systems of communication suggests that shifting from an innate system to an equally simple learned one is a difficult task, and one worthy of careful study.

Acknowledgements

The research for this chapter was carried out at the Language Evolution and Computation Research Unit at the Department of Linguistics, University of Edinburgh funded by ESRC grant R000237551. I would like to thank Ted Briscoe, Simon Kirby, and Jim Hurford for their helpful comments on this work.

References

Batali, J. (1997). Computational simulations of the emergence of grammar. In J. Hurford, C. Knight, and M. Studdert-Kennedy (eds.), *Evolution of Language: Social and Cognitive Bases for the Emergence of Phonology and Syntax*. Cambridge University Press, Cambridge.

Bickerton, D. (1990). *Language and species*. Chicago University Press, Chicago.

Bienenstock, E., L. Cooper, and P. Munro (1982). Theory for the development of neuron selectivity: Orientation specificity and binocular interaction in visual cortex. *Journal of Neuroscience 2*, 32–48.

Billard, A. and K. Dautenhahn (1997). The social aspect of communication: a case study in the use and usefulness of communication for embodied agents. In *Fourth European Conference on Artificial Life*, Brighton, England.

Bloom, P. (1997). Intentionality and word learning. *Trends in cognitive sciences 1*(1), 9–12.

Blume, A., Y. Kim, and J. Sobel (1993). Evolutionary stability in games of communication. *Games and Economic Behavior 5*, 547–575.

Burling, R. (2000). Comprehension, production and conventionalization in the origins of language. In C. Knight, J. Hurford, and M. Studdert-Kennedy (eds.), *The Evolutionary Emergence of Language*. Cambridge University Press, Cambridge, pp. 27–39.

de Saussure, F. (1959). *Course in general linguistics*. McGraw-Hill, New York.

Di Paolo, E. (1997). An investigation into the evolution of communication. *Adaptive Behavior 6*(2), 285–324.

Gardener, B. and P. Gardener (1969). Teaching sign language to a chimpanzee. *Science 165*, 664–672.

Goodall, J. (1986). *The chimpanzees of Gombe*. Harvard University Press, Cambridge, MA.

Greenfield, P. and E. Savage-Rumbaugh (1990). Grammatical combination in *pan paniscus*: Processes of learning and invention in the evolution and development of language. In S. Parker and K. Gibson (eds.), *"Language" and intelligence in monkeys and apes*, Cambridge University Press, Cambridge, pp. 540–578.

Grossberg, S. (1976). Adaptive pattern classification and universal recoding: Ii. feedback, expectation, olfaction, illusions. *Biological Cybernetics 23*, 187–202.

Hauser, M. (1996). *The evolution of communication*. MIT Press, Cambridge, MA.

Hayes, K. and C. Hayes (1951). The intellectual development of a home-raised chimpanzee. *Proceedings of the American Philosophical Society 95*, 105.

Hebb, D. (1949). *The organization of behavior*. John Wiley & Sons, New York.

Herman, L., D. Richards, and J. Wolz (1984). Comprehension of sentences by bottlenosed dolphins. *Cognition 16*, 129–219.

Hurford, J. (1989). Biological evolution of the Saussurean sign as a component of the language acquisition device. *Lingua 77*, 187–222.

Hutchins, E. and B. Hazelhurst (1995). How to invent a lexicon: the development of shared symbols in interaction. In N. Gilbert and R. Conte (eds.), *Artificial Societies: The computer simulation of social life*. UCL Press, London.

Hutchins, E. and B. Hazelhurst (1997). The emergence of propositions from the coordination of talk and action in a shared world. forthcoming.

Kim, Y. and J. Sobel (1995). An evolutionary approach to pre-play communication. *Econometrica 65*(5), 1181–1193.

Kohonen, T. (1989). *Self-organization and associative memory* (3rd ed.). Springer-Verlag, Berlin.

Lewis, D. (1969). *Convention: A philosophical study*. Harvard University Press, Cambridge, MA.

Markman, E. (1989). *Categorization and naming in children: Problems of induction*. MIT Press, Cambridge, MA.

Murciano, A. and J. Millan (1996). Learning signaling behaviors and specialization in cooperative agents. *Adaptive Behavior 5*(1), 5–28.

Newmeyer, F. J. (1991). Functional explanation in linguistics and the origins of language. *Language and Communication 11*, 3–28.

Noble, J. (1998). Evolved signals: Expensive hype vs. conspiratorial whispers. Paper presented at the ALife VI conference.

Ochs, E. and B. Shieffelin (1995). The impact of language socialization on grammatical development. In P. Fletcher and P. MacWhinney (eds.), *The Handbook of Child Language*, Blackwell, Oxford, pp. 73–94.

Oliphant, M. (1997). *Formal approaches to innate and learned communication: Laying the foundation for language.* Ph. D. thesis, University of California, San Diego.

Oliphant, M. (1998). Self-organized coordination in populations of interacting associative networks. Manuscript in preparation.

Oliphant, M. and J. Batali (1997). Learning and the emergence of coordinated communication. *Center for Research on Language Newsletter 11*(1).

Peirce, C. (1932). *Collected papers of Charles Sanders Peirce, Volume 2: Elements of logic.* Harvard University Press, Cambridge, MA.

Pepperberg, I. (1987). Evidence for conceptual quantitative abilities in the African parrot: Labeling of cardinal sets. *Ethology 75*, 37–61.

Pinker, S. and P. Bloom (1990). Natural language and natural selection. *Behavioral and Brain Sciences 13*, 707–784.

Premack, D. (1971). Language in chimpanzees? *Science 172*, 808–822.

Savage-Rumbaugh, E., K. McDonald, R. Sevcik, W. Hopkins, and E. Rubert (1986). Spontaneous symbol acquisition and communicative use by pygmy chimpanzees (*pan paniscus*). *Journal of Experimental Psychology: General 115*, 211–235.

Seyfarth, R. and D. Cheney (1986). Vocal development in vervet monkeys. *Animal Behavior 34*, 1640–1658.

Seyfarth, R., D. Cheney, and P. Marler (1980a). Monkey responses to three different alarm calls: evidence for predator classification and semantic communication. *Science 210*, 801–803.

Seyfarth, R., D. Cheney, and P. Marler (1980b). Vervet monkey alarm calls: semantic communication in a free-ranging environment. *Animal Behavior 28*, 1070–1094.

Skyrms, B. (1996). *Evolution of the social contract.* Cambridge University Press, Cambridge.

Snow, C. (1977). Mothers' speech research: From input to interaction. In C. Snow and C. Ferguson (eds.), *Talking to Children: Language input and acquisition*, Cambridge University Press, Cambridge, pp. 31–49.

Steels, L. (1996). Self-organizing vocabularies. In *Proceedings of the V Alife Conference*, Nara, Japan.

Strusaker, T. (1967). Auditory communication among vervet monkeys (*cercopithecus aethiops*). In S. Altmann (ed.), *Social Communication among Primates*, University of Chicago Press, Chicago, pp. 281–324.

Tinbergen, N. (1952). Derived activities: Their causation, biological significance, origin and emancipation during evolution. *Quarterly Review of Biology 27*, 1–32.

Tomasello, M. (1990). Cultural transmission in the tool use and communicatory signaling of chimpanzees? In S. Parker and K. Gibson (eds.), *Language and intelligence in monkeys and apes: Comparative developmental perspectives*. Cambridge University Press, Cambridge.

Tomasello, M. (1995). Pragmatic contexts for early verb learning. In M. Tomasello and W. Merriman (eds.), *Beyond Names For Things: Young Children's Acquisition of Verbs*. Lawrence Erlbaum, Mahwah, NJ.

Tomasello, M. (1996). Do apes ape? In C. Heyes and B. Galef (eds.), *Social Learning in Animals: The Roots of Culture*, Academic Press, San Diego, pp. 319–436.

Tomasello, M., J. Call, K. Nagell, R. Olguin, and M. Carpenter (1994). The learning and use of gestural signals by young chimpanzees: a trans-generational study. *Primates 35*, 137–154.

Tomasello, M., B. George, A. Kruger, J. Farrar, and E. Evans (1985). The development of gestural communication in young chimpanzees. *Journal of Human Evolution 14*, 175–186.

Tomasello, M., D. Gust, and T. Frost (1989). A longitudinal investigation of gestural communication in young chimpanzees. *Primates 30*, 35–50.

von Frisch, K. (1974). Decoding the language of the bee. *Science 185*, 663–668.

Warneryd, K. (1993). Cheap talk, coordination, and evolutionary stability. *Games and Economic Behavior 5*, 532–546.

Willshaw, D. (1971). *Models of distributed associative memory*. Ph. D. thesis, University of Edinburgh.

Willshaw, D., O. Buneman, and H. Longuet-Higgins (1969). Non-holographic associative memory. *Nature 222*, 960–962.

Worden, R. (2000). Words, memes and language evolution. In C. Knight, J. Hurford, and M. Studdert-Kennedy (eds.), *The Evolutionary Emergence of Language*, Cambridge University Press, Cambridge, pp. 353–371.

Yanco, H. and L. Stein (1993). An adaptive communication protocol for co-operating mobile robots. In J. Meyer, H. Roitblat, and S. Wilson (eds.), *From Animal to Animats 2: Proceedings of the Second International Conference on Simulation of Adaptive Behavior*. MIT Press, Cambridge MA.

3

Bootstrapping grounded word semantics

Luc Steels
Sony Computer Science Laboratory
Paris and VUB AI Laboratory Brussels
and
Frederic Kaplan
Sony Computer Science Laboratory
Paris

3.1 Introduction

The paper reports on experiments with a population of visually grounded robotic agents capable of bootstrapping their own ontology and shared lexicon without prior design nor other forms of human intervention. The agents do so while playing a particular language game called the guessing game. We show that synonymy and ambiguity arise as emergent properties in the lexicon, due to the situated grounded character of the agent–environment interaction, but that there are also tendencies to dampen them so as to make the language more coherent and thus more optimal from the viewpoints of communicative success, cognitive complexity, and learnability.

How do words get their meanings? An answer to this question requires a theory of the origins of meanings, a theory of how forms get recruited for expressing meanings, and a theory of how associations between forms and meanings may propagate in a population. Each theory must characterize properties of a cognitive agent's architecture: components a cognitive agent needs to have, and details of how the different components coordinate their activities. More specifically, the theories should detail what kind of associative memory the agents must have for storing and acquiring form–meaning relations, what type of mechanisms they might use to categorize the environment through sensory inputs, how they might acquire a repertoire of perceptually grounded categories (an ontology), and what behaviors the agents must be capable of so as to communicate successfully through language.

To allow validation, theories of agent architecture should be formally specified and hence testable through computer simulations or even better through experiments with robotic agents interacting with real world environments through a sensory apparatus. When shared lexicons and ontologies emerge from these experiments, the architecture is at least functionally adequate. Ideally other emergent properties also seen in the evolution of natural languages should be observed, such as the damping of synonymy, or an expansion of the language when the environment introduces new challenges and thus the creation of new meanings. Experiments with physical robots ensure that real world constraints are not ignored or overlooked.

In the last five years, substantial progress has been reported on these objectives (see the overview in Steels, 1997b). There has been a first wave of research in the early 1990's strongly inspired by artificial life concepts (Maclennan, 1991; Werner and Dyer, 1991; Hurford, 1989; Noble, 1998; Yanco Stein, 1993). This early research has often used a genetic approach and assumed that the set of meanings is fixed and given a priori by the designer. The primary emphasis was on understanding the emergence and evolution of animal communication rather than human natural language. There has been a second wave of research in the mid 1990's featuring more systematic investigations of different possible architectures (Oliphant, 1996) and a deeper study of the complex adaptive system properties of linguistic populations and their evolving lexicons (Steels and Kaplan, 1998; Arita and Koyama, 1998). The issue of meaning creation in co-evolution with lexicon formation has also been studied (Steels, 1997b; Hutchins and Hazelhurst, 1995) and more sophisticated experiments have been reported to ground lexicon formation on real robots (Steels and Vogt, 1997). In this second wave of research, the cultural approach dominates. Lexicons are no longer transmitted genetically but by learning. There is a growing interest to model the complex phenomena seen in human lexicon formation. In several experiments the set of possible meanings is open, expanding and contracting in relation to the demands of the task and the environment. The population of agents is also open so that issues of lexicon acquisition by virgin agents and preservation of a system across generations can be studied.

This paper builds further on these various research results focusing more specifically on two issues:

[1] *The Gavagai problem.* In *Word and Object*, Quine raises the question how a linguist might acquire a language of a foreign tribe (Quine, 1960:29). He points out that if a native says *Gavagai*, while pointing to a rabbit scurrying by, it is in no way possible to uniquely determine

its meaning. *Gavagai* could mean 'rabbit', 'animal', 'white', as well as hundreds of other things. So, how can one ever acquire the meaning of a word? As pointed out by Eve Clark (1993), children have a very similar problem and it is therefore not surprising that overextensions or underextensions are observed in the first words. In computer simulations so far, most researchers have assumed that agents have direct access to each other's meanings, so that the problem of lexicon construction and acquisition becomes one of learning associations between words and meanings, with direct feedback on whether the right association has been learned. But in more realistic circumstances, humans as well as autonomous agents only get feedback on the communicative success of an interaction, not on what meanings were used. Even communicative success may not be completely clear although this additional source of uncertainty has not been explored further in our experiments. The problem of lexicon construction and acquisition must therefore be reformulated: The agents must acquire word–meaning and meaning–object relations which are compatible with the word–object co-occurrences they overtly observe but without observing word–meaning relations directly. This problem is obviously much harder.

[2] *The grounding problem.* When agents are embodied and situated, and when they have to build up their ontology autonomously from scratch, the problem of lexicon acquisition becomes even harder. The perception of an agent depends on the viewpoint from which he observes the scene and categorization therefore becomes dependent on this viewpoint. For example, something which is to the left for one agent may be to the right for another one and vice-versa. Even the colors of a surface (more precisely wavelength reflection) are not perceptually constant when seen from slightly different angles. This perceptual incoherence makes it more difficult for agents to coordinate their words and meanings. Nevertheless, the success of a language depends to a great extent on whether the agents manage to abstract away from contingencies of viewpoints and situations.

In the past few years, we have designed an agent architecture addressing these two issues and have tested this architecture on physically embodied robotic agents. Although we have studied multi-word expressions and the emergence of syntax within the same experimental context (Steels, 1998), this paper only discusses single word utterances so that we can focus completely on semiotic dynamics. The first section of this paper briefly summarizes the experimental set up and the proposed

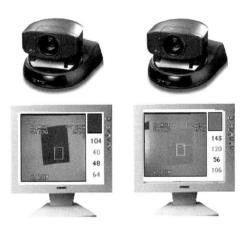

figure 3.1. Two Talking Head cameras and associated monitors showing what each camera perceives.

architecture. The rest of the paper focuses on the macroscopic properties of the lexicons and ontologies that emerge from our robotic experiments.

3.2 The Talking Heads experiment

The robotic setup used for the experiments in this paper consists of a set of 'Talking Heads' connected through the Internet. Each Talking Head features a Sony EVI-D31 camera with controllable pan/tilt motors for horizontal and vertical movement (figure 3.1), a computer for cognitive processing (perception, categorization, lexicon lookup, etc.), a screen on which the internal states of the agent currently loaded in the body are shown, a TV-monitor showing the scene as seen through the camera, and devices for audio input and output. Agents can load themselves in a physical Talking Head and teleport themselves to another Head by traveling through the Internet. By design, an agent can only interact with another one when it is physically instantiated in a body located in a shared physical environment. The experimental infrastructure also features a commentator which reports and comments on dialogs, displays measures of the ontologies and languages of the agents and game statistics, such as average communicative success, lexical coherence, average ontology and lexicon size, etc.

For the experiments reported in this paper, the shared environment consists of a magnetic white board on which various shapes are pasted: colored triangles, circles, rectangles, etc. Although this may seem a strong restriction, we have learned that the environment should be simple enough to be able to follow and experimentally investigate the complex dynamics taking place in the agent population.

The guessing game

The interaction between the agents consists of a language game, called the guessing game. The guessing game is played between two visually grounded agents. One agent plays the role of *speaker* and the other one then plays the role of *hearer*. Agents take turns playing games so all of them develop the capacity to be speaker or hearer. Agents are capable of segmenting the image perceived through the camera into objects and of collecting various sensory data about each object, such as the color (decomposed in RGB channels), average gray-scale or position. The set of objects and their data constitute a *context*. The speaker chooses one object from this context, further called the *topic*. The other objects form the *background*. The speaker then gives a linguistic hint to the hearer.

The linguistic hint is an utterance that identifies the topic with respect to the objects in the background. For example, if the context contains [1] a red square, [2] a blue triangle, and [3] a green circle, then the speaker may say something like *the red one* to communicate that [1] is the topic. If the context contains also a red triangle, he has to be more precise and say something like *the red square*. Of course, the Talking Heads do not say *the red square* but use their own language and concepts which are never going to be the same as those used in English. For example, they may say *malewina* to mean [UPPER EXTREME-LEFT LOW-REDNESS].

Based on the linguistic hint, the hearer tries to guess what topic the speaker has chosen, and he communicates his choice to the speaker by pointing to the object. A robot points by transmitting in which direction he is looking in his own agent-centered coordinates. The other robot is calibrated in the beginning of the experiment to be able to convert these coordinates into his own agent-centered coordinates. The game succeeds if the topic guessed by the hearer is equal to the topic chosen by the speaker. The game fails if the guess was wrong or if the speaker or the hearer failed at some earlier point in the game. In case of a failure, the speaker gives an extra-linguistic hint by pointing to the topic he had in mind, and both agents try to repair their internal structures to be more successful in future games.

The architecture of the agents has two components: a conceptualization module responsible for categorizing reality or for applying categories to find back the referent in the perceptual image, and a verbalization module responsible for verbalising a conceptualization or for interpreting a form to reconstruct its meaning. Agents start with no prior designer-supplied ontology nor lexicon. A shared ontology and lexicon must emerge from scratch in a self-organized process. The agents therefore not only play the game but also expand or adapt their ontology or lexicon to be more successful in future games.

The conceptualization module

Meanings are categories that distinguish the topic from the other objects in the context. The categories are organized in discrimination trees (figure 3.2) where each node contains a discriminator able to filter the set of objects into a subset that satisfies a category and another one that satisfies its opposition. For example, there might be a discriminator based on the horizontal position (HPOS) of the center of an object (scaled between 0.0 and 1.0) sorting the objects in the context in a bin for the category 'left' when HPOS < 0.5, (further labeled as [HPOS-0.0,0.5]) and one for 'right' when HPOS > 0.5 (labeled as [HPOS-0.5,1.0]). Further subcategories are created by restricting the region of each category. For example, the category 'very left' (or [HPOS-0.0,0.25]) applies when an object's HPOS value is in the region [0.0,0.25]. For the experiments in this paper, the agents have only channels for horizontal position (HPOS), vertical position (VPOS), color (RGB indicated as RED, GREEN, BLUE), and grayscale (GRAY). The system is open to exploit any channel with additional raw data, such as audio, or results from more complex image processing.

A distinctive category set is found by filtering the objects in the context from the top in each discrimination tree until there is a bin which only contains the topic. This means that only the topic falls within the category associated with that bin, and so this category uniquely filters out the topic from all the other objects in the scene. Often more than one solution is possible, but all solutions are passed on to the lexicon module.

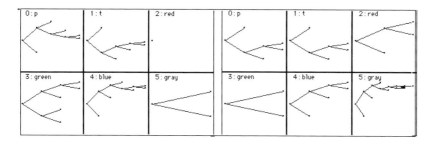

figure 3.2. The discrimination trees of two agents.

The discrimination trees of each agent are formed using a growth and pruning dynamics coupled to the environment, which creates an ecology of distinctions. Discrimination trees grow randomly by the addition of new categorizers splitting the region of existing categories. Categorizers compete in each guessing game. The use and success of a categorizer is monitored and categorizers that are irrelevant for the environments encountered by the agent are pruned. More details about the discrimination game can be found in Steels (1997a).

Verbalization module

The lexicon of each agents consists of a two-way association between forms (which are individual words) and meanings (which are single categories). Each association has a score. Words are random combinations of syllables, although any set of distinct word symbols could be used. When a speaker needs to verbalize a category, he looks up all possible words associated with that category, orders them and picks the one with the best score for transmission to the hearer. When a hearer needs to interpret a word, he looks up all possible meanings, tests which meanings are applicable in the present context, i.e. which ones yield a possible single referent, and uses the remaining meaning with the highest score as the winner. The topic guessed by the hearer is the referent of this meaning.

Based on feedback on the outcome of the guessing game, the speaker and the hearer update the scores. When the game has succeeded, they increase the score of the winning association and decrease the competitors, thus implementing lateral inhibition. When the game has failed, they each decrease the score of the association they used. Occasionally new associations are stored. A speaker creates a new word when he does not have a word yet for a meaning he wants to express. A hearer may encounter a new word he has never heard before and then store a new association between this word and the best guess of the possible meaning. This guess is based on first guessing the topic using the extra-linguistic hint provided by the speaker, and on performing categorization using his own discrimination trees as developed thus far. These lexicon bootstrapping mechanisms have been explained and validated extensively in earlier papers (Steels and Kaplan, 1998) and are basically the same as those reported by Oliphant (1996).

The conceptualization module proposes several solutions to the verbalization module which prefers those that have already been lexicalized. Agents monitor success of categories in the total game and use this to target growth and pruning. The language therefore strongly influences the ontologies agents retain. The two modules are structurally coupled and thus get coordinated without a central coordinator.

Examples

Here is the simplest possible case of a language game. The speaker, **a1**, has picked a triangular object at the bottom of the scene as the topic. There is only one other rectangular object in the scene, nearer to the top. Consequently, the category [VPOS-0.0,0.5]$_{\mathbf{a1}}$, which is valid when the vertical position VPOS < 0.5, is applicable because it is valid for the triangle but not for the rectangle. Assuming that **a1** has an association in his lexicon relating [VPOS-0.0,0.5]$_{\mathbf{a1}}$ with the word *lu*, then **a1** will retrieve this association and transmits the word *lu* to the hearer, which is agent **a2**.

Now suppose that **a2** has stored in his lexicon an association between "lu" and [RED-0.0,0.5]$_{\mathbf{a2}}$. He therefore hypothesises that [RED-0.0,0.5]$_{\mathbf{a2}}$ must be the meaning of *lu*. When he applies this category to the present scene, in other words when he filters out the objects whose value for the redness channel (RED) do not fall in the region [0.0, 0.5], he obtains only one remaining object, the triangle. Hence **a2** concludes that this must be the topic and points to it. The speaker recognises that the hearer has pointed to the right object and so the game succeeds.

The complete dialog is reported by the commentator as follows:

```
Game 125.
  a1 is the speaker. a2 is the hearer.
  a1 segments the context into 2 objects
```

```
a1 categorizes the topic as [VPOS-0.0,0.5]
a1 says: 'lu'
a2 interprets 'lu' as [RED-0.0,0.5]
a2 points to the topic
a1 says: 'OK'
```

This game illustrates a situation where the speaker and the hearer picks out the same referent even though they use a different meaning. The speaker uses vertical position and the hearer the degree of redness in RGB space.

Here is a second example, The speaker is again **a1** and he uses the same category and the same word *lu*. But the hearer, **a3**, interprets *lu* in terms of horizontal position [HPOS-0.0,0.5]$_{\mathbf{a3}}$ (left of the scene). Because there is more than one object satisfying this category in the scene the agents look at, the hearer is confused. The speaker then points to the topic and the hearer acquires a new association between *lu* and [VPOS-0.0,0.5]$_{\mathbf{a3}}$, which starts to compete with the one he already had. The commentator reports this kind of interaction as follows:

```
Game 137.
 a1 is the speaker. a3 is the hearer.
 a1 segments the context into 2 objects
 a1 categorizes the topic as [VPOS-0.0,0.5]
 a1 says: 'lu'
 a3 interprets 'lu' as [HPOS-0.0,0.5]
 There is more than one such object
 a3 says: 'lu?'
 a1 points to the topic
 a3 categorizes the topic as [VPOS-0.0,0.5]
 a3 stores 'lu' as [VPOS-0.0,0.5]
```

Table 3.1 shows part of a vocabulary of a single agent after 3,000 language games. It shows also the score (Sc.). We see in this table that for some meanings (such as [RED-0.0,0.125]) a single form *wovota* has firmly established itself. For other meanings, like [GRAY-0.25,0.5], a word was known at some point but is now no longer in use. For other meanings, like [VPOS-0.0,0.5], two words are still competing: *gorepe* and *zuga*. There are words, like *zafe*, which have two possible meanings [VPOS-0.0,0.25] and [GREEN-0.5,1.0].

Table 3.1. *Agent vocabulary*

Form	Meaning	Sc.	Form	Meaning	Sc.
wovota	[RED-0.0,0.125]	1.0	sogavo	[GREEN-0.5,1.0]	0.0
tu	[GRAY-0.25,0.5]	0.0	naxesi	[GREEN-0.5,1.0]	0.0
gorepe	[VPOS-0.0,0.5]	0.3	ko	[GREEN-0.5,1.0]	0.0
zuga	[VPOS-0.0,0.5]	0.1	ve	[GREEN-0.5,1.0]	0.0
lora	[VPOS-0.25,0.5]	0.1	migine	[GREEN-0.5,1.0]	0.0
wovota	[VPOS-0.25,0.5]	0.2	zota	[GREEN-0.5,1.0]	0.9
di	[VPOS-0.25,0.5]	0.0	zafe	[GREEN-0.5,1.0]	0.1
zafe	[VPOS-0.0,0.25]	0.2	zulebo	[HPOS-0.0,1.0]	0.0
wowore	[VPOS-0.0,0.25]	0.9	xi	[HPOS-0.0,1.0]	0.0
mifo	[HPOS-0.0,1.0]	1.0			

3.3 Tendencies in natural language

Clearly, to have success in the game the speaker and the hearer must share a list of words, and the meanings of these words must pick out the same referent in the same context. However agents can only coordinate their language based on overt behavior. This leads to various forms of incoherence. An incoherence remains until the environment produces situations that cause further disentanglement, as in the example above where a speaker uses a word which is interpreted by the hearer as referring to more than one object instead of just one.

There are clear tendencies in natural languages towards coherence and indeed a coherent language is 'better'. First of all coherence gives a higher chance of success in multiple contexts. For example, if every agent preferentially associates the same meaning with the same word, there is a higher chance that the same word will designate the same referent, even in a context that has not been seen before. Second, coherence diminishes cognitive complexity. For example, if all agents preferentially use the same word for the same meaning, there will be fewer words and therefore less words need to be stored. If all words preferentially have the same meaning, there is less cognitive effort needed in disambiguation. Third, coherence helps in language acquisition by future generations. If there are fewer words and they tend to have the same meanings, a language learner has an easier time to acquire them.

Natural languages are clearly not totally coherent even in the same language community, and languages developed autonomously by physically embodied agents will not be fully coherent either.

1. Different agents may prefer a different word for the same meaning. These words are said to be *synonyms* of each other. An example is "pavement" versus "sidewalk". The situation arises because an agent may construct a new word not knowing that one is already in existence. Synonymy is often an intermediate stage for new meanings whose lexicalization has not stabilized yet. Natural languages show a clear tendency for the elimination of synonyms. Accidental synonyms tend to specialize, incorporating different shades of meaning from the context or reflecting socio-linguistic and dialectal differences of speaker and hearer.

2. The same word may have different preferred meanings in the population. These words thus become *ambiguous*. This situation may arise completely accidentally, as in the case of *bank* which can mean river bank and financial institution. These words are then called *homonyms*. The situation may also arise whenever there is more than one possible meaning compatible with the same situation. An agent on hearing an unknown word may therefore incorrectly guess its meaning. Ambiguity also arises because most words are *polysemous*: The original source meaning has become extended by metaphor and metonymy to cover a family of meanings (Victorri and Fuchs, 1996). Real ambiguity tends to survive in natural languages only when the contexts of each meaning are sufficiently different, otherwise the hearer would be unable to derive the correct meaning.

3. The same meaning may denote different referents for different agents *in the same context*. This is the case when the application of a category is strongly situated, for example 'left' for the speaker may be 'right' for the hearer. Deictic terms like *this* and *that* are even clearer examples from natural language. In natural languages, this *multi-referentiality* is counter-acted by verbalizing more information about the context or by avoiding words with multi-referential meanings when they may cause confusion.

4. It is possible and very common with a richer categorial repertoire, that a particular referent in a particular context can be conceptualized in more than one way. For example, an object may be to the left of all the others, *and* much higher positioned than all the others. In the same situation different agents may therefore use different meanings. Agents only get feedback about whether they guessed the object

the speaker had in mind, not whether they used the same meaning as the speaker. This *indeterminacy* of categories is a cause of ambiguity. A speaker may mean 'left' by *bovubo*, but a hearer may have inferred that it meant 'upper'.

So, although circumstances cause agents to introduce incoherence in the language system, there are at the same time opposing tendencies, attempting to restore coherence. Synonyms tend to disappear and ambiguity is avoided. In the remainder of this paper, we want to show that the dynamics of the guessing game, particularly when it is played by situated embodied robotic agents, leads unavoidably to incoherence, but that there are tendencies towards coherence as well. Both tendencies are emergent properties of the dynamics. There is no central controlling agency that weeds out synonyms or eliminates ambiguity, rather they get pushed out as a side effect of the collective dynamics of the game. Before we can see whether all this is indeed the case we need a set of analysis tools.

3.4 Analysis tools

Semiotic landscapes

We propose the notion of a *semiotic landscape* (which we also call RMF-landscape) to analyse grounded semiotic dynamics. The semiotic landscape is a graph, in which the nodes in the landscape are formed by referents, meanings and forms, and there are links if the items associated with two nodes indeed co-occur (figure 3.3). The relations are labeled RM for referent to meaning, MR for meaning to referent, RF for referent to form, FR for form to referent, and FM for form to meaning and MF for meaning to form. For real world environments, the set of possible referents is infinite, so the semiotic landscape is infinite. However, for purposes of analysis, we can restrict the possible environments and thus the possible referents artificially and then study the semiotic dynamics very precisely. This is what we will do in the remainder of the paper.

In the case of a perfectly coherent communication system, the semiotic landscape consists of unconnected triangles. Each referent has a unique meaning, each meaning has a unique form, and each form a unique referent. Otherwise more complex networks appear. The RMF-landscape in figure 3.3 contains an example where the agents use two

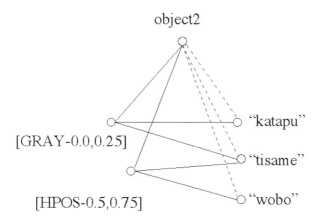

figure 3.3. A semiotic landscape represents the co-occurrences between referents, meanings and forms.

possible meanings for denoting **object2** namely [GRAY-0.0,0.25] (very light) and [HPOS-0.5,0.75] (lower upper), and the words *katapu* and *tisame* for [GRAY-0.0,0.25] and *wobo* and *tisame*, for [HPOS-0.5,0.75]. Each meaning has therefore two synonyms and *tisame* is ambiguous; it can mean both [GRAY-0.0,0.25] and [HPOS-0.5,0.75]. Three words are used to refer to *object2*. This kind of situation is typical in certain stages of our experiments and complexity rapidly increases when the same meaning is also used to denote other referents (which is obviously very common and indeed desirable).

As mentioned earlier, incoherence is not necessarily decreasing the communicative success of the language. The RMF-landscape in figure 3.3 still leads to total success in communication whenever both meanings are equally adequate for picking out the referent. Even if a speaker uses *tisame* to mean [GRAY-0.0,0.25] and the hearer understands *tisame* to mean [HPOS-0.5,0.75], they still have communicative success. The goal of the language game is to find the referent. It does not matter whether the meanings are the same. The agents cannot even know which meaning the other one uses because they have no access to each other's internal states.

Measuring coherence

The degree of coherence of a language can be measured by observing the actual linguistic behavior of the agents while they play language games, more specifically, by collecting data on the frequency of co-occurrence of items such as the possible forms used with a certain referent or all the possible meanings used with a certain form. Frequency of co-occurrence will be represented in competition diagrams, such as the RF-diagram in figure 3.8, which plots the evolution of the frequency of use of the Referent–Form relations for a given referent in a series of games. Similar diagrams can be made for the FR, FM, MF, RM and MR relations.

One co-occurrence relation for a particular item will be most frequent, and this is taken as the dominating relation along that dimension. The average frequency of the dominating relations along a particular dimension is an indication of how coherent the community's language system is along that dimension. For example, suppose we want to know the coherence along the meaning–form dimension, in other words whether there are many synonyms in the language or not. For a given series of games, we calculate for each meaning that was indeed used somewhere in the series, the frequency of the most common form for that meaning. Then we take the average of these frequencies and this represents the MF-coherence. If all meanings had only one form the MF-coherence is equal to 1.0. If two forms were used for the same meaning with equal frequency, it will be 0.5. When plotting the MF-coherence, we can therefore track tendencies towards an increase or decrease of synonyms.

3.5 Global evolution of coherence

We are now ready to study the semiotic dynamics of the guessing game, as played by situated embodied agents interacting in a shared physical environment. We typically start with a limited set of objects (for example four) that allow agents to play four different games, each object being in turn the topic. Then we progressively add new objects to the environment (by pasting new objects on the white board or moving them around) and study the impact on the lexicon and ontologies of the agents. Figure 3.4 shows the result of such an experiment involving 5 agents. It shows the progressive increase in environmental complexity and the average success in the game. We see clearly that the agents manage to bootstrap a successful lexicon from scratch. Success then

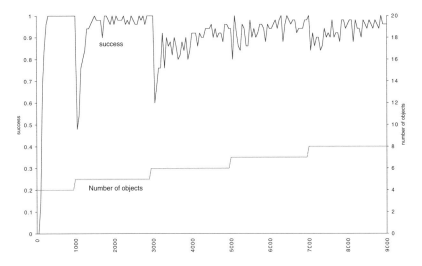

figure 3.4. The graph shows average success and increase in environmental complexity, for a group of 5 embodied agents engaged in the guessing game.

drops every time the environment increases in complexity but regains as the agents invent new words or create new meanings. Progressively it is less and less difficult to cope with expansions of the environment because words are less ambiguous and the repertoire is covering more and more meanings.

Figure 3.5 shows the evolution of the RF and FR complexity measures discussed earlier, for the same series of games as in figure 3.4. In an initial phase, the first 1000 games, the FR and RF relations fixate (even though agents do not necessarily use the same meaning to establish the relation). This is expected because agents get immediate feedback on this relation. The same word is used for the same referent and the same referent for the same word. As the complexity of the environment increases, this breaks down because many different words can be used for the same referent. Each of these words has another possibly appropriate meaning. This graph therefore shows that the lexicon becomes more general.

Figure 3.6 shows the evolution of the RM/MR and FM/MF complexity for the same series of games. We see very clearly that both the meaning–form and the form–meaning coherence increases, particularly after the initial period when ambiguities have been cleared from the language. The MR and RM co-occurrence is an indication of the degree of multi-referentiality and indeterminacy of categories. The same mean-

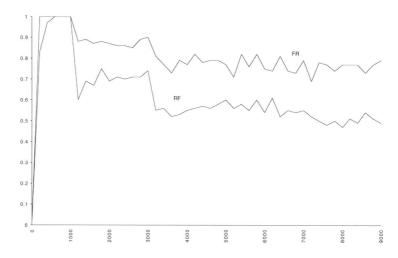

figure 3.5. The graph shows the coherence of the co-occurrence relation between referents and forms (RF), and forms and referents (FR).

ing co-occurs with different referents and the same referent is designated by different meanings.

3.6 Damping synonymy and ambiguity

We now inspect in more detail the kind of semiotic dynamics that is observed in the very beginning, when the agents do not have a lexicon nor ontology yet. Figure 3.7 shows a series of 5000 games played by a group of 20 agents. The first tendency that we see clearly is the damping of synonymy, by a winner-take-all process deciding on which form to use for a particular referent. This is shown in the RF-diagram displayed in figure 3.8, for the series of games displayed in figure 3.7, which shows that one word *va* comes to dominate for expressing this one referent. This damping is expected because the agents get explicit feedback about the RF relation and there is lateral inhibition as well as a positive feedback loop between use and success.

When we inspect the different meanings of *va*, through the FM-diagram (figure 3.9), we clearly see that even after 3000 games ambiguity stays in the language. Three stable meanings for *va* have emerged: [RED-0,0.125], [BLUE-0.3125,0.375], and [VPOS-0.25,0.5]. They are all equally good for distinguishing the topic *va* designates, and there are no situations yet that would have allowed disambiguation.

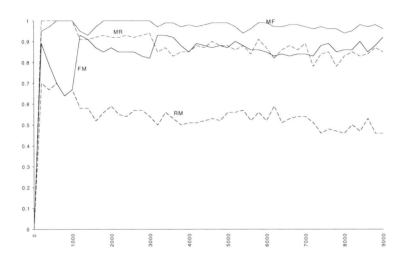

figure 3.6. The graph shows the coherence of the co-occurrence relation between referents and meanings (RM), meanings and referents (MR), meanings and forms (MF) and forms and meanings (FM) for the same series as in figure 3.6.

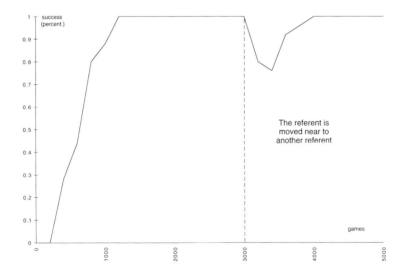

figure 3.7. This graph shows the average success per 200 games in a series of 5000 games played by 20 agents. The agents evolve towards total success in their communication after about 1000 games. A change in the environment induced after 3000 games gives a decrease in average success which rebounds quickly.

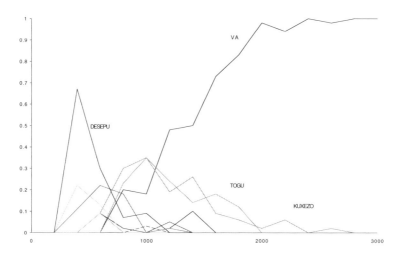

figure 3.8. This RF-diagram shows the frequency of all forms used for the same referent in 3000 language games.

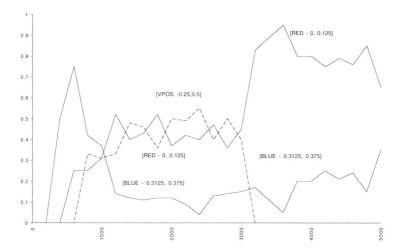

figure 3.9. This FM-diagram shows the frequency of each form–meaning co-occurrence for "va" in a series of 5000 games. A disambiguating situation occurs in game 3000 causing the loss of one meaning of *va*.

In game 3000, the environment produces a scene in which a category which was distinctive for the object designated by *va* is no longer distinctive. More precisely, we, as experimenters, have moved the object very close to another object so that the position is no longer distinctive.

Figure 3.7 shows that success drops (meaning there have been some failures in the game), but that it rebounds quickly. Failures occur because *va* no longer picks out the right object for those who believe that it means [VPOS-0.25,0.5], so they have to shift to an alternative meaning for *va*, compatible with the new situation. The FM-diagram in figure 3.9 shows that the positional meaning of *va* (namely [VPOS-0.25,0.5]) has disappeared. The other meanings, based on color, are still possible because they are not affected when the object designated by *va* moved its position.

3.7 Conclusions

The approach we have used for lexicon formation is different from the more traditional Quinean approach. Quine assumes that agents learn the meaning of words by making progressive inductive abstraction from the situations in which they observe a particular word-object relation. The common properties of referents constitute the meaning of the word and these common properties are learned by seeing many examples and retaining their similarities. Such an approach also underlies neural network approaches to word acquisition as discussed for example by Hutchins and Hazelhurst (1995), or Regier (1995). In contrast, we have adopted a Wittgensteinian approach, where agents invent words and meanings as part of a language game, formulate different hypotheses about the meanings of words used by others and test these meanings in their own language production. The evolution towards lexicon coherence in the population (where one word has one dominant meaning and one meaning has one dominant word) is a collective phenomenon triggered by responses of the system to new situations in which the multiple meanings of a word are no longer compatible with each other.

In the literature, intelligent generalization, specialization, or elimination operators are often ascribed to the individuals acquiring language (Clark, 1993). This is not the case in the present paper. Agents have very minimal forms of intelligence. We have observed that an agent sometimes starts to prefer a more general category for a word (or a more specific one), but this is not due to an explicit generalization operation in the agent, it takes place as a side effect of the repair action undertaken after a failing game. Similarly, the phenomenon of blocking (Copestake and Briscoe, 1995), which means that the availability of a specialized word (like *pork*) blocks the use of a more general one (like *pig*), arises as a side effect of the collective dynamics but cannot be ascribed to structure inside the agent.

A large amount of work needs to be done to further study the complex dynamics of lexicon formation. We need better tools to track the semiotic dynamics and study the interaction between lexicon and meaning formation. Nevertheless, we believe that the results discussed in this paper constitute a major step forward, because we have shown for the first time the evolution of an open-ended set of meanings and words by a group of autonomous distributed agents in interaction with physical environments through their sensory apparatus. The most valuable result of our experiments is that we are able to demonstrate a scale up. New meanings arise when the environment becomes more complex and the lexicon keeps adapting and expanding to sustain successful communication.

Acknowledgement

This research was conducted at the Sony Computer Science Laboratory. We are strongly indebted to Angus McIntyre for creating the Babel tool that is the technical backbone of our experiments and for technical support in the low level vision aspects.

References

Arita, T. and Y. Koyama (1998). Evolution of linguisitic diversity in a simple communication system. In Christopher Adami, *et al.* (1998) *Proceedings of Alife VI.* MIT Press, Cambridge MA. 9–17.

Cangelosi, A. and D. Parisi (1996). The Emergence of a "Language" in an Evolving Population of Neural Networks. *Conference of the Cognitive Science Society*, San Diego.

Clark, E. (1993). *The lexicon in acquisition.* Cambridge University Press, Cambridge.

Copestake, A. A. and E. J Briscoe (1995). Regular polysemy and semi-productive sense extension. *Journal of Semantics.* 12, 15–67.

Hurford, J. (1989) Biological evolution of the Saussurean sign as a component of the language acquisition device. *Lingua*, 77, 187–222.

Hutchins, E. and B. Hazelhurst (1995). How to invent a lexicon. The development of shared symbols in interaction. In Gilbert, N. and R. Conte (eds.) *Artificial societies: The computer simulation of social life.* UCL Press, London.

Langton, C. (ed.) (1995). *Artificial Life. An overview.* MIT Press, Cambridge MA.

MacLennan, B. (1991). Synthetic Ethology: An approach to the study of communication. In Langton, C., *et al.* (1991) *Artificial Life II.* Addison-

Wesley Pub. Cy, Redwood City CA. pp. 603–631.

Noble, J. (1998). Evolved signals: expensive hype vs. conspirational whispers. In Christopher Adami, *et al.* (1998) *Proceedings of Alife VI*. MIT Press, Cambridge MA. pp. 358–367.

Oliphant, M. (1996). The dilemma of Saussurean communication. *Biosystems*, 37(1-2), 31–38.

Quine, W. (1960). *Word and Object*. MIT Press, Cambridge MA.

Regier, T. (1995). A model of the human capacity for categorizing spatial relations. *Cognitive Linguistics*, 6-1, 63–88.

Steels, L. (1996). Emergent adaptive lexicons. In Maes, P., M. Mataric, J-A. Meyer, J. Pollack, and S. Wilson, (eds.) (1996) *From Animals to Animats 4: Proceedings of the Fourth International Conference on Simulation of Adaptive Behavior*. MIT Press, Cambridge, MA.

Steels, L. (1997a). Constructing and sharing perceptual distinctions. In van Someren, M. and G. Widmer (eds.) (1997) *Proceedings of the European Conference on Machine Learning*. Springer-Verlag, Berlin.

Steels, L. (1997). The synthetic modeling of language origins. *Evolution of Communication*, 1(1), 1–35.

Steels, L. (1998). The origins of syntax in visually grounded robotic agents. *Artificial Intelligence* 103, 1–24.

Steels, L. and F. Kaplan (1998). Spontaneous lexicon change, In *Proceedings of COLING-ACL*, Montreal, August 1998, 1243–1249.

Steels, L. and P. Vogt (1997). Grounding adaptive language games in robotic agents. In Harvey, I. *et al.* (eds.) *Proceedings of ECAL 97*, Brighton UK, July 1997. MIT Press, Cambridge MA.

Victorri, B. and C. Fuchs. (1996). *La polysemie. Construction dynamique du sens*. Hermes, Paris.

Werner, G. and M. Dyer (1991). Evolution of communication in artificial organisms. In Langton, C., *et al.* (ed.) *Artificial Life II*. Addison-Wesley Pub. Co. Redwood City, CA., 659–687.

Yanco, H. and L. Stein (1993). An adaptive communication protocol for cooperating mobile robots. In: Meyer, J-A, H. L. Roitblat, and S. Wilson (1993) *From Animals to Animats 2. Proceedings of the Second International Conference on Simulation of Adaptive Behavior*. MIT Press, Cambridge MA., pp. 478–485.

4

Linguistic structure and the evolution of words

Robert Worden
Charteris Ltd, London, UK

4.1 Introduction

This paper describes a precise sense in which language change can be regarded as a form of evolution – not of the language itself, but of the individual words which constitute the language. Many prominent features of language can be understood as the result of this evolution. In a unification-based theory of language, each word sense is represented in the brain by a re-entrant feature structure, which embodies the syntax, semantics and phonology of the word. When understanding or generating a sentence, we unify together the feature structures of the words in the sentence to form a derivation structure. The feature structure for any word can then be learnt by feature structure generalization, which complements unification to replicate the word feature structure precisely in a new mind. By this replication, word feature structures propagate precisely from one generation to the next, just as DNA propagates precisely in cell replication. The precision and transparency of DNA replication underlies the structure and diversity of life. Similarly, the precise and transparent replication of word memes underlies the structure and diversity of language. As word feature structures propagate from generation to generation, they undergo slow changes from selection pressures which cause many types of language regularities. In this analogy, each language is an ecology and each word is one species in the ecology. In language as in nature, different species exert selection pressures on one another. The pressures on a word are those factors which cause people to use it more or less often, and to learn it more or less easily – useful meaning, distinctive sound, lack of ambiguities, syntactic fit with other words, ease of learning, social acceptability and economy of expression. I illustrate by examples how these selection pressures act on words, creating many prominent features of language such as (some of) the Greenberg-Hawkins typological universals. There are two alternative explanations of language structure – that it reflects genetic evolution of the human brain, or that it arises from the evolution of word memes. Evolution of word memes goes much faster than evolution of brains, and so actually removes the selection pressures which might lead to genetic evolution of language structures in brains. For many features of language, there is no need to suppose that they reflect any innate structure in the brain.

4.2 Words as memes

The idea that language change is somehow analogous to evolution has a long and chequered history. Pre-Darwinian evolution, Lamarckian evolution and teleology have all been invoked in dubious explanations, which have given the idea of language evolution a bad name – but nevertheless, some kind of Darwinian evolution of languages is now regarded as a valid tool for thinking about language change (McMahon, 1994). Batali (this volume), Briscoe (this volume), Hurford (this volume) and Kirby (this volume) report on computer simulations of such an evolutionary process. One form of this idea goes as follows: each word is represented in the brain by a package of information that embodies the sound, syntax and meaning of the word. When people speak to one another, they combine the word packages to make sentence packages. A child, observing the sentence packages passing between adults, can somehow extract the component word packages and thus learn the words. Thus the word packages propagate from generation to generation. Over many generations, as word packages reproduce via the speaking/learning mechanism, some words are more successful than others – more commonly used or more easy to learn – and there is competition between the different 'species' of words. This competition leads to changes in the balance of word species in a language, and so leads to language change. In this model, words are a form of Dawkins' (1976) 'memes' – culturally transmitted replicators that propagate through a population. Such a picture is quite appealing, and could be used to model aspects of language change. However, as it stands it is unsatisfactory because of its looseness. Just what are these packages of information – what is in a word package and what is not? What is the mechanism of reproduction and what information can it propagate? Such a theory is like

the theory of Darwinian evolution before the discovery of DNA replication – it is quite plausible, but fundamental questions remain about
how it really works. Until we find the answers to these questions, the
idea remains an appealing story rather than a predictive theory. When
the structure and replication mechanism of DNA was discovered, Darwinian evolution could be put on a much firmer footing. Core questions,
such as the relation between Mendelian discrete inheritance and continuously variable traits, could begin to be answered. DNA replication
is done by a sequence of chemical analysis (splitting the DNA helix in
two) and synthesis (accumulating new bases from the surrounding cell)
– precisely matched to preserve the information in the order of the base
pairs. The DNA molecule may be many millions of base pairs long,
but can still replicate precisely with very few transcription errors. Any
sequence of legal base pairs can be replicated; in this sense the replication is completely transparent to any sequence, and so can pass through
any genetic information. It is the great precision and transparency of
DNA replication which underlies the huge diversity of life. Because each
DNA molecule can carry a large amount of information, and can propagate it faithfully from generation to generation, this information can
be used for the design of living things. Crossing and mutation create
diversity – but without the precise DNA replication, that diversity would
never be preserved for long enough for selection to act on it. We now see
the challenge faced by a 'words as memes' theory of language evolution.
If the word packages do not carry enough information, or cannot be reproduced faithfully enough, they cannot serve as the DNA of language;
changes introduced by selection of word memes might be wiped out by
an imprecise replication mechanism. From what we have said so far,
word replication (by a child observing the words used by her parents)
might well be 'sloppy' enough to wipe out subtle changes. This paper
describes a language learning mechanism which is precise enough and
transparent enough to support the evolution of words as memes, and
then explores some of its consequences for language change.

4.3 Language learning by generalization

In this section, I shall describe a theory of language learning in the framework of unification-based grammars. In this theory, words are feature
structures, and these feature structures replicate precisely from generation to generation. With this theory of learning, the idea of language

evolution can be precisely formulated and its consequences worked out. While there is not space here to describe the learning theory in full, I shall give the rationale for the theory and show how it leads to precise replication of words.

4.3.1 Feature structures and unification based grammars

In a unification-based grammar, each word of the language is represented by a feature structure. A feature structure denotes a directed acyclic graph (DAG). In this paper I shall show feature structures as tree-like structures of nodes and arcs, with features denoted by 'slot:value' pairs on the nodes and structure-sharing (re-entrancy) denoted by curved lines between nodes. Typical word feature structures are shown in the figures which follow. To see these feature structures in a more DAG-like form, imagine pulling the curved lines like threads until the two nodes at each end of a curved line coincide. The subgraphs below each end of a curved line must always be equal, to enable this to happen. Feature structures have proved to be very effective as a basis for computational models of language. The most successful computational models of language are based on feature structures, and it is not hard to see why. They are rich enough to represent both the tree-like syntactic structure of sentences and the tree-like embedded structure of sentence meanings. Other computational models such as neural nets, which have no intrinsic tree structure in the information they can learn and use, have a hard time coping with the intrinsically tree-like complexity of language. Unification-based grammars are based on the operation of feature structure unification. This operation is mathematically and computationally well defined, and has been extensively studied (e.g. Siekmann, 1989). The unification of two feature structures A and B is a third structure, denoted by A ⊓ B, which is at least as large as each input and contains any structure in either input A or B. It does so in the most economical way possible, fitting together parts of A and B wherever they match. Unification requires some match between A and B – some feature structures are incompatible and cannot be unified together. An example of unification is shown in figure 4.3 below. Note how the result of the unification (shown in the right hand side of the figure) contains all the structure in either of the inputs to unification (both shown to the left of the '=' sign in the figure). In a unification-based grammar, feature structures are used to represent both the syntactic structure of a word, and its meaning. Syntactic constraints are applied by unification (if two words are syntactically incompatible, their feature structures will not unify together). Meaning structures are also built up by unification of word meaning structures. This leads to an elegant declarative formalization of language, which has had great success in working computational models of language. Currently the most fully developed types of unification-based grammar are Lexical Functional Grammar (LFG) (Kaplan and Bresnan, 1981), Head-driven Phrase Structure Grammars (HPSG) (Pollard and Sag, 1993), and Categorial Grammars (CG) (Oehrle, *et al* 1988; Zeevat, *et al* 1988; Uszkoreit, 1986). These differ in significant respects, but share a strong core of mechanisms and approach (Shieber, 1986) and each can give elegant and powerful accounts of a wide range of linguistic phenomena. The Unification-based grammar formalism used in this paper is not identical to any of these formalisms, but shares their core features and can give similar accounts of many language phenomena. The particular features of this formalism are motivated by its learning mechanism.

4.3.2 The principle of generalization-based learning

There is another operation on feature structures, which, like unification, is mathematically well defined and has neat mathematical properties. This is the operation of generalization. The generalization of two feature structures A and B is a third feature structure written as $A \sqcup B$. This feature structure always exists, and is smaller than either of the inputs. It only contains structure (nodes, slots and values) which exists in both of the inputs. Examples of generalization are shown in figures 4.1, 4.2 and 4.4 below. In each of these figures, note how the result of the generalization (shown on the right hand side of each figure) contains all the structure (and only the structure) which appears in both of the inputs to the generalization (shown to the left of the '=' sign in each figure). Generalization is the complement of unification. Where unification builds up large feature structures, generalization breaks them down into small component parts. Mathematically, there are many useful identities involving unification and generalization, such as $A \sqcap (A \sqcup B) = A$. Generalization is a very promising mechanism for learning feature structures, because it projects out the common core of two or more examples. The learning theory described here can be summarized by the slogan: Unify to use, Generalize to learn.

Words are used in language by unification, but are learnt by generalization. I shall illustrate by analysis and examples how this works. Suppose some feature structure, A, cannot be observed directly, but can only be observed unified with other feature structures. We can observe (A ⊓ B), (A ⊓ C), (A ⊓ D) and so on. How can we learn A itself? It is intuitively obvious that each of the structures (A ⊓ B), (A ⊓ C) ... in the learning data contain A as a substructure – because they were all got by unifying A with other things. If we generalize (A ⊓ B) with (A ⊓ C), the result will still contain A as a substructure – because both the inputs have A as a substructure. This is summarized in the equation:

$$(A \sqcap B) \sqcup (A \sqcap C) = A' \sqsupseteq A$$

where the symbol '⊒' means 'contains as a substructure' or 'is more specific than' (technically, the inverse of subsumption). If there are any coincidental matches between B and C, they will survive in the result A′; so while A′ may be a good approximation to A, it need not be exactly equal to it. However, if we now generalize A′ with a third learning example we get:

$$A' \sqcup (A \sqcap D) = (A \sqcap B) \sqcup (A \sqcap C) \sqcup (A \sqcap D) = A'' \sqsupseteq A$$

Because all three learning examples contain A as a substructure, their generalization A″ also has A as a substructure. Anything else it contains (any features not in A) must be in B, C and D simultaneously. There may be some such features – but not as many as were in B and C simultaneously. A″ is a better approximation to A than A′ was. This is the core principle of generalization learning. If we have a series of learning examples (A ⊓ B), (A ⊓ C) ... , each got by unifying A with something else, then by generalizing them together we get a good approximation to A. We can show statistically that it only takes a very few examples (about five or six) to get a very good approximation to A – and so to learn A with very little chance of error. The idea of generalization learning can be applied individually to syntax, to meaning and to phonology – but more powerfully, to all three together. I shall illustrate by examples how these aspects of a word can be learnt.

4.3.3 Learning the meaning of a word

A core assumption of unification-based grammars is that meanings of sentences are represented by feature structures. This learning theory assumes the same, and assumes that the feature structures have some pre-linguistic basis in the brain – so that a child, observing any ongoing situation, can construct a feature structure representation of that feature in his head. This capability is assumed to pre-date language in both ontogeny and phylogeny. For instance, in the theory of primate social intelligence described in Worden (1996), any primate continually forms feature structure representations of the social situations around him. Suppose the child observes several situations involving the same component of meaning – such as an individual 'John', or an object 'cooker' or an action 'giving' – and constructs (by observation) the feature structures F1, F2, F3 . . . for these situations. This common component of meaning will be represented as some common substructure in the feature structures for each individual meaning. If the meaning of the feature structure for 'cooker' is C, then C will be a substructure of each meaning structure. That is, $F1 \sqsupseteq C$, and $F2 \sqsupseteq C$ and so on. If the child generalizes together all these observed meaning structures to form:

$$C' = F1 \sqcup F2 \sqcup F3 \ldots$$

Then it follows that $C' \sqsupseteq C$: the generalization also contains C as a substructure. If sufficient numbers of F are used, then C' will be a very good approximation to C. Generalization allows the child to learn the meaning of a new word. The same method can be used to learn the meaning of an action word, such as *give*. The meaning structures for different giving situations will differ in the representation of the donor, the gift, and the recipient, but will have a common core which is the meaning feature structure for 'giving'. This common core can be projected out by generalizing the feature structures. The meaning of any part of speech can be learnt in this way. You may ask – a child may observe very many different situations, each with its own meaning feature structure, each day. How does she choose which of the many feature structures to generalize together, to learn the meaning of some word? This question is answered in section 4.4.

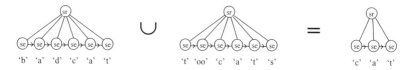

figure 4.1. Generalization to project out word sounds

4.3.4 Learning the sound of a word

The sound of a word is a sequence of phonemes, and this sequence can be represented as a feature structure with one node per phoneme. This is illustrated on the right-hand side of figure 4.1. In this diagram, the arrows between adjacent phoneme nodes represent a time constraint, that the end of one phoneme must coincide with the beginning of the next. (Thus it represents a co-indexing between two features: the end time of one phoneme and the start time of the next). Each phoneme node is labeled below with the sound it represents. The precise choice of sound units is not important (e.g. phonemes, syllables, diphones): the key point is to break up the sound stream into small units that can be recombined. The sound of a sentence can be represented as a sequence of phonemes in a similar manner. Assume the child has an innate capacity to construct these sound feature structures from sentences she hears. What happens if you generalize together the feature structures for two or more different sentences? If those sentences all contain the same word, then the result of the generalization will be just the sound of that word – the common sub-structure of all the sentence structures. This is illustrated in figure 4.1. Therefore generalization of feature structures offers a solution to the problem of sound segmentation – how a child can project out the sound of an individual word from a continuous sound stream. Again you may ask – of the many sentences which the child hears every day, how does she know which ones to generalize together to project out the sounds of words? This question is answered in the next section.

4.4 Learning a sound–meaning association

Consider a pre-linguistic child who hears many sentences each day, and constructs the feature structure representations of their sounds. She also observes many situations each day, and constructs the feature structure

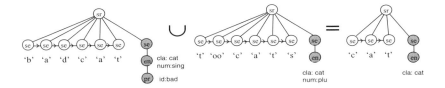

figure 4.2. SMP generalization

representations of those situations. Suppose the child ties together the
feature structure for the sound of a sentence with the meaning feature
structure for the situation going on at the time, in one feature structure.
Call this joint feature structure a sentence–meaning pair (SMP) and denote SMPs by S_1, S_2, and so on. The child may observe hundreds of
SMPs each day. Each SMP has a sound part (the sound of a sentence)
and a meaning part (the meaning of the situation going on at the same
time). What happens when the child forms generalizations such as G_{12}
$= S_1 \sqcap S_2$ of these SMPs? Each G_{ij} will have both a sound part and a
meaning part. But if sentences in the SMPs S_1 and S_2 have no words
in common, then the sound part of G_{12} will have no sounds in it. Similarly if the meanings in S_1 and S_2 have nothing in common, then the
meaning part of G_{12} will be empty. Only if S_1 and S_2 have some word in
common, and some element of meaning in common, will G_{12} have some
content in both its sound part and its meaning part. An example of this
is shown in figure 4.2. When S_i and S_j have some sound in common,
the situations going on will often have some meaning in common – because quite often the sentence in S_i describes a situation going on at the
same time. If the sentence contains some word, the meaning structure
will then contain the meaning of the word. If the same word occurs in
both S_i and S_j, and in their meaning situation, then the sound of that
word and its meaning will both appear in their generalization, G_{ij}. So
forming all pair-wise generalizations G_{ij}, and retaining only those which
have significant information content in both their sound part and their
meaning part, is an effective way to filter out both the sound and the
meaning of individual words. Even if many sentences are misheard, or
if many situations are misconstrued, or many sentences do not describe
the situation currently going on, still in a significant fraction of cases
the G_{ij} will have both sound and meaning. All the misheard or misconstrued or irrelevant cases are filtered out by demanding some content in
both sound and meaning parts of G_{ij}. Each of the remaining G_{ij} for a

word may contain some other sounds, and other meanings, which are not connected with that word because of coincidental similarities between S_i and S_j. These can be filtered out by generalizing each G_{ij} with further SMPs or pairwise generalizations G_{kl}, using a statistical criterion (which will not be described in detail here) to eliminate cases where the wrong word or word sense is involved. (In essence, if any generalization loses most of the information content in either the sound part or the meaning part of G, you should reject the SMP you used because it has the wrong word or meaning). In this way, the child can form a generalization G_{ijkl} = $S_i \sqcap S_j \sqcap S_k \sqcap S_l$ where all of the SMPs involved contain the same word in the same meaning sense. Generalization projects out this sound and meaning. Then to a very good approximation, the sound part of G_{ijkl} is just the sound of the word, and the meaning part is its meaning. Language learning theorists have often been concerned that the learning signal for the child may be too 'noisy' – that useful learning examples may be outnumbered by cases which are misheard, or where the speaker's intended meaning is not obvious or is misconstrued. Generalization learning offers an effective solution to this problem. By forming pair-wise generalizations of SMPs, and retaining only those which have significant information content in both their sound part and their meaning part, the learning mechanisms seeks out *significant coincidences* – cases where the same sound occurs repeatedly with the same meaning. In so doing, it filters out all the other cases where the sound was misheard, or the meaning was not evident in the current situation, or the meaning was misconstrued – to home in on the useful learning examples where the clear sound of a word was paired with its meaning. How many learning examples are needed for the child to successfully filter out the sound and meaning of a word, and to know that they are associated with one another? If we use a Bayesian theory of learning (which in many learning contexts can be shown to have optimum performance) then we can show that only about 6 learning examples are needed to learn a word. The argument goes as follows. Every feature structure which the child might learn must first be assigned a Bayesian prior probability, and it will only be learnt when the evidence for it is strong enough to overcome this small prior probability. A good model for the prior probability of some feature structure F is $2^{**}[-k*I(F)]$, where I is the information content of F, and k is a constant around 3. (We require k > 1 to make the sum of the prior probabilities converge). So in terms of log probabilities, there is an initial handicap of $k*I(F)$ bits to be overcome before the feature structure can be learned; any evidence less than this might arise just from random coincidences. Each new learning example S_i must pass a test that its generalization $S_i \sqcap G_{jk}$ has at least I bits of information – approximately I/2 bits in its sound nodes, and I/2 bits in its meaning nodes. The probability of a random feature structure passing this test is approximately 2**[–I], so passing the test provides I bits of evidence in favor of the learning hypothesis that the word exists. So approximately k=3 learning examples are sufficient to overcome the Bayesian prior. It also turns out that about six examples are sufficient to safely eliminate any random coincidences between learning examples, which would otherwise add spurious structure to the learned word.

In this way the child can simultaneously learn the sound of a word, its meaning, and the fact that they are paired together. This information is all together in the one feature structure. The same learning mechanism works for any part of speech – although it does not learn the syntax associated with any part of speech. This mechanism for learning sound–meaning pairs is probably available to other primates, such as chimps. There is ample evidence from the ape language experiments that chimps can learn sound–meaning pairs, and lexigram–meaning pairs. Evidence on chimp learning of syntax is more disputed. The learning of syntax proceeds by the same route of collecting sound–meaning pairs, followed by generalization; but to learn syntax, the SMPs are first 'embellished' by some further unifications, as described in the next section.

4.4.1 Learning syntax

In a unification-based grammar, the syntactic constraints of a word are embodied in feature structures, and these constraints are applied by unification. From the previous discussion, it seems likely that some form of generalization-based learning should be able to learn these syntactic constraints. If the syntax associated with a word is embodied in a feature structure, Q, and if the learning samples consist of cases where Q is unified with other feature structures $(Q \sqcap X)$, $(Q \sqcap Y)$, $(Q \sqcap Z)$ and so on, then if you generalize together the learning examples to form:

$$Q' = (Q \sqcap X) \sqcup (Q \sqcap Y) \sqcup (Q \sqcap Z)$$

Then to a very good approximation $Q' = Q$; the syntax of a word can be learnt by generalizing the examples of its use. This learning approach works in a fully-lexicalized grammar, where the syntax of each word is embodied in the word itself, and not in any separate structures. I am not sure whether this learning strategy can be applied within any of the main unification-based grammar formalisms (HPSG, LFG and CG); that is an open research question. These formalisms apply unification selectively, so that parts of feature structures are sometimes unified with parts of other feature structures, and other operations besides unification are sometimes used. Because unification is applied selectively, it is not clear exactly where generalization should be applied to reverse the work of unification. However, I have shown by a working computer program that generalization learning can learn the syntax of any word in a *Pure Unification Grammar*, which is characterized as follows:

Every word sense in a language is represented by one feature structure, which embodies the phonology, meaning and syntax of the word.

When a sentence is heard, the word sounds are used to retrieve the feature structure for each word in the sentence. Then the feature structures of all the words are unified together.

If the sentence violates some syntactic constraint, this unification will fail. Otherwise, the meaning of the sentence appears as one branch of the unified structure.

To generate a sentence, the same word feature structures are unified together in a different order – starting from the full meaning, and ending with a large feature structure containing all the word sounds.

The full structure got by unifying all the words in the sentence is the same for generation as for understanding. I call this structure the Derivation D of the sentence. If a sentence contains words with feature structures W, X, Y... then its derivation can be written D = W ⊓ X ⊓ Y.

The derivation D contains the feature structure for every word in the sentence amongst its sub-structures, because it is made by unifying them together.

The pure unification grammar is illustrated in figure 4.3. Two simple word feature structures, for the words *Fred* and *sleeps* are shown on the left of the figure. The time arrow between the two nodes in the left branch of the feature structure for *sleeps* embodies its syntactic constraint, that the subject must come before the verb. The curved arrow (co-indexing link) then embeds the subject in a feature structure whose meaning is 'sleeping'. To keep these feature structures compact, I am now not using a 'phoneme by phoneme' representation of word sounds,

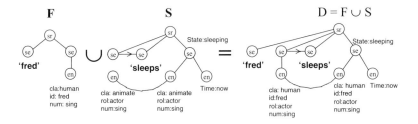

figure 4.3. Word Feature structures and their unification in a Pure Unification Grammar

but simply label one node with the sound of a whole word. This does not affect the learning mechanism. The feature structures F for *Fred* and S for *sleeps* arc unified together to understand the sentence *Fred sleeps*. The sentence meaning is the right-hand branch of the result, the derivation which is written as $D = F \sqcap S$. Within D are the sounds of all the words of the sentence – which was the starting point for sentence understanding. I have shown by building a computer implementation that this form of unification grammar can handle sentences much more complex than this example – handling phenomena such as relative clauses, control verbs, anaphora, agreement, quantifiers, co-ordination, and ambiguities. Operations other than unification are used to handle some of these phenomena, but the core mechanism remains simple unification of word feature structures. Suppose there are several derivations D_1, D_2, D_3 ... for sentences all containing some word W. Since D_1, D_2, D_3 ... all have the feature structure for W within them, their generalization $(D_1 \sqcup D_2 \sqcup D_3...)$ will also contain W as a substructure – and if there are several distinct derivations, their generalization contains little else, so that to a very good approximation $\sqcup D_2 \sqcup D_3...) = $ W. By generalizing the derivations, we can recover the original feature structure, W – recovering simultaneously the sound, syntax and meaning of the word. Suppose a child learning a language docs not know the word, W, but knows other words. Hearing sentences containing W and the other words, she can often infer the intended meaning from the context. In this way, she can reconstruct the derivations D_1, D_2, D_3 ..., even though she does not know W. By generalizing them together, she recovers the feature structure and thus learns a new word. The learnt feature structure embodies the syntax, semantics and sound of the word in one package. The learning process is illustrated in figure 4.4, where

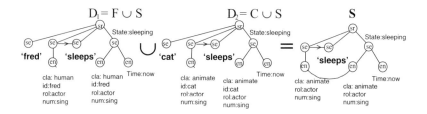

figure 4.4. The word 'sleeps' is recovered from two derivations by generalization

a child observes two distinct uses of the word *sleeps*. In each case she can infer the intended meaning non-linguistically from the context, so she can construct the whole derivation, D (except for the co-indexing links in the word to be learnt). Generalizing these derivations together, she learns the feature structure for the previously unknown word *sleeps*. The one new feature which appears in the result, S, but is not in either of the derivations, D_1 or D_2, is the co-indexing link (the curved line). Generalization discovers these co-indexing links, which are a vital part of the semantic information in many parts of speech such as verbs. In the case of the verb *sleeps*, the link ensures that the subject entity, whatever it is, is associated appropriately with the sleeping event. As before, the Bayesian learning theory implies that to learn a word requires only about six clear learning examples (where the child knows the other words in a sentence, and can infer the intended meaning of the sentence). The learning mechanism is robust against poorly-understood or misheard examples, and can learn the feature structure for any part of speech. If the feature structures for several words have structure in common, there is a secondary learning process – generalizing all the similar word feature structures together – which projects out their shared structure to learn a lexical or morphological rule relating the different words (e.g. the *+ed* rule for the English past tense). This saves the child having to learn all the regular forms individually. The secondary learning process can project out both the stems and the inflections of regular inflected words, by generalizing together the appropriate feature structures for full words. Writing the feature structure for a word as F(word), the secondary learning process can be illustrated by the equations:

$$F(\text{fitted}) \sqcup F(\text{fitting}) \sqcup F(\text{fits}) = F(\text{fit}+) \text{ [learn stem]}$$

F(fitting) ⊔ F(waiting) ⊔ F(spilling) = F(+ing) [learn inflection]
F(fit+) ⊓ F(+ing) = F(fitting) [use stem and inflection]

Generalizing together different words with the stem *fit+*, you learn the sound, meaning and syntax of the stem. Generalizing together different verbs ending in *+ing*, you learn the sound and its contribution to meaning. Finally, full word feature structures can be reconstructed by unifying feature structures for stems and endings. This theory of language learning is described in more detail in Worden (1997), where it is compared with many empirical facts of language learning, showing broad agreement. I have built a computer program which, using this learning mechanism, can 'bootstrap' itself from no knowledge of English to knowing the sound, syntax and meaning of 50 common English words. More incisive tests of the theory remain to be done. As the whole content of a word – its syntax, meaning and sound – are represented by one feature structure, then learning of word feature structures by generalization combines the learning of syntax, semantics and sound into one operation.

4.4.2 Evolutionary origins of language learning

In Worden (1996) I argued that primate social intelligence requires internal representations of complex structured social situations. The required representation can be thought of as a feature structure, which encodes something akin to the 'scripts' of Schank and Abelson (1977). It is then economical to assume that social inferences are made by unification of these feature structures with one another, and that feature structures representing social regularities may be learnt by generalization. I developed this model of primate social intelligence in Worden (1996) and showed how it can account for known data about primate social intelligence in species such as vervet monkeys (Cheney and Seyfarth, 1990). It is then not a big step to assume that the feature structures used in the brain for language have evolved from the feature structures used for primate social intelligence. In Worden (1998) I presented other evidence supporting this identification. The learning mechanisms and inference mechanisms are then the same for language and for social intelligence.

4.4.3 The analogy with chemistry and DNA

There is a rather close analogy between the processes of unification and generalization – used in this theory of language learning – and the processes of chemical synthesis and analysis. Unification of two feature structures is like chemical synthesis of two molecules – binding them together to form a larger whole, which contains both the input molecules as sub-structures. Generalization of two feature structures is like a form of chemical analysis, in which two molecules are compared to extract their largest common building block. Unification and generalization are complementary, just as chemical synthesis and analysis are complementary. Unification merges feature structures together to form larger wholes, while generalization breaks them down again into their constituent parts. Suppose one generation of speakers has a set of words represented by feature structures W, X, Y in their heads. They unify together these feature structures together to form sentences with derivations such as W ⊓ X, Y ⊓ Z and so on. Children then observe the derivations, and generalize them together to learn words. By this process of analysis, they can only recover the same feature structures as were input to the syntheses. We can show mathematically that the children can only learn the words used by the adults. Learning of the word feature structures through unification and generalization is a faithful replication process. It is also a very transparent process; there are very few restrictions on the form of word feature structures which can be propagated in this way. DNA replication is a chemical process which also involves successive stages of analysis (splitting of the DNA helix) and synthesis (doubling of each strand by picking up complementary bases). This process also propagates DNA structures stably from generation to generation. DNA propagation is faithful (the sequence of base pairs is copied with very few errors) and transparent (any sequence of base pairs can be reproduced). The learning process of unification and generalization is the language equivalent of DNA replication. It works for any word feature structure – no matter how complex, or what part of speech – and given a few examples of each word, it works reliably to reconstruct the original feature structure. That is the faithful and transparent replication of word feature structures on which the evolution of words is built. The resulting model of language evolution, by replication of word feature structures through language learning, is shown in figure 4.5

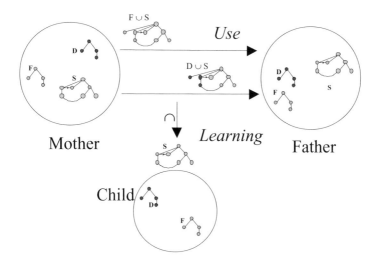

figure 4.5. Replication of word feature structures by unification and generalization

4.5 Language change by evolution of word feature structures

Learning of word feature structures by unification and generalization is sufficiently robust, faithful and transparent to allow word feature structures to replicate over many generations, preserving traits which lead to greater viability, and thus allowing them to evolve. As words evolve, the language changes. In this theory, 'evolution of words' is not just an analogy with biological evolution – it is a precise evolutionary theory of language change, and can be used to analyse directly the observed forms of language change. The analogy with biological evolution is still useful for understanding how the theory works. In this analogy, each word is like a separate species – not mixing its 'genotype' (feature structure) with that of other words – and a language is like an entire ecology. Every word has a 'niche' which is a part of meaning space; different word species may compete with one another to occupy useful niches in the space of meanings which people want to express. By combining productively with other words, a word may effectively expand its meaning niche and so prosper; this is the selection pressure which has led to the unbounded productivity of language, and to all of syntax. As the whole of a language is defined by its word feature structures, evolution of the words constitutes the whole of language change. The full Oxford English Dictionary is a museum of (mainly extinct) word species. Each word species is a parasitic life form, much like a virus. A virus needs a living cell to host it, and a word needs a human brain.

As I write, I have individuals from 50,000 separate species of word parasite in my head, and I am spreading them into this document. You in turn are absorbing them, because you have individuals from virtually the same 50,000 parasite species already in your head. Some of these species are thousands of years old, and some are much younger. As we shall see, this model of language change can account for many language-specific features, as well as for cross-language universals. A language universal is not necessarily a clue to some underlying constraint of the human brain; it may arise just from the convergent evolution of words. To see how word feature structures evolve over generations, we need to understand the selection pressures which shape their evolution. 'Fitness' of a word species depends on how frequently it is used by speakers, and on how easy it is for children to learn the word when they hear it. There are six main factors which determine the fitness of a word feature structure. These six selection pressures act in different ways at different times to shape the words of a language:

Useful Meaning: A word will tend to be used frequently if it expresses a meaning which people find useful, and need to express often.

Productivity: The use of a word depends not just on its own meaning, but also on how it combines with other words to express useful compound meanings – on the productivity of the constructs in which it figures. Evolution of word species is essentially symbiotic; the fitness of a word species depends on how well it co-operates with other species.

Economy: If a meaning can be expressed in two ways, and one is quicker and more economical than the other, then the quicker construct will tend to be used more and therefore learnt more.

Minimizing Ambiguity: As language grows in productivity and complexity of sentences, the scope for ambiguity multiplies. The mind performs prodigious feats in resolving ambiguities on the fly; but any word feature structure which tends to cause extra ambiguity will be avoided, and be selected against.

Ease of learning: The learning mechanism is unconscious and automatic; to learn a word, a child needs to collect about six examples of its use, in unambiguous sentences where she knows all the other words in the sentence and can infer the intended meaning non-linguistically. Ease of learning requires frequent use in unambiguous constructs, where the intended meaning can be inferred. Because of the secondary learning mechanism, regular constructs can also reduce the amount of learning required, so making learning easier.

Social Identification: We judge people by their language, and know that we are judged by our own language. Wherever people wish to identify themselves with some social group, they will tend to adopt the language of the group. Word evolution is continually shaped by peoples' social aspirations.

4.6 Examples of word evolution

Many different features of languages can be understood as products of the evolution of word feature structures; some of these are outlined in Worden (2000). However, here I shall just illustrate in more detail how two kinds of language phenomena can be understood from this viewpoint. The examples I shall use are (1) some of the Greenberg-Hawkins universals of language structure, and (2) the mixture of regularity and irregularity which we observe in all languages.

4.6.1 Language universals

Greenberg (1966), Hawkins (1994) and others have found universals of language structure, some of which hold with high statistical reliability over all known languages. Typical of these is Greenberg's (1966) Universal Number 2, which states that: "In languages with prepositions, the genitive almost always follows the governing noun, while in languages with postpositions it almost always precedes." Hawkins (1994) has given a functional analysis of universals such as this one in terms of his "Early Immediate Constituents" (EIC) principle. He defines a metric of difficulty of parsing a sentence, which depends on the length of constituent recognition domains (CRD). Every node in the parse tree can be recognized when some of its immediate constituents have been identified. The CRD is the duration between recognition of the first immediate constituent, and the recognition of the constituent which defines the type of the mother node. Hawkins then shows that languages which obey universals like that above have shorter CRDs than languages which do not. If short CRDs lead to ease of parsing, then languages which obey the universals are easier to parse. If ease of parsing is a selection pressure which acts on features of languages, and this selection pressure acts to change the populations of language features in a speaking community, then the emergence of language universals in response to Hawkins' EIC preference is an example of language change by evolution of language memes. Kirby (1996, 1998) has made this identification, and has illustrated by simulations how language populations obeying the universals can emerge from initially unstructured conditions. Further, if words are identified as the basic unit of language learning (including the learning of syntax), then this is an example of language change by evolution of word memes. I propose an alternative account, where the key selection pressure on word memes is not complexity or parsing, but the difficulty of the whole understanding process – including, crucially, the resolution of ambiguities. I shall argue that the pressure to avoid certain kinds of ambiguity is a much stronger pressure than the 'ease of parsing' selection pressure involved in Hawkins' and Kirby's accounts. Then, even if both EIC and ambiguity accounts are admissible (in that both selection pressures exist) it is the stronger selection pressure which will actually lead to the language universals as observed.

To understand the origin of this selection pressure, it is necessary to describe how sentences are understood in the unification grammar described in section 2. In this model, the core operation for language understanding is unification. Feature structures for words are unified together, to form meaning representations for groups of words in the sentence. These meaning representations are feature structures derived from the right-hand (meaning) sides of the word feature structures. When a group of words (which constitute a phrase) is understood, unification of their feature structures produces a meaning structure for the phrase. This meaning structure is the only trace of the phrase which carries through to the rest of the understanding process. So parsing is mediated entirely by semantic representations. As an example, to understand the sentence *Fred broke the lid of the box*, you first form a meaning representation for *Fred*, the subject of the sentence; you then form a meaning representation for the object phrase *the lid of the box*. You finally unify the meaning structures for subject and object with the feature structure for the verb *broke* to form a meaning structure for the whole sentence. This requires doing one unification operation for each word in the sentence. For simple sentences, this process of unification works easily; the constraints built into the word feature structures leave

little choice in the order of doing the unifications, and the final meaning
is uniquely determined. However, when sentences get a little more complicated, there can be many structural ambiguities. These correspond to
different orders of doing the unifications, and the understanding process
is not so simple. Consider the sentence *I saw the lid of the box on the
table*. This can be read in at least two ways, with different constructions
of the object phrase: 'I saw ((the lid of the box) on the table)' and 'I
saw (the lid of (the box on the table))'. The meaning distinction between these two readings is a fine one: what was on the table – the lid
or the box? But the language understanding process cannot ignore it;
we are sensitive to these meaning distinctions. If, as before, you unify
the feature structures for the words in the object noun phrase, by doing
these unifications in two different possible orders you will arrive at two
possible meaning structures – one describing ((the lid of the box) on
the table) and the other describing (the lid of (the box on the table)).
Call these meaning feature structures L1 and L2, describing two vari-
eties of lid. Having created two alternative meaning structures, how do
you carry on to understand the rest of the sentence? One possibility is
to carry out two independent understanding processes in parallel, one
each for L1 and L2. However, it seems unlikely that the brain does this.
We easily understand sentences in which there are three or four distinct
structural ambiguities. If the understanding process were to split into
two parallel processes for each ambiguity, then to understand such sentences we would need to do 8 or 16 (or more) understanding processes
in parallel. Given the difficulty of understanding just two conversations
at once, it seems highly unlikely that this is the way the brain works.
The operation of generalization, introduced in section 2 as a learning
mechanism, provides a possible answer. If a phrase yields two possible
meaning structures L1 and L2, then we can form their generalization
$L = L1 \sqcap L2$, and carry on understanding the the sentence as if the
phrase had just the one meaning L – coming back later to resolve the
ambiguity and find the full meaning. For instance, consider the example
where L1 is the meaning of '((the lid of the box) on the table)' and L2
is the meaning '(the lid of (the box on the table))'. These are both
complex feature structures with subsidiary branches describing 'of the
box-ness' and 'on the table-ness'; but they both describe some kind of
lid. So the generalization $L = L1 \sqcup L2$ still describes a lid of a box
– although it loses the table element. The formation of L is shown,
using simplified feature structures, in figure 4.6. Empirically, this gen-

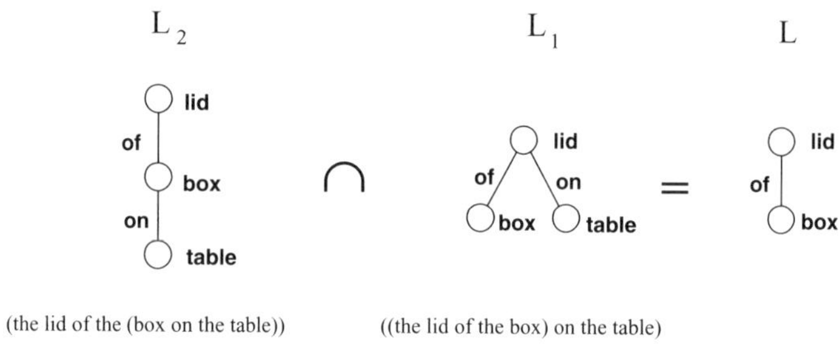

figure 4.6. Generalization of ambiguous readings of a phrase

eralization procedure works well. Where there are multiple structural
ambiguities, it avoids the combinatorial explosion of possible meaning
structures, and allows you to form a sentence meaning by doing a small
number of unification operations. This is not the full meaning of the
sentence; in the example above, it just describes the core meaning 'I saw
the lid of the box', and you still have to go back and work out where
the table was (under the lid or under the box). But having the core
meaning is a very good start for creating mental images, or whatever
else you may need to do to decide which of the two ambiguous meanings makes most sense. Even the core meaning on its own may be very
useful to know. What has this to do with Greenberg's universals? This
whole procedure of forming generalizations and avoiding a combinatorial explosion of parses can only work well in languages which obey the
universals. Greenberg's universals guarantee that ambiguous pairs of
meanings have the maximum amount of meaning in common, which will
survive generalization and lead to useful sentence meanings – even before resolution of ambiguities. English is a language with prepositions
rather than postpositions (*fiddler on the roof* refers to a fiddler, not a
roof) and the genitive follows the governing noun (*man of action* is a
man, not an action). In languages such as Japanese both go the other
way round; universal no. 2 says that in essentially all languages the genitives and adpositions are similarly linked. Now consider the previous
examples, $L_1 = $ ((the lid of the box) on the table) and $L_2 = $ (the lid
of (the box on the table)). Because English genitives and prepositions
branch the same way, both of these readings refer to a lid. In Japanese,
both readings would refer to a table. However, in a language which did
not obey Greenberg's universal No. 2, the two readings might be rad-

	← ← on of	→ → on of	← → on of	→ ← on of
(the lid of (the box on the table))	**lid**	**table**	**box**	**lid**
((the lid of the box) on the table)	**lid**	**table**	**box**	**table**
	Greenberg		Anti-Greenberg	

figure 4.6.1

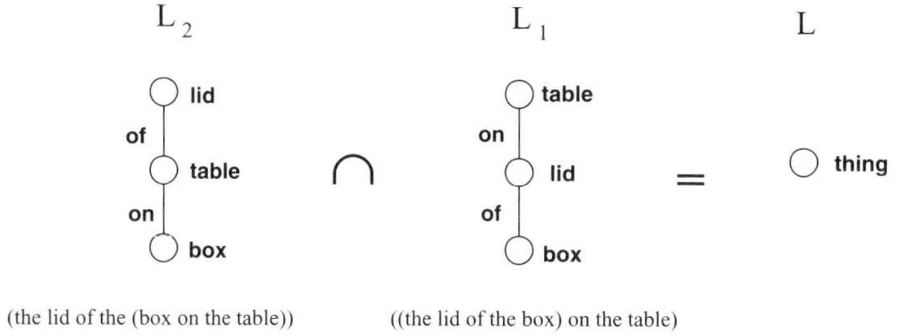

figure 4.7. Generalization to project out the common meanings of two constructions of a phrase, in a language with postpositions which does not obey Greenberg's Universal No. 2

ically different (e.g one reading would refer to a kind of lid, the other reading to a kind of table). This is shown in figure 4.6.1. In a language like that shown in the fourth column, the meanings of the two possible constructions of the phrase are completely different, and have nothing in common. Therefore nothing useful survives into the generalization of the two meanings. This is shown in figure 4.7. If the only trace of the phrase which is carried forward for the rest of sentence processing is its meaning feature structure, and if generalization of two ambiguous meanings reduces this structure to a single node meaning 'thing', then this will provide almost no constraints to guide the understanding of the rest of the sentence, and almost no useful meaning until the ambiguity is resolved. In this case, there are two possible ways to proceed: to try to resolve the ambiguity immediately, before any other sentence processing, or to carry on sentence processing with each of the two possible meanings. Either of these is potentially expensive. The first may require the construction of a mental image or model to work out which of the two senses is more plausible – and there may not yet be enough information available to construct a useful model. The second will involve running two, four, eight or more parallel parse operations if there are other structural ambiguities in the sentence. I shall call such ambiguities, which require either immediate resolution or multiple parallel parses, hard ambiguities, and other ambiguities soft ambiguities. While hard ambiguities can be tolerated occasionally (for instance, in short sentences), they are generally to be avoided. A language which does not obey Greenberg's universal no. 2, and so has hard ambiguities in adpositional phrases, will be highly awkward for people to use. Listeners will often have to pause in mid-sentence to work out what speakers are talking about – and may typically miss the rest of the sentence – or speakers will have to remember that certain constructs are incomprehensible, and should be avoided. This gives rise to interdependent selection pressures on the feature structures for genitives and adpositions to align with one another so as to obey Greenberg's universal no. 2 and so to avoid hard ambiguities. A very similar selection pressure forces all adpositions in a language to go the same way – to be all prepositions, or all postpositions.

Similar accounts apply to many of the structural universals discovered by Greenberg and others. For instance, the structural ambiguity in *I saw the man near the steps* would be hard to handle in a language which had VO order and postpositions; so VO order is generally linked with prepositions, OV order with postpositions. VO/OV order must also be consistent with genitive order to avoid other similar hard ambiguities; the three features of VO/OV order, pre/postpositions, and genitive binding direction all exert selection pressures on each other to be mutually consistent and so to avoid hard ambiguities. The ordering of relative clauses before or after a noun is similarly constrained by the need to avoid hard ambiguities. The only way to obey these constraints simultaneously is to be clearly a head-first or head-last language – to have a well-defined Head Parameter. Feature structures for verbs, prepositions, genitives and relative pronouns are mutually selected to line up in this way. In a language which is simply head-first or head-last, there is a regular relation between linear word order and the resulting meaning tree – so that structural ambiguities translate into different positions of attachment of some structure onto the tree. Then generalization of the two possible structures will preserve most of the meaning. If a language is not simply head-first or head-last, but is a mixture, a structural ambiguity can translate into a more radical difference between meaning trees, so little meaning will survive generalization – as is illustrated in figure 4.7.

Therefore we have two alternative accounts for many of the Greenberg-Hawkins Universals – either they arise because of the need to avoid hard ambiguities, or they arise from the human parser's preference for short constituent recognition domains (CRDs), as in Hawkins' EIC principle. How can we choose between these two accounts ? When a language changes in response to some selection pressure on the word feature structures, the rate of change is proportional to the strength of the selection pressure. This strength can be measured in terms of the differential survival and reproduction of words which have (or do not have) the trait being selected for. For instance, in the case of Greenberg's Universal no. 2 in a language with prepositions, the selection pressure on genitives depends on the rates of survival and reproduction of the two possible forms (following or preceding the governing noun). It is possible in principle (although difficult in practice) to calculate the selection pressures arising from Hawkins' EIC principle, and from the need to avoid hard ambiguities. While I have not made any detailed calculation of these pressures, I suggest that the selection pressure to avoid hard ambiguities is much stronger than the selection pressure from the EIC principle. The EIC principle proposes that the human parser prefers short CRDs, and that languages change to minimize average lengths of CRDS (Hawkins uses a different, but closely related metric – the IC to word ratio – to facilitate comparisons between languages). However, the differences in CRD-related metrics (between languages obeying the Greenberg universals, and languages which do not) are not large compared with the differences in CRD metrics which we handle every day, when we understand long sentences. Therefore the differences are all well within the capabilities of the human language parser. In other words, our parser may prefer short CRDS, but we know empirically that it can actually handle very long CRDs, in long sentences. Therefore the selection pressure for short CRDs cannot be a very strong one. On the other hand, if a language had many hard ambiguities, we would frequently encounter sentences which drove our language understanding capability well outside its normal operating range – having to handle large numbers of possible parses in parallel, or diverting to resolve ambiguities in mid-sentence with insufficient information. Also, while the consequences of a long CRD are purely local (within the phrase itself), the consequences of a hard ambiguity can spread out over the whole sentence – making the whole sentence understanding operation more difficult. An effect which drives the parser out of its normal operating range, and whose harmful effects impact whole sentences, will give rise to a much stronger selection pressure on words than an effect whose impacts are localized and are well within the normal operating range of the parser. So hard ambiguities provide a stronger selection pressure than the EIC principle. Even if both selection pressures are acting concurrently, it is the pressure to avoid hard ambiguities which predominantly drives language change. That is a tentative reason for preferring the hard ambiguity account of the language universals over the EIC account. It is only a tentative reason, because I have not made any quantitative calculations of the selection pressures.

If we can calculate selection pressures it should also be possible to compare the selection pressures leading to different universals within each account. The best-obeyed regularities should arise from the strongest selection pressures. We would expect the two accounts to give different predictions for the relative sizes of different selection pressures, and so to predict different levels of exceptions from various regularities.

4.6.2 Regularity and irregularity

The model of word evolution described in this paper gives an account of one of the most puzzling features of language – the mixture of regularity and irregularity observed in every language. Many theories of language are based on the regularities observed in languages. For instance, the 'principles and parameters' theory of language learning assumes that the core of a language is regular, defined by a few parameters; it explains language learning as a process of setting those parameters. However, this leaves no place for irregularity. Irregular features have to be relegated to a language 'periphery' which is not addressed by the theory. In general, irregularity is something of an embarrassment for theories based on regularity. The theory of unification-based grammar with generalization learning, outlined in section 2, starts from the opposite end of the spectrum – since it can support languages of arbitrary irregularity. The theory is fully lexicalized, so the syntax associated with every word is packaged in the feature structure for that word; a language can be learnt and used even if every word has different syntax packaged with it – if the language is completely irregular. The issue for this theory is not to account for the irregularities, but explain why languages have even partial regularity. Because of the selection pressures on words, no language would stay completely irregular for long. Words with similar meanings exert mutual selection pressures on one another to conform to common syntactic patterns. The discussion in section 4.1 illustrates how the pressure to avoid hard ambiguities tends to produce language-wide syntactic patterns – for instance, of prepositions rather than postpositions.

There are three main selection pressures on words, which lead to increased language regularity: (a) Minimizing Ambiguity: as in the example of the Greenberg-Hawkins universals. (b) Productivity: Suppose some commonly used word has a certain syntactic 'shape' (for instance, a common verb requiring SVO order). Then if other verbs of similar meaning adopt the same syntactic shape, they will be easily interchangeable with the common verb in the same syntactic pattern. This will make them easy to use and so make them propagate easily from generation to generation – leading to increasing regularity of the language. (c) Ease of learning: Regular syntax and morphology can be learnt by the secondary learning process, described in section 2, which reduces the amount of learning required – so that for instance only the stem of every new verb or noun need be learnt, not having to learn all its inflections.

On this basis, therefore, we might expect every language to continually converge to a state of greater and greater regularity. However, three main influences prevent this, leading to a mixture of regularity and irregularity. The first major force leading to irregularity is language contact – typically caused by conquest or invasion. Here the conquering group brings its own language, which the conquered emulate and absorb, producing an irregular mixture from two (possibly more regular) antecedent languages. This is the main initial agent of irregularity. However, I suggest that there are two further causes of irregularity which imply that even if languages never mixed, each language would not necessarily converge to a state of complete regularity.

The first of these is the self-stabilization of different, and inconsistent, domains of regularity in a language. This self-stabilization can be understood from the analogy of a ferromagnetic crystal, in which neighboring atoms, through their magnetic moments, tend to line each other up along a common axis of magnetism. The mutual selective forces (a) – (c) exerted by words on one another are of this form – tending to align words with similar meanings into similar syntactic patterns. However, in ferromagnetic solids, all atoms do not take the same alignment. The forces tending to line up atoms together are local forces. Once the atoms in a small region have become lined up in one direction, they stabilize each other in that direction – so it then becomes more difficult for any influence from neighboring regions to realign them. So the solid splits up into a number of small domains, each of which has a regular alignment, but which have irregular borders. Even though a fully aligned state may actually be the minimum-energy state for a crystal of iron, it does not reach that state, because other states with differently aligned domains form local minima – and the iron crystal gets stuck in one of these local minima.

I suggest that words in a language show similar behavior, because the selective forces leading to regularity are local in the space of word meanings – so words of similar meanings form 'domains of regularity', stabilizing each other in those patterns and resisting change from other domains. Each new word is drawn into some domain of regularity – but the domains have irregular and unpredictable boundaries. One example of this is the mixed ergative languages. Most case-marked languages – where the main semantic roles of agent, patient and theme are determined by case marking, rather than word order – use a binary marking which may be nominative/accusative or ergative/absolutive. There are advantages in having the same form of marking across the whole language; for instance, it is then easier to mark adjectives for agreement with any noun, without needing a mixed marking system for the adjectives. So most case-marked languages take one of the pure forms. However, there are languages, such as the Aboriginal language Yidijn, which use both nominative/accusative and ergative/absolutive case markings. The choice of case marking is not random across the language; in all such languages, the nominative/accusative nouns are at the animate end of the scale, and the ergative/absolutive nouns tend to be inanimate – they form distinct domains, rather than overlapping at random (Anderson, 1985). Each domain is self-stabilizing (e.g. through interaction with the different sets of adjectives which tend to apply to animate and inanimate nouns respectively) but they have different alignment. We can understand why these domains are at the animate and inanimate ends of the noun meaning spectrum. Nominative/accusative languages always mark the nominative case more briefly than the accusative for economy, as nominative is used for two of the three possible semantic roles (agent of transitive sentences, and agent/theme of intransitive sentences). Similarly, in ergative languages the absolutive case is marked more briefly, as it is used for two of the three main roles (patient of a transitive sentence, and agent/theme of an intransitive sentence). Since inanimate nouns tend to be patients more often than animate nouns do, the ergative/absolutive case marking achieves better economy for inanimate nouns than it does for animate nouns. Therefore the ergative/absolutive marking tends to occupy the inanimate end of the spectrum, where it gives a better advantage of economy. The mixed case marking of languages like Yidijn actually gives them a slight advantage of economy over pure case-marked languages; this may help to explain their preservation.

There is a second influence which may preserve irregularity in a language for ever. The borders of a domain of irregularity may also be defined by some other selective pressure, which acts more strongly than the force leading to regularity on those words at the boundary of the regular domain. This, for instance, may define the limits of regular noun endings in case-marked languages. For any comparatively rare word, ease of learning is an important selection pressure. If six good learning examples were needed to learn each different inflection of a rare noun, it would take a long time to learn and might not propagate well through a population. By having regular endings, the stem with all its case markings can be learnt from just six examples in total, and so it will reproduce much more successfully. However, for the very common words which we learn early in childhood, the balance of selection pressures may be completely different. Given plenty of learning examples, we have no difficulty in learning all the case markings separately – which may then be irregular. Some of these irregular markings may have advantages (such as brevity) which outweigh the small selective advantage of learnability. So irregular forms of very common nouns may be permanently stable. From these examples we can begin to see how the mixture of regularity and irregularity which we find in all languages – and which can be problematic for theories based on regularity – may emerge in an unforced manner from the theory of word evolution.

4.7 Discussion

4.7.1 The speed of language evolution

There are two alternative accounts of the structure of language – that it reflects language-specific structures in the human brain (i.e. that it arises from biological evolution), or that it reflects just the functional requirements for language. The theory of this paper is of the latter kind, because it is the functional requirements for language which create selection pressures for the evolution of words. If a particular feature of universal grammar (say, the Head Parameter) can arise from two distinct mechanisms, how do we decide which mechanism is responsible? One relevant piece of information is the relative speed of the two mechanisms. The speed of any evolutionary process depends on three factors (Worden, 1995):

1. The inter-generation time for replication
2. The maximum number of offspring from one successful replicator in one generation
3. The strength of the selection pressures (difference in fitness between least and most fit)

The second and third factors are related, since a species can only survive strong selection pressures if it produces many offspring per generation; so the sum of the selection pressures cannot be greater than the log of the average number of offspring. These factors can be combined into a numerical speed limit, which bounds the rate at which survival-enhancing information can accumulate in the design of the species by evolution. The speed limit can be proved quite generally from uncontroversial assumptions about the nature of evolution (Worden, 1995). Because the second and third factors are related, we can express the speed limit in terms of either of them. The overall speed limit is:

$dG/dn < 2\ V$

Here G is the useful design information expressed in the phenotype of the species (measured in bits), and n is the number of generations. V is the total selection pressure on the traits in G, and is approximately given by $V = \log2(S_{max}\ /\ S_{avg})$, where S_{max} is the maximum survival rate and S_{avg} is the average survival rate. Then V is bounded by $V < \log \gamma$, where γ is the average number of offspring per generation. We can convert this speed limit into a time constant for evolution T_e, measured in years. T_e is the time required for a large proportion of the design of the species to be improved or replaced by evolutionary effects, and so measures the characteristic timescale over which evolution acts. If the average amount of design information required to define a phenotype is I, and the inter-generation time is P years, then the time constant T_e is given by:

$T_e = 2I\ P/V$

We can now calculate the evolutionary time constants T_e both for the evolution of individual words (i.e. for the process which constitutes language change) and for the biological evolution of the human language device. For the evolution of words:

The information content I of a word includes the information content of its sound pattern, its meaning, and its syntactic constraints. These typically amount to something in the order of 100–300 bits in total.

The inter-generation time for word replication is similar to the human generation time, for those few words we learn from our parents as very young children. But most words in a language, which we pick up from our peers, can spread rapidly producing many 'offspring' within a generation time of the order of 1 year.

The selection pressures on individual words can be strong; if a new word is coined to express some meaning more conveniently or less ambiguously than some old word, then the old word may be only rarely used and lose its chance to reproduce. To reflect this, we set $V = 1$. Combining these factors leads to a time constant T_e of about 500 years for the evolution of languages through word evolution. This is consistent with what we know about language change.

For the human language capacity in the brain, the factors are:

The design of the language capability cannot be very simple, given its impressive capabilities, which even now we have great difficulty reproducing in computer models. Conservatively we assume that the design information needed to specify this capability is at least $I = 5,000$ bits.

The inter-generation time for human reproduction is taken as 20 years.

Because humans typically produce only about 3 offspring, the sum of all selection pressures V can only be about 2. This includes all selection pressures for disease resistance, physical strength, accident-proneness and so on. It seems likely that within this, the selection pressure for language proficiency (i.e. the difference in survival probabilities between the most eloquent and the average in one generation) is not more than about 20%.

Combining these factors leads to a time constant T_e of about 1 million years for the evolution of the human language capability. This is consistent with what we know about the evolution of language, and is a factor 2,000 slower than the evolution of words. These arguments give a clear quantitative basis for the assertion that cultural evolution of language is much faster than biological evolution of the language organ in the brain. If two competing explanations of some change both seem to fit the facts, you should believe the faster one – the faster mechanism will get there first and make the change, even if the slower one might have done so in time. In fact, the faster mechanism will probably remove any selection pressure which could have driven the slower mechanism. If the words of our languages naturally line themselves up to be head-first or head-last, over hundreds of years, then our brains are under no selection pressure to evolve a head parameter (i.e to force the words into line) over millions of years.

Deacon (1997, 1998) has similarly argued that selection pressures for specific features of language – such as the Head Parameter – are unlikely to have shaped the neural structures in our brains, because of the diversity of languages and their rapid rate of change compared to evolutionary timescales.

4.7.2 Constraining the theory

The theory of learning described in section 2 is quite highly constrained. It uses two key operations (unification and generalization) which are computationally well-defined, and its behavior is governed by a Bayesian learning theory, which predicts how fast any given word feature structure can be learnt. However, the theory of language evolution described in sections 3 and 4 does not at first sight appear to be well constrained. There are six distinct types of selection pressure acting on words (usefulness of meaning, minimal ambiguity, ease of learning, productivity, economy and social identification). It might appear from the examples in section 4 that any of these pressures can be invoked at will to tell some kind of 'Just So Story' about the evolution of any language feature. Unless we can constrain the relative strengths of the different selection pressures, this will be a problem; different pressures could be freely invoked to account for any data. To avoid this problem, we need some principled way to estimate the relative strengths of the different selection pressures, and then to predict their influence on the evolution of words. One way to do this is to use the speed limit for evolution, as in section 4.7.1; but this does not give us a detailed picture of the relative effects of different selection pressures. A more detailed approach is to write down the equations which govern the evolution of every word species, and then to solve those equations – either analytically, numerically, or by simulation. The selection pressures appear as terms in the equations. Any account of the emergence of a language feature then places constraints on the selection pressures; each selection pressure will appear in the accounts of several features. As we account for more language features, the selection pressures become more constrained and so our theory becomes more constrained. Eventually it will become falsifiable.

The equations governing word evolution are population equations for the words in the language community. Denote different possible words by an index i = 1,2,... W (where W is of course very large). In a population of P speakers per generation, denote the number of speakers who know word i by N_i. This is the 'population' of that word species, and will grow or shrink according to the selection pressures on the word. Individual copies of a word reproduce as their speakers use the word in front of people who do not already know the word, so those people learn it. Words die out as their speakers die. We can write down an equation which sums these birth and death processes to give the rate of change of the population. If time, t, is measured in generations, then:

$$dN_i/dt = (U_i/L)(1\text{-}N_i/P) - N_i$$

Here, U_i is the number of times per generation when a speaker will use a word, in circumstances where it can be used as a learning example. L is the number of learning examples needed to learn the word. $(1\text{-}N_i/P)$ is the probability that the hearer does not already know the word (and so is ready to learn it), and the final $- N_i$ arises from the death process.

While this equation seems simple in form, it is often quite hard to analyse. All of the selection pressures act through the term U_i, which depends on the word and on other words in the speaking population in complex ways. For instance, if a word combines productively with other words, then U_i depends on the populations of those other words in the community, increasing as their populations increase. In principle, however, we can model how the U_i depend on the various selection pressures. In a few simple cases we can solve these coupled equations analytically; but more typically we would need to solve them numerically, or run a simulation of the population through many generations. This would be similar to the simulations reported in other chapters of this book. However we solve the equations, the resulting analysis places constraints on the U_i, and so places constraints on the selection pressures. As we learn

more about the selection pressures, our room for manoeuvre in accounting for new phenomena will become more limited; the theory becomes
more constrained.

4.8 Conclusions

The idea that languages evolve has always seemed an attractive idea,
but has been hard to cash out into a predictive theory. This is because
the basic mechanism of language replication – the DNA of language –
has been unknown; and without it, the language evolution story lacks
crucial detail. Constraints on language replication might prevent or
divert evolutionary changes. However, there is now a simple working
theory of language learning, formulated in the framework of unification-
based grammars, which enables us to understand how words replicate,
and so how they evolve. In this theory, the basic mechanisms of language use and language acquisition are not highly language-specific or
restrictive; they are built on more general operations of unification and
generalization. Each word in a language is a feature structure, with few
restrictions on its form. Any one of these word feature structures will
be faithfully transmitted across generations by the learning mechanism,
and over many generations word species evolve. I have illustrated how
this picture of word evolution can account simply for a few prominent
features of languages – such as the diverse syntactic means used to define
semantic roles, the domains of syntactic regularity and irregularity seen
in languages, and some language universals. It seems likely that a similar
word evolution account can be given for many other features of language.
In this picture, therefore, many language features arise not from the restrictions of an innate language apparatus of the brain (as, for instance,
in a 'Principles and Parameters' picture of language – Chomsky, 1988),
but from the evolution of word feature structures (memes) under the
selection pressures of use. Language tells us less about the structure of
the mind than we thought it did. To those who want to learn about the
mind, this result may seem a disappointment. However, it need not be
– because in a scientific theory, less is more. We need not assume that
the mind has a whole range of complex language-specific devices; just
that we have a few general and powerful mechanisms for learning and
using feature structures, evolved from our primate social intelligence.
These mechanisms place few constraints on the word feature structures,
which then evolve freely as we use them, giving the structure of modern

languages. As long as this model fits the data, a simpler theory of the human mind is a better one.

References

Anderson, S. R. (1985). Inflectional morphology, in Shopen, T. (ed.) *Language Typology and Syntactic Description*, Vols. I–III, Cambridge University Press, Cambridge.

Chomsky, N. (1988). *Language and Problems of Knowledge: the Managua Lectures*, MIT press, Cambridge, MA.

Dawkins, R. (1976). *The Selfish Gene*, Oxford University Press, Oxford.

Deacon, T. (1997). *The Symbolic Species – the Co-evolution of Language and the Human Brain*, Penguin, London.

Deacon, T. (1998). Constraints on language evolution, paper presented at the *Second conference on the evolution of language*, London.

Greenberg, J. H. (1966). Some universals of grammar with particular reference to the order of meaningful elements, in Greenberg, J. H. (ed.) *Universals of Language*, 2nd edition, MIT Press, Cambridge, MA.

Hawkins, J. A. (1994). *A Performance Theory of Order and Constituency*, Cambridge University Press, Cambridge.

Kaplan, R. M. and J. Bresnan (1981). Lexical Functional Grammar: a Formal System for Grammatical Representation, in Bresnan, J. and R. M. Kaplan, (eds.) *Lexical Functional Grammar*. MIT Press, Cambridge, MA.

Kirby, S. (1996). The emergence of universals: function, selection and innateness. University of Edinburgh, PhD thesis.

Kirby, S. (1998). Fitness and selective adaptation of language, in Hurford, J., M. Studdert-Kennedy, and C. Knight, (eds.) *Approaches to the Evolution of Language*, Cambridge University Press, Cambridge.

McMahon, A. M. S. (1994). *Understanding Language Change*, Cambridge University Press, Cambridge.

Oehrle, R. T., E. Bach and D. Wheeler (eds.) (1988). *Categorial Grammars and Natural Language Structures*, Reidel, Dordrecht.

Pollard, C. and I. Sag (1993). *Head-Driven Phrase Structure Grammar*, University of Chicago Press, Chicago.

Schank, R. C. and R. P. Abelson (1977). *Scripts, Plans, Goals and Understanding: an Inquiry into Human Knowledge Structures*, Lawrence Erlbaum Associates, Hillside, NJ.

Seyfarth, R. M. (1990). *How Monkeys See the World*, University of Chicago Press, Chicago.

Shieber, S. (1986). *An Introduction to Unification-Based Approaches to Grammar*, University of Chicago Press, Chicago.

Siekmann, J. H. (1989). Unification theory, *J. Symbolic Computation*, 7, 207–274.

Uszkoreit, H. (1986). Categorial unification grammars, *Proceedings of COLING 1986*, Bonn.

Worden, R. P. (1995). A speed limit for evolution, *Journal of Theoretical Biology*, 176, 137–152.

Worden, R. P. (1996). Primate social intelligence, *Cognitive Science*, 20(4): 579–616.

Worden, R. P. (1997). A theory of language learning, draft paper at http://dspace.dial.pipex.com/jcollie/

Worden, R. P. (1998). The evolution of language from primate social intelligence, in Hurford, J., M. Studdert-Kennedy and C. Knight, (eds.) *Approaches to the Evolution of Language*, Cambridge University Press, Cambridge.

Worden, R. (2000). Words, memes and language evolution. In Knight, C., J. Hurford, and M. Studdert-Kennedy (eds.), *The Evolutionary Emergence of Language*, Cambridge University Press, Cambridge, pp. 353–371.

Zeevat, H., E. Klein and J. Calder (1988). Unification categorial grammar, in Haddock, N., E. Klein and G. Morrill (eds.) *Categorial Grammar, Unification Grammar and Parsing*, Edinburgh Working Papers in Cognitive Science Volume 1, Centre for Cognitive Science, University of Edinburgh.

5

The negotiation and acquisition of recursive grammars as a result of competition among exemplars

John Batali
Department of Cognitive Science
University of California at San Diego

5.1 Introduction

Of the known animal communication systems, human languages appear to be unique in their use of recursively characterizable structural relations among sequences of sounds or gestures and the meanings those sequences can be used to express.

The patterns of structural relations that recursion makes possible can serve a range of communicative functions, tremendously extending the expressive resources of the system. Structural relations may be used to express specific meanings, or to modify, extend, or restrict the meanings conveyed by words and other simple constituents.

Despite the unbounded complexity it makes possible, a recursive communicative system can be learned relatively easily because the constituents of a complex construction may themselves be simpler instances of that same kind of construction, and the properties of complex constructions are often predictable from simpler counterparts.

The research described in this chapter is an investigation of how recursive communication systems can come to be. In particular, the investigation explores the possibility that such a system could emerge among the members of a population as the result of a process I characterize as 'negotiation', in which each individual both contributes to, and conforms with, the system as it develops. The members of the population are assumed to possess general cognitive capacities sufficient for communicative behavior and for learning to modify their behavior based on observations of others. However they are given no external guidance about how their communication system is to work, and their internal cognitive mechanisms impose few constraints.

A detailed model of the cognitive capacities required to participate in the negotiation of a communication system is presented in this chapter. This model has been implemented as a computer program and used to simulate the negotiation process. The simulations usually yield highly accurate communication systems that use structural properties of utterances to encode their meanings, often in ways that resemble syntactic processes in human languages.

This chapter is organized as follows:

Section 5.2 presents the assumptions underlying this research, and a summary of the computational model.

The formalism used to represent the meanings that agents in the computational model attempt to convey to each other is presented in section 5.3. Section 5.4 describes how agents analyze relationships between signals and meanings, and how they use such analyses as they communicate. The algorithms implementing the agents' learning abilities are described in section 5.5.

Section 5.6 fills in some remaining details about the computational simulations, and describes the progress of a typical simulation. Analyses of the communication systems that emerge from the simulations are presented in section 5.7. A few issues concerning the relevance of the model and the simulation results to the emergence of human language are discussed in section 5.8.

5.2 Negotiated communication systems

I assume that the inventors of language were pretty smart. Their cognitive capacities almost certainly included the ability to categorize individuals and events, and to internally represent situations as involving one or more events and a cast of participants. Individuals might have used such capacities to record past situations, to understand and respond to ongoing events, and to anticipate and plan for the future.

I also assume that the inventors of language were gregarious and mutually reliant, but not entirely naïve. They watched each other closely. Sometimes their attention was based on concern, sometimes on curiosity, sometimes on fear. They learned enough from their observations to be able to to predict, control, assist, and sometimes avoid or thwart, each other, with varying degrees of success.

Coordinated social activity required coordination of the representations that guided each individual's actions. A major impetus for the development of language was its use as an external and public medium for the expression of what had previously been private and internal. In particular, the ability to describe situations and events enables the members of a group to pool their perceptual abilities, to plan joint activities, and to entertain each other afterwards.

5.2.1 Systematic communication

In the research described in this chapter, I treat communication as involving the transfer of information from one agent to another. One of the agents, who will be called the **sender**, begins an episode of communication with an internal representation M_1 of some meaning. The sender performs a publicly visible signaling behavior S in order to express M_1. The second agent, who will be called the **receiver**, observes the performance of S and interprets it as conveying a meaning the receiver represents as M_2. To the degree that the representations M_1 and M_2 are equivalent, the meaning is conveyed accurately, and the communicative episode is considered successful.

Communicative behavior is **systematic** if it occurs as the result of repeatable mechanisms in the agents and depends, at least partly, on meanings and signals having certain general properties, or instantiating certain types or categories. Therefore, if the sender were to express the same type of meaning in another situation, it might use the same signal.

If the communicative behavior of each member of a population is systematic, and if, as a result, the agents often communicate accurately with each other, I will speak of the population as possessing a **communication system**. However the system exists only as a manifestation of the individual behavior of the agents, and each agent might implement its communicative behavior differently.

A population's communication system will be called **conventional** if it is learned, and if, in principle, each member could have learned a different system. I assume that accurate communication is mutually beneficial for both senders and receivers, at least often enough for the agents to attempt to convey meanings to each other, to interpret signals, and to learn how to improve their abilities at both tasks. In a population where this is true, a conventional communication system can result from a process of of **negotiation**, as the agents alternate between contributing to, and conforming with, the emerging system.

The negotiation of communication systems in which a set of simple signals is used to convey elements from a small set of meanings has been explored by researchers in a number of different fields. Lewis (1969), in philosophy, discusses the issue in the context of an investigation of conventional behavior. In economics, Spence (1973), Crawford and Sobel (1982), and Canning (1992) apply the mathematical theory of games. Hurford (1989), in linguistics, describes computational simulations comparing the effect that different learning procedures have on the communication systems that emerge from their use. In the field of robotics, Steels (1996) applies symbolic learning methods to explore the development and subsequent modification of communication systems. In cognitive science, Hutchins and Hazlehurst (1991) use neural-network learning algorithms in a simulation of the negotiation process; Oliphant (1997) explores various learning mechanisms, as well as the relations between communication and altruistic behavior.

5.2.2 Conventional analyses of structural mappings

A conventional communication system could be implemented as a simple table in which each meaning to be conveyed is associated with a unique signal. However if the sets of meanings and signals are large, agents won't get a chance to observe all of the entries in the table, and probably wouldn't be able to remember them all.

If the sets of meanings and signals are large, the agents probably don't use a distinct internal representation for each of them. Their representations are most likely constructed from a relatively small number of component types. The interpretation of an internal representation depends on the specific components use to construct it, and how they are configured. I will refer to this as the **structure** of the representation.

When an agent is given a meaning to express, it will, in general, use aspects of the structure of its representation of the meaning in its derivation of the structure of the signal used to express that meaning. The receiver's interpretation of the signal will make use of the signal's structure to derive a representation of the meaning it conveys. The derivations performed by the sender and receiver therefore constitute implicit analyses of the relations between the structures of meanings and signals. The process is illustrated schematically in figure 5.1.

The structural derivations performed by the sender and the receiver might have no relation to one another, except that they both involve the same signal, and, if the agents are lucky, equivalent meanings.

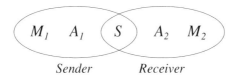

Sender   Receiver

figure 5.1. Communicating structured meanings. The sender derives a signal S to express meaning M_1 according to analysis A_1 of the mapping from the structure of M_1 to S. The receiver derives its interpretation M_2 of the signal according to analysis A_2 of the mapping from the structure of S to M_2.

For them to achieve better than chance accuracy, I assume that the members of a population obey a set of negotiated conventions regarding possible derivational relationships between the structures of signals and meanings. These conventions can emerge if senders perform their derivations of signals while considering how receivers might interpret them, and if receivers derive their interpretations of signals while considering how they might have been constructed by senders. By including recursive characterizations of structural properties, the set of conventions can be used to coordinate communication of an unbounded set of meanings with a relatively small set of conventions.

Analyses of structural mappings between signals and meanings are used by learners as they attempt to discover the conventions the users of a communication system obey, and as they attempt to perform derivations of signals and meanings in accord with the conventions.

In general, a set of conventions might allow more than one analysis of the mapping between the structure of a meaning and a signal, and might allow more than one signal to be mapped to a given meaning, and vice versa. The set of conventions would therefore include procedures for determining which of a set of alternative analyses is preferred.

A communication system is negotiated by the members of a population as they learn from observations of each other's communicative attempts. The individuals analyze their observations as well as they can, and use their recorded analyses whenever possible, as follows:

For a meaning M_1, a sender finds a signal S and an analysis A_1 of the derivation of S from M_1, such that according to the sender's observations, A_1 is licensed by the population's communication system, and is preferred over alternatives with the same meaning. The signal S is performed by the sender to express M_1.

For a signal S, a receiver finds a meaning M_2, and an analysis A_2 of the derivation of M_2 from S, such that according to the receiver's observations, A_2 is licensed by the population's communication system, and is preferred over alternatives with the same signal. The signal S is interpreted by the receiver as M_2.

The ability to create and manipulate mappings between the structures of representations may be an important aspect of cognition in domains other than communication. Gentner (1983) presents a theory of analogical reasoning that involves such mappings. A model of how structure mappings are computed is described by Falkenhainer, Forbus and Gentner (1989). An alternative model of analogy and perception, which also relies on the computation of structural mappings, is presented by Chalmers, French and Hofstadter (1992). An implementation of the model is described by Mitchell (1993).

5.2.3 Exemplars

Individuals must record analyses of their learning observations in a way that can be used to guide their subsequent attempts to express meanings and to interpret signals. This could take the form of a set of rules or principles that govern the allowed structural mappings between meanings and signals. These rules or principles would be induced from the set of observations the learner has analyzed, and would later be used to derive analyses of other signal/meaning pairs.

The alternative explored in this research is that learners simply store all of their analyzed observations as **exemplars**. No rules or principles are induced from them. Instead, exemplars are used directly to convey meanings and to interpret signals. An exemplar may be used intact, to express the exact meaning, or to interpret the signal, recorded in the exemplar. Exemplars may also be modified to construct new analyses of the mapping between a signal and a meaning.

The use of recorded exemplars based on individual observations, rather than rules or abstractions induced from them, is central to proposals made in a number of different cognitive domains. Medin and Schaffer (1978) and Barsalou (1989) have explored models of categorization based on recorded exemplars. Aha, Kibler and Albert (1991) develop an 'instance-based' theory of learning, and Hammond (1990) describes a 'case-based' model of planning, in which stored solutions to previous problems are modified and reused. Bod (1998) develops a 'data-oriented' model of parsing that uses a corpus of previously parsed examples to find the most likely structure of a sentence.

In general, exemplar sets are almost certain to contain inconsistent and redundant entries. Mechanisms must exist for choosing which of a set of alternative exemplars, or modified analyses based on them, will be used in a communicative episode. I assume that learning involves a process of **competition** among exemplars: those that are repeatedly found to be consistent with learning observations become more likely to be used to create new signal/meaning mappings; exemplars that are found to be inconsistent with learning observations, or with other exemplars, are used less often. This process is similar to that described by MacWhinney and Bates (1987) in a competition-based account of first language acquisition.

5.2.4 The computational model

These ideas are implemented in a computational model that is used to simulate the negotiation process and analyze its results.

Agents are implemented with a set of data structures and algorithms that correspond to the cognitive abilities required to participate in a negotiation. However the agents begin a negotiation with no shared communication system, and are given no guidance whatsoever as they develop one.

The agents begin the negotiation with the ability to manipulate internal representations of situations, called **formula sets**, which will serve as the meanings they convey to each other. The agents can also create and manipulate sequences of characters (called **strings**), to be used as signals.

The mapping between a formula set and a string of characters is represented with a data structure called a **phrase**. A phrase may simply record that a given meaning was observed to be expressed with a given string, or it may involve an analysis of how the string is broken into constituents, and how their meanings are combined. Phrases are constructed and manipulated by the agents as they determine the strings they will use to express meanings, and as they interpret strings generated by others.

Phrases are also used by the agents as they learn to communicate. In some situations, an agent is assumed to observe both the string sent by another agent, as well as the meaning that the other agent used that string to express. The learner creates one or more **exemplar phrases** to record this observation, and will use its set of exemplars to guide its subsequent communicative behavior.

Each phrase is assigned a numeric **cost**, whose value depends on how the phrase was constructed. Costs are used to implement the choice of a preferred phrase among several that equally satisfy an agent's requirements. The primary algorithm that implements an agent's communicative behavior and its analysis of learning observations is a search through the agent's exemplars to find or construct the cheapest possible phrase with a specific meaning and/or string.

An agent can create a new phrase by combining and modifying some of its exemplar phrases. The cost of the resultant phrase equals the sum of the costs of the exemplars that were used, plus a small additional cost for each modification. If an agent has no exemplars, or none that satisfy its current search requirements, the agent can create entirely new phrases, or combine some of its exemplar phrases with newly created structure. The costs assigned to these new phrases are relatively high, so that the agents will tend to use exemplar phrases, or phrases that can be constructed out of them, if possible.

All exemplar phrases are given the same initial cost. An exemplar's cost may later be increased or decreased in subsequent learning observations, thereby changing the likelihood that the exemplar will be used by the agent. The cost of an exemplar is reduced if it is found to be consistent with exemplars used by other agents in the population, and an exemplar's cost is increased if it is found to be inconsistent with other exemplars the agent has acquired.

At the start of a negotiation, the agents have no exemplars to guide their communicative attempts, and so they just babble randomly and fail miserably to understand anything. As the agents acquire sets of exemplars, and as the costs of their exemplars are adjusted, their communicative accuracy steadily increases, and a shared system emerges.

5.3 Internal representations

The agents begin a negotiation with the ability to create and manipulate internal representations of situations and their participants. I assume that such cognitive abilities are prior to, and independent of, language, at least for the simple kinds of meanings described here. Many species of mammals and birds exhibit behaviors that seem to require such representations, and a great deal of experimental and observational evidence

	Formula Set	*Gloss*
a.	{(goose 1) (sang 1)}	A goose sang.
b.	{(insulted 1 2) (pig 2)}	(Something) insulted a pig.
c.	{(duck 1) (tickled 2 1) (cow 2)}	A cow tickled a duck.
d.	{(rat 1) (slapped 1 1)}	A rat slapped itself.
e.	{(goose 1) (sang 1) (noticed 1 2) (snake 2)}	A goose that sang noticed a snake.
f.	{(snake 1) (goose 2) (sang 2) (noticed 2 1) (bit 1 3) (moose 3) (danced 3)}	A snake that a goose that sang noticed bit a dancing moose.

figure 5.2. Example formula sets.

suggests that apes and other primates use internal representations even more sophisticated than those described here. (Premack, 1983; Thompson, 1995; Pough, Heiser and McFarland, 1996.)

5.3.1 Formula sets

In the computational model, internal representations are implemented as **formula sets**. Each **formula** is composed of a **predicate**, written as an English word, followed by one or two **variables**, which will be referred to as the formula's **arguments**, written as Arabic numerals. The predicate and arguments of a formula are written inside parentheses. Example formula sets are shown in figure 5.2.

The variables used in a formula set are interpreted as designating participants in a situation. A formula set's predicates are interpreted as designating properties of, and relations among, those participants. A given variable is interpreted as designating the same participant everywhere it occurs in a formula set.

In the manipulations of formula sets performed by the agents, the only distinction made among predicates has to do with the number of arguments they take. A predicate that takes a single argument will be referred to as a **property** whether it is the name of a kind of animal or an intransitive verb. A two argument predicate will be called a **relation**, with the different arguments designating the roles of the participants in the action or event. The words used to represent predicates are entirely fanciful, and the modeled agents do no inference or other interpretation of formulae based on their predicates.

English sentences are used to gloss the meanings of the formula sets in figure 5.2, and elsewhere in this chapter, to simplify the presentation and analysis of the model. However the formalism captures only those aspects of the meanings of sentences that involve characterizing configurations of actions, events, and participants. For most formula sets, a number of different sentences would serve equally well as glosses. For example, the meaning of formula set c in figure 5.2 could equally well be glossed as 'A duck was tickled by a cow'.

5.3.2 Renaming arguments

Two formula sets that have exactly the same possible interpretations will be said to be **equivalent**. Two situation descriptions with the same set of formulae are equivalent no matter the order in which the formulae are written or stored. Two formula sets may also be equivalent if the variables in one of them can be uniquely renamed to yield the other. In the following examples, formula set 5.3.a can be used to represent a situation involving two participants, one of which, a cow, bit the other:

5.3.a   {(cow 1) (bit 1 2)}
5.3.b   {(cow 2) (bit 2 1)}
5.3.c   {(cow 2) (bit 1 2)}
5.3.d   {(cow 1) (bit 1 1)}

The same interpretation can be given to 5.3.b, and so the formula sets 5.3.a and 5.3.b are equivalent. Formula set 5.3.c also involves two participants in a biting incident, however the cow is the victim, not the perpetrator. In formula set 5.3.d, only one participant is involved. These two formula sets are therefore not equivalent to 5.3.a.

The operation of renaming the arguments in a formula set is formalized by introducing a set of operators called **argument maps**. An argument map is written as a two-column table of variables. When applied to a formula, each of the variables in the left-hand column of the table is replaced by the variable in the right hand column of the same row. An argument map is **invertible** if no variable appears twice in its right-hand column, and is **non-invertible** otherwise. As just illustrated, the application of an invertible argument map to a formula set yields an equivalent formula set, while the application of a non-invertible argu-

Formula Set	*Arg. Map*	*Result*
{(rat 1) (sang 1)}	1:2	{(rat 2) (sang 2)}
{(cow 1) (chased 1 2)}	1:1 / 2:1	{(cow 1) (chased 1 1)}
{(duck 1) (bit 1 2) (fox 2)}	1:2 / 2:1	{(duck 2) (bit 2 1) (fox 1)}
{(chicken 1) (noticed 1 2)}	1:1 / 2:2	{(chicken 1) (noticed 1 2)}

figure 5.3. Example argument maps. The argument maps in the center column are applied to the formula sets on the left to yield the formula sets on the right.

ment map yields a formula set whose interpretation is more restricted. The set of argument maps also includes **identity argument maps** that rename each variable to itself, and therefore yield formula sets that are identical to those they are applied to. Example argument maps are shown in figure 5.3.

5.3.3 Combining formula sets

Two formula sets can be combined by taking their union. The result can be used to represent a more complex situation.

In the following examples, 5.3.e represents a situation in which a rat was present, and 5.3.f represents a situation in which something sang. The formula set obtained by combining them, 5.3.g, represents a situation in which the rat was the singer.

5.3.e {(rat 1)}
5.3.f {(sang 1)}
5.3.g {(rat 1) (sang 1)}

To represent a particular configuration of participants in a situation, the arguments of one or both of a pair of formula sets may be renamed with argument maps before their formulae are combined. For example, formula set 5.3.g could be combined with 5.3.h to yield 5.3.i. The result could represent that a singing rat was chasing something.

Alternatively, if the variable in 5.3.g is renamed with the argument map $\boxed{1:2}$ before the formula sets are combined, the result, 5.3.j, can be used to represent a situation in which the sonorous rodent was the object of pursuit.

5.3.h {(chased 1 2)}
5.3.i {(rat 1) (sang 1) (chased 1 2)}
5.3.j {(rat 2) (sang 2) (chased 1 2)}

5.3.4 Formula sets as meanings

The agents in the computational simulations are given formula sets as meanings to convey. Formulae are constructed from a set of 22 property predicates and 10 relation predicates. The formula sets given to the agents are randomly selected from candidates that contain from two to seven formulae and involve at most three different variables. (So the last example in figure 5.2 is as hard as they get.)

There are 2.3×10^{13} different (i.e., non-equivalent) formula sets that may be selected. This number represents the magnitude of the task the agents face in negotiating a communication system. They must somehow develop a way to express any of these possible meanings after having attempted to convey only a tiny subset.

Although there are a lot of them, the representational capacities of formula sets are extremely impoverished. They can't be used to represent propositional attitudes, counter-factual situations, or anything else that involves embedded meanings.

The decision to use such a restricted formalism was made deliberately. Any formal system for representing embedded meanings would have to include operators for creating and manipulating embedded meanings, along with rules governing the use of those operators. The agents' internal representations would therefore have recursive structure. It is possible that the syntax of the formalism for representing embedded meanings might influence the ways the agents find to express such meanings in their communication systems. This possibility is consistent with theoretical proposals about the relationship between syntax and semantics (for example in the work of Montague, 1974), but can't occur in this model. Any recursive regularities in the systems the agents develop to express these non-recursive meanings will be entirely of their own invention.

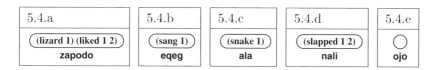

figure 5.4. Tokens. A token contains a formula set, printed inside a balloon, and a string of characters, printed below it.

5.4 Phrases

Analyses of mapping between formula sets and strings are represented with data-structures called **phrases** that the agents create and manipulate as they communicate, and as they record their observations of each other's communicative attempts.

5.4.1 Tokens

A simple phrase, which will be called a **token**, contains only a formula set and a string, with no further analysis of the structure of either. Some example tokens are shown in figure 5.4.

A token's formula set may contain any number of elements, including zero. If its formula set contains a single element, the token will be referred to as a **singleton token**. Examples 5.4.b, 5.4.c, and 5.4.d in figure 5.4 are singleton tokens. If the predicate in a singleton token's formula takes one argument, the token will be called a **property token**; if the predicate in a singleton token's formula takes two arguments, the token will be called a **relation token**. Examples 5.4.b and 5.4.c are property tokens, and 5.4.d is a relation token. Tokens whose formula sets contain no elements will be called **empty tokens**; an example is 5.4.e.

5.4.2 Complex phrases

A **complex phrase** is used to record a structural analysis of how the mapping between a string and meaning depends on the meanings and strings of a pair of constituents. The mapping is represented as involving the combination of two other phrases, which will subsequently be referred to as the **left-subphrase** and **right-subphrase**. The complex phrase's string is obtained by concatenating the strings of its left and right subphrases. The meanings of the constituents are combined ac-

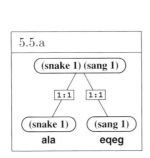
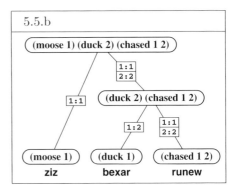

figure 5.5. Complex Phrases. The left and right subphrases of a complex phrase, and the argument maps applied to each constituent's formulae, are drawn below the balloon containing the complex phrase's meaning. Phrase 5.5.a represents an analysis of how the structures of the string 'alaeqeg', and the meaning {(snake 1) (sang 1)} ('A snake sang.'), are derived from the strings and meanings of two token constituents. Phrase 5.5.b represents an analysis of how the structures of the string 'zizbexarrunew', and the meaning {(moose 1) (duck 1) (chased 1 2)} ('A moose chased a duck.'), are derived from two constituents, one of which is also a complex phrase.

cording to the technique described in section 5.3.3: an argument map is applied to the formulae of each phrase's meaning, and the resulting formulae are combined to obtain the formula set of the complex phrase. The constituents of a complex phrase may be tokens, or they may be other complex phrases. Example complex phrases are shown in figure 5.5.

I will use the term 'phrase' to mean either tokens or complex phrases, unless the discussion is specific to one or the other. When discussing the structure of a complex phrase, I will use the term **subphrase** to refer to a complex phrase's left or right subphrase, or one of their constituents.

5.4.3 Exemplars

Phrases are used to represent the structural mapping between a meaning and a string used to express it. For a shared communication system to emerge, the agents must come to agreement on how these mappings are constructed and analyzed. They do so by recording their observations of the communicative attempts of other agents, and by using their recorded observations in their subsequent communicative behavior.

An **exemplar** is a phrase created by an agent to record an observation of another agent using a string to convey a meaning. An exemplar phrase may consist simply of a token with the observed string and meaning. Such an exemplar is nothing more than a literal record of the observation. Alternatively, the learner might construct a complex phrase with the given string and meaning. In this case the exemplar phrase records the learner's analysis of how the observed string and meaning might have been obtained by combining simpler phrases.

Each exemplar has a numerical **cost**. New exemplars are all given a cost of 1.0, and exemplar costs are subsequently modified by the learning procedures described in Section 5.5.2. Exemplar costs are used to choose among the structural analyses an agent considers as it communicates and as it learns to communicate.

5.4.4 Combining and modifying exemplar phrases

Given a set of exemplar phrases and their associated costs, it is possible to create new phrases from them. Each new phrase will be assigned a cost that depends on the costs of the exemplars used to construct it, and the specific modifications that were made to them.

Any pair of exemplar phrases may be combined into a new complex phrase by specifying the order in which the phrases are to be combined, and the pair of argument maps to be applied to the formula sets of each constituent. The cost of the new complex phrase equals the sum of the costs of the constituent phrases, plus the value of the 'New Structure Cost' parameter, 1.5.

An exemplar phrase may be modified by replacing one of its subphrases with another phrase. The modified phrase's string is obtained by replacing the string of the subphrase that was removed with the string of the phrase that replaced it. The modified phrase's meaning is obtained by removing any formulae contributed by the replaced phrase from the meaning of the original phrase, and replacing them with the formulae of the new subphrase's meaning, after applying the argument maps above the modified phrase. The cost of the new phrase thus created equals the sum of the costs of the two phrases that were used, plus the value of the 'Replacement Cost' parameter, 0.1. The process is illustrated in figure 5.6.

A phrase can replace a subphrase of another phrase provided that the replacement phrase's formula set uses the same variables as the subphrase it replaces. I will refer to this restriction as the **Replacement**

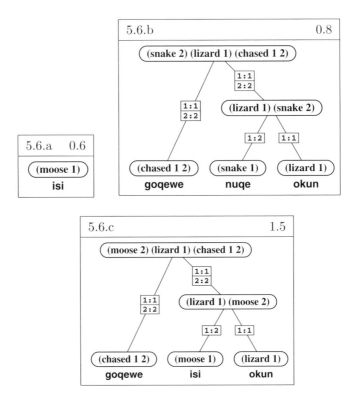

figure 5.6. Modifying a phrase. Phrase 5.6.a replaces the token with the string 'nuqe' in phrase 5.6.b, yielding 5.6.c. The cost of each phrase is shown at its upper right.

Condition. If it is satisfied, the argument maps that were applied to the variables in the deleted phrase's meaning can be applied to those in the phrase that replaces it.

5.4.5 Searching a set of exemplars

The algorithm that underlies all communicative behavior in the model involves a search over a set of exemplars for a phrase with a given meaning or string. The string or meaning thus given will be called the **target** of the search, and a phrase whose meaning or string matches the target of a search will be called a **solution** to the search. For some targets, the set of exemplars will contain one or more phrases that can be used intact as solutions. In other searches, new phrases must be created by combining and modifying exemplars. Whenever more than one solution to a search can be found or constructed, the cheapest alternative is selected.

When an agent acts as a sender in a communicative episode, it searches its set of exemplars for the cheapest phrase with the meaning it is given to express. The string from that phrase is passed to another agent, who searches its own set of exemplars for a phrase with that string. The formula set of the receiver's phrase represents the receiver's interpretation of the meaning of the string.

An agent also searches its set of exemplars to record a learning observation of a string being used to express a meaning. The agent locates the cheapest phrase with both the observed string and meaning, and uses its solution to construct new exemplars, and to guide the adjustment of the costs of other exemplars, as described in Section 5.5.

An exemplar set may not contain phrases with some of the strings and/or meanings required to satisfy a given search target. (This will occur, for example, at the start of a negotiation, before the agents have acquired any exemplars at all.) In such cases, an entirely new token with any required string and meaning may be created. The cost of a new token equals the sum of the number of characters in its string and the number of formulae in its meaning. The new token is added to the exemplar set for the duration of the search in which it was created and is discarded afterward.

If an agent is given a meaning to express, and needs to create new tokens because it has none with one or more of the formulae in the meaning, it will generate a random string, consisting of alternating vowels and consonants, and create a new token with that string and the required formula or formulae.[1] If an agent is given a string to interpret, and has no token exemplars with that string, or one of its subsequences, the receiver will create a new token with an empty meaning. Learners also create new tokens if needed, and such tokens may be incorporated in exemplars.

The values of the Replacement Cost and New Structure Cost parameters, and the costs assigned to new tokens, are such that agents will, in general, rely on their exemplars as they communicate and analyze their learning observations. If a search's requirements can be satisfied by us-

---

[1] The alternation of vowels and consonants in newly created random strings has no deep theoretical motivation, but is done so that the agents' strings can be pronounced by the Festival Speech Synthesis system developed at the University of Edinburgh (Black and Taylor, 1997); URL: `www.cstr.ed.ac.uk/projects/festival`.

ing exemplar phrases, or phrases that can be constructed by modifying exemplar phrases, such solutions will almost always be cheaper than phrases that require the creation of new tokens or complex phrases.

5.4.6 The origins of phrases

While it may be plausible that the ability to create and manipulate internal representations of situations and participants, described in section 5.3, is prior to, and independent of, communication, the same cannot be said of the data structures and algorithms described in this section. The model of tokens and phrases is inspired by human language, and is intended to be as simple as possible, consistent with the following generalizations about human languages:

1. Utterances tend to be linear sequences of sounds or gestures.
   This generalization is implemented in the strings the agents use as signals.
2. The constituent structure of utterances tends to group adjacent elements.
   Implemented in the binary-branching structure of complex phrases.
3. The meanings of utterances often depend on the meanings of their constituents.
   Implemented in the operation of combining the formula sets of the constituents of complex phrases.

The abilities to combine tokens into complex phrases, and to further combine complex phrases, could be seen as an implementation of what Chomsky (1975) refers to as the 'structure dependency' of the analyses performed by humans as they learn a language. The fact that all known human languages rely on structure dependent rules is used by Chomsky as evidence for the existence of innate computational mechanisms, useful only for language, and found only in humans.

An alternative, suggested by O'Grady (1987), recognizes that the human ability to learn and use language might require biological support, but suggests that 'the contribution of the genetic endowment is restricted to the specification of concepts and learning strategies that are required independent of language' (p. xi).

As discussed in section 5.2, the mechanisms of structural mappings and exemplar-based learning are similar to those proposed in the domains of perception, analogical reasoning, and planning, and so might turn out to be the result of cognitive mechanisms of general utility, consistent with O'Grady's suggestion.

Although the use of tokens and phrases with hierarchical structure might not seem to be of general cognitive utility, these properties of language might occur as solutions to the problem of encoding complex meanings into linear sequences. In previous research (Batali, 1998), agents negotiating a system for communicating meanings with predicate/argument structure developed signals in which the predicate tends to be expressed at the start of the signal, and the referent at the end.

In any case, although the agents begin a simulation with the ability to use embedded phrase structure, they are unable to communicate with each other unless and until they negotiate a shared system. Whether and how they do so is the main focus of this research.

5.5 Learning

The agents acquire their exemplars by recording observations of other agents expressing meanings. A learner finds the cheapest phrase with the observed string and meaning that can be created by combining or modifying phrases from its existing set of exemplars, creating new tokens and phrases if necessary.

Section 5.5.1 presents a sequence of observations made by a hypothetical agent at the beginning of a simulation, and the exemplars that are constructed to record those observations. The algorithms for subsequently modifying exemplar costs are described in section 5.5.2.

5.5.1 Acquiring exemplars

The agent in this sequence of examples begins the negotiation with no exemplars. If it is given a meaning to express before it has made any learning observations, the agent will create a new token containing a random string. The agent makes no record of the new token it just created, and so if it were later given the same meaning to express, it would almost certainly create a token with a different random string. If the agent is given a string to interpret before it has any exemplars, it will create a new empty token, and simply fail to interpret the string as conveying any meaning at all.

An initial observation

Our agent's first learning observation is of another agent using the string
'usifala' to express the meaning {(snake 1) (sang 1)}.

Observation 5.5.1.1.

usifala	{(snake 1) (sang 1)}

A new token is created with this string and meaning, and recorded
as the agent's first exemplar. All new exemplars are given a cost of 1.0.

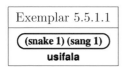

Exemplar 5.5.1.1

(snake 1) (sang 1)
usifala

If the agent is now chosen to be the sender in a communicative episode,
and is given the meaning {(snake 1) (sang 1)} to express, it will find the
exemplar just created as a solution to its search. Any new token with
the meaning would cost at least 2.0, and so the exemplar token will be
cheaper.[2] The agent therefore uses the string 'usifala' to express the
meaning.

If the agent is later selected as a receiver, and happens to be given
the string 'usifala' to interpret, it will again find exemplar 5.5.1 as
a solution to its search. An empty token with this string would cost
7.0, so the agent will interpret the string as expressing the meaning
{(snake 1) (sang 1)}.

There is no guarantee that this is the meaning another agent used this
string to express. The observed agent may have been using a random
string the other agent just created. But there is some chance that our
agent's interpretation might be correct. After all, Exemplar 5.5.1 was
created because another agent was observed using that meaning and
string, and other agents may have made similar observations.

Constructing a complex phrase

The agent next observes:

Observation 5.5.1.2.

usifalaozoj	{(snake 1) (sang 1) (chased 1 2)}

---

[2] As mentioned in section 5.4.5, the cost of a new token equals the sum of the number
formulae in its meanings and the number of characters in its string.

The agent has no exemplars with exactly this string and meaning. However its one exemplar covers the the first seven characters of the string, and two of the three formulae of the meaning.

If that exemplar were used to analyze the first part of the string as {(snake 1) (sang 1)}, the remainder, 'ozoj', would be analyzed as contributing the formula (chased 1 2).

The agent creates a new token with for this string and meaning, and combines the new token and its token exemplar into a complex phrase, using identity argument maps for both subphrases.

This solution is used to create two new exemplars. One of them corresponds to the solution phrase, and one is created from the newly created token. In general, exemplars are created for all subphrases of a learner's solution phrase except those that are unmodified exemplars.

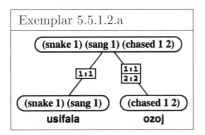

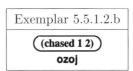

Using a complex phrase exemplar

Observation 5.5.1.3.

| oduozoj | {(pig 1) (chased 1 2)} |

As with the previous observation, the agent's exemplars cover part of the observed string and meaning. A new token is created with the string 'odu' and the meaning {(pig 1)}.

This time the agent need not create a new complex phrase. Instead, the complex phrase exemplar created after the previous learning observation can be modified by replacing its left subphrase with the new token.

Two new exemplars are created:

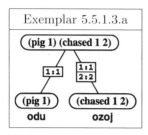

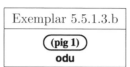

The previous two examples illustrate how the acquisition of even a few complex phrase exemplars facilitates the acquisition of singleton tokens. Singleton tokens are extremely useful for communication because they can be inserted into phrases whenever a specific formula is part of a meaning to be expressed.

Renaming an exemplar's variable

Observation 5.5.1.4.

vuxahozojodu	{(lizard 1) (chased 1 2) (pig 2)}

A new token with the string 'vuxah' and meaning {(lizard 1)} is created, and used to replace the left-subphrase of one of the agent's complex phrase exemplars. The agent has a token with the remainder of the observed string, 'odu', but the variable in that token's formula must be renamed from 1 to 2 using a new complex phrase.

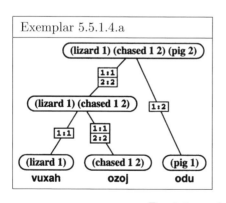

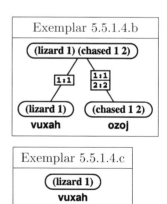

Bootstrapping

Observation 5.5.1.5.

esebvuxah	{(bit 1 2) (lizard 2)}

The agent's exemplar 5.5.1.4.a can be used to combine a new token with the string 'eseb' and meaning (bit 1 2) with the exemplar token 'vuxah'.

The agent has not yet seen a string where a relation token is put first, followed by a property token. However the system emerging from its exemplar set is consistent with interpreting the second token as expressing a property of variable 2.

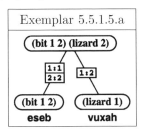

Creating an empty token

Observation 5.5.1.6.

| vuxahozojif | {(lizard 1) (chased 1 1)} |

The agent's exemplar 5.5.1.4.b covers all but the last two characters of the observed string. If the variable 2 were mapped to 1, the meaning of that exemplar would match the observation. However the remainder of the observed string doesn't seem to be contributing anything.

The agent creates an empty token with the string 'if', and a new complex phrase with the required argument maps.

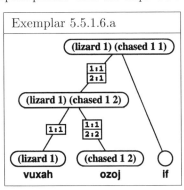

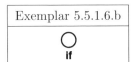

More of the same

As its observations continue, the agent accumulates more exemplars, using its existing exemplars to guide its creation of new ones. The rest of the agents in the population are doing likewise, and in some cases, their observations are of this agent's communicative attempts.

The sequence presented here is fictional, but corresponds in its essential details to what occurs in simulation runs. The main difference between this set of examples, and what occurs in a real simulation, is that this agent is stupifyingly lucky. The specific sequence of observations described will never occur so quickly, or in such a convenient sequence. But eventually, agents will make observations, and acquire exemplars, similar to those presented.

Once they have begun to acquire complex phrase exemplars, the agents soon do so at a very rapid rate, and the members of a population begin to succeed occasionally at conveying meanings. The use of complex phrases to analyze observations can simplify, and thus accelerate, the agents' acquisition of singleton token exemplars. Soon after they start using complex phrases, a population of agents begins to negotiate a shared set of singleton tokens that one might refer to as the 'vocabulary' of their communication system. The existence of a shared vocabulary enables them to come to similar agreement on sets of complex phrase exemplars that encode a productive 'grammar' of their communication system.

5.5.2 Reinforcement and discouragement

As an agent continues to record learning observations, its exemplar set will accumulate redundant and contradictory elements. The other agents whose observations are observed may be randomly babbling. Even if they aren't, the learner's analyses of its observations are not likely to have much resemblance to the phrases that were used to produce them (other than having the same strings and meanings). The phrases used by the sender and by the learner may have different meanings assigned to different constituents and in fact might not even agree as to where the boundaries of the constituents are, or how they are combined. The search algorithm makes random choices when it assigns meanings to new tokens and when it chooses how to combine the constituents of new complex phrases.

From this mess, the agents must select a subset of their exemplars to guide their communication. This is done by decreasing the costs of some exemplars and increasing the costs of others.

Reinforcing shared exemplars

Decreasing an exemplar's cost is called **reinforcing** the exemplar. When an exemplar is reinforced, its cost is reduced according to the formula:

$$C_A = C_B - r\, C_B \qquad (5.1)$$

where C_B is the exemplar's cost before it is reinforced, r is the value of the "Reinforcement Rate" parameter, 0.1, and C_A is the new cost assigned to the exemplar.

An exemplar is reinforced when it is used in the phrase an agent constructs to record a learning observation. For example, the agent's first complex phrase exemplar, 5.5.1.2.a, would have been reinforced when it was used to create the solution phrase for learning observations 5.5.1.3 and 5.5.1.4, so its cost after the observations described in section 5.5.1 would be 0.81.

The more often an exemplar is part of a learner's solution phrase, the more likely it is that other agents share similar exemplars. The lower costs of reinforced exemplars will result in their being used more often in communicative situations, as well as to record subsequent learning observations. The other agents are also reinforcing exemplars that are used to analyze their learning observations, so the process of reinforcement tends to guide the population towards similar exemplars with similarly low costs.

Discouraging inconsistent exemplars

Increasing an exemplar's cost is called **discouraging** the exemplar. When an exemplar is discouraged, its cost is modified according to the formula:

$$C_A = C_B + d \qquad (5.2)$$

where C_B is the exemplar's cost before it is reinforced, d is the value of the 'Discouragement Rate' parameter, 0.1, and C_A is the new cost assigned to the exemplar.

As it records a learning observation, an agent may discover that its current set of exemplars is inconsistent with the observation. To locate such inconsistencies, and to discourage the exemplars responsible for them, an agent performs two searches of its exemplars when it makes

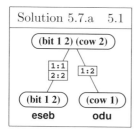 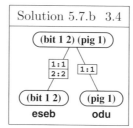 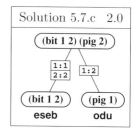

figure 5.7. Solution phrases for inconsistent learning observations. Solution 5.7.a is the cheapest phrase that the learner of Section 5.5.1 can construct to match Observation 5.5.2.1. Solution 5.7.b is the cheapest phrase for Observation 5.5.2.2. Solution 5.7.c is the cheapest phrase with the string 'esebodu', independent of meaning. The cost of each phrase, shown at its upper right, reflects adjustments to exemplar costs due to reinforcement.

a learning observation. In addition to finding the cheapest phrase with the observed string and meaning, the agent also searches its exemplars for any cheaper phrases whose strings match the observation, but whose meanings do not.

For example, suppose that the agent of section 5.5.1 were to make one of the following learning observations:

Observation 5.5.2.1.

esebodu	{(bit 1 2) (cow 2)}

Observation 5.5.2.2.

esebodu	{(bit 1 2) (pig 1)}

To match learning observation 5.5.2.1, the agent must create a new token pairing 'odu' with {(cow 1)}, and use it in phrase 5.7.a in figure 5.7. To match learning observation 5.5.2.2, the agent must create a new complex phrase, 5.7.b. Given the string 'esebodu' alone, the agent would use exemplars 5.5.1.5.a, and 5.5.1.3.b to create solution 5.7.c.

If the agent were acting as receiver, and given only the string 'esebodu', it would use solution 5.7.c to interpret string as {(bit 1 2) (pig 2)}. If the actual meaning expressed were that of learning observation 5.5.2.1 or 5.5.2.2, the agent would interpret the string incorrectly. To reduce the likelihood that the inconsistency will result in its misinterpretation of subsequent communicative attempts, the agent determines which of the exemplars used to construct solution 5.7.c are responsible for its having the wrong meaning, and those exemplars are discouraged.

If the learning observation had been 5.5.2.1, the incorrect meaning would be blamed on the use of the token exemplar 5.5.1.3.b, which pairs the string 'odu' with the meaning $\{(\mathsf{cow}\ 1)\}$. If the learning observation had been 5.5.2.2, the complex phrase exemplar 5.5.1.a would be blamed, because both tokens are consistent with the correct meaning but are not renamed correctly by the complex phrase's argument maps.

The increased cost of discouraged exemplars makes them less likely to be used. This improves the agent's accuracy in interpreting strings generated by others, as well as making its communicative behavior more reliable as a source of learning data for the other agents.

Competition

Some of an agent's exemplars will be repeatedly reinforced, and rarely if ever discouraged. Such exemplars will used more and more often, and will form the basis of the agent's communication system. Other exemplars will be used rarely or never, usually because there are cheaper alternatives.

Most of an agent's exemplars will be alternately reinforced and discouraged, and their costs will fluctuate around the cost of new exemplars. For this to occur, there must be some other exemplars, also in active use, that are inconsistent with it. The reinforcement and discouragement therefore implements competition among groups of exemplars.

Eventually, one of a group of competing exemplars will begin to be reinforced more often, and discouraged less often, than the rest. This could occur purely by chance, or because the winner is more compatible with the agent's other exemplars. The costs of the other competitors will begin to be increased more often.

The equations for updating exemplar costs, the values of the parameters in those equations, and the cost assigned to new exemplars, were chosen to keep the cost of competing exemplars high.

If an exemplar is being reinforced at the same rate as it is being discouraged, its cost, C, will change over time at the rate:

$$\frac{d}{dt}C = k(d - rC) \tag{5.3}$$

Where k is a measure of the rate at which the exemplar is used to analyze learning observations, and r and d are the values of the reinforcement and discouragement parameters, respectively. For the exemplar's cost to remain constant, it must be the case that:

$$C = d/r. \tag{5.4}$$

The values of the parameters r and d are equal, and so the cost of an exemplar that is being discouraged as often as it is being reinforced will rise to 1.0, at which point new exemplars may be used instead. If an exemplar is being discouraged more often than it is being reinforced, its cost will continue rising. If the cost rises above the cost of creating new structure (1.5), the agent will begin creating new complex phrases to record observations it otherwise might have used the exemplar for. This makes it possible for discouraged exemplars to be replaced by others more consistent with the emerging system.

Pruning

Exemplars are removed, or **pruned**, from an agent's set if they haven't been used in a solution phrase during the agent's last two hundred interactions as either sender, receiver, or learner. Exemplars in active use tend to be used at a rate of once per thirty or so chances, so the pruned exemplars are unlikely to be used ever again. In general, unused exemplars are unused because their costs are higher than alternatives, and so pruning exemplars tends to have little effect on the emergence of communication systems. In any case, pruning is necessitated by limitations in computer memory.

5.6 Computational simulations

A computational simulation of the negotiation process is begun by creating data structures to represent a population of agents and their (initially empty) sets of exemplars.

The simulation proceeds as a sequence of **rounds**, each of which involves two agents chosen at random from the population. One of them is given a formula set as a meaning to express, and finds the cheapest phrase that it can construct with the meaning. The string from that phrase is given to the other agent. In nine out of ten rounds, the other agent also receives the same formula set that the sender was given, and applies the learning algorithms described in section 5.5 to create new exemplars and to modify the costs of existing ones. The remaining rounds are used to assess the accuracy of the emerging system. The second agent is given only the string from the sender's phrase, and its interpretation of that string is compared with the meaning that the sender was given to express.

5.6.1 Measuring communicative accuracy

A numerical measure of the accuracy of the communication between a sender and receiver is computed as:

$$\textbf{Communicative Accuracy} = \frac{1}{2}\,(c/s + c/r) \qquad (5.5)$$

Where:

s	=	the number of elements in the sender's formula set.
r	=	the number of elements in the receiver's formula set.
c	=	the number of formulae common to both sets.

If the formula sets of the sender and receiver are equivalent, $s = r = c$, and the communicative accuracy value is 1.0. If the two formula sets differ, the quantity c/s is the fraction of the sender's meaning that got through to the receiver, and the quantity c/r is the fraction of the receiver's interpreted meaning that the sender actually expressed.[3] The communicative accuracy measure is the average of these two values.

5.6.2 An example simulation

Figure 5.8 tracks the progress of a population of ten agents as they negotiate a communication system.

As shown in the top plot of figure 5.8, the communicative accuracy of the population begins at zero, and stays there for the first several hundred rounds. It is still below 0.01 at round 2500, but then begins to rise. Soon after round 10,000 the accuracy value begins rising sharply, reaching 0.80 near round 26,000 and at the end of the simulation has reached a value of 0.95.

The center plot in figure 5.8 records the average number of exemplars per agent. For the first few thousand or so rounds of the simulation, each agent acquires about one exemplar per round. After round 2000, the agents begin pruning unused exemplars, and the rate of exemplar acquisition begins to level off. Near round 3000, the agents begin to acquire and use complex phrase exemplars. This is followed by a period

---

[3] These measures are based on the 'precision' and 'recall' values used to assess information retrieval systems (Kent, *et al.*, 1955).

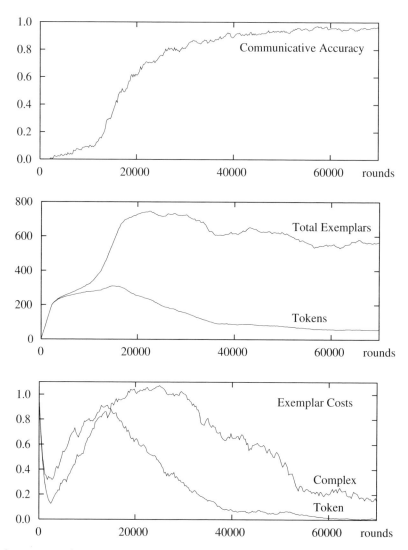

figure 5.8. A population of ten agents negotiates a shared communication system. The top plot tracks the average communicative accuracy among the agents, as measured by Equation 5.5. The center plot shows the average total size of the agents' exemplar sets, and the average number of token exemplars in each set. The bottom plot shows the average cost of complex phrase exemplars and token exemplars used in senders' solution phrases.

of rapid accumulation of exemplars, and a sharp rise in the population's communication accuracy. At round 22,500 the agents have an average of 745 exemplars each, of which 232 are tokens, and the communicative accuracy has reached 0.70. Soon afterwards, as the agents begin to come to agreement on a shared set of exemplars, the number of token exemplars drops fairly rapidly, followed later and more slowly by the number of complex phrase exemplars. At the end of the simulation, the agents have an average of 561 exemplars each, of which 57 are tokens.

The bottom graph in figure 5.8 tracks the average cost of exemplars used by senders in the phrases they use to express meanings. Before round 2500, the few exemplars that are being used are almost always reinforced afterwards, and their costs decrease rapidly. Once the agents begin to accumulate exemplars, inconsistencies accumulate as well, and many learning observations result in discouragement of exemplars. The average costs of exemplars in active use rises, until by round 20,000 the average cost of complex phrase exemplars being used is about equal to the cost of new exemplars. The costs of token exemplars in active use is a bit less, and begins to drop near round 15,000, suggesting that the agents have begun to come to agreement on them. The cost of complex phrase exemplars continues to remain high until near round 30,000, when it begins to decrease slowly, as it continues to do for the rest of the simulation.

The progress of the simulation shown in figure 5.8 is fairly typical. Simulations differ in the final value of the communicative accuracy reached, how long it takes to reach it, and the numbers of exemplars possessed by the agents at the end of the simulation. Most populations reach a communicative accuracy value above 0.90, though some do not get much higher than that. A few have reached values above 0.98.

The most variability observed among runs involves the number of rounds that elapse until the initial spurt in the number of complex phrase exemplars. For populations of the same size, this may vary by as much as a factor of two. Once it occurs, most simulations proceed as the example does, and the differences at the start of the runs have little effect on the time taken to reach the maximum accuracy value. The number of rounds taken by a negotiation to reach a communicative accuracy of 0.90 scales approximately linearly with the size of the population.

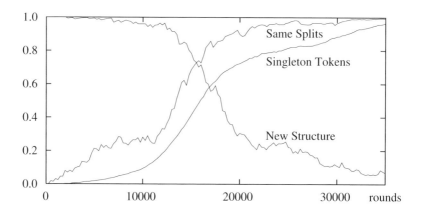

figure 5.9. The emergence of agreement in the simulation shown in Figure 5.8.

5.6.3 The emergence of agreement

Most aspects of a population's communication system are established in a relatively short period early in the negotiation, during which the average communicative accuracy rises most rapidly. In the example simulation, this occurs from rounds 10,000–20,000.

Figure 5.9 presents additional measurements taken during the first part of simulation shown in figure 5.8. The plot labeled 'New Structure' tracks the average fraction of rounds in which an agent needed to create either a new complex phrase, or a new token, to analyze a learning observation. This value begins to drop soon after round 10,000, right when the communicative accuracy of the population begins to increase. This suggests that the increase in communicative accuracy is triggered by the accumulation of similar exemplars by all of the agents.

The plot labeled 'Same Splits' in figure 5.9 records how often the sender and receiver in a testing round break a string into constituents at the same places. This value is fairly low at first, because most learning analyses are random, and few if any of the randomly chosen constituent boundaries are aligned. This value also increases sharply soon after round 10,000, suggesting that the agents have at least come to agreement on the basic units of their communication system, if not what they ought to mean.

The plot labeled 'Singleton Tokens' in figure 5.9 tracks the average fraction of each agent's token exemplars that contain a single formula. As mentioned in section 5.5, the use of singleton tokens, and agreement

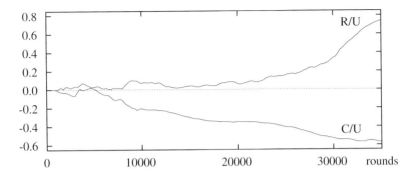

figure 5.10. Correlation between the rates exemplars are used and their costs (C/U); and between the rates exemplars are used and the rate at which they are reinforced (R/U), in the simulation shown in Figure 5.8.

on them, is important for the emergence of the systems in general. This value also shows a sharp increase soon after round 10,000.

By round 20,000 the agents are using singleton tokens a large majority of the time, so they usually don't need to create new structures to analyze learning observations, and the phrases they construct almost always match up on constituent boundaries. The communicative accuracy is fairly high at this point, but improves for several tens of thousands of rounds as competition among exemplars continues to weed out inconsistencies.

The effects of competition can be seen in the values plotted in figure 5.10. The plot labeled 'C/U' tracks the correlation between the cost of an exemplar and the number of times in which it was used in a solution phrase over the previous 100 rounds. The plot labeled 'R/U' tracks the correlation between the number of times an exemplar was used and the number of times it was reinforced, over the previous 100 rounds.

The C/U correlation begins to decline steadily almost as soon as the first exemplars are acquired; this reflects the fact that agents choose the cheapest combination of exemplars that satisfy their search requirements. However the R/U correlation remains near zero until round 20,000. This is consistent with the bottom plot of figure 5.8 showing that exemplar costs increase until soon after round 20,000. Before this occurs many exemplars are discouraged more often than they are reinforced, and so their costs remain high enough for alternatives to be explored. The R/U correlation begins rising sharply near round 30,000 and reaches a value of 0.75 at round 35,000.

As the agents begin to come to agreement on the basic sequences of characters their system uses and what some of the singleton tokens mean, the costs of exemplars consistent with the emerging system start declining. The costs of their competitors remain high, and many of them are pruned away. Eventually the cheapest solution phrases constructed by learners are almost always consistent with exemplars used by other members of the population, and the agents use and reinforce such exemplars almost exclusively.

5.7 Negotiated systems

In this section, I describe some of the communication systems that have emerged in simulation runs. I focus on properties of the systems that are seen relatively often, and those that have superficial similarities to syntactic phenomena in human languages.

Every simulation yields a different communication system and its own set of challenges. The process of understanding how a negotiated system works is a sort of cartoon version of linguistic fieldwork, and some of the methods of that discipline can be applied. A set of related meanings can be given to the agents to obtain the phrases used to express them, and sets of strings can be given to the agents to see how they are interpreted. Of course my 'subjects' are as patient and cooperative as I need them to be, and I can directly examine their computational mechanisms and exemplar sets.

Usually the agents have come to agreement on a few dozen tokens that they use to express individual formulae. The agents may also share a few tokens with more complex meanings, and some with no meaning at all. Each agent's exemplar set also includes many complex phrase exemplars, but few if any of these exemplars are identical to those of other agents. The agents' success at communication comes not from their possessing identical sets of exemplars, but from regularities in the structures of phrases constructed from their exemplars.

After introducing some terminology, several example systems are discussed. I then describe some general properties shared by most of the communication systems that have been examined.

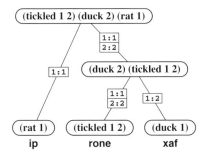

figure 5.11. A phrase from system 5.7.2.

5.7.1 Introducing formulae

A phrase from system 5.7.2 [4] is shown in figure 5.11. Before discussing this system in detail, I will use this phrase as an example to illustrate some terminology.

In the analysis of the phrases and exemplars used in negotiated systems, it is useful to determine the origin of the formulae in a phrase's meaning. Sometimes a token with the formula occurs as a subphrase of the phrase being considered, and the variables of the formula are not modified by any intervening argument maps. This occurs for the formulae (rat 1) and (tickled 1 2) in figure 5.11. Alternatively, the variables occurring in a token's formula set may be renamed by argument maps to yield formulae in the meaning of the top-level phrase. This occurs for the formula (duck 2) in the example. The formula starts out as (duck 1) in the token whose string is 'xaf', and its variable is renamed by the complex phrase above it.

I will say that a token **introduces a formula** f_P into the meaning of a phrase that contains the token if the token's formula set contains a formula f_T with the same predicate as f_P, such that the argument maps applied to the token, and to any nodes above it in the phrase, rename the variables of f_T to yield f_P. Thus the token 'ip' introduces the formula (rat 1), the token 'rone' introduces tickled 1 2, and the token 'xaf' introduces (duck 2) into the meaning of the phrase in figure 5.11.

I will also say that a token **introduces a variable** into the meaning of a phrase if that variable occurs in a formula the token introduces into the phrase. It is possible for a single formula in the meaning of a phrase

---

[4] The number of the subsection in which a communication system is discussed is used to refer to that system.

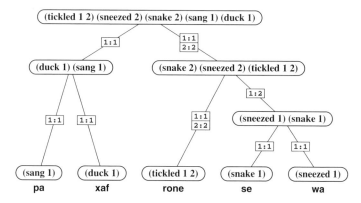

figure 5.12. A partitioned phrase, from system 5.7.2.

to be introduced by more than one token, though this rarely occurs in negotiated systems. On the other hand, it is common for a variable to be introduced by several tokens. For example, the variable 1 is introduced by the tokens 'ip' and 'rone' in figure 5.11.

I will say that a formula or variable is **introduced below** a node in a phrase if the formula or variable is introduced into the given phrase by the node itself, or by tokens that are constituents of the node.

5.7.2 Partitioning

Figure 5.12 presents another phrase from system 5.7.2. Note that this phrase has the same the same top-level structure as the phrase in figure 5.11. Specifically, the argument maps applied to both subphrases are identical, as are the argument maps applied to the constituents of their right-subphrases. This suggests that similar exemplars were used to construct the two phrases.

The phrase in figure 5.12 includes constituent phrases that combine the formulae of pairs of singleton tokens. These phrases occur in the same positions occupied by singleton tokens with the same variables in the simpler phrase in figure 5.11. As a result, the tokens in figure 5.12 are ordered such that the tokens expressing properties of the same variable are adjacent. Compare this phrase with the one shown in figure 5.13, where no such ordering occurs.

I will say that a phrase **partitions** two variables if there is a node in the phrase such that all predicates applied to one of the variables are introduced below that node, and no one-argument predicate applied

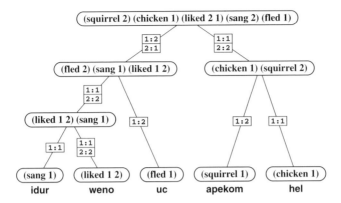

figure 5.13. A non-partitioned phrase, used early in a simulation run.

to the other variable is introduced below that node. A phrase will be said to be **partitioned** if it partitions each pair of variables used in its formula set.

If a phrase is partitioned, property tokens introducing its variables occur in separate sequences, sometimes with relation tokens or empty tokens among them. A partitioned phrase cannot have a sequence of three property tokens with the first and third introducing one variable and the middle one introducing a different variable. Such a sequence is seen in the last three tokens of the non-partitioned phrase in figure 5.13.

Figure 5.14 presents more data from the simulation run described in section 5.6.2. Whenever an agent was given a meaning to express that contained at least two properties of two different variables (as is true for the meanings of the phrases in figures 5.12 and 5.13), the phrase constructed by that agent was examined to see if it partitioned its variables. The plot labeled 'Partitioned' in figure 5.14 tracks the fraction of phrases that did. The probability that a randomly constructed phrase will be partitioned is approximately 0.2, and the agents start using partitioned phrases at about that frequency. However the fraction of partitioned phrases rises quite rapidly, and reaches 1.0 by round 20,000.

All simulation runs that have been analyzed have had similar results, yielding communication systems that rely almost exclusively on partitioned phrases. One consequence of partitioning is that regularities in a communication system can sometimes be summarized by giving the orders in which variables in a phrase's meaning are introduced by singleton tokens. For example, the phrases in figure 5.11 and 5.12 both exhibit

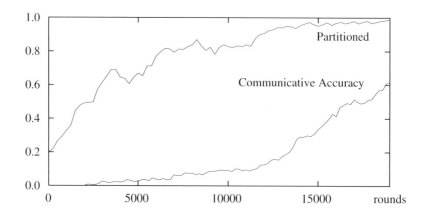

figure 5.14. Another record of the simulation shown in figure 5.8 of section 5.6.2. The plot labeled 'Partitioned' tracks the fraction of times that a sender used a partitioned phrase when expressing complex meanings. The Communicative Accuracy plot is the same as in the top graph in Figure 5.8.

the order '1 R 2', where 'R' indicates the position of the token introducing the relation applied to the two variables. The causes of partitioning are discussed in section 5.7.8.

5.7.3 Empty tokens as delimiters

Two phrases from system 5.7.3 are shown in figure 5.15. Phrases in this system usually have the relation token first, followed by tokens expressing properties of its arguments.

As described in section 5.5.1, empty tokens appear early in simulation runs as a result of mismatches of various kinds between the phrase that one agent used to generate a string, and the one a learner created to analyze it. Many of the exemplars that introduce these empty tokens ultimately disappear from the negotiated systems as the agents begin to analyze each other's utterances in consistent ways. But in most of the simulations observed, a few empty tokens remain, sometimes acquiring specific communicative functions.

In phrase 5.15.a, the empty token 'ajvaf' occurs between two tokens, the first of which introduces a property of variable 2, and the second introduces a property of variable 1. The token 'ajvaf' is also used in phrase 5.15.b, again serving to separate tokens introducing different variables.

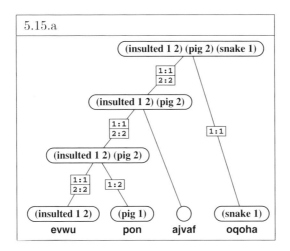

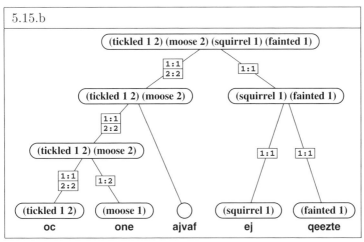

figure 5.15. Phrases from system 5.7.3.

The two phrases shown in figure 5.16, also from system 5.7.3, illustrate how the agents that negotiated this system express a pair of simpler meanings. In phrase 5.16.a, the right hand token is interpreted as expressing a property of variable 1. The use of the empty token 'ajvaf' in 5.16.b changes the interpretation of the token to its left, such that it expresses a property of variable 2. The exemplar used to construct 5.16.a is slightly cheaper than that used in 5.16.b. The two exemplars therefore implement a default rule for the interpretation of a token that occurs to the right of a relation token: it is treated as introducing a

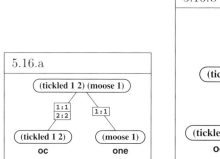

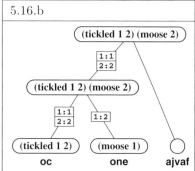

figure 5.16. Two more phrases from system 5.7.3.

property of variable 1 unless it is followed by 'ajvaf'.

Most exemplar phrases containing the token 'ajvaf' have the structure of 5.16.b. This phrase applies the argument map 1:2 to the right subphrase of the node above the relation token. Agents with similar exemplars will use one of them to analyze a sequence beginning with a relation token, and ending with 'ajvaf'.

Both exemplars may be used in a single phrase. For example, phrases 5.15.a and 5.15.b use 'ajvaf' to signal the non-default interpretation of the token to its left, however the top-level node in both phrases uses the default structure of phrase 5.16.a to map the rightmost token's argument to variable 1.

To see how the two exemplars interact, agents from the population that negotiated this system were given a string that contained two property tokens between a relation token and the empty token 'ajvaf'. The phrase most agents used to interpret this string is shown in figure 5.17. The first property token, 'one' is assigned the default interpretation, and its argument is not modified by the argument map above it. However the next property token, 'qeezte' does have its argument renamed from 1 to 2, by the exemplar containing the empty token. Note that the phrase shown in figure 5.17 is not partitioned. This phrase would not be used by the agents to communicate the meaning shown (they would use a phrase with the structure of 5.15.b), but it is the cheapest phrase they can find to interpret the given string.

To express a meaning in which two or more tokens express properties of argument 1, the agents use a phrase with the structure shown in figure 5.18. This phrase uses an additional empty token, 'te'. The

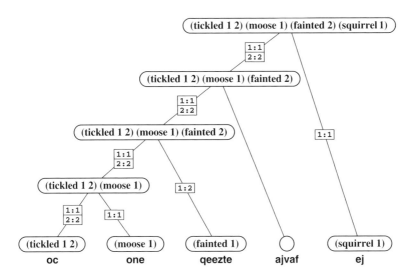

figure 5.17. A solution phrase for the string 'oconeqeezteajvafej'.

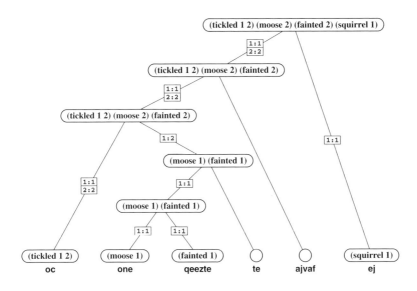

figure 5.18. Use of the empty token 'te' to delimit a sequence of property tokens to which an identity argument is applied.

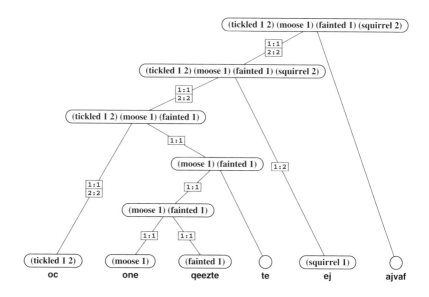

figure 5.19. Using 'te' and 'ajvaf' to express an alternative meaning from that of the phrase shown in Figure 5.18.

argument map on the right subphrase of the phrase that 'te' is attached to applies the identity argument map to the formula of the phrase below it. Therefore the token 'te' can serve to signal the end of a sequence of tokens introducing properties of the same argument. By combining the two formulae in this way, it is then possible for the 'ajvaf' exemplar to apply to both tokens' formulae, and they are mapped together to variable 2 in the meaning of the top-level phrase.

Figure 5.19 shows another way that the tokens 'te' and 'ajvaf' can interact. In Figure 5.18 variables are introduced in the order 'R 2 1'. The same sequence of property tokens in figure 5.19 is interpreted as introducing variables in the order 'R 1 2'. The only difference between the two strings is the position of the empty token 'ajvaf', which seems to behave somewhat like a case ending or particle, indicating that the phrase to its left expresses properties of variable 2.

5.7.4 Marking reflexive predicates

In system 5.7.4, the standard order in which arguments are introduced is '2 1 R', as shown in figure 5.20.a. However the empty token 'ojo' is

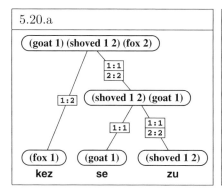

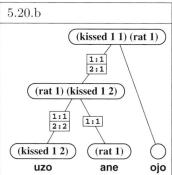

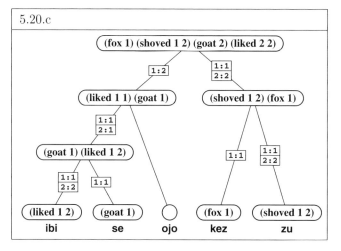

figure 5.20. Phrases from system 5.7.4, illustrating the use of the empty token 'ojo' as a marker of reflexive predicates.

part of an exemplar containing a non-invertible argument map. If it is used after a phrase containing a relation token and a property token, the relation is interpreted as involving a single argument, as shown in phrase 5.20.b. In phrase 5.20.b, both patterns are seen: the left subphrase uses 'ojo' to create a reflexive predicate whose argument is mapped to variable 2. The top-level phrase uses the standard ordering.

All of the agents in this population possess a number of exemplars containing the empty token 'ojo', and in all such exemplars, that token is the right subphrase of a phrase whose argument map collapses the two variables of the meaning of its left subphrase.

Therefore if an agent is given a string containing the sequence 'ojo', it will almost always use one of those exemplars in its interpretation or analysis of that string, and the resulting phrase will contain the collapsing argument map. An agent will likewise almost always use an exemplar containing the token 'ojo' to express such meanings, as such exemplars contain the argument map needed to create a reflexive predicate out of one with two arguments.

Not all systems use empty tokens to signal reflexive predicates. In some systems, the agents use additional singleton tokens specifically for the reflexive forms of all relations. Other systems use characteristic orderings to signal reflexive predicates. Figure 5.20 illustrates a reason why the use of an empty token to signal reflexives might have been used in this system. Recall that in this system, if a relation is applied to two different variables, they are introduced before the relation. If the empty token 'ojo' were missing from the phrase in figure 5.20.c, token 'se' might be interpreted as expressing variable 2 of the relation token 'zu'. The occurrence of 'ojo' in the string blocks this interpretation.

5.7.5 Marking inverting maps

A related use of empty tokens is illustrated in figure 5.21. In this system, if the empty token 'la' appears after a relation token, it signals that an inverting argument map is applied to the variables in the relation, as shown in phrase 5.21.b. This phrase is used to replace the relation token in 5.21.a, to yield 5.21.c, in which the roles played by the referents of variables 1 and 2 are the opposite from that in 5.21.a.

In this system, the empty token 'la' almost always occurs as the right subphrase of a phrase whose left subphrase is a relation token. This token therefore resembles the inflectional morphology that verbs in some languages take to indicate passive voice.

5.7.6 Overruling the default mapping

In system 5.7.6, the empty token 'uy' has two different functions, shown in figure 5.22. If it occurs before a relation token that is followed by a property token, an inverting argument map is applied to the variables of the phrase. If the empty token occurs after the property token, an identity map is applied to the phrase. Note that in both phrases an inverting argument map is applied to the variables of the relation token.

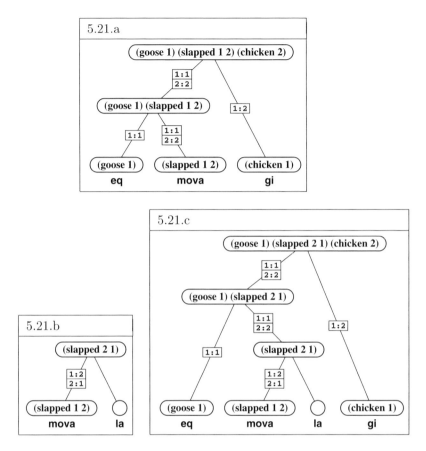

figure 5.21. Phrases from system 5.7.5, illustrating the use of the empty token 'la' as a marker of inverting argument maps.

Phrase 5.22.c illustrates the cheapest interpretation most agents assign to a sequence of a relation token and a property token. Note that this phrase uses an argument map that collapses variable 2 to 1. This phrase is the solution that the agents would use if given the meaning {(kissed 1 1) (squirrel 1)} to express. In this system, the default interpretation of the relation token followed by a property token is that the relation is reflexive. The empty token 'uy' is therefore needed to overrule the default interpretation.

The agents only rarely convey meanings that involve reflexive predicates. So in this system, the default interpretation does not correspond to the most common case. This should not necessarily be surprising,

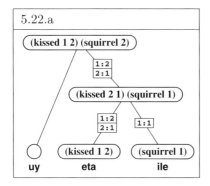
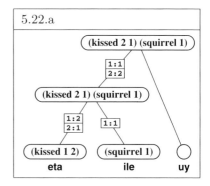

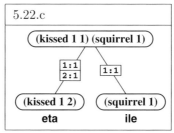

figure 5.22. Phrases from system 5.7.6 illustrating how the empty token 'uy' is needed to overrule the default interpretation of a relation token followed by a property token.

because the factors influencing the properties of a communication system do not exert their influences independently. In this case, it seems the token 'uy' might have first acquired the function of delimiting the set of arguments to a relation. If it were used to do so in almost every phrase where there were multiple arguments, it could have acquired the function of signaling the non-reflexive interpretation of the relation token.

5.7.7 Equivalent empty tokens

In system 5.7.7, the empty tokens 'laxo' and 'ah' seem to be more or less equivalent. The phrases shown in figure 5.23 illustrate that either token, put before a property token followed by a relation token, maps the variable 1 to 2. If either empty token is after a relation token followed by a property token, an identity argument map is applied to the property token.

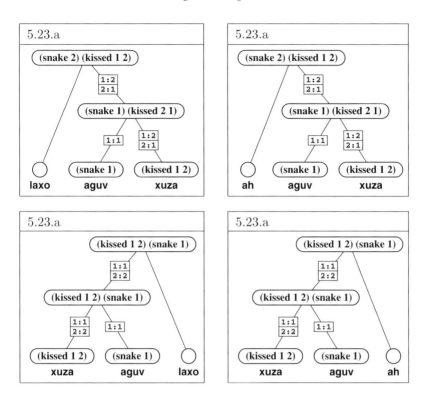

figure 5.23. Phrases from system 5.7.7 illustrating the use of two equivalent empty tokens.

In most negotiated systems, the empty tokens only occur in specific exemplars, and each empty token's string can serve to indicate particular structural properties of phrases containing it. However in this system, the agents have a pair of exemplar empty tokens, and can use either to replace the other.

The two empty tokens are not always interchangeable. The standard ordering of a two argument relation is shown in figure 5.24. Although the structure of the exemplar this phrase is based on is consistent with those shown in figure 5.24, it contains the token 'laxo' at the beginning, and 'ah' at the end. The agents don't create phrases with the empty tokens in the other order (although they have no problem interpreting such phrases correctly).

The pattern seen in figure 5.24 is used to express a more complicated meaning in figure 5.25. In the right subphrase, the empty tokens 'ah',

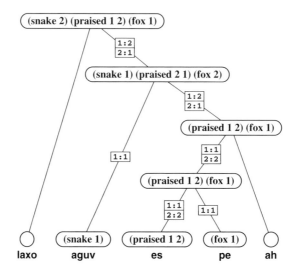

figure 5.24. A phrase from system 5.7.7 illustrating the use of empty tokens to delimit the arguments to a relation.

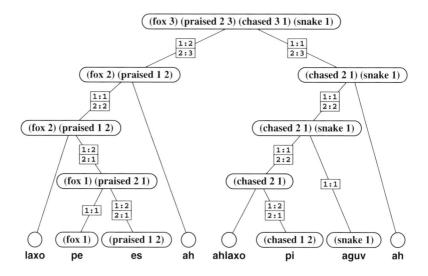

figure 5.25. A phrase from system 5.7.7 illustrating the use of empty tokens to delimit a subordinated relation.

and 'laxo' appear to be combined into the empty token 'ahlaxo', used to indicate the start of a sequence describing a second relation that one of the participants is involved in. The structure of the subordinated relation is otherwise the same as the phrase in figure 5.24, and even includes the sequence 'laxo ... ah', with the additional 'ah' apparently serving as a marker of subordination.

5.7.8 Properties of negotiated systems

Agreement on singleton tokens

As mentioned above, the agents in a simulation tend to come to agreement relatively quickly on a shared set of singleton tokens. In some cases, they use as few as 32 tokens – one for each of the possible predicates. More often, they settle on from 40–70 exemplars, with a few that express multiple formula meanings, a few empty tokens, and a few that express reflexive or inverted senses of other relation tokens. In a few of the systems, the agents have a token for almost every possible argument pattern of a relation, and therefore do not need to use argument maps to modify them.

Partial regularity

The preceding discussion might have left the impression that most negotiated systems can be seen as obeying a relatively small set of rules. This is only partially true. Every system analyzed so far uses a few phrases whose structure seems to be idiosyncratic.

In some cases, the irregularities in the system can be isolated. In figure 5.26, three phrases from a negotiated system are shown. For all but three predicates, the reflexive form of the predicate is expressed using a phrase with the structure of 5.26.a. The empty token 'ay', occurring before the relation token, indicates that the two arguments of the relation are collapsed by a non-invertible argument map.

For the remaining predicates, including the predicate bit, the agents do not use such a phrase. Instead, they have found distinct singleton tokens for the reflexive forms. For the two-argument form of the predicate bit, the agents use the token 'otu'; for the reflexive form, they use 'atay'. Since 'atay' is a one-argument predicate, there is no need to use the empty token 'ay'.

Apparently, in the early stages of the negotiation, the agents came to agreement on how the reflexive version of a few of the predicates would

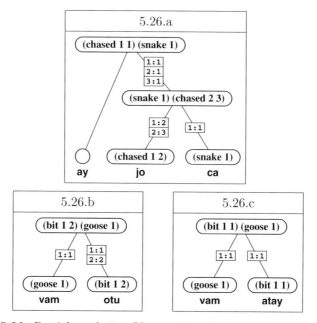

figure 5.26. Partial regularity. Phrase 5.26.a illustrates the pattern used to express most reflexive predicates. For the predicate bit, however, the agents use one token to express the two argument form (shown in phrase 5.26.b), and a different token for the reflexive form (shown in phrase 5.26.c).

be expressed, before they came to agreement on the use of 'ay'.

The exemplar-based model provides a simple account of how regular and irregular forms can coexist in a communication system. Each exemplar, in isolation, can be thought of as an 'irregular form'. Regularities occur because the agents tend to acquire sets of exemplars whose structures are similar. However this is only a tendency; if a given form is used, and therefore reinforced often enough, it will continue to be used, no matter how similar or dissimilar it is to the rest of an agent's exemplars.

Causes of partitioning

There is nothing in the model that requires the agents to use only partitioned phrases, and they don't use them at the start of simulation runs, as the plot in figure 5.14 illustrates. However in all runs observed, the agents quickly come to rely almost exclusively on partitioned phrases. This occurs as a consequence of the competition among exemplars induced by their reinforcement and discouragement during learning rounds

figure 5.27. Partitioning exemplars.

figure 5.28. Non-partitioning exemplars.

in the early part of a negotiation. Certain exemplars and sets of exemplars tend to be used and reinforced often relative to their alternatives, and the structures of those exemplars begins to impose partitioning on phrases created from them. Once the trend is established, it is exploited and amplified as new exemplars are created and used.

Exemplars with the structures shown in figure 5.27 can be used to construct partitioned phrases. In these diagrams, the letters X and Y are used to designate the variable introduced at or below the indicated node labeled with the letter. Both variables are introduced below nodes labeled XY.

Exemplars with structure 5.27.a are acquired quickly by all agents. Such exemplars can be used to combine pairs of phrases whose formula sets involve the same variable, and so they are used and reinforced often. Note that the structure of 5.27.a is seen in the nodes used to combine the first and last pair of property tokens in figure 5.12.

The use of exemplars with the structures in figure 5.27 does not guarantee that the resulting phrases will be partitioned, but the structures of small phrases containing such exemplars begins the trend towards partitioning. If an agent has acquired exemplars with structure 5.27.a, and they have acquired relatively low costs, the agent can combine phrases whose formula sets contain different variables with exemplars whose structures are shown in 5.27.b and 5.27.c, as well as the structures corresponding to their mirror-images.

Exemplars with the structures shown in figure 5.28 tend to be used in non-partitioned phrases. If the structure 5.28.a is used, the phrase that contains it will not be partitioned. The structure 5.28.b is used in non-partitioned phrases to combine phrases containing 5.28.a, though it can occur in partitioned phrases as well.

Exemplars with the structure 5.28.a are likely to appear later in a simulation than 5.27.a, and will probably be used and reinforced less often. In addition, exemplars whose structure is the mirror-image of 5.28.a will also occur and the use of exemplars from one of the two sets will often cause one or more exemplars from the other set to be discouraged. Until one or the other pattern is established, the costs of exemplars in both sets will remain relatively high. On the other hand, the symmetry of exemplars with the structure of 5.27.a makes them immune to such competition.

Given that a learner is not able to observe the structure of the phrase used by the sender whose string and meaning is being analyzed, it is often the case that the learner's phrase differs from the sender's. The learner may therefore create, and reinforce, exemplars whose structures are quite different from those used by the sender. However the structures of some exemplars are such that their use in a sender's phrase increases the chance that similar exemplars will be used by learners.

Consider for example, phrases whose meanings involving three formulae: a relation and two property tokens, one for each argument of the relation. (E.g., {(tickled 1 2) (duck 2) (rat 1)}.)

Three tokens introducing a relation and two different variables can occur in six different orders. For each, there are two phrase structures that can be used to combine the tokens into a complex phrase. There are therefore twelve phrase structures that can be used to express the meanings being considered. Some of them are shown in figures 5.29 and 5.30.

Figure 5.29 shows the two phrase structures consistent with the ordering '1 R 2'. The structures consistent with the ordering '2 R 1' are the mirror-images of those shown. Figure 5.30 shows the structures consistent with the ordering 'R 1 2'. The mirror images of these structures correspond to the ordering '2 1 R'. The structure of the two phrases with the ordering 'R 2 1' and the two with '1 2 R' are similar to those shown in figure 5.30.

Note that both of the phrases shown in figure 5.29 can be constructed from the 'partitioning' exemplars in figure 5.27. So if a sender were to use the structure 5.29.a in its phrase, the learner would reinforce such exemplars, whether it had the same structure used by the sender, or the

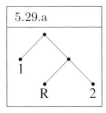 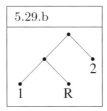

figure 5.29. The two phrase structures consistent with the ordering '1 R 2'.

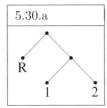 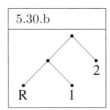

figure 5.30. The two phrase structures consistent with the ordering 'R 1 2'.

structure of 5.29.b.

On the other hand, if the sender used a phrase with the structure of 5.28, built from the non-partitioning exemplars in figure 5.28, the learner might use the structure 5.28 to record its observation. If so, it would reinforce the partitioning exemplars instead of exemplars corresponding to those the sender used.

The partitioning exemplars in figure 5.27 are therefore more likely to be used more often by the learners when they later express meanings, and such exemplars, and new ones created from them, will be used with increasing frequency.

Strict ordering versus empty tokens

As a very rough generalization, the use of empty tokens in a system is inversely related to the strictness with which the system uses ordering to indicate how the variables in property tokens are mapped. The strictness of ordering varies widely. In some systems, the agents will always use a particular ordering for a two argument predicate, in other systems, the ordering is much more free.

The few systems observed with no empty tokens at all use one of the two orderings: '1 R 2' or '2 R 1' exclusively. It seems that the agents require some way to determine the boundaries of partitioned sequences of tokens introducing properties of more than one variable. If this isn't

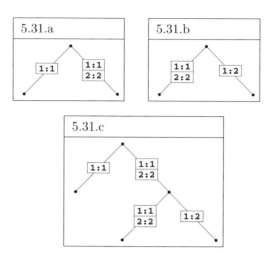

figure 5.31. Phrase patterns in Promoting systems.

done by an empty token, a relation token is the only available solution.

However the distinction between systems that use ordering versus those that use empty tokens isn't especially useful for the systems that emerge in the simulations. In most systems, a particular ordering may be used most of the time, but other orderings are also used (and understood); and almost all systems use a number of empty tokens as well.

Promoting versus inverting systems

A sharper distinction has to do with how variable 2 is introduced into the meaning of a phrase. Most of the systems examined in detail use one of two methods.

A **promoting** system uses exemplars with the structures shown in figure 5.31. Both of the simple exemplars, 5.31.a and 5.31.b can be used to combine a property token with a relation token. One of them applies the identity argument map to the relation token's formula, the other exemplar renames variable 1 to 2. These exemplars can be combined to express properties of both arguments of a relation, as shown in 5.31.c.

An **inverting** system uses exemplars with the structures shown in figure 5.32. In these phrases, an inverting argument map is applied to the formula of a relation. The variable introduced below the other subphrase is therefore mapped to variable 2 in the original relation, which has been

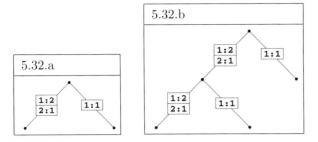

figure 5.32. Phrase patterns in Inverting systems.

renamed to 1 by the inverting map. If this same exemplar (or one with similar structure) is used again, the variables of the relation are renamed back to what they were to start with, but the property token's variable is mapped to 2. The variable introduced by the other subphrase of the top-level phrase is not renamed.

Of those discussed in this section, systems 5.7.2, 5.7.3, 5.7.4 and 5.7.5 use the promoting pattern of exemplars. Systems 5.7.6 and 5.7.7 use the inverting pattern.

In general, systems that use the promoting pattern must come to agreement on the ordering of property tokens that express a particular argument of a relation. In the examples shown in figure 5.31, the ordering leads to the pattern '1 R 2'. Unless one or the other ordering is chosen (or empty tokens are used to signal participant roles), the agents will incorrectly map the variables.

Inverting systems are in a sense simpler than promoting systems, because they use only one basic pattern of argument maps, shown in 5.32.a. Where promoting systems must use either ordering or empty tokens to signal how arguments are renamed, in inverting systems, the mapping of each variable can be determined from its depth in the phrase. Inverting systems still use empty tokens, often to delimit the arguments of multiple relations, or to indicate when a non-default argument map is applied to a subphrase.

5.8 Discussion

In this section I discuss some of the reasons for the agents' success at negotiating communication systems, some deficiencies of the model, and what the results presented in this chapter might tell us about the emergence of human language.

5.8.1 Meanings and learnability

According to the framework described in section 5.2, syntactic structure represents analyses of mappings between signals and meanings. Such analyses are neither independent of, nor reducible to, the other domains.

This approach qualitatively changes the problem of learning a communication system. In the model of Gold (1967), the learner is given strings generated by a grammar, and must hypothesize this grammar, given only the class of the grammar and those strings. Gold shows that this task is impossible for all but a proper subset of regular grammars.

In the present model, the learner's task is to hypothesize a mapping between strings and meanings, given observations of example mappings. If the domain of meanings can be characterized structurally, the goal of a learner in this model and in Gold's are formally identical. However the data available to the learner are different in the two approaches: in the task of learning mappings between signals and meanings, positive examples can provide negative evidence.

Given an observation of a meaning M_O and a string S_O used to express that meaning, the learner can use its current hypotheses about the system to interpret S_O as conveying a meaning M_H. If M_H is not equivalent to the observed meaning M_O, the learner has discovered that there is a problem with its hypotheses. Depending on how the hypotheses are represented, the learner may be able to track down and modify those that are to blame. A similar comparison can be made between the string S_O and the string the learner's hypothesized system would use to express M_O.

Hamburger and Wexler (1973) demonstrate that certain classes of transformational grammars that are unlearnable according to Gold's model can be acquired if the learner is given a representation of the meaning of each string. In their model, learners represent their hypotheses about the grammar being learned as a set of rules, and a rule may be removed if it is used in the derivation of a phrase whose meaning does not match a learning observation.[5] Hamburger and Wexler use techniques from the theory of stochastic processes to show that such a learner will acquire the correct set of rules after a bounded number of observations.

Although the model described in this chapter differs from that of Hamburger and Wexler in its representations of syntactic structure and meanings, the results of the computational simulations are consistent with their findings. It might be possible to extend their result to show that some classes of grammars can not only be acquired, but can be developed in the first place, provided that learners have access to meanings as well as strings.

5.8.2 Controlling recursion

To exploit recursion it must be controlled. The number of possible structural analyses of an utterance can increase exponentially with the number of recursive patterns in a communication system, drastically decreasing the likelihood that the analyses performed by senders and receivers have any similarity to each other. Unless there is at least occasional agreement on such analyses, a coordinated communication system cannot emerge, and won't be learnable by new members of the population.

The communication systems that emerge in the computational simulation exhibit a number of regularities that enable the combinatorial power of a recursive communication system to be exploited by limiting the set of structural analyses that may be performed.

For example, the reliance on partitioned phrases, and on either the promoting or inverting pattern of expressing two argument predicates, restricts the possible structural configurations that need be considered. Many empty tokens occur only in exemplars that exhibit a particular structural configuration, and therefore can serve as markers of that configuration. And the use of singleton tokens makes it possible to determine where the recursion bottoms out.

---

[5] The method described in section 5.5.2 for locating exemplars to discourage is similar to Hamburger and Wexler's algorithm for removing rules.

5.8.3 The learning dynamic

The regularities just discussed are consequences of the mechanisms implementing the agents' communicative and learning abilities without being specifically encoded or enforced by the implementation. The agents can and do produce phrases that fail to satisfy them, especially in the early rounds of a negotiation. It would be misguided to characterize the agents' learning mechanisms in terms of the properties of the communication systems they give rise to, as such characterizations reverse the actual direction of influence, and provide little help in understanding how communication systems could occur in the first place.

The regularities emerge as dynamical consequences of the processes of learning and negotiation among the agents. Certain kinds of exemplars tend to occur early in negotiations, or tend to be reinforced often relative to alternatives. Sets of exemplars may mutually reinforce each other, or may cause other exemplars to be discouraged and ultimately removed from a system. Some exemplar structures are differentially better at being learned than others, and will tend to accumulate in the population.

Exploring the effects of the learning dynamic requires a different characterization of the problem of language acquisition. Rather than focusing on whether and how languages with specific formal properties can be acquired, attention should be directed at understanding the influences that learning mechanisms can have on the languages that emerge from their use.

5.8.4 Deficiencies of the model

The implemented model described in this chapter is intended to be as simple as possible while remaining true to the framework described in section 5.2. The primary goal of the research is to explore whether and how communication systems that exploit recursive structural regularities can emerge as a result of the negotiation process. The simplicity of the model limits its applicability to many syntactic issues.

Some of the deficiencies are deliberate. For example, I mentioned in section 5.3.4 that the agents' system for internal representations cannot handle embedded meanings. Given that the agents can't represent such meanings, they will be extremely unlikely to negotiate ways to communicate them.

The universal tendency of systems to use phrases that partition their arguments is, at best, only a step towards an account of the properties of phrases in human languages. The current model does not incorporate either semantic or syntactic categories for tokens or complex phrases, and it does not seem as if any such categories emerge as a result of the negotiation process. Without any notion of category, it seems impossible to explore many central syntactic phenomena. For example, the relations among the head, modifiers and complement of a phrase seem to depend on the categories to which each constituent is assigned. A phrase's category is also relevant in determining how the phrase can be manipulated, and how it can be interpreted.

These and other deficiencies of the model might be fixed by modifying the agents' system of internal representations, the algorithms and data-structures underlying their communicative behavior, and/or their learning mechanisms.

In addition to closing the specific gap it was designed for, a modification to the agents may alter the learning dynamic in ways that allow new kinds of properties to emerge in negotiated communication systems. Therefore this research will proceed as conservatively as possible, endowing the agents with new capacities only if they seem biologically plausible, or of general cognitive utility, and attempting to understand how each modification affects the learning dynamic and the properties of the communication systems it yields.

5.8.5 Conclusion

Agents in the computational simulations negotiate communication systems that enable them to accurately convey 2.3×10^{13} meanings after each agent has made fewer than ten thousand learning observations. Each agent acquires several hundred exemplars, of which a few dozen are singleton tokens identical to those of other agents in the population. The agents express meanings by combining their singleton tokens into complex phrases, using the order and structure of phrases, as well as the presence and position of empty tokens, to convey information about configurations of participants in one or more events.

The negotiated systems are far from human languages. But each system incorporates a unique set of solutions to the problem of conveying elements from a huge set of meanings using a linear sequence of primitive signals, and some of the solutions resemble those used in human languages. Like human languages, the negotiated systems possess enough simplicity and regularity for accurate communication and learning to be possible, but not much more: the systems remain fairly complicated, often incorporating a number of irregularities and rarely-used forms.

The communication systems emerge as the result of a learning mechanism that involves no induction or rules, or noticing of similarities, or setting of parameter values, and is subject to very few internal constraints. The agents learn to communicate by recording their observations of other agents communicating, and using those records to guide their own attempts. The learning dynamic thus induced is responsible for the regularities the negotiated systems acquire as well as the complexities they retain.

The results presented in this chapter suggest that some aspects of human language syntax might have emerged as a result of such a learning dynamic. Adequately characterizing the formal power and limitations of negotiated communication systems is a topic of ongoing research. It may turn out that a significant fraction of the syntactic phenomena used in human languages can, in principle, emerge among agents with the cognitive and social sophistication required to instantiate the model. If so, language may be a result of our ancestors trying to be understood, trying to understand, and trying to get better at doing both.

Acknowledgements

The author wishes to thank William O'Grady and James Hurford for inspiration, Kara Federmeier for carefully reading the final draft, and Ted Briscoe for his patience.

References

Aha, D. W., D. Kibler, and M. K. Albert (1991). Instance-based learning algorithms. *Machine Learning*, 6, 37–66.

Barsalou, L. W. (1989). On the indistinguishability of exemplar memory and abstraction in category representation. In T. K. Srull and R. S. Wyer (eds.), *Advances in Social Cognition*. Lawrence Erlbaum, Hillsdale, NJ.

Batali, J. (1998). Computational simulations of the emergence of grammar. In James Hurford, Michael Studdert-Kennedy, and Chris Knight (eds.), *Approaches to the Evolution of Language, Social and Cognitive Bases*, Cambridge University Press, Cambridge, pp. 405–426.

Black, A. and P. Taylor (1997). Festival speech synthesis system: system documentation. Human Communication Research Centre Technical Report HCRC/TR-83.

Bod, R. (1998). *Beyond Grammar: An Experience-Based Theory of Language*. CSLI Publications, Center for the Study of Language and Information, University of Chicago Press, Chicago.

Canning, D. (1992). Learning language conventions in common interest signaling games. Unpublished manuscript, Columbia University.

Chalmers, D. J., M. French, and D. R. Hofstadter (1992). High-level perception, representation, and analogy: A critique of artificial intelligence methodology. *Journal of Experimental and Theoretical Artificial Intelligence*, 4, 185–211.

Chomsky, N. (1975). *Reflections on Language*. Pantheon Books, New York.

Crawford, V. P., and J. Sobel (1982). Strategic information transmission. *Econometrica*, 50(6), 1431–1451.

Falkenhainer, B., K. D. Forbus, and D. Gentner (1989). The structure-mapping engine: algorithm and examples. *Artificial Intelligence*, 41, 1–63.

Gentner, D. (1983). Structure-mapping: A theoretical framework for analogy. *Cognitive Science*, 7, 155–170.

Gold, E. M. (1967). Language identification in the limit. *Information and Control*, 16, 447–475.

Hamburger, H. and Kenneth Wexler (1973). Identifiability of a class of transformational grammars. In K. J. J. Hintikka, J. M. E. Moravcsik, and P. Suppes (eds.), *Approaches to Natural Language*, Reidel, Dordrecht, pp. 153–156.

Hammond, K. (1990). Case-based planning: A framework for planning from experience. *Cognitive Science*, 14(3).

Hurford, J. R. (1989). Biological evolution of the Saussurean sign as a component of the language acquisition device. *Lingua*, 77, 187–222.

Hutchins, E. and Brian Hazlehurst (1991). Learning in the cultural process. In C. G. Langton, C. Taylor, J. D. Farmer, and S. Rasmussen (eds.), *Artificial Life II: SFI Studies in the Sciences of Complexity, Volume X*, pp. 689–706.

Kent, A., M. Berry, F. U. Leuhrs, and J. W. Perry (1955). Machine literature searching viii: Operational criteria for designing information retrieval systems. *American Documentation*, 6(2), 93–101.

Lewis, D. K. (1969). *Convention: A Philosophical Study*. Harvard University Press, Cambridge MA.

MacWhinney, B. and E. Bates (1989). Functionalism and the competition model. In B. MacWhinney and E. Bates (eds.) *The Crosslinguistic Study of Sentence Processing*, Cambridge University Press, Cambridge, 3–73.

Medin, D. L. and M. M. Schaffer (1978). Context theory of classification learning. *Psychological Review*, 85, 207–238.

Mitchell, M. (1993). *Analogy-Making as Perception: A Computer Model*. The MIT Press, Cambridge, MA.

Montague, R. (1974). *Formal Philosophy: Selected Papers of Richard Montague*. Richard Thomason (ed.), Yale University Press, New Haven.

O'Grady, W. (1987). *Principles of Grammar & Learning*. The University of Chicago Press, Chicago.

Oliphant, M. (1997). Communication as altruistic behavior. Ph.D. Dissertation, Department of Cognitive Science, U.C.S.D.

Pough, F. H., J. B. Heiser, and W. M. McFarland (1996). *Vertebrate Life*. Prentice-Hall, NJ, fourth edition.

Premack, D. (1983). The codes of man and beast. *Behavioral and Brain Sciences*, 6, 125–167.

Spence, J. M. (1973). Job market signaling. *Quarterly Journal of Economics*,

87, 296–332.

Steels, L. (1996). Emergent adaptive lexicons. In P. Maes (ed.), *Proceedings of the Simulation of Adaptive Behavior Conference*. MIT Press, Cambridge, MA.

Thompson, R. K. R. (1995). Natural and relational concepts in animals. In Herbert L. Roitblat and Jean-Arcady Meyer, editors, *Comparitive Approaches to Cognitive Science*, MIT Press, Cambridge, MA, pp. 175–224.

6

Learning, bottlenecks and the evolution of recursive syntax

Simon Kirby
Language Evolution and Computation
Research Unit, Department of Linguistics,
University of Edinburgh

6.1 Introduction

Human language is a unique natural communication system for two reasons. Firstly, the mapping from meanings to signals in language has structural properties that are not found in any other animal's communication systems. In particular, syntax gives us the ability to produce an infinite range of expressions through the dual tools of compositionality and recursion. Compositionality is defined here as the property whereby an expression's meaning is a function of the meanings of parts of that expression and the way they are put together. Recursion is a property of languages with finite lexica and rule-sets in which some constituent of an expression can contain a constituent of the same category. Together with recursion, compositionality is the reason that this infinite set of expressions can be used to express different meanings.

Secondly, at least some of the *content* of this mapping is learned by children through observation of others' use of language. This seems *not* to be true of most, maybe all, of animal communication (see review in Oliphant, this volume). In this chapter I formally investigate the interaction of these two unique properties of human language: the way it is learned and its syntactic structure.

6.1.1 Evolution without natural selection

Evolutionary linguistics is currently a growing field of research tackling the origins of human language (Bickerton, 1990; Pinker & Bloom, 1990; Newmeyer, 1991; Hurford *et al.*, 1998). Of particular interest to many researchers is the origins of syntactic structure. Perhaps the dominant

approach to the evolution of this structure is expounded by Pinker &
Bloom (1990); they suggest that the best way to view human language
is as a biological adaptation that evolved in response to the need to
communicate "propositional structures over a serial interface" (p. 707).
In their (and many linguists') view, syntax is to a significant extent
specified by an innate (and therefore genetically determined) language
acquisition device (LAD) which constrains the language learner with
prior knowledge about the nature of language.

> Evolutionary theory offers clear criteria for when a trait should be attributed
> to natural selection: complex design for some function, and the absence of
> alternative processes capable of explaining such complexity. Human language
> meets these criteria.
>
> *Pinker & Bloom (1990:707)*

In this chapter I agree that the structure of the human learning mech-
anism(s) will bring particular prior biases to bear on the acquisition task.
Indeed there are good theoretical reasons why this *must* be the case for
any learner that can generalize (e.g. Mitchell, 1997). However, because
language is unique (an autapomorphy in biological terms) we should
search very carefully for 'alternative processes' before turning to natural
selection as an explanation. In fact, recent work of which this chapter is a continuation, (Batali, 1998; Kirby, 1998, 2000; Hurford, 2000;
Batali, this volume; Hurford, this volume) has suggested that some of
the complex structure of language may be the result of a quite different
process from biological evolution. This work shows that learning influences the dynamic process of linguistic transmission, historically, from
one generation to the next. In many ways this approach is mirrored in
the recent work of linguists from quite different research perspectives
(e.g. Niyogi & Berwick, 1995; Niyogi & Berwick, 1997; Christiansen &
Devlin, 1997; Briscoe, 1998). This chapter aims to demonstrate that,
for any reasonable learning bias, basic structural properties of language
such as recursion and compositionality will inevitably emerge over time
through the complex dynamical process of cultural transmission – in
other words, without being built in to a highly constraining innate language acquisition device.

6.1.2 A computational approach

If we are to understand the ways in which a learned, socially transmitted, system such as language can evolve we need some sophisticated

models of learners embedded in a dynamic context. Verbal theorizing about the likely behavior of complex dynamical systems is often not good enough. As Niyogi & Berwick (1997) point out, our intuitions about the evolution of even simple dynamical systems are often wrong. Recently, many researchers have responded to this problem by taking a computational perspective (e.g. Hurford, 1989; Hurford, 1991; MacLennan, 1991; Batali, 1994; Oliphant, 1996; Cangelosi & Parisi, 1996; Steels, 1996; Kirby & Hurford, 1997b; Briscoe, 1997, 1998). This methodology provides a third way between verbal theorizing on the one hand and on the other, analytical mathematical approaches – which are often difficult to formulate for these types of system. This chapter follows on from this line of research, developing a working computational simulation of individuals capable of learning to communicate by observing each other's behavior, and tracking the development of the artificial languages that emerge in the population.

The rest of this chapter is divided into three main sections. Firstly, the computational model is described in some detail, with particular attention being paid to the process of learning (although some details are left to an appendix). The next section deals with two representative experiments, with the model dealing with the emergence of compositionality given simple semantics, and with the emergence of recursive subordinate clauses given a more complex semantic space. Finally, an explanation of the behavior of the simulation is given in theoretical terms along with a discussion of the impact of these results on linguistic theory.

6.2 A working model of linguistic transmission

Language exists in two different domains (Chomsky, 1986; Hurford, 1987; Kirby, 1999):

I-language This is (internal) language as represented in the brains of the population. It is the language user's knowledge of language.

E-language This is the (external) language that exists as utterances in the arena of use (Hurford, 1987).

These two domains of language influence each other in profound ways via the process of linguistic transmission diagrammed in figure 6.1. E-language is a product of the I-language of speakers. However, the I-language of language learners is a product of the E-language that they have access to. A model of the constraints on these two domains and

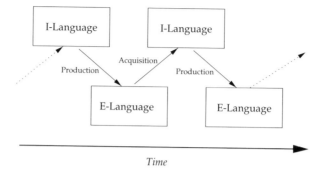

figure 6.1. The transmission of language over time.

the transformations that map between them should be sufficient to determine the dynamical properties of linguistic transmission.

A computational simulation of linguistic transmission works within the framework shown in figure 6.2, an elaboration of the model in figure 6.1. The simulation implements these processes:

1. An individual in the simulation is given a set of meanings that must be expressed. These meanings can be thought of as being provided by the external 'world', but in the simulation will simply be chosen randomly from some predefined set.
2. The individual then attempts to express each meaning either using their own internalized knowledge of language or by some random process of invention.
3. A new learner takes this set of utterances and uses it as input to learning.
4. Finally, the learner becomes a new speaker, the old speaker is discarded and a new individual is added to become a new learner and the cycle repeats.

The utterances that the individuals produce and learn from in these simulations are pairs of strings of letters (which can be thought of as basic unanalysable phonemic segments) and meaning representations. In these simulations the world is made up of a set of predefined atomic concepts. These might include:

john   tiger

eats   fears

knows

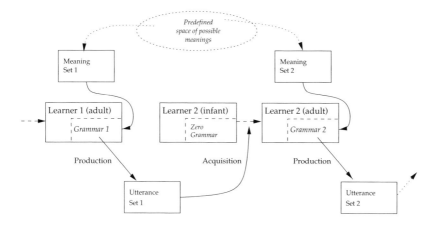

figure 6.2. A computational implementation of linguistic transmission.

These concepts can be combined into simple predicate–argument propositions, which may have hierarchical structure. For example:

$$\text{fears(john,tiger)}$$
$$\text{knows(john,eats(tiger,john))}$$

So, an example utterance by an individual in the simulation that happened to know something like English might be the pair:

$$< \texttt{tigereatsjohn}, \text{eats(tiger,john)} >$$

Obviously the biggest component of the simulation will be the part that takes sets of pairs such as these and is able to learn from them in some useful way – in other words, the part of the simulation that takes instances of E-language and maps them into I-language. This is the subject of the next section.

6.2.1 Learning

For simulations such as the one presented in this chapter, which model many generations of speakers and acquirers, the design of the learning algorithm is crucial. Two important criteria for a learning algorithm for us are: efficiency, because the simulations will need to model thousands of learners over time; and ease of analysis, since we are interested in how the language evolves over time and it is therefore important to be able to easily inspect the internal states of the learners.

The algorithm presented here[1] has been designed specifically with simulation tasks in mind – it is extremely simple and efficient, and it enables the internal states of learners to be easily analysed. Although no claims are made here for its efficacy as a *practical* grammar induction tool, it does model in a simple way the dual processes of rote learning of examples and induction of generalizations that must be at the core of any model of language acquisition.

Grammatical representation

For these simulations, the hypothesis space that the learning algorithm searches consists of context-free grammars enriched with the kind of simple semantics described above. In fact, these grammars are a restricted form of definite-clause grammar in which non-terminals may have a single argument attached to them which conveys semantic information. It is important to realize that although the internal knowledge of the individuals is a type of context-free grammar, this does not mean that compositionality or recursion is built-in. Consider a learner that can produce the string `tigereatsjohn` meaning eats(tiger,john). Here are two (of many, many possible) grammars that this learner could have internalized:

$$S/\text{eats(tiger,john)} \to \texttt{tigereatsjohn} \quad \begin{Vmatrix} S/p(x,y) \to N/x \ \ V/p \ \ N/y \\ V/\text{eats} \to \texttt{eats} \\ N/\text{tiger} \to \texttt{tiger} \\ N/\text{john} \to \texttt{john} \end{Vmatrix}$$

The S symbol in these grammars is the start symbol, whereas the N and V are arbitrarily named non-terminals. The lower case letters are shorthand for preterminals that expand to atomic phonemic segments. The material following the slashes attached to non-terminals is the semantic representation for that non-terminal.[2]

The grammar on the left is the simplest grammar that could produce the utterance. It states that '`tigereatsjohn`' is a valid sentence mean-

---

[1] In some respects the algorithm is a simplification and development of the one described in Kirby (1998, 2000).

[2] Formally, the semantic structures attached to non-terminals can take one of three forms: a fully specified form (i.e. a semantic structure with no variables), a partially specified form (i.e. a semantic structure with some variables, although the variables may only occur at the top level), or a variable. The left hand side semantics can take any of these forms in the grammar, but right hand side non-terminals can only take semantic variables in this formalism.

ing eats(tiger,john). Notice that this is entirely non-compositional – in no way is the meaning of the whole a function of meanings of its parts. In fact the string is not broken down or analysed at all, instead it is simply treated as a holistic chunk.

The grammar on the right, however, is compositional. The sub-parts of the string each are assigned meanings. So, for example, tiger corresponds to the meaning tiger. The whole string is composed by piecing these substrings together and combining their meanings using the variables x, p, and y.

It should be clear from this example, that although the grammatical formalism (obviously) allows us to represent languages that are structured syntactically, it *does not constrain languages to be of this form.* In other words, the space of languages that the learners have access to includes many that would not be considered possible human languages because, for example, they are non-compositional. The choice of formalism therefore does not build-in the result we are looking for.

Rule subsumption

In the first stage of learning, the grammar contains no rules. Data is presented to the the inducer as a pairing of a string of terminals and a semantic structure. A single pair can be incorporated into the grammar rather trivially. Say the pair

$< $ tigereatssausages, eats(tiger,sausages) $ >$

is to be incorporated. The simplest rule that covers this 'fact' about the language to be induced is:

$S/$eats(tiger,sausages) $\rightarrow$ tigereatssausages

A trivial learning algorithm could involve gathering one of these language facts for every string–meaning pair presented and storing them as one big grammar. This would give us a grammar which can generate exactly and only the sentences in the input. We could add one simple refinement to this technique by deleting duplicate rules in the grammar. In fact these two basic operations – incorporation, and duplicate deletion – are at the core of the final induction algorithm used by the simulation.

The problem with using just these two operations is that the inducer has no power to generalize. As such, this is a rather poor model of learning. A basic strategy for extracting generalizations from rules that are overly specific (similar in some ways to the more general method used in some inductive logic programming – see, e.g. discussion and citations in Mitchell (1997)) is to take pairs of rules and look for the least-general generalization that can be made that subsumes them within some prespecified constraints. For example, imagine a grammar with these two rules:

$$S/\text{eats(tiger,sausages)} \rightarrow \texttt{tigereatssausages}$$
$$S/\text{eats(john,sausages)} \rightarrow \texttt{johneatssausages}$$

What is the *least general* rule that would subsume both of these? Firstly, we need to replace tiger and john in the semantics with a variable. So the left hand side becomes: $S/\text{eats}(x, \text{sausages})$. But this means we need a nonterminal with an x attached to it in the right hand side of the rule. If we replace **tiger** and **john** on the right hand sides with a single new category (let's call it N), the we have our new rule:

$$S/\text{eats}(x,\text{sausages}) \rightarrow N/x \text{ eatssausages}$$

We can now delete the original two rules because we have one that subsumes them both. However, there is a problem here. We have introduced a new nonterminal, N, but there is no rule saying what an N is. At every stage of induction, our generalization should ensure that the new grammar can still parse the sentences that it could parse previously. In other words, the set of sentences $L(g)$ that a grammar g could generate before generalization will always be a subset (though not necessarily a proper subset) of the set of sentences $L(g')$ that could be generated after generalization. So, we must add two new N rules:

$$N/\text{tiger} \rightarrow \texttt{tiger}$$
$$N/\text{john} \rightarrow \texttt{john}$$

This is the most commonly applied subsumption method in the induction algorithm, but there are others. For example, if there are two rules such as:

$$N/\text{mary} \rightarrow \texttt{mary}$$
$$M/\text{mary} \rightarrow \texttt{mary}$$

then a rule that subsumes these two will simply choose one of the non terminal category symbols N or M. Let us say that it chooses to replace

M with N,[3] then to keep the induction preservative we must rewrite all occurrences of M throughout the grammar with N.

The induction algorithm thus proceeds by taking an utterance, incorporating the simplest possible rule that generates that utterance directly, and then searches through all pairs of rules in the grammar for possible subsumptions like the ones described above until no further generalizations can be found, and finally deletes any duplicate rules that are left over. More details about the algorithms for rule-subsumption and the constraints on its application can be found in the appendix to this chapter.

6.2.2 *Invention*

The particular meanings of the sentences that the speakers produce is controlled by the experimenter. The space of possible meanings can be thought of as the population's 'world model', in other words, what they want to talk about. One way to think of it is that the world compels the speaker to try to produce a string for a certain meaning. This means that there is no guarantee that the speaker will have a way of generating a string for the meaning it is compelled to produce. This will be especially true of the early stages of any simulation run, since the population is initialized with no grammatical knowledge at all.

If there was no way for speakers to produce strings *in the absence* of a grammar that can generate them, then a language could never get off the ground. It is important, therefore, that our model of an individual be enriched to allow for *invention*. The invention process is essentially a mechanism for introducing random new words for chunks of meaning, but it should not build in new syntactic structure. In other words, we assume that the individuals are able to invent strings of sounds but are not able to spontaneously invent hierarchical structure that they have not observed.

The invention algorithm used here, given a meaning that the speaker does not have a way of producing, tries to find the closest meaning that the speaker *does* have a way of producing. With this new meaning, a string and a parse tree for that string can be generated. The parse tree will show the parts of the string that correspond to the 'wrong' parts

---

[3] In general which it chooses will not matter *except* in the case of the start category, S. The start category is never changed.

of the meaning – in other words, the parts of the near meaning that are different to the meaning that should have been produced. These parts of the string are excised, and replaced with a random sequence of symbols.[4] Finally, the speaker's induction algorithm 'hears' its own invented string/meaning pair (this ensures that the speaker's output is consistent).

An example should make this clearer. Imagine that a speaker has the following grammar:

$$S/\text{loves(john,}x) \rightarrow \texttt{johnloves}\ N/x$$
$$N/\text{mary} \rightarrow \texttt{mary}$$
$$N/\text{jane} \rightarrow \texttt{jane}$$

This speaker is then asked to produce a string for the meaning loves(john, anna). The nearest meanings to this that the speaker can produce strings for are loves(john, mary) or loves(john, jane). We'll pick the first, which produces the tree structure:

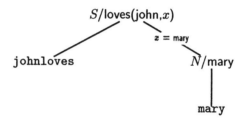

The wrong part of this tree is the material dominated by the node that introduces the meaning mary. We therefore delete the string `mary` and replace this with a random sequence of characters. So, the invented string for the meaning loves(john,anna) might be `johnlovesspog`. So, in this case, the compositionality of the grammar is reflected in the invented string.

A second example demonstrates an important property of the algorithm which avoids the introduction of novel structure. We'll use the same grammar, but instead try and invent a string for the meaning loves(fred,mary). The nearest meaning to this one using the grammar is loves(john,mary), which generates the same tree as above. This time the wrong bit of meaning is john, which dominates the whole string. An invented string for loves(fred,mary), therefore, might be a totally non-

---

[4] For the simulation runs presented here, the sequence varies from 1 to 3 letters randomly chosen from the alphabet.

compositional string like `bling`.

6.2.3 Summary of simulation cycle

In general the simulation can contain a population of any number of individuals, but to keep things simple in the experiments described here, there are only ever two individuals at any one time: an adult **speaker** and a new **learner**. At the start of any simulation run, neither the speaker nor the learner has any grammar at all — in other words, they have no knowledge of language. This means that any language that is observed in the simulation is purely emergent from the interactions of the individuals in the simulation.

Each generation in the simulation goes through the following steps:

1. The speaker tries to produce a set of utterances that will form input to the learner. This involves repeating the following sequence of actions some number of times (set by the experimenter):

   (a) The speaker is given a meaning chosen at random from a prede-fined set.

   (b) If the speaker is able to generate a string for that meaning using its grammar, it does so, otherwise it invents a string.[5] If the speaker has invented a string, the *speaker* uses that string–meaning pair as input to induction. This means that, if an individual invents a new way of saying something, they will learn from that and use that invention again if the need arises.

   (c) The learner is given the string, and tries to parse it with any grammar it might have. If it is unable to parse the string, then it takes the string–meaning pair and uses it as input to induction.

2. The speaker's grammar is logged and then it is deleted from the simulation.

3. The learner becomes the new speaker, and a new learner with a blank grammar is added to the simulation.

The two main parameters that the experimenter can vary in this

---

[5] Generation is always deterministic. If the grammar allows more than one way of producing a certain string, only one way is ever used. However, which one is used will be random. This is implemented by randomly ordering the grammatical rules once after the learner becomes a speaker, and using this order to inform the choice of rules employed in generation.

model are: the number of utterances that the speaker will be called upon to produce in its lifetime, and the structure and size of the meaning space. In the discussion section of this chapter we will see that these two parameters bear upon each other in an interesting way.

6.3 Example experiments

This section describes in detail two experiments which demonstrate that interesting linguistic structure emerges in initially non-linguistic populations over time in the cycle of acquisition and use. Each experiment has been run many times with differing initial random-number 'seeds'. In analysing the results we are able to directly examine individual grammars as well as plotting numerical values such as the proportion of meanings that are produced without invention, and size of grammar.

6.3.1 Degree-0 compositionality

In the first simulation run we experiment with the properties of languages that emerge when the individuals only communicate about simple meanings. The meaning space is made up of simple degree-0 two-place predicates (i.e. predicates with no embedding) in a world with five possible 'objects' and five possible 'actions'. Example meanings are:

likes(gavin,mary)
loves(mary,john)
hates(heather,pete)
and so on...

In these simulations, the arguments of the predicates must be distinct – in other words, reflexives like loves(john,john) are not allowed.

This means there are 100 distinct meanings that the individuals may wish to express (5 predicates x 5 possible first arguments x 4 possible second arguments). Each speaker produces 50 utterances in a lifetime, each of which is chosen at random from this space of two-place predicates. This means that, even if the meanings were carefully chosen, rather than being picked at random, learners can never be exposed to the entire range of possible meanings.

The results of the simulation can be plotted on a graph of grammar size against grammar expressivity. The former is calculated simply by counting the number of rules in each speaker's grammar, and the lat-

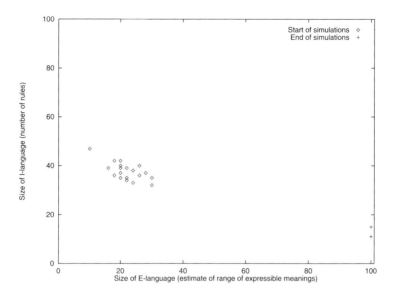

figure 6.3. A scatter plot of the start and end of the simulations in a space of I- vs. E-language size.

ter can be estimated by counting the proportion of utterances that the speaker produced without resorting to invention. These two values can be thought of as the I-language size and E-language size, respectively. Figure 6.3 is a scatter plot on this space, of the state of the languages at the start of the simulation runs (i.e. at the end of the first speaker's 'life') and again at the end of the simulation runs. In fact, almost all the simulation runs ended up at the same point (with an expressivity of 100, and 11 grammar rules). The one exception is a language that had not converged on a stable system of 11 rules by the end of the run (we return to this situation later). Figure 6.4 shows the movement through this space of the languages of five typical simulations.

These graphs are best understood by working through a particular example language as it changed over time. Here is a typical first generation grammar (nonterminals except for the start nonterminal S are arbitrarily chosen capital letters):

Generation 1
S/detests(john,gavin) → nqb
S/hates(heather,mary) → b
S/loves(mary,pete) → k

S/admires(john,mary) → u
S/detests(pete,john) → ayj
S/likes(heather,gavin) → g
S/loves(john,mary) → o

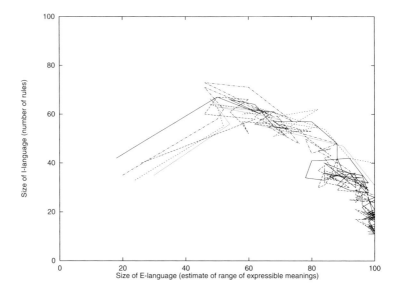

figure 6.4. The movement of some of the simulations through the I/E-language space. In the early stages, all the languages have low expressivity (E-language size) and big grammars. However, the languages universally move towards higher expressivity and smaller grammars.

S/loves(pete,john) → vcs	S/hates(pete,mary) → r
S/likes(john,pete) → os	S/likes(gavin,pete) → qi
S/loves(heather,gavin) → e	S/admires(gavin,john) → j
S/likes(mary,gavin) → ke	S/detests(john,mary) → f
S/admires(john,gavin) → hy	S/detests(heather,pete) → wkm
S/admires(pete,heather) → dx	S/detests(pete,mary) → sm
S/admires(gavin,pete) → x	S/loves(heather,john) → i
S/likes(heather,mary) → d	S/hates(john,heather) → xf
S/detests(heather,john) → m	S/loves(mary,gavin) → bni
S/detests(john,pete) → fu	S/admires(gavin,heather) → yn
S/detests(mary,gavin) → qqq	S/hates(heather,pete) → yya
S/hates(gavin,john) → jrx	S/admires(x,john) → f A/x
S/likes(gavin,john) → w	A/mary → lg
S/admires(gavin,mary) → h	A/pete → nv
S/hates(heather,gavin) → nln	

This is the grammar of the very first speaker at the end of life. The reason the speaker has any grammar at all is due to the fact that every utterance that it invents it also uses for its own induction. The grammar is essentially an idiosyncratic vocabulary for a random subset of the meaning space. So, for example, the speaker's sentence corresponding to the English *Gavin hates John* is `jrx`, whereas the sentence for *Gavin likes John* is the completely unrelated `w`. This, then, is a non-compositional, non-syntactically structured communication system. Notice, however, that a chance similarity of two sentences – `flg` meaning admires(mary,john) and `fnv` meaning admires(pete,john) – has lead to the creation of an *A* category for mary and pete.

Further on in this same simulation, we have grammars such as this one:

Generation 14
S/hates(pete,john) → a
S/p(john,x) → A/x B/p
S/likes(gavin,pete) → lw
S/hates(heather,john) → z
$S/p(x,$ mary$)$ → l B/p A/x
S/p(pete,gavin) → dx E/p
S/admires(heather,mary) → hhi
S/likes(mary,pete) → h
$S/p(x,$ heather$)$ → F/p A/x
S/hates(gavin,mary) → rw
S/detests(gavin,john) → vow
S/hates(heather,gavin) → s
S/detests(x,y) → D/x A/y
S/hates(mary,x) → D/x rs
S/hates(heather,pete) → kw
S/likes(heather,gavin) → ufy
S/loves(x,y) → A/y A/x
S/likes(x,y) → l C/y A/x
S/admires(x,y) → A/y C/x
$S/p(x,y)$ → C/x B/p n A/y

A/gavin → b
A/mary → ni
A/john → y
A/heather → x
A/pete → h
B/loves → y
B/hates → n
B/likes → z
B/detests → m
C/pete → t
C/gavin → yo
C/heather → gpi
C/john → d
D/heather → kr
D/gavin → q
E/hates → c
E/detests → rp
F/detests → r
F/hates → mofw
F/admires → u,d

Here, we have some productive generalizations. For example, there are several words of category *A*, which can be used in different contexts. The *A* category in fact covers all the objects in the semantic space, although objects are not exclusively expressed in this way. For example, in different contexts, heather can be expressed as `gpi`, `kr` or `x`.

Turning time forward even further, we get some highly regular grammars:

Generation 112
$S/p(x,y)$ →
C/y B/p n A/x
$S/p(x,y)$ →
A/y C/x B/p n
A/gavin → b
A/mary → ni

A/pete → re
A/john → y
B/loves → xfh
B/hates → n
B/admires → srw
B/likes → z
B/detests → m

C/heather → fkn
C/pete → t
C/mary → ns
C/gavin → yo
C/john → d

Now the category B can clearly be thought of as a *verb*. There are two nominal categories C and A, giving us two types of expression for most of the objects in the semantic space as shown in the table below:

Meaning	type 1 (category C)	type 2 (category A)
mary	ns	ni
pete	t	re
gavin	yo	b
john	d	y
heather	fkn	—

There are now only two sentence rules. The first sentence rule gives us an OVS language, with the object nouns of type 1, and the subject nouns of type 2. In the other sentence rule, the word order is OSV. Interestingly, the two types of noun have switched roles, so the object nouns are of type 2, and the subject nouns are type 1.

This form of the language is fairly stable, losing the type 2 form of gavin, but otherwise remaining the same for thousands of generations. In fact, this is similar to the state of the 'unusual' language in figure 6.3, which has a larger grammar at the end of its simulation run than those of the rest of the simulations. Eventually, however, the language goes through a rapid and complex series of changes to end up with the following form, which only has one type of noun:

Generation 7944
$S/p(x, y) \rightarrow$ v A/y g A/x B/p n
$A/$gavin $\rightarrow$ gw
$A/$john $\rightarrow$ gbb
$A/$pete $\rightarrow$ k
$A/$heather $\rightarrow$ gyt

$A/$mary $\rightarrow$ pd
$B/$hates $\rightarrow$ n
$B/$loves $\rightarrow$ c
$B/$detests $\rightarrow$ m
$B/$admires $\rightarrow$ srw
$B/$likes $\rightarrow$ z

This result is fairly typical of the simulation run started with different random-number seeds. The language in the population evolves from an idiosyncratic vocabulary for complex meanings to a completely compositional syntax with nominal and verbal categories. The main variation between runs is how quickly the coverage of the basic categories becomes complete. Sometimes an idiosyncratic sentence rule for a particular action, or particular object survives for a long time, and very occasionally optionality in word order emerges and appears to be stable for a long time.

6.3.2 Infinite language, finite means

The simulation in the previous section used a finite meaning space. The next step is to expand the meaning space so that there is an infinite range of meanings that may be expressed. To do this we include predicates which may take other predicates as arguments. The simulation is run again with five 'embedding predicates' (such as know, say etc.) Each speaker tries to produce 50 degree-0 meanings as before, but also then tries to produce 50 degree-1 meanings and finally, 50 degree-2 meanings.[6]

Because the potential expressivity of a language with this kind of semantics is infinite, we cannot visualize the behavior of the simulation in the same way as we did for degree-0 meanings. Instead, figure 6.5 shows the proportion of degree-0, degree-1 and degree-2 meanings expressed without invention against time averaged over ten simulation runs. Also plotted on these graphs is a line showing the average size of the grammars in these runs.

Once again, this graph can best be understood by looking at the evolution of language in a particular simulation run. The first generation grammars for a simulation starting with these parameters are very large (over 100 rules), because there are three times as many utterances to be produced. Here is a small subset of a typical first generation grammar for this new set of conditions:

Generation 1
S/praises(pete,heather) → k
S/hits(john,mary) → u
S/admires(heather,pete) → y
S/hates(gavin,mary) → qv
S/says(mary,admires(gavin,mary)) → n
S/says(mary,praises(pete,gavin)) → te
S/decides(heather,hits(gavin,john)) → h
S/says(john,hits(mary,pete)) → q
S/knows(gavin,loves(pete,heather)) → r
S/believes(john,praises(heather,mary)) → ei
S/says(mary,loves(heather,gavin)) → l
S/thinks(gavin,loves(gavin,mary)) → a
S/decides(heather,hates(heather,pete)) → vi
S/decides(john,admires(heather,john)) → jj
S/says(heather,hits(gavin,john)) → lzf
S/decides(heather,hits(john,mary)) → apv
A/praises(heather,pete) → p
S/knows(gavin,p) → g A/p

---

[6] Notice, this presentation scheme simulates a "starting small" learning paradigm (Elman, 1993; Kirby & Hurford, 1997a).

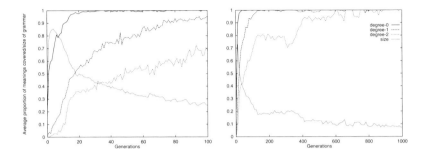

figure 6.5. Proportions of meaning space covered and size of grammars averaged of ten simulation runs, plotted on two different time-scales. The grammar size is scaled down by a factor of 300 in order that it can be plotted on the same scale. Coverage of the different meaning types increases and the size of the grammar decreases over time.

A/admires(mary,gavin) → ws
S/says(mary,thinks(mary,praises(john,gavin))) → bx
S/thinks(pete,thinks(john,admires(pete,heather))) → gv
S/believes(pete,thinks(john,hates(john,heather))) → bc
S/believes(gavin,thinks(gavin,hates(heather,pete))) → im
S/believes(pete,decides(gavin,hates(pete,heather))) → lsq
S/decides(heather,believes(heather,admires(mary,pete))) → hjg
B/admires(mary,heather) → p
S/knows(pete,p) → m B/p d
B/knows(john,loves(john,mary)) → m
.
.
.

Firstly, notice that the vocabulary obviously includes more complex meanings such as says(mary, thinks(mary, praises(john,gavin))) (in English *Mary says she thinks that John praises Gavin*). As with the last simulation runs, the inducer has already done some work. So, the similarity between the sentences mpd meaning knows(pete, admires(mary,heather)) and mmd meaning knows(pete, knows(john, loves(john,mary))) has lead to the creation of a category B for admires(mary,heather) and knows(john, loves(john,mary)).

The grammars in the simulation rapidly increase in size and complexity, peaking in the mid 200's in terms of number of rules, and they also are quickly able to express the full range of degree-0 meanings using regular sentence rules rather like those that emerged in the simulation runs in the previous section. However, after some time the grammars typically reduce dramatically in size:

Generation 115

$S/p(x,q) \rightarrow S/q \quad C/p \quad \texttt{gp} \quad B/x \quad \texttt{d}$
$S/p(x,y) \rightarrow \texttt{stlw} \quad A/p \quad B/y \quad B/x$
$A/\text{loves} \rightarrow \texttt{r}$
$A/\text{admires} \rightarrow \texttt{i}$
$A/\text{hates} \rightarrow \texttt{wja}$
$A/\text{detests} \rightarrow \texttt{w}$
$A/\text{likes} \rightarrow \texttt{btl}$
$B/\text{pete} \rightarrow \texttt{f}$

$B/\text{heather} \rightarrow \texttt{v}$
$B/\text{gavin} \rightarrow \texttt{eks}$
$B/\text{mary} \rightarrow \texttt{k}$
$B/\text{john} \rightarrow \texttt{a}$
$C/\text{says} \rightarrow \texttt{fdbtl}$
$C/\text{decides} \rightarrow \texttt{b}$
$C/\text{believes} \rightarrow \texttt{o}$
$C/\text{knows} \rightarrow \texttt{z}$
$C/\text{thinks} \rightarrow \texttt{t}$

There are two sentence rules in this grammar, and three other categories. The second sentence rule is similar to the ones we saw in the previous section, allowing the language to express the full range of degree-0 sentences. The category A is a verbal category, and B is the nominal category. This language has VOS order in main clauses.

The other sentence rule is the one that allows the language to express meanings greater than degree-0. It introduces a category C for verbs that have a subordinating function (such as $\texttt{fdbtl}$ meaning says), and crucially has a category S on its right hand side. This means that the language is recursive, allowing it to build up an infinite range of meanings. The tree in figure 6.6 shows how this particular language copes with complex meanings. It displays the parse for the sentence $\texttt{stlwrkazgpfd}$ which, translated into English, means *Pete knows that John loves Mary*.

Again, the language in the simulation has evolved simply by being learned and used repeatedly by individuals in the population. An initially random, idiosyncratic non-compositional and relatively inexpressive communication system, has become a compact, compositional language with nominal and verbal categories, word order encoding meaning distinctions and recursive subordinate clauses allowing the speakers to express an infinite range of meanings. The question is why?

6.4 Bottlenecks and universal grammar

The individuals in the simulation simply observe each other's behavior and learn from it, occasionally inventing, at random, new behaviors of their own. From this apparent randomness, organization emerges. Given that so little is built into the simulation, why is compositional, recursive

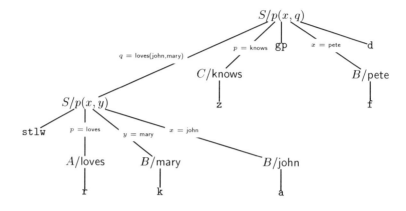

figure 6.6. "stlwrkazqpfd" meaning *Pete knows that John loves Mary.*

syntax inevitable? To answer this question we need to look back at how languages persist over time in a population (figure 6.1).

We can divide up I-language into units – *replicators* – that may or may not persist through time. The persistence of an I-language in this view is related to the success of the replicators that make up that language. In other words, the languages which are more easily transmitted from generation to generation will persist.

Within a population, certain replicators actually compete for survival. That is, the success of one must be measured relative to the success of others in the population at that time. These competing replicators are those rules which potentially express the same meaning. If there are two ways of saying *John loves Mary*, then on a particular exposure to this meaning, the learner can obviously only hear one of them. Therefore, on one exposure, only one of the rules (or, more properly, set of rules) that can be used to express *John loves Mary* has a chance of being induced by the learner.

At face value, it would seem that the two competing rules (or rulesets) will have an equal chance of being the one chosen for producing the meaning, so the replicative success of all rules in a language should be equal. This would be true *if each rule only ever expressed one meaning*. However, if one rule can be used to express more meanings than another, then, all other things being equal, that rule will have a greater chance of being expressed in the E-language input to the learner. In this case, the more general rule is the better replicator.

For a more concrete example, consider a situation where, in the population of I-languages, there are two competing rules. One is a rule that expresses *John loves Mary* as an unanalysed string of symbols – essentially as one word. The other rule expresses *John loves Mary* as a string of symbols, but can also be used to express any meaning where someone *loves Mary*. So, the latter rule can also be used to express *Gavin loves Mary* and so on. Further imagine that both rules have an equal chance of being used to express *John loves Mary*. The more general rule is a better replicator, because for any randomly chosen set of meanings, we can expect it to be used more often than the idiosyncratic rule. Its chances of survival to the next generation are far more secure than the idiosyncratic rule.

Of course, the more general rule will not be learned as easily as the idiosyncratic rule. In the simulations described above, an idiosyncratic pairing of one meaning to one form takes only one exposure to learn, but the most general rule takes several. However, the idiosyncratic rule only covers one meaning, whereas the most general rule covers an infinite number. It is clear, therefore, that the probability of a acquiring a particular rule given any sample of meanings increases with the generality of that rule. The success of I-languages which contain general rules seems secure.

The picture that emerges, then, is of the language of the population acting as an adaptive system in its own right. Initially, the rules are minimally general, each pairing one string with one meaning. At some point, a chance invention will lead a learner to 'go beyond the data' in making a generalization that the previous generation had not made. This generalization will then compete with the idiosyncratic rule(s) for the same meaning(s). Given that generalizations are better replicators, the idiosyncratic rules will be pushed out over time. The competition will then be replayed amongst generalizations, always with the more general rules surviving. (Notice that this picture of a move from holistic protolanguage to an emergent syntactic system is similar to the one proposed by Wray (1998).)

The inevitable end state of this process is a language with a syntax that supports compositionally derived semantics and recursion in a highly regular fashion. The grammar for such a language appears to be the shortest (in terms of numbers of rules) that can express the entire meaning space. The shorter the grammar, the higher the generality of each of the rules – the shortest grammar that can still do the job of

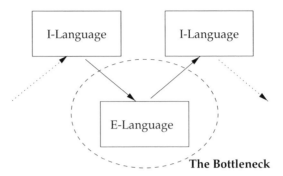

figure 6.7. The E-language domain acts as a bottleneck on the transmission of I-language.

expressing meanings is therefore the one made up of optimal replicators.

We can think of the transformations between I- and E-language as a bottleneck on the transmission of language over time (see figure 6.7). Since the number of meanings that the learners are exposed to is always lower than the total number of meanings, a totally idiosyncratic language *cannot* survive. In order to see this, we can visualize the contrast between idiosyncratic and syntactic languages in terms of types of mappings between structured spaces. Figure 6.8 is a schematic representation of a possible mapping between two spaces. This mapping does not preserve structure from one space to the other. In other words, there is a random relation between a point in the space and its corresponding point in the other space.

Now, imagine that this mapping must be learned. In the diagram, some of the pairings are shown in bold – if these where the only ones a learner was exposed to, would that learner be able to reconstruct the whole mapping? Not easily: for a finite space, the only way a random mapping could be reliably learnt from a subset of pairings would be if the learner had a very informative and domain specific prior bias to learn that particular mapping. Even this is not possible where the spaces are potentially unbounded.

Figure 6.9 on the other hand, shows a mapping in which structure in one space is preserved in the other. Given the sample in bold, it seems that a learner has a higher chance of reconstructing the mapping. A learner that is biased to construct concise models, for example, would learn this mapping more easily than that in the first figure. Importantly,

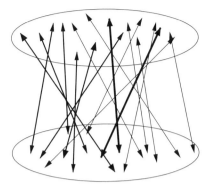

figure 6.8. A non-structure preserving mapping between two spaces with spatial structure. The bold lines indicate an imaginary subsample of the mapping that might be evidence for a learner. This mapping could only be learnt by a learner with a very specific prior bias.

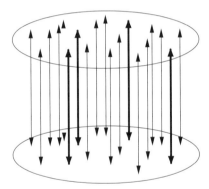

figure 6.9. A mapping in which structure is preserved. The bold lines indicate an imaginary subsample of the mapping that might be evidence for a learner. This mapping is more likely to be successfully learnt by a learner with a more general prior bias.

this bias is more likely to be domain general than one that explicitly codes for a particular idiosyncratic mapping. Furthermore a model can be constructed that would map the spaces even if they were potentially infinite in extent.

In the second set of simulations, as in real language, what is being learnt is a mapping between a meaning space and a signal space both of which are potentially infinite in extent. This means that it is in principle impossible for a learner to acquire a language that looks like the mapping of the first type, that is an idiosyncratic pairing of meanings and strings. This is why the initial, random languages in the simulations are unstable over time. This is not a feature of syntactically structured languages, however. Structure in the mapping improves the survivability of that mapping from one generation to the next.

What we are left with is a very general story about the (cultural) evolution of mappings. Structure-preserving mappings are more successful survivors through the learning bottleneck. This fact, coupled with random invention of pairings in languages that have incomplete coverage of the meaning space, and the unboundedness of the meaning and signal spaces, leads inevitably to the emergence of syntax.

At the start of this chapter the approach taken here was contrasted with the dominant approach in evolutionary linguistics, where the structure of language is taken to match closely with the structure of the language faculty which in turn is shaped by natural selection. We can now more precisely unpack the differences between these two perspectives on the origins of syntax. In particular, the relationship between the model of the acquirer and constraints on cross-linguistic variation is quite different.

Traditionally, the Chomskyan language acquisition device (LAD) directly constrains what makes a possible human language by limiting directly what can or cannot be acquired. This limit is said to closely map the observed constraints on variation (Hoekstra & Kooij, 1988). Part of the generative research program involves accounting for variation between languages explicitly within the model of the language acquirer. In fact, Universal Grammar (UG) and the LAD are often treated as synonymous within this tradition. It is not generally considered that the dynamics of language acquisition and use impose further constraints within the boundaries imposed by the structure of the LAD (although see Niyogi & Berwick (1995) & Clark (1996) for interesting exceptions).

Figure 6.10 contrasts this view with that proposed in this paper. The language learning device clearly does impose constraints directly in a similar fashion – there are certain types of language that the learner simply cannot acquire – however these constraints are far less severe than those imposed by the Chomskyan model of the LAD. As can be seen in the initial stages of the simulation, very un-language-like systems can be acquired by this learner. The constraints on variation are not built into the learner, but are instead emergent properties of the social

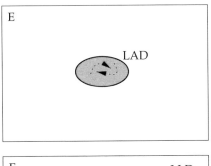

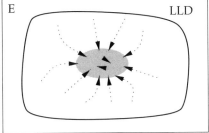

figure 6.10. Two Venn diagrams showing the different approaches to explaining observed constraints on cross-linguistic variation. E is the set of all logically possible languages, the gray area signifies the set of occurring human languages. In the top diagram, the Chomskyan language acquisition device constrains the learner directly and nothing else is required to explain the limits on variation. In the bottom diagram, the language *learning* device is less constraining, and the particular characteristics of human languages are the end result of a historical evolution of languages in populations (represented by arrows).

dynamics of learned communication systems and the structure of the semantic space that the individuals wish to express.

The theory presented here gives us a neat explanation of why human languages use syntactic structure to compositionally derive semantics, use recursion to express infinite distinctions in a digital way, have words with major syntactic categories such as noun and verb, and use syntactic rules of realization (such as ordering rules) to encode meaning distinctions. However, it does not seem to allow us to understand more specific universals. For example, why particular constituent orders are far more frequent than others across the languages of the world (Hawkins, 1983; Dryer, 1992).

Perhaps the best explanation for these types of universal should look at the effect of parsing and generation on the transmission of replicators (see Kirby, 1999 and Kirby, 1997 for details). On the other hand, at least some of these word order constraints may eventually be explained in terms of linguistic adaptation without appealing to processing (see, Christiansen, 1994 and Christiansen & Devlin, 1997 for some suggestions along these lines). X-bar theory – a sub part of UG which constrains the structure of syntactic trees cross categorially (Jackendoff, 1977) — has been implicated in various word order universals. Daniel Nettle (personal communication) has suggested that X-bar is just the sort of over-arching generalization that the theory put forward in this chapter predicts. It can be characterized as a pair of phrase structure rules:

$$XP \rightarrow Spec\ X' \ \ \text{or} \ \ XP \rightarrow X'\ Spec$$
$$X' \rightarrow X\ YP \ \ \text{or} \ \ X' \rightarrow YP\ X$$

These rules are like standard context free rules except that X and Y are variables that can range over the lexical categories in the language.

This use of variables in phrase structure rules is not possible with the formalism adopted here, so this result is not possible in the simulation. Nevertheless, if the language learning device were able to make a generalization such as that expressed by X-bar, we would expect it to thrive as a replicator. More generally, we should expect languages to behave in such a way that their word orders can be expressed in the most compact way, since this will reflect the behavior of the optimal, most general, replicator. Dryer (1992) shows with a large-scale cross-linguistic survey, that this is indeed the case; languages tend to order their non-branching nodes on the same side of their branching nodes across the phrasal categories of the language.

6.5 Conclusion

Compositionality and recursion are arguably the most basic features of the syntax of language. These structural properties, along with the way it is transmitted, are what makes human language a unique natural communication system. This chapter has presented an explanation of the origins of the properties which does not require them to be built-in as hard constraints on learning. This lifts the burden of explanation away from the biological evolution of the human genome and instead relies on very general properties of the dynamics of mappings that must replicate over time through learning.

For a language to survive from generation to generation it must be learned by individuals observing the behavior of other individuals. The sample of observations will be finite, yet the range of meanings that individuals may wish to communicate about is likely to be very large or infinite. This learning bottleneck leads inevitably to the emergence of a language in which structure is preserved in the mapping between semantics and strings in utterances.

The working model of linguistic transmission presented in this chapter has provided a demonstration of this process of emergence; compositional, recursive grammars arise given a particular model of learning and a particular model of semantics. Treating language as an adaptive system in its own right, in which properties of information transmission impact on its emergent structure, opens up new avenues of explanation in linguistics. Before seeking a biological or functional explanation for a particular feature of human language, or appealing to direct coding in an innate acquisition device, we should be aware of what we might be getting 'for free' through the kinds of processes described here.

Acknowledgements

The research for this chapter was carried out at the Language Evolution and Computation Research Unit at the Department of Linguistics, University of Edinburgh funded by ESRC grant R000237551. I would like to thank Jim Hurford, Mike Oliphant, Ted Briscoe and Robert Worden for useful discussions relating to the material presented here (although they do not necessarily agree with the content).

References

Batali, J. (1994). Innate biases and critical periods: Combining evolution and learning in the acquisition of syntax. In R. Brooks and P. Maes (eds.), *Artificial Life IV*, MIT Press, Cambridge MA, pp. 160–171.

Batali, J. (1998). Computational simulations of the emergence of grammar. In J. Hurford, C. Knight, and M. Studdert-Kennedy (eds.), *Approaches to the Evolution of Language: Social and Cognitive Bases*, Cambridge University Press, Cambridge, pp. 405–426.

Bickerton, D. (1990). *Language and Species*. University of Chicago Press, Chicago.

Briscoe, E. J. (1997). Co-evolution of language and of the language acquisition device. In *35th Association for Computational Linguistics*, pp. 418–427. Morgan Kaufmann, San Mateo, CA.

Briscoe, E. J. (1998). Language as a complex adaptive system: co-evolution of language and of the language acquisition device. In P. Coppen, H. van Halteren, and L. Teunissen (eds.), *8th Meeting of Comp. Linguistics in the Netherlands*, Rodopi, Amsterdam, pp. 3–40.

Cangelosi, A. and D. Parisi (1996). The emergence of a language in an evolving population of neural networks. Technical Report NSAL–96004, National Research Council, Rome.

Chomsky, N. (1986). *Knowledge of Language*. Praeger, New York.

Christiansen, M. (1994). *Infinite Languages, Finite Minds: Connectionism, Learning and Linguistic Structure*. Ph. D. thesis, University of Edinburgh.

Christiansen, M. and J. Devlin (1997). Recursive inconsistencies are hard to learn: A connectionist perspective on universal word order correlations. In *Proceedings of the 19th Annual Cognitive Science Society Conference*, Lawrence Erlbaum Associates, Mahwah, NJ, pp. 113–118.

Clark, R. (1996). Internal and external factors affecting language change: A computational model. Master's thesis, University of Edinburgh.

Dryer, M. (1992). The Greenbergian word order correlations. *Language 68*, 81–138.

Elman, J. L. (1993). Learning and development in neural networks: the importance of starting small. *Cognition 48*, 71–99.

Hawkins, J. A. (1983). *Word Order Universals*. Academic Press, San Diego.

Hoekstra, T. and J. G. Kooij (1988). The innateness hypothesis. In J. A. Hawkins (ed.), *Explaining Language Universals*. Blackwell, Oxford.

Hurford, J. (1987). *Language and Number: the Emergence of a Cognitive System*. Blackwell, Oxford.

Hurford, J. (1989). Biological evolution of the Saussurean sign as a component of the language acquisition device. *Lingua 77*, 187–222.

Hurford, J. (1991). The evolution of the critical period for language acquisition. *Cognition 40*, 159–201.

Hurford, J. (2000). Social transmission favours linguistic generalisation. In C. Knight, J. Hurford, and M. Studdert-Kennedy (eds.), *The Evolutionary Emergence of Language*, Cambridge University Press, Cambridge. pp. 324–352.

Hurford, J., C. Knight, and M. Studdert-Kennedy (eds.) (1998). *Approaches to the Evolution of Language: Social and Cognitive Bases*, Cambridge University Press, Cambridge.

Jackendoff, R. (1977). *X-Syntax: A Study of Phrase Structure*. MIT Press, Cambridge MA.

Kirby, S. (1997). Competing motivations and emergence: explaining implicational hierarchies. *Language Typology 1*, 5–32.

Kirby, S. (1998). Language evolution without natural selection: From vocabulary to syntax in a population of learners. Technical Report EOPL–98–1, Department of Linguistics, University of Edinburgh.

Kirby, S. (1999). *Function, Selection and Innateness: the Emergence of Language Universals*. Oxford: Oxford University Press.

Kirby, S. (2000). Syntax without natural selection: How compositionality emerges from vocabulary in a population of learners. In C. Knight, J. Hurford, and M. Studdert-Kennedy (eds.), *The Emergence of Language*, Cambridge University Press, Cambridge, pp. 303–323.

Kirby, S. and J. Hurford (1997a). The evolution of incremental learning: Language, development and critical periods. Occasional Paper EOPL-97-2, Department of Linguistics, University of Edinburgh, Edinburgh.

Kirby, S. and J. Hurford (1997b). Learning, culture and evolution in the origin of linguistic constraints. In *Fourth European Conference on Artificial Life*, MIT Press, Cambridge, MA, pp. 493–502.

MacLennan, B. (1991). Synthetic ethology: an approach to the study of communication. In C. Langton, C. Taylor, J. Farmer, and S. Ramussen (eds.), *Artificial Life II*, Addison-Wesley, Redwood City, CA, pp. 631–657.

Mitchell, T. M. (1997). *Machine Learning*. McGraw Hill, New York.

Newmeyer, F. J. (1991). Functional explanation in linguistics and the origins of language. *Language and Communication 11*, 3–28.

Niyogi, P. and R. Berwick (1995). The logical problem of language change. Technical Report AI Memo 1516 / CBCL Paper 115, MIT AI Laboratory and Center for Biological and Computational Learning, Department of Brain and Cognitive Sciences.

Niyogi, P. and R. Berwick (1997). Populations of learners: the case of Portugese. Unpublished manuscript, MIT.

Oliphant, M. (1996). The dilemma of Saussurean communication. *BioSystems 37*, 31–38.

Pinker, S. and P. Bloom (1990). Natural language and natural selection. *Behavioral and Brain Sciences 13*, 707–784.

Steels, L. (1996). Emergent adaptive lexicons. In P. Maes (ed.), *Proceedings of the Simulation of Adaptive Behavior Conference*. MIT Press, Cambridge, MA.

Wray, A. (1998). Protolanguage as a holistic system for social interaction. *Language and Communication 18*, 47–67.

Appendix: Details of rule subsumption

This appendix gives a more thorough treatment of the rule subsumption approach introduced in section 6.2.1. The algorithm uses two methods of subsumption:

Merge *If* the two rules would be the same if two category symbols were merged, *then* merge those categories. In other words, pick one of the categories and rewrite the other one to be the same as it throughout the grammar.

Chunk *If* the two rules would be the same if either one or both of them chunked a sequence of terminals, *then* chunk those terminals. Chunking involves creating a new rule made up of a substring of nonterminals on the right hand side of the old rule, and adjusting the old rule to refer to the new one.

Whilst rule subsumption through merging is straightforward, chunking is rather more difficult to implement. It is best to describe the procedure step-by-step:

1. Take a pair of rules, r_1 and r_2 from the grammar with the same left

hand side category symbol, C.

2. Can chunking can be applied to both rules?

    (a) Do the left hand side semantics of the two rules differ in only one position? If so, call the differences m_1 and m_2. If there is no difference, or if there is more than one difference then stop.

    (b) Are there two strings of terminals that, if removed, would make the right hand sides of the two rules the same? If so, call this string difference λ_1 and λ_2. If there isn't one string difference, then go to step 3.

    (c) Create a new category N.

    (d) Create two new rules:

$$N/m_1 \rightarrow \lambda_1$$
$$N/m_2 \rightarrow \lambda_2$$

    (e) Replace the old rules r_1 and r_2 with one rule. This rule is identical to r_1 (or r_2) except that λ_1 (or λ_2) is replaced with C/x on the right hand side, and m_1 (or m_2) is replaced with the variable x on the left hand side.

    (f) Stop.

3. Can chunking can be applied to just one of the rules?

    (a) Can the left hand side semantics of the two rules can be unified? If not, stop.

    (b) Is there a string of terminals λ in one of the rules which corresponds to a nonterminal label N/m in the other rule? In other words, is this the only difference in the two rules' right hand sides? If not, stop.

    (c) Delete the rule containing the substring λ.

    (d) Create a new rule:

$$N/m \rightarrow \lambda$$

    (e) Stop.

We can work through this chunking procedure using the example in section 6.2.1.

1. start with the two rules, r_1 and r_2:

$$S/\text{eats(tiger,sausages)} \rightarrow \texttt{tigereatssausages}$$
$$S/\text{eats(john,sausages)} \rightarrow \texttt{johneatssausages}$$

These have the same left hand side category symbol, S.
2. check to see if chunking can be applied to both of these rules.

(a) the left hand side semantics differ in one position, so $m_1 =$ tiger and $m_2 =$ john.

(b) the shortest pair of strings of terminals that could be removed from both rules to make them the same is tiger and john, so $\lambda_1 =$ tiger and $\lambda_2 =$ john.

(c) we make up a new category name – for convenience, we'll call it N.

(d) the two new rules are therefore:

$$N/\text{tiger} \rightarrow \text{tiger}$$
$$N/\text{john} \rightarrow \text{john}$$

(e) the two old rules are replaced with a single more general one:

$$S/\text{eats}(x,\text{sausages}) \rightarrow N/x \text{ eatssausages}$$

(f) stop.

With merging and chunking, the inducer can successfully discover new rules that subsume pairs of rules that it has learnt through simple incorporation. However, in practice it is useful to add an other procedure to the induction algorithm which also makes rules more general. Wherever possible, the inducer tries to simplify its rules by utilizing other rules that are already in the grammar. So, for example, if we had the following pair of rules:

$$S/\text{loves}(\text{john},\text{mary}) \rightarrow \text{johnlovesmary}$$
$$N/\text{mary} \rightarrow \text{mary}$$

the inducer would simplify the first one to:

$$S/\text{loves}(\text{john},x) \rightarrow \text{johnloves } N/x$$

7

Theories of cultural evolution and their application to language change

Partha Niyogi

Bell Laboratories, 600 Mountain
Avenue, Murray Hill, NJ 07974, USA.

7.1 Introduction

We discuss the problem of characterizing the evolutionary dynamics of linguistic populations over successive generations. Here we introduce the framework of Cavalli-Sforza and Feldman (1981) for the treatment of cultural evolution and show how to apply it to the particular case of language change. We relate the approach to that of Niyogi and Berwick (1995) and show how to map trajectories in one to those in the other. In both models, language acquisition serves as the mechanism of transmission of language from one generation to the next. For memoryless learning algorithms and the case of two languages in contact, we derive particular dynamical systems under the assumptions of both kinds of models. As an application of such computational modeling to historical change, we consider the evolution of English from the 9th century to the 14th century A.D. and discuss the role of such modeling to judge the adequacy of competing linguistic accounts for historical phenomena.

7.1.1 The problem of language change

A central concern for historical linguists is to characterize the dimensions along which human languages change over time and explain why they do so. Under the assumptions of contemporary linguistic theory, change in linguistic behavior of human populations must be a result of a change in the internal grammars that successive generations of humans employ. The question then becomes: why do the grammars of successive generations differ from each other? In order to answer this question, we need to know how these grammars are acquired in the first place and how the grammars of succeeding generations are related to each other. If such a relationship is uncovered, one might then be able to systematically predict the envelope of possible changes and relate them to actually observed historical trajectories.

Problems in historical or evolutionary linguistics have only recently begun to attract computational attention. This is in contrast to some other areas of linguistics, notably language acquisition, where for example, a significant body of work exists regarding computational models of grammatical inference under a variety of different assumptions (see, for example, Wexler and Culicover, 1980; Osherson, Stob and Weinstein, 1986). At the same time, computational and mathematical work in biological evolution has a long and rich tradition beginning with the pioneering work of Fisher, Wright, and Haldane and continuing to the present day. In a treatise in 1981, Cavalli-Sforza and Feldman outlined a general model of cultural change that was inspired by models of biological evolution and has potential and hitherto unexploited applicability to the case of language.

Indeed many motivating examples in Cavalli-Sforza and Feldman (19–81) were taken from the field of language change. However, the applicability of such models to language change was not formally pursued there. In this paper, we introduce their basic model and provide one possible way in which the principles and parameters approach to grammatical theory (construed in the broadest possible way) is amenable to their modeling framework.

More recently, a framework for the computational characterization of changing linguistic populations has also been developed in a series of papers by Niyogi and Berwick (1995, 1997, 1998). We explore here the formal connections between these two approaches for the case of two linguistic variants in competition. In particular, we show how evolutionary trajectories in one framework can be formally translated into the other and discuss their similarities and differences. To ground the discussion in a particular linguistic context, we show the application of such models to generate insight into possible evolutionary trajectories for the case of the diachronic evolution of English from the 9th century A.D. to the 15th century A.D. Finally, we provide some extensions of the basic Cavalli-Sforza and Feldman framework that might allow us to characterize the effect of spatial (geographical) location on the linguistic interactions between individuals in a population and the evolutionary consequences of such interactions.

The reader might ask – what is the role of formal modeling of the sort described in this paper in gaining insight in historical or evolutionary linguistics? From our perspective, these techniques provide research tools to increase our understanding about the range of explanations for historical phenomena. The formal model places constraints on the kinds of informal, largely descriptive accounts of attested historical changes which linguists develop. Tools of this sort therefore help us figure out the plausibility of various accounts and rule out logical inconsistencies that might be difficult to spot in a more informally developed treatment.

7.1.2 The Cavalli-Sforza and Feldman theory of cultural transmission and change

Cavalli-Sforza and Feldman (1981) outline a theoretical model for cultural change over generations. Such a model closely mimics the transmission of genetic parameters over generations: except now, we have 'cultural' parameters that are transmitted from parents to children with certain probabilities. In the model (hereafter referred to as the CF model in this paper), the mechanism of transmission is unknown – only the probabilities of acquiring one of several possible variations of the trait are known.

We reproduce their basic formulation for *vertical* transmission (from one generation to the next) of a particular binary valued trait. Assume a particular cultural trait has one of two values. Some examples of traits they consider are political orientation (Democrat/Republican) or health habits (smoker/non-smoker) and so on. Let the two values be denoted by H and L. Each individual is assumed to have exactly one of these two values. However, such a value is presumably not innate but learned.

A child born to two individuals (mother and father) will acquire one of these two possible values over its lifetime. The probability with which it will acquire each of these traits depends upon its immediate environment – in the standard case of their model (though variations are considered[1]), its parents. Thus one can construct table 7.1.

---

[1] Pure vertical transmission involves transmission of cultural parameters from parents to children. They also consider (i) *oblique* transmission where members of the parental generation other than the parents affect the acquisition of the cultural parameters (ii) *horizontal* transmission where members of the same generation influence the individual child. We discuss in a later section the approach of Niyogi and Berwick (1995) that involves oblique transmission of a particular sort and is different from the Cavalli-Sforza and Feldman (1981) treatment.

Table 7.1. *Cultural transmission*

Pat. Val.	Mat. Val.	$P(ChildVal. = L)$	$P(Types)$	Rdm. Mtg.
L	L	b_3	p_3	u_t^2
L	H	b_2	p_2	$u_t(1 - u_t)$
H	L	b_1	p_1	$u_t(1 - u_t)$
H	H	b_0	p_0	$(1 - u_t)^2$

The cultural types of parents and children related to each other by their proportions in the population. The values depicted are for vertical transmission and random mating.

The first three columns of table 7.1 are self-explanatory. As one can see easily enough, parental compositions can be one of 4 types depending upon the values of the cultural traits of each of the parents. We denote by b_i the probability with which a child of the ith parental type will attain the trait L (with $1 - b_i$, it attains H.) In addition, let p_i be the probability of the ith parental type in the population. Finally, we let the proportion of people having type L in the parental generation be u_t. Here t indexes the generation number and therefore proportion of L types in the parental generation is given by u_t and proportion of L types in the next generation (children who mature into adults) is given by u_{t+1}.

Under random mating, one sees that the proportion of parents of type (L, L) , i.e., male L types married to female L types is u_t^2. Similarly one can compute the probability of each of the other combinations.

Given this, they go on to show that the proportion of L types in the population will evolve according to the following quadratic update rule:

$$u_{t+1} = Bu_t^2 + Cu_t + D \tag{7.1}$$

where $B = b_3 + b_0 - b_1 - b_2$, $C = b_2 + b_1 - 2b_0$, and $D = b_0$. In this manner, the proportion of L types in generation $t + 1$ (given by u_{t+1}) is related to the proportion of L types in generation t (given by u_t).

A number of properties and variations of this basic evolutionary behavior are then evaluated (Cavalli-Sforza and Feldman, 1981) under different assumptions.

Thus, we see that evolution (change) of the cultural traits within the population is essentially driven by the probabilities with which children acquire the traits given their parental types. The close similarity of this particular model[2] to biological evolution is clear: (1) trait values, like gene-types are discrete (2) their transmission from one generation to another depends (in a probabilistic sense) only on the trait-values (gene-types) of the parents.

The basic intuition they attempted to capture in their model is that cultural traits are acquired (learned) by children from their parents. Thus, by noting the population mix of different parental types and the probabilities with which they are transmitted one can compute the evolution of these traits within the population. They had hoped to apply this model to language. In the next section we show how to do this.

7.2 Instantiating the CF model for languages

In order to apply the model to the phenomena of language change, the crucial point to appreciate is that the mechanism of linguistic transmission from generation to generation is 'language learning', i.e., children learn the language of their parents as a result of exposure to the primary linguistic data they receive from their linguistic environment. Therefore, in this particular case, the transmission probabilities b_i's in the model above will depend upon the learning algorithm they employ. We outline this dependence for a simplified situation corresponding to two language types in competition.

7.2.1 One parameter models

Assume there are two languages in the world – L_1 and L_2. Such a situation might effectively arise if two languages differing by a linguistic parameter are in competition with each other and we will discuss later the historical example of syntactic change in English for which this is a reasonable approximation. We consider languages to be subsets of Σ^* in the usual sense where Σ is a finite alphabet. Furthermore, underlying each language L_i is a grammar q_i that represents the internal knowledge that speakers of the language possess of it.

Individuals are assumed to be native speakers of exactly one of these two languages. Furthermore, let speakers of L_1 produce sentences with a probability distribution P_1 and speakers of L_2 produce sentences with a

---

[2] To avoid misinterpretation, it is worthwhile mentioning that extensions to continuous valued traits have been discussed. Those extensions have less relevance for the case of language since linguistic objects are essentially discrete.

distribution P_2. There are now four parental types and children born to each of these parental types are going to be exposed to different linguistic inputs and as a result will acquire a particular language with different probabilities.

In the abstract, let us assume that children follow some acquisition algorithm $\mathcal{A}$ (for a brief overview of the structure of learning theory, see appendix) that operates on the primary linguistic data they receive and comes up with a grammatical hypothesis – in our case, a choice of g_1 or g_2 (correspondingly L_1 or L_2). Formally, let $\mathcal{D}_k$ be the set of all subsets of Σ^* of cardinality k. Each subset of Σ^* of cardinality k is a candidate dataset consisting of k sentences that might constitute the primary linguistic data a child receives. Clearly $\mathcal{D}_k$ is the set of all candidate datasets of size k. Then $\mathcal{A}$ is a computable mapping from the set $\cup_{k=1}^{\infty} \mathcal{D}_k$ to $\{g_1, g_2\}$. We now make the following assumptions.

1. Children of parents who speak the same language receive examples only from the unique language their parents share, i.e., children of parents speaking L_1 receive sentences drawn according to P_1 and children of parents speaking L_2 receive examples drawn according to P_2.
2. Children of parents who speak different languages receive examples from an *equal* mixture of both languages, i.e., they receive examples drawn according to $\frac{1}{2}P_1 + \frac{1}{2}P_2$.
3. After k examples, children 'mature' and whatever grammatical hypothesis they have, they retain for the rest of their lives.

Thus the learning algorithm $\mathcal{A}$ operates on the sentences it receives. These sentences in turn are drawn at random according to a probability distribution that depends on the parental type. We now define the following quantity:

$$g(\mathcal{A}, P, k) = \sum_{\{w \in \mathcal{D}_k : \mathcal{A}(w) = g_1\}} \prod_{i=1}^{k} P(w_i) \qquad (7.2)$$

Recall that each element $w \in \mathcal{D}_k$ is a set of k sentences. In eq. 7.2 we denote by w_i the ith sentence of the set w. Therefore, $g(\mathcal{A}, P, k)$ is the probability with which the algorithm $\mathcal{A}$ hypothesizes grammar g_1 given a random draw of k indpendent examples according to probability distribution P. Clearly, g characterizes the behavior of the learning algorithm $\mathcal{A}$ if sentences were drawn according to P. It is worthwhile noting that

Table 7.2. *Language transmission*

Pat. Lg.	Mat. Lg.	P	Prob. Child speaks L_1
L_1	L_1	P_1	$b_3 = g(\mathcal{A}, P_1, k)$
L_1	L_2	$\frac{1}{2}P_1 + \frac{1}{2}P_2$	$b_2 = g(\mathcal{A}, \frac{1}{2}P_1 + \frac{1}{2}P_2, k)$
L_2	L_1	$\frac{1}{2}P_1 + \frac{1}{2}P_2$	$b_1 = g(\mathcal{A}, \frac{1}{2}P_1 + \frac{1}{2}P_2, k)$
L_2	L_2	P_2	$b_0 = g\mathcal{A}, P_2, k)$

The probability with which children attain each of the language types, L_1 and L_2 depends upon the parental linguistic types, the probability distributions P_1 and P_2 and the learning algorithm $\mathcal{A}$.

learnability (in the limit, in a stochastic generalization of Gold, 1967) requires the following:

Statement 1. *If the support of P is L_1 then $\lim_{k \longrightarrow \infty} g(\mathcal{A}, P, k) = 1$ and if the support of P is L_2 then $\lim_{k \longrightarrow \infty} g(\mathcal{A}, P, k) = 0$.*

In practice, of course, we have made the assumption that children 'mature' after k examples: so a reasonable requirement is that g be high if P has support on L_1 and low if P has support on L_2. Given this, we can now write down the probability with which children of each of the four parental types will attain the language L_1. These are shown in table 7.2.

Thus we can express the b_i's in the CF model of cultural transmission in terms of the learning algorithm. This is reasonable because after all, the $b_i's$ attempt to capture the fact that traits are 'learned' – in the case of languages, they are almost certainly learned from exposure to linguistic data.

Under random mating[3], we see that the population evolves according to eq. 7.1. Substituting the appropriate $g's$ from table 7.2 above in place of the $b_i's$ we obtain an evolution that depends upon $P_1, P_2, \mathcal{A}$, and k.

7.2.2 An alternative approach

In a recent attempt to explicitly characterize the problem of language change, Niyogi and Berwick (1995, 1997, 1998) develop a model (here-

---

[3] We have only considered the case of random mating here for illustrative convenience. The extension to more assortative forms of mating can be carried out using the standard techniques of population biology.

after, we refer to this class of models as NB models) for the phenomenon making the following simplifying assumptions.

1. The population can be divided into children (learners) and adults (sources).
2. All children in the population are exposed to sentences drawn from the same distribution.
3. The distribution with which sentences are drawn depends upon the distribution of language speakers in the adult population.

The equations for the evolution of the population under these assumptions were derived. Let us consider the evolution of two-language populations. At any point, one can characterize the state of the population by a single variable ($s_t \in [0,1]$) denoting the proportion of speakers of L_1 in the population. Further assume, as before, that speakers of L_1 produce sentences with distribution P_1 on the sentences of L_1 and speakers of L_2 produce sentences with distribution P_2 on the sentences of L_2.

The evolution of s_t over time (the time index t denotes generation number) was derived in terms of the learning algorithm $\mathcal{A}$, the distributions P_1 and P_2, and the maturation time k. Essentially, this evolution turns out to be the following:

$$s_{t+1} = f(s_t) = g(\mathcal{A}, s_t P_1 + (1 - s_t)P_2, k)$$

The interpretation is clear. If the previous state was s_t, then children are exposed to sentences drawn according to $s_t P_1 + (1 - s_t)P_2$. The probability with which the average child will attain L_1 is correspondingly provided by g and therefore one can expect that this will be the proportion of L_1 speakers in the next generation, i.e., after the children mature to adulthood.

Niyogi and Berwick (1995, 1997, 1998) derive the specific functional form of the update rule f (equivalently g) for a number of different learning algorithms. In the next section, we show how these two approaches to characterizing the evolutionary dynamics of linguistic populations are related. Specifically, we show how the evolutionary update rule f in the NB framework is explicitly related to the update rule in the CF framework.

7.2.3 Transforming NB models into the CF framework

Let the NB update rule be given by $s_{t+1} = f(s_t)$. Then, we see immediately that:

1. $b_3 = f(1)$
2. $b_2 = b_1 = f(0.5)$
3. $b_0 = f(0)$.

The CF update rule is now given by eq. 7.1. The update as we have noted is quadratic and the coefficients can be expressed in terms of the NB update rule f. Specifically, the system evolves as

$$s_{t+1} = (f(1) + f(0) - 2f(0.5)) \, s_t^2 + (2f(0.5) - 2f(0)) \, s_t + f(0) \quad (7.3)$$

Thus we see that if we are able to derive the NB update rule, we can easily transform it to arrive at the CF update rule for evolution of the population. The difficulty of deriving both rules rests upon the difficulty of deriving the quantity g that appears in both update rules. Notice further that the CF update rule is *always* quadratic while the NB update rule is in general not quadratic.

The essential difference in the nature of the two update rules stems from the different assumptions made in the modeling process. Particularly, Niyogi and Berwick (1995, 1997, 1998) assume that all children receive input from the same distribution. Cavalli-Sforza and Feldman (1981) assume that children can be grouped into four classes depending on their parental type. The crucial observation at this stage is that by dividing the population of children into classes that are different from each other, one is able to arrive at alternate evolutionary dynamics. In a later section we utilize this observation to divide children into classes that depend on their geographical neighborhood. This will allow us to derive a generalization of the NB model for neighborhoods. Before proceeding any further, let us now translate the update rules derived in Niyogi and Berwick (1995, 1996) into the appropriate CF models. The update rules are derived for memoryless learning algorithms operating on grammars. We consider an application to English with grammars represented in the principles and parameters framework.

7.3 CF models for some simple learning algorithms

In this section we consider some simple on-line learning algorithms (like the Triggering Learning Algorithm of Gibson and Wexler (1994); henceforth TLA) and show how their analysis within the NB model can be plugged into eq. 7.3 to yield the dynamics of linguistic populations under the CF model.

7.3.1 TLA and its evolution

How will the population evolve if the learning algorithm $\mathcal{A}$ in question is the Triggering Learning Algorithm[4] (or related memoryless learning algorithms in general)? The answer is simple. We know how the TLA driven system evolves in the NB model (from an analysis of the TLA in Niyogi and Berwick, 1996). All we need to do is to plug such an evolution into eq. 7.3 and we are done.

Recall that the TLA is as follows:

1. **Initialize:** Start with randomly chosen input grammar.
2. Receive next input sentence, s.
3. If s can be parsed under current hypothesis grammar, go to 2.
4. If s cannot be parsed under current hypothesis grammar, choose another grammar uniformly at random.
5. **If** s can be parsed by new grammar, retain new grammar, **else** go back to old grammar.
6. Go to 2.

It is shown in Niyogi and Berwick (1996) that such an algorithm can be analyzed as a Markov Chain whose state space is the space of possible grammars and whose transition probabilities depend upon the distribution P with which sentences are drawn. Using such an analysis, the function f can be computed. For the case of two grammars (languages) in competition under the assumptions of the NB model, this function f

---

[4] The Triggering Learning Algorithm has been chosen here for illustrative purposes to develop the the connections between individual acquisition and population change in a concrete manner in both NB and CF models. Replacing the TLA by another learning algorithms does not alter the spirit of the major points we wish to make in this paper but rather the details of some of the results we might obtain here. In general, acquisition algorithms can now be studied from the point of view of adequacy with respect to historical phenomena.

is seen to be:

$$f(s_t) = \frac{s_t(1-a)}{(1-b) + s_t(b-a)}$$
$$+ \frac{[b - s_t(b-a)]^k[(1-b) + s_t(a+b-2)]}{2[(1-b) + s_t(b-a)]} \tag{7.4}$$

In eq. 7.4, the evolving quantity s_t is the proportion of L_1 speakers in the community. The update rule depends on parameters a, b and k that need further explanation. The parameter a is the probability with which ambiguous sentences (sentences that are parsable by both g_1 and g_2) are produced by L_1 speakers, i.e., $a = \sum_{w \in L_1 \cap L_2} P_1(w)$; similarly, b is the probability with which ambiguous sentences are produced by L_2 speakers, i.e., $b = \sum_{w \in L_1 \cap L_2} P_2(w)$. Finally, k is the number of sentences that a child receives from its linguistic environment before maturation. It is interesting to note that the only way in which the update rule depends upon P_1 and P_2 is through the parameters a and b that are bounded between 0 and 1 by construction.

It is not obvious from eq. 7.4, but it is possible to show that f is a polynomial (in s_t) of degree k. Having obtained $f(s_t)$, one obtains the quadratic update rule of the CF model by computing the b_i's according to the formulae given in the earlier section. These are seen to be as follows:

$$b_3 = 1 - \frac{a^k}{2}; b_0 = \frac{b^k}{2}; b_1 = b_2$$
$$= \frac{(1-a)}{(1-a) + (1-b)} + (\frac{a+b}{2})^k \frac{(a-b)}{2[(1-a) + (1-b)]}$$

The following remarks are in order:

1. For $k = 2$, i.e., where children receive exactly two sentences before maturation, both the NB and CF models yield quadratic update rules for the evolution of the population. For the NB model, the following is true: (i) for $a = b$, there is *exponential* growth (or decay) to one fixed point of $p* = \frac{1}{2}$, i.e., populations evolve until both languages are in equal proportion and they coexist at this level; (ii) for $a \neq b$, there is *logistic* growth (or decay) and in particular, if $a < b$ then there is one stable fixed point $p^*(a, b)$ whose value depends upon a, b and is greater than $\frac{1}{2}$. If $a > b$ then there is again one stable fixed point $p^*(a, b)$ that is less than $\frac{1}{2}$. Populations tend to the stable fixed point from all initial conditions in logistic fashion. The value of p^*

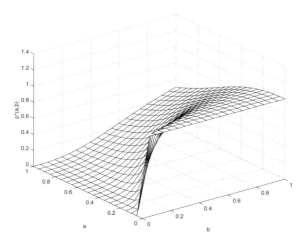

figure 7.1. The fixed point $p^*(a, b)$ for various choices of a and b for the NB model with $k = 2$.

as a function of a and b is shown in figure 1.

2. For $k = 2$, the evolution of the CF model is as follows: (i) for $a = b$, there is exponential growth (or decay) to one fixed point of $p^* = \frac{1}{2}$. (ii) for $a \neq b$, there is still one stable fixed point whose value can be seen as a function of a and b in figure 2. For $b > a$, the value of this fixed point is greater than $\frac{1}{2}$, for $a > b$, the value is less than $\frac{1}{2}$. While the overall qualitative behavior of the two models for this value of k, are quite similar, the value of $p^*(a, b)$ is not identical. This can be seen from figure 3 where we plot the difference (between p^*_{NB} and p^*_{CF}) in values of the fixed point obtained for each choice of a and b.

3. If one considers the limiting case where $k \longrightarrow \infty$, i.e., where children are given an infinite number of examples to mature, then the evolution of both the NB and the CF models has the same qualitative character. There are three cases to consider: (i) for $a = b$, we find that $s_{t+1} = s_t$, i.e., there is no change in the linguistic composition; (ii) for $a > b$, the population composition s_t tends to 0 (iii) for $a < b$, the population composition s_t tends to 1. Thus one of the languages *drives the other out* and the evolutionary change proceeds to completion. However the rates at which this happens differs under the differing assumptions of the NB and the CF models. This difference is explored in a later section as we consider the application of the models to the historical

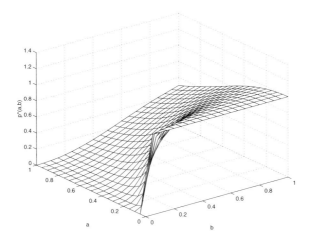

figure 7.2. The fixed point $p^*(a, b)$ for various choices of a and b for the CF model with $k = 2$.

evolution of English syntax. It is worthwhile to add that in real life, $a = b$ is unlikely to be exactly true – therefore language contact between populations is likely to drive one out of existence.

Additionally, the limiting case of large k is also more realistic since children typically get adequate primary linguistic data over their learning years in order to acquire a unique target grammar with high probability in homogeneous linguistic communities where a unique target grammar exists. In the treatment of this paper, we have always assumed that learners attain a single target grammar. Often, when two languages come in contact, learners typically attain both grammars in addition to a reasonable understanding of the social and statistical distribution of the two grammars in question. This can be handled within the framework we discuss here by requiring the learner to actually learn (estimate) a mixture factor ($\lambda \in [0, 1]$, say) that decides in what proportion the two grammars are to be used. A value of $\lambda = 0$ or $\lambda = 1$ would then imply that the learner had actually attained a unique grammar. One can then analyze a population of such learners to characterize their evolutionary consequences. We do not discuss such an analysis here.

4. We have not yet been able to characterize the evolutionary behavior of populations for arbitrary values of k.

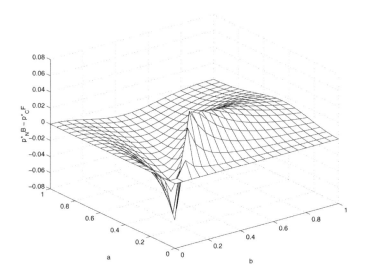

figure 7.3. The difference in the values of $p*(a,b)$ for the NB model and the CF model $p_{NB}^* - p_{CF}^*$ for various choices of a and with $k = 2$. A flat surface taking a value of zero at all points would indicate that the two were identical. This is not the case.

From the preceding discussion we see that the evolutionary characteristics of a population of linguistic agents can be precisely derived under certain simplifying assumptions. We show how the differing assumptions of the NB model and the CF model yield dynamical systems with different behaviors and how these models relate to each other.

7.3.2 A historical example

So far the development has been fairly abstract. To ground our discussion in a particular context, let us consider the phenomena surrounding the evolution of Old English to Modern English and its treatment within both kinds of model.

One of the significant changes in the syntax of English as it evolved from the 9th century to the 15th century is the change in word order. Consider, for example, the following passage taken from the Anglo Saxon Chronicles (878 A.D.) and reproduced in Trask (1996):

> *Her ... AElfred cyning ... gefeaht wid ealne here, and hine*
> Here ... Alfred king ... fought against whole army and it
> *geflymde, and him aefter rad od pet geweorc, and paer saet*
> put to flight and <u>it after rode</u> to the fortress and there camped

XIIII niht, and pa sealde se here him gislas and myccle
fourteen nights and then gave the army him hostages and great
adas, pet hi of his rice woldon, and him eac geheton
oaths that they from his kingdom would [go] and him also promised
pet heora cyng fulwihte onfon wolde, and hi paet gelaston ...
that their king baptism receive would and they that did

The original text is in italics and a word-for-word translation (gloss) is provided immediately below each line of the passage. Some phrases have been underlined to indicate the unusual word order prevalent in the writing of the times. Sampling the historical texts over the period from Old to Middle English, one finds that the early period shows three major alternations: (i) verb phrases (VP) may show Object–Verb (OV) or Verb–Object (VO) order; (ii) the inflectional head (I) may precede (I-medial) or follow (I-final) the verb phrase; (iii) there may or may not be movement of the inflected verb to head of CP (complementizer position in clauses) (following the terminology of Government and Binding theory; see Haegeman, 1991).

For the purposes of the discussion in this paper, we will collapse the OV/VO and I-final/I-medial distinctions into a single head-complement parameter in accordance with commonly made assumptions of the principles and parameters approach to grammatical theory. The movement of the finite verb to second position is related to the V2 parameter – modern German and Dutch are +V2 while modern English is -V2. Therefore, the two grammatical parameters at issue are:

1. The **head-complement** parameter: this denotes the order of constituents in the underlying phrase-structure grammar. Recall from X-bar theory that phrases XP have a **head** (X) and **complement**, e.g. the verb phrase *ate with a spoon* and the prepositional phrase *with a spoon* have as a head the verb *ate* and the preposition *with* respectively. Grammars of natural languages could be **head**-first or **head**-final. Thus X-bar phrase structure rules have the form (X and Y are arbitrary syntactic categories in the notation below):
   head-first: (i) $XP \longrightarrow X' \, YP$ (ii) $X' \longrightarrow X$
   head-final: (i) $XP \longrightarrow YP \, X'$ (ii) $X' \longrightarrow X$

2. The **V2** parameter: this denotes the tendency in some languages of the finite verb to move from its base position to the head of the complementizer (C of CP) by V to I to C raising. The specifier

of CP has to be filled resulting in the verb appearing to be in the second position in linear order of constituents. Grammars of natural languages can be **+V2** or **-V2**. Thus

+V2: Obligatory movement of V to I to C and specifier of CP filled.
-V2: V2 movement absent.

Modern English is exclusively head-first and -V2. Old English seems to be largely head-final and +V2. How did such remarkable changes in grammars occur? There are several competing accounts for these changes (see chapters by Kroch and Taylor, Lightfoot, and Warner in Van Kemenade (1997) for further details) but there seems to be some agreement that there were two competing grammars – a northern Scandinavian based +V2 grammar and a southern indigenous -V2 grammar. The first of these grammars was lost as the populations came into contact. Invoking learnability arguments as an explanation for such a change, Lightfoot (1997) writes: 'Children in Lincolnshire and Yorkshire, as they mingled with southerners, would have heard sentences whose initial elements were non-subjects followed by a finite verb less frequently than the required threshold; if we take seriously the statistics from the modern V2 languages and take the threshold to be about 30% of matrix clauses with initial non-subject in Spec of CP, then southern XP-Vf forms, where the Vf is not I-final and where the initial element is not a wh-item or negative, are too consistently subject-initial to trigger a V2 grammar.' [implying that the +V2 grammar was therefore lost over time]. These are the kinds of arguments that can be modeled precisely and tested for plausibility within the framework we have discussed here.

We will not attempt in this section to do justice to the various accounts of the historical change of English in a serious manner as the subject of such a discussion is well beyond the scope of the current paper. However, for illustrative purposes, we discuss below the evolutionary trajectories of populations with two competing grammar types that come into contact. The grammar types have been chosen to capture the parametric oppositions that played themselves out over the course of the historical evolution of English.

Case I: +V2/-V2 for head-first grammars

Imagine that two linguistic populations came together and the two languages in competition differed only by one parameter – the $V2$ parameter. Further assume that all other grammatical parameters of these two languages were identical to modern English. Children growing up in the mixed communities would hear sentences from both grammatical types. Suppose they set (learnt) all other grammatical parameters correctly and it was only in the V2 parameter that children differed from each other in how they set it – i.e., some acquired the +V2 grammar and some acquired the −V2 grammar. How would the population evolve? Would the +V2 grammar die out over time? What conditions must exist for this to happen?

These questions can be addressed within the framework that we have developed in this paper. To begin with, we need to identify the sets L_1 and L_2. Following Gibson and Wexler (1994), we derive the set of degree-0 sentences[5] (with no recursion) that are associated with the +V2 and −V2 grammars. These are listed below where S = subject, V = verb, O1 = direct object; O2 = indirect object; Aux = auxiliary; Adv = adverb.

g_1: *-V2; Head-first; Spec-first*

$L_1 = \{$ S V, S V O, S V O1 O2, S Aux V, S Aux V O, S Aux V O1 O2, Adv S V, Adv S V O, Adv S V O1 O2, Adv S Aux V, Adv S Aux V O, Adv S Aux V O1 O2 $\}$

The grammar underlying these sentences corresponds to that of modern English. For example, the sentence type (S Aux V O1 O2) maps to actual sentences like *John will eat beef in London.*

g_2: *+V2; Head-first; Spec-first*

$L_2 = \{$ S V, S V O, O V S, S V O1 O2, O1 V S O2, O2 V S O1, S Aux V, S Aux V O, O Aux S V, S Aux V O1 O2, O1 Aux S V O2, O2 Aux S V O1, Adv S V, Adv V S O, Adv V S O1 O2, Adv Aux S V, Adv Aux S V O, Adv Aux S V O1 O2$\}$

This grammar requires obligatory movement of the inflected verb to second position (actually to C and the specifier of CP must be filled).

---

[5] Of course, both L_1 and L_2 contain infinite sentences. Recall that the evolutionary properties of the population will depend upon the probability distributions P_1 and P_2 with which sentences are produced. In practice, due to cognitive limitations, speakers produce sentences with bounded recursion. Therefore P_1 and P_2 will have effective support on a finite set only. Furthermore, the learning algorithm of the child $\mathcal{A}$ operates on sentences and a common psycholinguistic premise is that children learn only on the basis of degree-0 sentences (Gibson and Wexler, 1994) and all sentences with recursion are ignored in the learning process. We have adopted this premise for the purposes of this paper. Therefore only degree-0 sentences are considered in this analysis.

Thus, an example of an actual sentence (not following English word order of course) corresponding to the sentence type Adv V S O1 O2 is *often saw we many students in London.*

Given these lists of sentences, one can obtain by taking an intersection of the two languages, the set of ambiguous types, i.e., sentence types that may have different but valid parses under the two assumptions. We see that:

$L_1 \cap L_2 = \{$ S V, S V O, S V O1 O2, S Aux V, S Aux V O, S Aux V O1 O2$\}$

We have considered several variants of both the CF and NB models for two languages in competition in the previous sections. Recall that for large k, the qualitative behavior of the two models is similar and L_1 would drive L_2 out from all initial conditions if and only if $a < b$. Here a is the probability measure on the set of ambiguous sentences produced by speakers of L_1 and b is the probability measure on the set of ambiguous sentences produced by speakers of L_2. This situation would lead to the loss of +V2 grammar types over time.

Under the unlikely but convenient assumption that P_1 and P_2 are uniform distributions on degree-0 sentences of their respective languages (L_1 and L_2), we see that

$$a = \frac{1}{2} > b = \frac{1}{3}$$

Therefore, the +V2 grammar, rather than being lost over time would tend to be gained over time. Shown in figure 7.3.2 are the evolutionary trajectories in the CF and NB models for various choices of a and b. Some further remarks are in order:

1. The directionality of change is predicted by the relationship of a with b. While, uniform distributions of degree-0 sentences predict that the V2 parameter would be gained rather than lost over time, the empirical validity of this assumption is doubtful. From corpora of child-directed sentences in synchronic linguistics and aided perhaps by some historical texts, one might try to empirically assess the distributions P_1 and P_2 by measuring how often each of the sentence types occur in spoken language and written texts. These empirical measures are being conducted at the present time and will be the subject of a later paper.

2. The dynamical systems that we have derived and applied to this par-

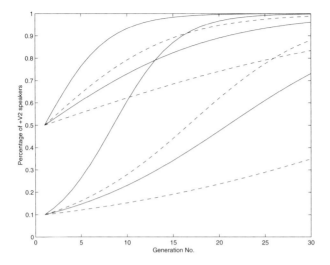

figure 7.4. Trajectories of V2 growth. Shown in the figure are the evolving trajectories of s_t = proportion of +V2 grammars in the population over successive generations. The solid curves denote the evolutionary trajectories under the NB model; the dotted curves denote the trajectories under the CF model. Two different initial population mixes are considered (a) 0.1 initial +V2 speakers (b) 0.5 initial +V2 speakers. For each initial mix and each model (CF and NB) the upper curve (faster change) corresponds to a choice of $a = 0.5$ and $b = 0.33$ and $a = 0.4$ and $b = 0.33$ respectively. Notice that the NB model has a faster rate of change than the CF model.

ticular case hold only for the case of memoryless learning algorithms like the TLA. For other kinds of algorithms and their evolutionary consequences, see Niyogi and Berwick (1997).

Case II: OV/VO for +V2 grammars

Here we consider a head-first grammar in competition with a head-final grammar where both are +V2 grammars that have the same settings for all other parameters – settings that are the same as that of modern English. Therefore, one of the two grammars (head-first setting) is identical to modern English except for the V2 parameter. It is also the same as g_2 of the previous section. The other grammar differs from modern English by two parameters.

As in the previous section, following Gibson and Wexler (1994), we can derive the degree-0 sentences associated with each of the two languages. We do this below:

g_1: *+V2; Head-first; Spec-first*

$L_1 = \{$ S V, S V O, O V S, S V O1 O2, O1 V S O2, O2 V S O1, S Aux V, S Aux V O, O Aux S V, S Aux V O1 O2, O1 Aux S V O2, O2 Aux S V O1, Adv S V, Adv V S O, Adv V S O1 O2, Adv Aux S V, Adv Aux S V O, Adv Aux S V O1 O2$\}$

This grammar is the same as g_2 of the previous section.

g_2: *+V2; Head-final; Spec-first*

$L_2 = \{$ S V, S V O, O V S, S V O2 O1, O1 V S O2, O2 V S O1, S Aux V, S Aux O V, O Aux S V, S Aux O2 O1 V, O1 Aux S O2 V, O2 Aux S O1 V, Adv V S, Adv V S O, Adv V S O2 O1, Adv Aux S V, Adv Aux S O V, Adv Aux S O2 O1 V$\}$

An example of a sentence type corresponding Adv V S O2 O1 is *often saw we in London many students*.

We can therefore straightforwardly obtain the set $L_1 \cap L_2$ as:

$L_1 \cap L_2 = \{$ S V, S V O, O V S, O1 V S O2, O2 V S O1, S Aux V, O Aux S V, Adv V S O, Adv Aux S V$\}$

Assuming P_1 and P_2 are uniform distributions on the degree-0 sentences of their respective languages, we see that

$$a = \frac{1}{2} = b$$

Therefore, under the assumptions of both the NB and the CF models there is no particular tendency for one grammar type to overwhelm the other. Language mixes would remain the same. If for some reason, a became slightly less than b, we see that the head-final language would be driven out and only the head-first language would remain. This would replicate the historically observed trajectory for the case of English. The rate is faster for the NB model than it is for the CF model.

A Final Note

Taking stock of our modeling results, we see that when a +V2 and a -V2 grammar come together (other parameters being the same) there is an inherent asymmetry with the -V2 grammar being more likely to lose out in the long run. On the other hand when a head-first and head-final grammar come together, there is no particular proclivity to change – the directionality could go either way. The reason for this

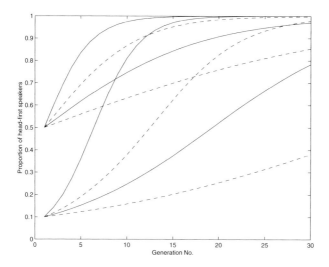

figure 7.5. Trajectories of head-first growth. Shown in the figure are the evolving trajectories of s_t = proportion of head-first grammars in the population over successive generations. The solid curves denote the evolutionary trajectories under the NB model; the dotted curves denote the trajectories under the CF model. Two different initial population mixes are considered (a) 0.1 initial head-first speakers (b) 0.5 initial head-first speakers. For each initial mix and each model (CF and NB) the upper curve (faster change) corresponds to a choice of $a = 0.4$ and $b = 0.6$ and $a = 0.47$ and $b = 0.53$ respectively. Notice that the NB model has a faster rate of change than the CF model.

asymmetry is seen to be in the asymmetry in the number of surface degree-0 sentences that are compatible with each of the grammars in question with +V2 grammars giving rise to a larger variety of surface sentences and therefore ambiguous sentences (those parsable with both +V2 and -V2 constraints) constitute a smaller proportion of the total sentence types of such grammars.

In conclusion, however, it is worthwhile reiterating again our motivation in working through this particular example of syntactic change in English. There are many competing accounts of how English changed over the years. Among other things, these accounts differ in: (i) the precise grammatical characterization of the two grammars in competition; (ii) the number of parametric changes that happened and their description in the context of a grammatical theory; (iii) the nature of the learning mechanism that children employ in learning grammars (e.g.

monolingual versus bilingual acquisition) and so on. However, these factors can be modeled and the plausibility of any particular account can then be verified. To give the reader a sense of how this might happen in a linguistically grounded manner, we worked through these examples – not to make a linguistic point but to demonstrate the applicability of this kind of computational thinking to historical problems.

7.4 A generalized NB model for neighborhood effects

The CF model described in this paper assumes that children can be divided into four classes depending upon their parental types. The children of each class then receive input sentences from a different distribution depending upon their parental type. The NB approach on the other hand assumes that all children in the population receive inputs from the same distribution that depends on the linguistic composition of the entire parental generation. In this section, we consider a generalization of both approaches with a particular view to modeling 'neighborhood' effects in linguistic communities.

The key idea here is that in multiple language communities speakers tend to cluster in linguistically homogeneous neighborhoods. Consequently children growing up in the community might receive data drawn from different distributions depending upon their spatial location within the community. Imagine as usual a two-language population consisting of speakers of L_1 or L_2. We now let the parental generation of speakers reside in adjacent neighborhoods. Children receive sentences drawn from different distributions depending upon their location in this neighborhood. At one end of the scale, children receive examples drawn only from L_1. At the other end of the scale, children receive examples drawn only from L_2. In the middle – at the boundary between the two neighborhoods as it were – are children who receive examples drawn from both sources.

Let us develop the notion further. Let children of type α be those who receive examples drawn according to a distribution $P = \alpha P_1 + (1-\alpha)P_2$. Here P_1 is the probability with which speakers of L_1 produce sentences, and P_2 is the probability with which speakers of L_2 produce sentences. The quantity $\alpha \in [0,1]$ is the proportion of L_1 speakers that an α-type child is effectively exposed to. Children will be of different α types depending upon their spatial location.

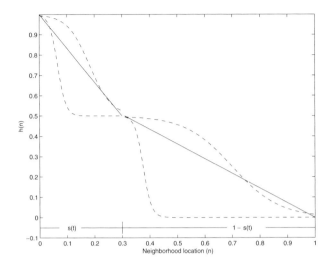

figure 7.6. Examples of h mappings between the location n and the α type of the children occupying that location. Here the value of s_t (proportion of L_1 speakers) is taken to be 0.3 for illustrative purposes. Therefore the interval $[0, 0.3]$ is the L_1 speaking neighborhood; the interval $[0.3, 1]$ is the L_2 speaking neighborhood. For any location n the value of $h(n)$ represents the proportion of L_1 speakers the child occupying that location is exposed to.

How do we characterize location? Let location be indicated by a one-dimensional real-valued variable n in the interval $[0, 1]$. Let speakers be uniformly distributed on this interval so that speakers of L_1 are close to $n = 0$ and speakers of L_2 are close to $n = 1$. Let the proportion of L_1 speakers in the population be s_t. Therefore, all children located in $[0, s_t]$ are in the L_1 speaking neighborhood and all children located in $[s_t, 1]$ are in the L_2 speaking neighborhood. Let us now define the mapping from neighborhood to α-type by $\alpha = h(n)$ where $h : [0, 1] \longrightarrow [0, 1]$. We leave undefined the exact form of h except noting that it should possess certain reasonable properties, e.g., $h(0)$ should be close to 1, $h(1)$ should be close to 0, $h(s_t)$ should be close to $\frac{1}{2}$ and h be monotonically decreasing.

Shown in figure 7.4 are some plausible mappings h that mediate the relation between location of the child in the neighborhood and its α-type. The x-axis denotes location. The y-axis denotes the α-type of a learner. We now have learners distributed uniformly in location and a mapping from location to α-type provided by h. One can therefore easily compute the probability distribution of children by α-type. This is just the probability distribution function for the random variable $\alpha = h(n)$ where n is uniform. Let this distribution be $P_h(\alpha)$ over $[0,1]$. Now a child (learner) of type α receives sentences drawn according to $P = \alpha P_1 + (1-\alpha)P_2$. According to our notation developed earlier, we see that it therefore has a probability $f(\alpha)$ of attaining the grammar of L_1. (This is provided by an analysis of the learning algorithm in the usual way, i.e., $f(\alpha) = g(\mathcal{A}, \alpha P_1 + (1-\alpha)P_2, k)$). Therefore, if children of type α are distributed in the community according to distribution $P_h(\alpha)$ and each child of type α attains L_1 with probability $f(\alpha)$, we see that in the next generation, the percentage of speakers of L_1 is provided by eq. 7.5:

$$s_{t+1} = \int_0^1 P_h(\alpha)f(\alpha)d\alpha \tag{7.5}$$

7.4.1 A specific choice of neighborhood mapping

For purposes of illustration, let us choose a specific form for h. In particular, let us assume that it is piecewise linear in the following way (eq. 7.6; the solid line of figure 7.4):

$$h(0) = 1; h(1) = 0; h(s_t) = \frac{1}{2}; h(n)$$
$$= 1 - \frac{1}{2s_t}n \text{ for } n < s_t; h(n) = \frac{1-n}{2(1-s_t)} \text{ for } n > s_t \tag{7.6}$$

Thus, clearly, h is parameterized by s_t. For such an h, it is possible to show that P_h is piecewise uniform – given by the following:

$$P_h(\alpha) = 2s_t \text{ if } \alpha > \frac{1}{2}; P_h(\alpha) = 2(1 - s_t) \text{ if } \alpha < \frac{1}{2}; P_h(\alpha)$$
$$= 0 \text{ if } \alpha \notin [0,1]. \tag{7.7}$$

In previous sections, we discussed the form of the NB update rule $f = g(\mathcal{A}, s_t P_1 + (1-s_t)P_2, k)$ for memoryless learning algorithms like the TLA. From eq. 7.4, we see that it is a polynomial of degree k. Putting this into eq. 7.5, we get the update rule with neighborhood effects to be

$$s_{t+1} = 2(1 - s_t)(\int_0^{1/2} f(\alpha)d\alpha) + 2s_t(\int_{1/2}^1 f(\alpha)d\alpha) \tag{7.8}$$

Since α is a dummy variable in the above integral, the effect of the neighborhood is to reduce the update rule to a linear one. This is in striking contrast to the original NB update rule (kth order polynomial) and the CF update rule (quadratic). It is worthwhile reflecting on a few aspects of such behavior.

1. The linear map implies an exponential growth (or decay) to a stable fixed point whose value is given by

$$s^* = \frac{2\int_0^{1/2} f(\alpha)d\alpha}{1 + 2(\int_0^{1/2} f(\alpha)d\alpha - \int_{1/2}^1 f(\alpha)d\alpha)}$$

2. Notice that $s^* = 0$ requires $\int_0^{1/2} f(\alpha)d\alpha = 0$. Correspondingly, $s^* = 1$ requires $\int_{1/2}^1 f(\alpha)d\alpha = \frac{1}{2}$. Neither is very likely – therefore, no language is likely to be driven out of existence completely. If one chooses the update rule f for large k ($= \infty$) one can compute these quantities exactly. It is then possible to show that the fixed point s^* is never 0 or 1. In contrast, both the NB and CF models result in one language becoming extinct if $a \neq b$.

Needless to say, the particular form of the update rule obtained with such neighborhood effects actually depends upon the functional mapping h. In general, however, this approach allows us to compute the evolutionary trajectories of populations where children have arbitrary α-types. It is worthwhile recalling the original CF and NB models of the previous sections in this light. The CF models are derivable from this perspective with a particular choice of $P_h(\alpha)$ which happens to be a probability mass function with $P_h(\alpha = 0) = s_t^2; P_h(\alpha = \frac{1}{2}) = 2s_t(1 - s_t); P_h(\alpha = 1) = (1 - s_t)^2$. The NB model of previous sections is equivalent to choosing $P_h(\alpha)$ to be a delta function, i.e., $P_h(\alpha) = \delta(\alpha - s_t)$.

Remark It is important to recognize two aspects of the neighborhood model introduced here. First, the function h is not a fixed function but depends upon the proportion s_t of the L_1 speakers at any time. Therefore, h changes from generation to generation (as s_t evolves). Second, the population of mature adults is *always* organized into two linguistically homogeneous neighborhoods in *every* generation. Of course, children in a particular neighborhood might acquire different languages. It is implicitly assumed that on maturation, the children (now adults) re-organize themselves into homogeneous neighborhoods. It is this re-organization into homogeneous neighborhoods that prevents the elimination of any one language from the system.

Another (more complete) way to characterize neighbourhood effects is to treat the proportion of L_1 speakers in the tth generation as a function that varies continuously with distance (n) in the neighbourhood. It is this function that evolves from generation to generation. Without additional simplifying assumptions, this treatment requires techniques well beyond the scope of this paper and will be the subject of future work.

7.5 Conclusions

In this paper, we have discussed the basic model of Cavalli-Sforza and Feldman (1981) for cultural transmission and change. We have shown how this provides us with a framework in which to think about problems of language evolution and change. Language acquisition serves as the mechanism of transmission of language from parents to children. By suitably averaging over a population we are then able to derive the population dynamics, i.e., the evolutionary trajectories of the linguistic composition of the population as a whole from generation to generation.

We have shown how the approach of Cavalli-Sforza and Feldman (1981) relates to that of Niyogi and Berwick (1995, 1997) and how to go back and forth between the two models. For the particular case of two languages in competition, we have derived several particular dynamical systems under varying assumptions. We have also considered the generalization of such models to explicitly take into account the effect of spatial clustering of speakers into linguistic neighborhoods and have investigated the consequences of such neighborhood effects.

The case of two languages in competition is of some significance since historical cases of language change and evolution are often traceable to a point in time when speakers of two language types came into contact with each other. As a particular case of this, we considered the evolution of English syntax from Old to Middle to Modern English. While the various linguistic explanations for such a change were not considered in a serious fashion, we demonstrated in this paper, how one might apply the computational framework developed here to test the plausibility of various accounts. In general, the possibility of pursuing such a strategy in a serious manner for the study of language evolution and change remains our main motivation for the future.

References

Cavalli-Sforza, L. and M. W. Feldman (1981). *Cultural Transmission and Change: A Quantitative Approach*. Princeton University Press, Princeton, NJ.

Gibson, E. and K. Wexler (1994). Triggers. *Linguistic Inquiry*, 25(3), 407–454.

Haegeman, L. (1991). *Introduction to Government and Binding Theory*. Blackwell, Oxford.

Kemenade, A. van and N. Vincent (1997). *Parameters of Morphosyntactic Change*. Cambridge University Press, Cambridge.

Kroch, A. W. and A. Taylor (1997). Verb Movement in Old and Middle English: Dialect Variation and Language Contact. In Kemenade, A. van and N. Vincent (1997).

Lightfoot, D. (1997). Shifting Triggers and Diachronic Reanalyses. In Kemenade, A. van and N. Vincent (1997).

Niyogi, P. (1997). *The Informational Complexity of Learning: Perspectives on Neural Networks and Generative Grammar*. Kluwer Academic Press, Boston.

Niyogi, P. and R. C. Berwick (1995). The Logical Problem of Language Change. MIT AI Memo No. 1516.

Niyogi, P. and R. C. Berwick (1996). A Language Learning Model for Finite Parameter Spaces. *Cognition*, 61(1), 161–193.

Niyogi, P. and R. C. Berwick (1997). Evolutionary Consequences of Language Learning. *Linguistics and Philosophy*, 20, 697–719.

Niyogi, P. and R. C. Berwick (1998). The Logical Problem of Language Change: A Case study of European Portuguese. *Syntax: A Journal of Theoretical, Experimental, and Interdisciplinary Research*, 1.

Osherson, D., M. Stob and S. Weinstein (1986). *Systems that Learn*, MIT Press, Cambridge, MA.

Trask, R. L. (1996). *Historical Linguistics*. Arnold, London.

Warner, A. (1997). The Structure of Parametric Change and V Movement in the History of English. In Kemenade, A. van and N. Vincent (1997).

Wexler, K. and P. Culicover (1980). *Formal Principles of Language Acquisition*. MIT Press, Cambridge, MA.

Appendix: language learning

The problem of language learning ("logical problem of language acquisition") is typically formulated as a search by a learning algorithm for a grammar that is close to the one that generates the sentences the learner is exposed to. To make matters concrete, let us define the following objects that play an important role in the theory of language learning:

1. $\mathcal{G}$: *Target Class* The target class consists of a class of grammars $g \in \mathcal{G}$. Each grammar gives rise to a corresponding language $L \in \mathcal{L}$ where all languages are subsets of Σ^* in the usual way. A unique target grammar $g_t \in \mathcal{G}$ is the grammar to which the learner is exposed via examples and which the leaner must "learn".

2. $\mathcal{S}$: *Examples* Examples are sentences $s \in L_t$ where L_t is the target language. The learner is provided with a stream of examples drawn in some manner. For our purposes here we will assume that examples are drawn in i.i.d. fashion according to a distribution P on the sentences of the target language L_t. In other words, P is a distribution on Σ^* that has support on L_t – it puts zero measure on all $s \notin L_t$ and non-zero measure on all $s \in L_t$.

3. $\mathcal{H}$: *Hypotheses Class* The hypothesis class consists of a class of grammars that the learning algorithm uses in order to approximate elements of the target class. For our purposes, we will assume that $\mathcal{H} = \mathcal{G}$.

4. $\mathcal{A}$: *Learning Algorithm* The learning algorithm is an effective procedure that maps sets of examples into elements of $\mathcal{H}$, i.e., it develops hypotheses on the basis of examples. Formally, let $\mathcal{D}_k$ be the set of all subsets of Σ^* of cardinality k. Each subset of Σ^* of cardinality k is a candidate dataset consisting of k example sentences that a learner might receive. Clearly $\mathcal{D}_k$ is the set of all candidate datasets of size k. Then $\mathcal{A}$ is a computable mapping from the set $\cup_{k=1}^{\infty} \mathcal{D}_k$ to $\mathcal{H}$.

Given this setup, the central question of learnability theory is whether or not the hypothesis of the learning algorithm converges to the target grammar as the number of examples k goes to infinity. Specifically, let $h_k \in \mathcal{H}$ be the grammar that the learner hypothesizes after exposure to k examples. Since the examples are randomly drawn and the learning algorithm itself might be randomized, it is clear that h_k is a random variable. One can then define the probability that the learner's hypothesis h_k is the same as the target grammar. Let us call this p_k as below:

$$p_k = P(h_k = g_t)$$

The target grammar g_t is said to be **learnable** if $\lim_{k \to \infty} p_k = 1$ for any distribution P with which examples are drawn. This simply implies that "in the limit" as the number of examples tends to infinity, the learner's hypothesis will be the same as the target grammar, i.e., the learner will converge to the target. This notion of convergence in the limit was first introduced by Gold (1967) in a non-probabilisitic framework which required that the learner converge to the target on all sequences of examples that included all sentences of the target. The treatment here is probabilistic in nature. For more information on this see Osherson, Stob, Weinstein (1986); Wexler and Culicover (1980); Niyogi (1997). If every grammar $g \in \mathcal{G}$ is learnable, then the **class** of grammars

$(\mathcal{G})$ is said to be learnable.

In a certain sense, linguistic theory attempts to describe and formulate classes of grammars $\mathcal{G}$ that contain the grammars of the natural languages of the world. Empirically, it is observed and believed that all such naturally occuring languages are learnable. Therefore, any class $\mathcal{G}$ that is proposed must be learnable. Learning theory investigates the questions that are associated with the learnability of classes of grammars. It is important to recognize that the framework developed for learning theory is actually very broad and therefore a wide variety of grammatical theories and learning algorithms can be accommodated within the same framework of analysis.

In the analysis of the TLA developed in Niyogi and Berwick (1996), the class $\mathcal{H} = \mathcal{G}$ consists of a finite number of grammars. The learning algorithm can be modeled as a Markov chain with as many states as there are grammars in $\mathcal{H}$. Transition probabilities from state to state depend upon the probability distribution P with which sentences are drawn and set differences between the different languages in the family $\mathcal{L}$ (equivalently $\mathcal{G}$). Probabilities like p_k can then be computed as a function of the transition probability matrix and this is done in Niyogi and Berwick (1996).

8

The learning guided evolution of natural language

William J. Turkel
MIT Brain and Cognitive Sciences

8.1 Introduction

Human natural language is a complex adaptive system, and the usual account of adaptive complexity in the biological world is natural selection (Pinker and Bloom, 1990). There have been a number of arguments that the human capacity for natural language could not have evolved via natural selection. In this paper I focus on two such arguments. The first is the argument that language could not exist in any intermediate forms, and thus could not be the product of a stepwise selective process. The second is that language is arbitrary, and that selection cannot explain its *specific* nature (Piatelli-Palmarini, 1989).

In this paper, I argue that even if one accepts the claim that language cannot exist in intermediate forms, it is still possible that it could have evolved via natural selection. I make two crucial assumptions. The first is that humans have some degree of plasticity, and are capable of learning. The model of learning that I invoke is impoverished, and is not meant to reflect actual human capacities. The second assumption is that successful communication confers a reproductive advantage on its possessors. In other words, language is adaptive as long as it is shared. This has become a fairly common assumption in the computational modeling of language evolution; an early example is provided by Hurford (1989). I do not consider arbitrariness to be any argument against adaptation (cf. Ridley, 1990), although I do not dispute the claim that many aspects of language are arbitrary.

8.2 Evolution as hillclimbing

Pinker and Bloom (1990) have argued that natural language fits into a continuum of viable communicative systems. This continuum (taken in concert with the assumption that an efficient communication system provides a reproductive advantage to organisms that have one) allows a species to gradually increase in communicative ability over time. If we think of the fitness function as a surface, then this surface has hills which increase gradually, and which can be climbed by any process which can look at a local region of the surface and see which way is up. Genetic algorithms (computer programs which model evolution) generally have no problem finding maxima of such surfaces.[1] By implication, natural selection could have given rise to natural language if these assumptions are correct.

If we assume that natural language could not exist in any intermediate form, we get a very different fitness surface. Since there is only one system which can confer any advantage on its possessor, the fitness function consists of a spike of high fitness in a uniformly bad landscape. Finding the maxima of such functions is extremely difficult for genetic algorithms (Hinton and Nowlan, 1987). Intuitively, the only way to find the fitness spike would be by trial-and-error. Considering the large space of possibilities, this would suggest that language could not have evolved in the time available.[2] One would seem to be led to the conclusion that language is not a product of selection, but rather *preadaptation* or *exaptation*: that the capacity for language evolved to serve some other function, and was later co-opted for language. Simulations of learning guided evolution suggest that this conclusion may be premature. Contrary to

---

[1] For an overview of genetic algorithms, see the review article by Forrest (1993). The textbooks by Goldberg (1989) and Mitchell (1996) are good, as is Holland's (1992) original treatment. For what follows it is helpful to know at least the following. Genetic algorithms operate over a population of *genotypes*, where each genotype is a string of genes. The index of a particular gene is called its *locus*. Different values of a single gene are called *alleles*. Genotypes are randomly 'mated' via a mechanism called *one-point crossover*. This results in 'offspring' which are similar (but not identical) to the 'parents'. Reproductive opportunities are allocated to genotypes based on their *fitness*. The fitness is a measure of how good a particular genotype is at solving an adaptive problem posed by the environment. Typically phenotypic variation is ignored, and individuals are equated with genotypes.

[2] Suppose that the only working human language system can be described by 30 binary parameters. Then that system is a spike of fitness in a landscape of 1073741823 non-working systems.

intuition, the possibility of individual learning alters evolutionary search in non-obvious ways.

8.3 Learning guided evolution

Before I describe learning guided evolution, I should stress that it is not Lamarckian in any way. Recall that Lamarckian inheritance allows characteristics acquired by the organism in its lifetime to be incorporated into the genome and passed to offspring. Despite the attractiveness of the idea, it has been generally rejected by biologists (see the discussion in papers by Morgan (1896) and Maynard Smith (1987)). Hinton & Nowlan (1987) put the problem as follows:

> To know how to change the genotype in order to generate the acquired characteristics of the phenotype it is necessary to invert the forward function that maps from genotypes, via the processes of development and learning, to adapted phenotypes. This is generally a very complicated, non-linear, stochastic function and so it is very hard to *compute* how to change the genes to achieve desired changes in the phenotypes even when these desired changes are known
>
> *p. 500*

Besides being biologically unrealistic, there are two other reasons that we might wish to avoid Lamarckianism. Elitzur (1994) has argued that it is inconsistent with the Second Law of Thermodynamics, and thus is physically impossible. Gruau & Whitley (1993) have also argued that it would undermine the ability of the genetic algorithm to search via hyperplane sampling. Briefly, hyperplane sampling allows the genetic algorithm to implicitly process more information than is explicitly represented in the population of individuals. It is one of the explanations for the efficiency of genetic algorithms (Goldberg, 1989; Holland, 1992).

The *Baldwin effect* (after the 1896 paper by J. Mark Baldwin) is an interaction between learning and evolution which works as follows (Morgan, 1896). Each organism inherits a certain amount of plasticity in addition to fixed structure. In cases where the environment is uniform and predictable, fixed structure will tend to be advantageous, and in cases where the environment is variable, plasticity will be advantageous. Under constant conditions, the organism will be in harmony with its environment, and variations will be kept within narrow limits. When the environment changes, however, those organisms whose innate plasticity is capable of dealing with the change will survive. At this point, variation in fixed structure in the direction of the changed environment will not be suppressed. Variation in the opposite direction will tend to be selected against. Over time, there is a tendency for the learned behavior to be incorporated into the genome as fixed structure. At the least, learning will affect the direction of evolution. In its strongest form, the claim is that learned behavior can become genetically determined (Grau and Whitley, 1993). Note that we are not concerned here with the likelihood of this scenario, merely with its possibility. Simpson (1953), for example, finds the Baldwin effect fully plausible (in that each of the individual steps is known to occur separately) but he doubts that it is frequent or important in biological evolution. Others, such as Pinker (1994), Briscoe (2000), and Deacon (1997), each argue that the Baldwin effect must have played a role in the evolution of human language, although they differ on the specifics.

Hinton & Nowlan [19] simulated the Baldwin effect and showed that the adaptations learned during the lifetime of an organism guide the course of evolution by altering the shape of the search space.

The problem studied by Hinton and Nowlan was as follows. Imagine that there is an organism with a neural net that has twenty potential connections. The effect of this net is such that it will only increase the fitness of the organism when it is wired exactly the right way. Each connection is specified by a single gene with three alleles: $\boxed{0}$, $\boxed{1}$, and $\boxed{?}$. The $\boxed{1}$ allele says that a connection is present, the $\boxed{0}$ that it is absent, and the $\boxed{?}$ that the organism should attempt to learn that connection. (So the fitness surface for this problem consists of one spike of fitness in a landscape of $2^{20} - 1$ uniformly bad wirings.) Initially, all organisms have ten genes which code for fixed connections (five each of $\boxed{0}$ and $\boxed{1}$) and ten genes which allow connections to be learned. Each of the organisms is given a number of trials to attempt to learn the proper wiring of the net. If the organism succeeds in learning the correct wiring, then their fitness is increased (by an amount proportional to how quickly they learned.) Since the evolution of the organisms is simulated with a genetic algorithm, the fitness for each organism is used as a measure of how likely that organism is to contribute genetic material to the next generation.

Note that it is impossible for an organism to learn the correct wiring if they have the wrong connections specified as $\boxed{0}$ or $\boxed{1}$ in their genome. Over time, the offspring of the good learners will come to dominate the population. Hinton and Nowlan discovered two things: first, that learning organisms evolve much faster than their non-learning counterparts can, and second, that learning alters the search space by constructing a large zone of increased fitness around the fitness spike.

8.4 The 'no external reality' thesis

A number of aspects of natural language are arbitrary. Piatelli-Palmarini (1989) has argued that this arbitrariness is evidence against adaptation. "Adaptationism cannot even begin to explain why the natural languages that we can acquire and use possess these central features [e.g., the Projection Principle and the Principle of Full Interpretation] and not very different ones." (p. 24) Elsewhere he speaks of the impossibility of deducing the specific facts of language from adaptive criteria.

I feel that this argument is somewhat misguided. Jacob (1977) argues that there are two paramount factors in evolutionary processes: constraints operating at each level and historical circumstances. As the complexity of the object increases, history plays a more and more important role. Gould & Lewontin (1979) seem to agree. "When 'multiple adaptive peaks' are occupied, we usually have no basis for asserting that one solution is better than another. The solution followed in any spot is a result of history; the first steps went in one direction, though others would have led to adequate prosperity as well." (p. 593) To some extent, all adaptations may be more or less arbitrary, in the sense that they are due to chance and historical accident, as well as to selection (Ridley, 1990).

As long as the arbitrariness is shared, it can be adaptive. Janet Fodor (1989) calls this the *no external reality* thesis: "Innate beliefs about language are 'true' and useful if and only if they are identical to those of other members of the species." Elsewhere, this has been called the requirement for *parity* (Liberman and Mattingly, 1989). Fodor notes that this has implications for language acquisition. The standard of correctness will be set by other members of the community. All that the child who is learning the language has to do is to make the same choices that others did before, regardless of what they were. If the way that the learner chooses is uniform across individuals and genetically determined, then the learner will choose as the others did.

The origin of shared arbitrary behavior poses a bit of a problem, because it would seem to require mutation to produce compatible changes in neighboring individuals at roughly the same time. When the individuals can learn to coordinate behavior, however, the Baldwin effect can greatly accelerate the nativization of a shared arbitrary system of coordination (Briscoe, 2000).

8.5 A simulation

I simulated the evolution of a Principles-and-Parameters (P&P) system (Chomsky, 1981) with a variant of Hinton and Nowlan's model. A P&P system consists of a set of innate principles and a finite set of finitely valued parameters. A setting of the parameters instantiates a natural language grammar. In our case, we consider two kinds of parameter settings. *Fixed* parameter settings have the value set as part of the individual's genetic inheritance. The other value for a fixed parameter can never be learned. I will denote fixed parameters with $\boxed{0}$ and $\boxed{1}$. On the other hand, *plastic* parameter settings are not set genetically, but left for the individual to vary during the course of acquisition. The parameters discussed in the P&P literature are all plastic in our sense. I will denote plastic parameters with $\boxed{?}$.

I assumed that the relevant aspects of human language can be captured with a set of binary parameters. Each parameter is coded for by a single allele with one of the three values $\boxed{0}$, $\boxed{1}$, $\boxed{?}$. To be concrete about the interpretation of the relation between the genotype (the string of genes) and the phenotype (a parser for a P&P grammar), I will follow Robin Clark's (1992) suggestion. On this reading, there is a fixed central algorithm which corresponds to the principles of universal grammar. Within the algorithm are a number of flags indicating points at which code must be inserted for the algorithm to function. Depending on the setting of each parameter, different chunks of code are substituted into the algorithm at flag points. The fixed alleles $\boxed{0}$ and $\boxed{1}$ correspond to hardwired parameter settings. If the genotype has one of these alleles for a particular parameter, then the parser has the corresponding code fragments permanently inserted. Any individual who possesses that genotype will never be able to learn the other setting for that parameter. In contrast, a $\boxed{?}$ allele at a given locus will mean that different code fragments can be inserted at that point, at run time as it were. Consequently, individuals who have the $\boxed{?}$ allele for a parameter can learn different settings of that parameter based upon their (primary linguistic) environment. In other words, a $\boxed{?}$ allele represents a true parameter.

Table 8.1. *Simulation conditions.*

Condition	Ratio of $\boxed{0}$: $\boxed{1}$: $\boxed{?}$
No plasticity	6:6:0
Equal ratio	4:4:4
Original	3:3:6
High plasticity	2:2:8

Table 8.2. *Fitness algorithm.*

1. Start with the genotype being evaluated.
2. Choose another genotype from the population at random.
3. If the two genotypes are entirely fixed (i.e., consist entirely of $\boxed{0}$'s and $\boxed{1}$'s) and identical, then return a fitness of 2.
4. If the two genotypes match (see below), then attempt to establish communication between their owners. The fitness of the first genotype is proportional to how quickly the two genotypes learn to communicate. This fitness will be over 2.
5. Otherwise return a fitness of 1.

The alleles can be in different ratios. I ran four conditions, each with a different ratio of alleles shared by every member of the initial population, as shown in table 8.1. To be clear, suppose we are testing the high plasticity ratio of alleles (*2:2:8*). Each initial chromosome will consist of two copies of the allele $\boxed{0}$, two copies of $\boxed{1}$, and eight copies of $\boxed{?}$, concatenated and shuffled so that different alleles occur at different loci for different individuals. The ratios were chosen so that the chromosome length is always twelve, regardless of condition. The population size was 200. Depending on the condition, initial populations were more or less likely to have a small number of identical members. Experiments with initial populations that had no identical members provided qualitatively similar results.

Each genotype in the population is assigned a fitness according to the algorithm given in table 8.2.

Two genotypes are compared on a locus-by-locus basis. They are said to *match* if every comparison is true. A truth table for the matching operator is shown in table 8.3.

When two genotypes match, it is possible in principle for the possessors of those genotypes to learn to communicate. The attempt to

Table 8.3. *Truth table*
for matching operator.

Match	0	1	?
0	T	F	T
1	F	T	T
?	T	T	T

Table 8.4. *Attempt to establish communication.*

1. Temporarily rewrite each ? allele in both genotypes with a 0 or 1 chosen randomly. This represents one learning trial.
2. If the two rewritten genotypes are identical, then communication has been established. Return the fitness.
3. Otherwise, decrement the number of remaining learning trials and attempt to establish communication again.
4. If there are no more learning trials, stop trying to establish communication.

establish communication proceeds as shown in table 8.4. There are a maximum of ten learning trials per pair of genotypes attempting to communicate. The fitness is scaled so that it drops linearly with each unsuccessful trial, ranging in value from 12 (for an immediately successful attempt) to 2 (for success on the last trial). If communication is not established, the genotype being evaluated will get a fitness of 1.

Once a fitness has been calculated for each member of the population, reproductive opportunities are allocated for each, and the genotypes are recombined via one-point crossover. The selection method was *roulette-wheel*[3], with generational replacement. The probability of crossover was 0.2. The whole process was iterated for 240 generations. No mutation was used.

Some comments on the algorithm are in order.

First, the original genotype is used for recombination, not the temporarily rewritten genotype which is used in the attempt to establish

---

[3] Imagine that the fitness of each individual is mapped onto a piechart. If we use that piechart as roulette wheel, and spin it to select individuals, those with the highest fitness will be selected most often.

communication. If the rewritten genotype were used, the program would be Lamarckian.

Second, the algorithm returns a fitness of 2 if the two genotypes are identical. In this case, no attempt is made to establish communication, because the possessors of the genotype can communicate perfectly in principle. If we were to allow the individuals to attempt to communicate, then the best possible fitness would be 12, and the worst, 2. By automatically returning 2, we are scaling the fitness to the bottom of the range. I decided on the relatively low fitness because I did not want the population to converge to identical genotypes. Setting aside the Baldwin effect, the usual explanation for learning is that it allows the organism to deal with unexpected aspects of the environment. So I would like to provide some selective advantage for learning, over and above the advantage for communication. In general, the number of communication attempts between identical genotypes remained relatively low while there was a reasonable amount of variation in the population.

Third, the random assignment of $\boxed{0}$ and $\boxed{1}$ to parameters during learning was adopted for simplicity and for compatibility with the Hinton and Nowlan simulation. Anyone who is familiar with the language acquisition literature will recognize that this is a grossly inadequate model. In the 1994 manuscript, I suggested that the learning could instead be based on a parameter-setting model such as that described in Gibson and Wexler (1994) or Niyogi and Berwick (1996). Kirby and Hurford (1997) subsequently implemented such a system.

Finally, my learning procedure and representation entail that the genotypic and phenotypic spaces are identical. This is an important assumption, because Mayley (1996) has shown that for an acquired characteristic to become genetically specified, the two spaces must exhibit what he calls *neighborhood correlation*. This means that a small distance between two phenotypes implies a correspondingly small distance between the genotypes of the same two individuals. Obviously, in my case, there is perfect neighborhood correlation.

The original simulation was coded from scratch in Scheme. The rewritten version was implemented in Mathematica, and based on the simple genetic algorithm described by Freeman (1993). Results for both simulations with a variety of settings were qualitatively similar.

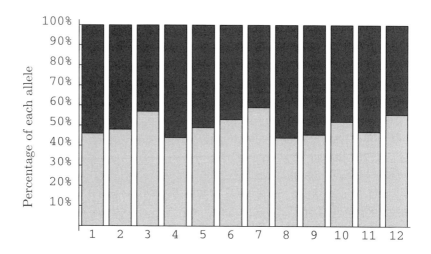

figure 8.1. No plasticity condition, Generation 1

8.6 Results

In general, there are two ways to think about the Baldwin effect. One is that learning makes possible some task that is the evolutionary equivalent of searching for a needle in a haystack: a spike of high fitness in an otherwise uniformly level landscape. This aspect is nicely illustrated in the original work of Hinton and Nowlan (1987). A second way of thinking about the Baldwin effect is that learning can accelerate the evolutionary process. The simulations show both kinds of effect.

If we consider graphs of allele by locus for the initial populations, we expect to see approximately the same ratio of alleles at each locus as there are in each individual. (This follows from the way the initial populations are constructed.) Graphs of allele by locus are shown in figures 8.1 through 8.4. for the initial population of each condition. In the figures, grey denotes the percentage of allele $\boxed{0}$ at a particular locus, black denotes the percentage of $\boxed{1}$, and white denotes the percentage of $\boxed{?}$.

By generation 100, however, the three conditions which involve plasticity have each converged to a single genotype, whereas there are still a number of distinct genotypes in the *no plasticity* condition (71 in the run shown). Figures 8.5 through 8.8 show the state of the simulation conditions at generation 100.

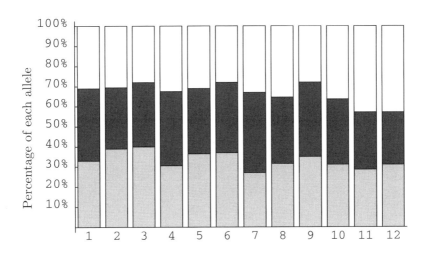

figure 8.2. Equal ratio condition, Generation 1

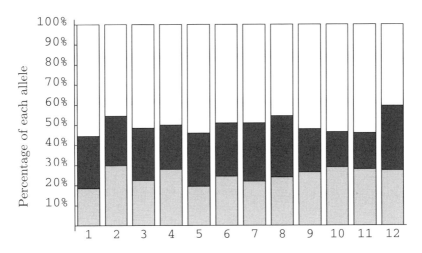

figure 8.3. Original condition, Generation 1

In these simulations, the speed with which the population converged to a single genotype varied inversely with the degree of plasticity. This can be seen in plots of the average value for the *match* operation during the run, shown in figures 8.9 through 8.12. When there is no plasticity, the number of distinct genotypes in the population falls very gradually,

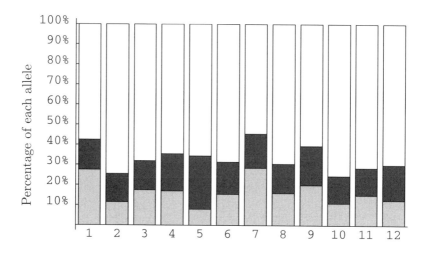

figure 8.4. High plasticity condition, Generation 1

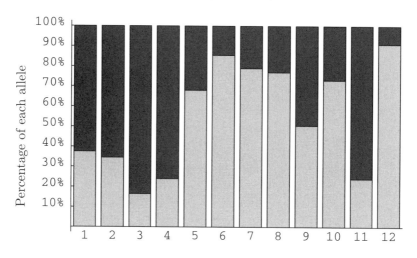

figure 8.5. No plasticity condition, Generation 100

giving rise to a correspondingly slow increase in the match value. At
about 160 generations, there is so little variation in the population,
that individuals begin to find identical others to communicate with.
These have an advantage in fitness, and the population rapidly converges
to a single genotype. In runs where the length of the chromosome is

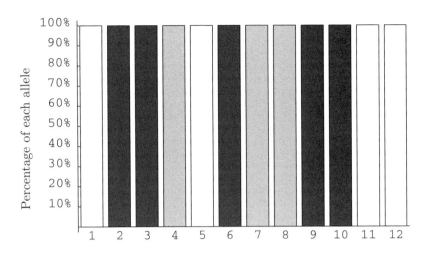

figure 8.6. Equal ratio condition, Generation 100

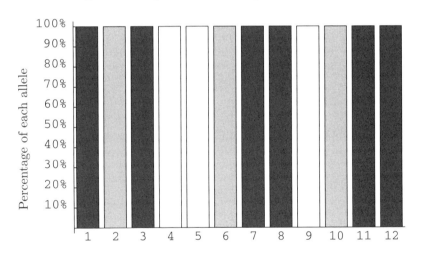

figure 8.7. Original condition, Generation 100

longer (24 or 48, for example), the search space is much larger and the population does not converge to a single genotype in 200 generations, or even many more.

The introduction of plasticity, in the other conditions, results in very different temporal profiles. The plasticity allows individuals to learn to

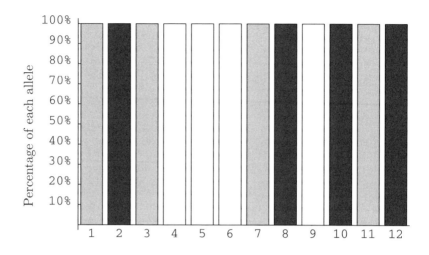

figure 8.8. High plasticity condition, Generation 100

communicate, providing a fitness advantage. At each locus, one or the other of the fixed alleles is rapidly eliminated. This gives rise to an intermediate state, where each locus is some ratio of $\boxed{0}:\boxed{?}$ or $\boxed{1}:\boxed{?}$ for each member of the population. The intermediate state is unstable, however, and each of the loci will eventually resolve to a single allele. The length of time that it takes for the population to converge to a single genotype depends on the degree of overall plasticity. In the runs shown in the figures, the *equal ratio* condition converged by generation 30, the *original* condition by generation 60, and the *high plasticity* condition by generation 80. Since plasticity allows individuals to communicate with those that are fixed, there is less pressure to eliminate plastic alleles.

Under our interpretation, the convergence of a locus to $\boxed{0}$ or $\boxed{1}$ represents the evolution of a *principle* of grammar, whereas the convergence to $\boxed{?}$ represents the evolution of a true parameter. Note that in each case, there are a number of parameters. Pinker & Bloom (1990) suggest metaphorically that "Such learning devices may have been the sections of the ladder that evolution had no need to kick away." Using a diffusion equation approach, Harvey (1993) shows that the selection pressure to remove the last $\boxed{?}$ alleles is not enough to overcome the forces of genetic drift. (See also the text by Maynard Smith, 1998).

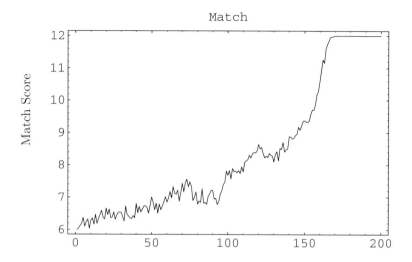

figure 8.9. No plasticity condition, Average match

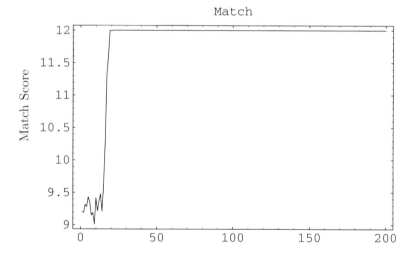

figure 8.10. Equal ratio condition, Average match

8.7 Discussion

The simulation demonstrates a number of interesting effects. First, it suggests that it is possible for a shared parameterized system to arise via natural selection even if intermediate forms confer no adaptive ad-

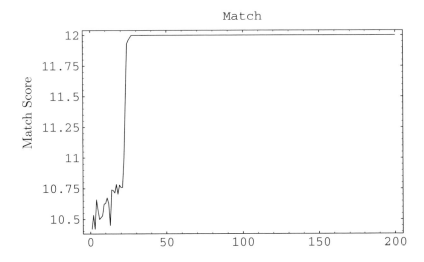

figure 8.11. Original condition, Average match

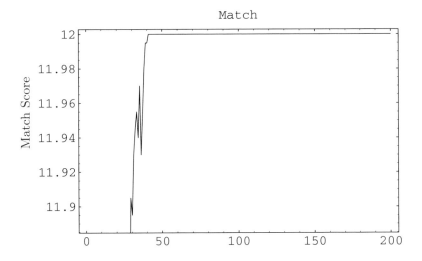

figure 8.12. High plasticity condition, Average match

vantage. In the presence of learning, the parameterized system comes into being quite quickly, and remains stable for indefinitely long periods.

Which aspects of the system become fixed, and which remain plastic, depends here on chance. In Kirby and Hurford's (1997) work it was shown that functional pressure during linguistic selection on a cultural/historical timescale can shift the proportion of alleles found at a particular locus. This result obtained only when the functionality could be attributed to a single parameter. When the functionality was the result of parameter interdependence, there was no way for the Baldwin effect to nativize it, because there was no way to represent complexes of parameters. This is an important limitation, because a fair amount of the P& P learnability literature focuses on the fact that parameters occasionally seem to be interconnected. (See, for example, Williams (1987) on 'paralyzing' interdependence, Clark (1994) on 'parameter coalitions', and Dresher & Kaye (1990) for an example in phonology.)

Chomsky (1986:25 and elsewhere) has argued that the initial state of the language faculty is common to the human species to a very close first approximation. The long-run tendency of the simulations to converge to a single genotype supports this idea. The simulations suggest an intriguing alternative phenomenon, however. Depending on the degree of plasticity and the evolutionary stage of the population, some principles may be parameters for some individuals. This happens when a given locus has been resolved toward one of the fixed alleles or the other. (Eventually, that locus will either become a principle or a parameter.) To my knowledge, there is no discussion of such a possibility in the parameter-setting literature.

Ackley & Littman (1994) have argued that the Baldwin effect depends on the stability of both a problem and its solution over evolutionary time. If it is possible for the solution to change, then being genetically fixed for a particular solution can be a liability. If, on the other hand, the problem were to disappear, any added fitness for possessing a solution would also disappear. They write, "The effect can only persist through extended evolutionary time if, somehow, improvements can continually be added to the solution without ever *really* solving the problem." (p. 504) Natural language seems to be such a case. Genetic acquisition of a specific solution would lead to a nonadaptive inflexibility. The adaptive problem which communication solves will not simply vanish. The only remaining alternative is to be flexible enough to track a moving target, but constrained enough to acquire the system correctly and quickly.

Any model is necessarily different from the phenomena modeled, and necessarily incomplete. There are a number of aspects of the simulations presented here which may need to be expanded or rethought.

First, there is a sense in which intermediate forms in the model may have a higher fitness. Genotypes that partially match some intermediate form and also partially match the final state of the population will have a relatively high fitness at both times. Whether or not such an individual can be thought of as an 'intermediate form' seems to be open to question. Second, if a pair of individuals that are fixed and identical are given a high fitness, then the population will quickly converge to fixed, identical individuals. In this case, the adaptive problem does go away. By choosing the fitness function that I did, I "put a hole at the top of the mountain" of the fitness surface.[4] This is probably not the best way to model the drawbacks of communicative inflexibility; it certainly has an effect on the dynamics of the simulations.

There are a number of areas where the simulations could be extended. Communication is modeled by interaction with a single other individual, but population measures of communicative ability are needed. I didn't address the origin of the fixed central algorithm, which presumably evolved as well. For comparison with Hinton and Nowlan's results (and the large body of similar work that followed), it would be interesting to experiment with acquiring a particular target language. Finally, the effects of stochastic drift may be important in simulations like this, and should be systematically studied.

I do not think that the choice between learning guided and gradual selection is all-or-none. No doubt, both have played a role in human cognitive evolution. I have argued, however, that it is possible to give an adaptationist account of the origin of natural language, even under the stricture that intermediate forms confer no adaptive advantage.

Acknowledgements

This is a revised version of a paper which was circulated in manuscript form in 1994. During the work, I enjoyed useful discussions with Michael Best, Seth Bullock, Angelo Cangelosi, Robin Clark, Henry Davis, Geoffrey Hinton, Steven Nowlan, Steve Pinker, and Doug Pulleyblank. I am particularly grateful to Paul Bloom, Simon Kirby and James Hurford, Ted Briscoe, and John Batali, who wrote extensive critiques and replicated aspects of the simulation. This paper has been much improved by their generous efforts. All errors are mine.

---

[4] Thanks to John Batali for the mental image.

References

Ackley, D. H. and M. L. Littmann (1994). Altruism in the evolution of communication. In Rodney Brooks and Pattie Maes, (eds.) *Proceedings of the fourth artificial life workshop*. MIT Press, Cambridge, MA.

Baldwin, J. M. (1896). A new factor in evolution. *American naturalist*, 30, 441–451.

Briscoe, E. J. (2000). Grammatical acquisition: inductive bias and coevolution of language and the language acquisition device. *Language*, 76(2), 245–296.

Chomsky, N. (1981). *Lectures on government and binding*. Foris, Dordrecht.

Chomsky, N. (1986). *Knowledge of language*. Praeger, New York.

Clark, R. (1992). The selection of syntactic knowledge. *Language acquisition*, 2, 85–149.

Clark, R. (1994). Finitude, boundedness and complexity: learnability and the study of first language acquisition. In Barbara Lust, Gabriella Hermon, and Jaklin Kornfilt (eds.), *Syntactic theory and first language acquisition: cross-linguistic perspectives*, volume 2. Laurence Erlbaum, Hillsdale, NJ.

Deacon, T. W. (1997). *The symbolic species: the co-evolution of language and the brain*. W. W. Norton, New York.

Dresher, E. and J. Kaye (1990). A computational learning model for metrical phonology. *Cognition*, 34, 137–195.

Elitzur, A. E. (1994). Let there be life: Thermodynamic reflections on biogenesis and evolution. *Journal of theoretical biology*, 168, 429–459.

Fodor, J. D. (1989). Learning the periphery. In Robert J. Matthew and William Demopoulos (eds.), *Learnability and linguistic theory*, Kluwer, Dordrecht, pp. 129–154.

Forrest, S. (1993). Genetic algorithms: Principles of natural selection applied to computation. *Science*, 261, 872–878.

Freeman, J. (1993). Simulating a basic genetic algorithm. *The Mathematica journal*, 3, 52–56.

Gibson, E. and K. Wexler (1994). Triggers. *Linguistic inquiry*, 25, 407–454.

Goldberg, D. E. (1989). *Genetic algorithms in search, optimization and machine learning*. Addison-Wesley, Reading, MA.

Gould, S. J. and R. C. Lewontin (1979). The spandrels of San Marco and the Panglossian paradigm: A critique of the adaptationist programme. *Proceedings of the Royal Society of London B*, 205, 581–598.

Gruau, F. and D. Whitley (1993). Adding learning to the cellular development of neural networks: Evolution and the Baldwin effect. *Evolutionary computation*, 1(3), 213–233.

Harvey, I. (1993). The puzzle of the persistent question marks: A case study of genetic drift. Technical Report CSRP 278, School of Cognitive and Computing Sciences, University of Sussex, Brighton, England.

Hinton, G. E. and S. J. Nowlan (1987). How learning can guide evolution. *Complex systems*, 1, 495–502.

Holland, J. H. (1992). *Adaptation in natural and artificial systems: an introductory analysis with applications to biology, control, and artificial intelligence*. MIT Press, Cambridge, MA, first MIT press edition.

Hurford, J. (1989). Biological evolution of the Saussurean sign as a component of the language acquisition device. *Lingua*, 77, 187–222.

Jacob, F. (1977). Evolution and tinkering. *Science*, 196, 1161–1166.

Kirby, S. and J. Hurford (1997). Learning, culture and evolution in the origin of linguistic constraints. In Phil Husbands and Inman Harvey (eds.), *Fourth European conference on artificial life*. MIT Press, Cambridge, MA.

Liberman, A. M. and I. G. Mattingly (1989). A specialization for speech perception. *Science*, 243, 489–496.

Lloyd Morgan, C. (1896). On modification and variation. *Science*, 4, 733–740.

Mayley, G. (1996). No pain, no gain: Landscapes, learning costs and genetic assimilation. Technical Report CSRP 409, School of Cognitive and Computing Sciences, University of Sussex, Brighton, England.

Maynard Smith, J. (1987). When learning guides evolution. *Nature*, 329, 762.

Maynard Smith, J. (1998). *Evolutionary genetics*. Oxford University Press, Oxford, 2nd edition.

Mitchell, M. (1996). *An introduction to genetic algorithms*. MIT Press, Cambridge, MA.

Niyogi, P. and R. C. Berwick (1996). A language learning model for finite parameter spaces. *Cognition*, 61, 161–193.

Piatelli-Palmarini, M. (1989). Evolution, selection and cognition: From "learning" to parameter setting in biology and in the study of language. *Cognition*, 31, 1–44.

Pinker, S. (1994). *The language instinct*. HarperCollins, New York.

Pinker, S. and P. Bloom (1990). Natural language and natural selection. *Behavioral and brain sciences*, 13(4), 707–784.

Ridley, M. (1990). Arbitrariness no argument against adaptation. *Behavioral and brain sciences*, 13(4), 756.

Simpson, G. G. (1953). The Baldwin effect. *Evolution*, 7, 110–117.

Williams, E. (1987). Introduction. In Thomas Roeper and Edwin Williams (eds.), *Parameter setting*, Reidel, Dordrecht, pp. vii–xix.

9

Grammatical acquisition and linguistic selection

Ted Briscoe
Natural Language and Information
Processing Group, Computer Laboratory,
University of Cambridge

9.1 Introduction

This paper is part of an ongoing research effort (Briscoe, 1997, 1998, 1999, 2000a, b) to develop a formal model of language acquisition, demonstrate that an innate language acquisition device (LAD) could have coevolved with human (proto)language(s) given plausible assumptions, and explore the consequences of the resulting model of both language and the language faculty for theories of language change. The paper builds on the earlier work by examining the model's ability to account for the process of creolization (Bickerton, 1981; 1984; 1988; Roberts, 1998) within a selectionist theory of language change.

Sections 9.1 and 9.2 describe the theoretical background to this research. Section 9.2 presents a detailed model of the LAD utilizing generalized categorial grammars embedded in a default inheritance network integrated with a Bayesian statistical account of parameter setting. Section 9.3 reports experiments with this model demonstrating feasible and effective acquisition of target grammars for a non-trivial fragment of universal grammar (UG). Section 9.4 describes the simulation of an evolving population of language learners and users. Section 9.5 reports experiments with the simulation model which demonstrate linguistic selection for grammatical variants on the basis of frequency and learnability. Section 9.6 reports further experiments demonstrating evolution of the LAD by genetic assimilation of aspects of the linguistic environment of adaptation. Section 9.7 describes the experiments modeling the demographic and linguistic context of creolization. Section 9.8 summarizes the main findings and outlines areas of further work.

9.1.1 Grammatical acquisition

Within the parameter setting framework of Chomsky (1981), the LAD is taken to consist of a partial genotypic specification of UG complemented with a parameter setting procedure which, on exposure to a finite positive sample of triggers from a given language, fixes the values of a finite set of finite-valued parameters to select a single fully-specified grammar from within the space defined by UG. Triggers are defined as pairings of surface and logical forms, embodying the assumption that the learner has access to the meaning of (some) utterances and that the acquisition task is one of discovering the correct grammatical mapping from surface forms to logical forms (e.g. Lightfoot, 1992).

Many parameters of grammatical variation set during language acquisition appear to have default or so-called unmarked values retained in the absence of robust counter-evidence (e.g. Chomsky, 1981:7f; Hyams, 1986; Wexler and Manzini, 1987; Lightfoot, 1992). Thus, the LAD incorporates both a set of constraints defining a possible human grammar and a set of biases (partially) ranking possible grammars by markedness. A variety of explanations have been offered for the emergence of an innate LAD with such properties based on saltation (Berwick, 1998; Bickerton, 1990, 1998) or genetic assimilation (Pinker and Bloom, 1990; Kirby, 1998). Formal models of parameter setting (e.g. Clark, 1992; Gibson and Wexler, 1994; Niyogi and Berwick, 1996; Brent, 1996) have demonstrated that development of a psychologically-plausible and effective parameter setting algorithm, even for minimal fragments of UG, is not trivial. The account developed in Briscoe (1997, 1998, 1999, 2000a,b) and outlined here improves the account of parameter setting, and suggests that biases as well as constraints evolve through a process of genetic assimilation of properties of human (proto)language(s) in the environment of adaptation for the LAD, but these constraints and biases in turn influence subsequent development of language via linguistic selection.

9.1.2 Linguistic selection

In recent generative linguistic work on diachronic syntax, language change is primarily located in parameter resetting (reanalysis) during language acquisition (e.g. Lightfoot, 1992, 1997; Clark and Roberts, 1993; Kroch and Taylor, 1997). Differential learnability of grammatical variants, on the basis of learners' exposure to triggering data from varying grammatical sources, causes change. Languages can be viewed as dynamical systems which adapt to their niche – of human language learners and users (e.g. Cziko, 1995; Hurford, 1987; 1998; Keller, 1994). Thus, languages *themselves* are evolving, on a historical timescale, and the primary source of *linguistic* selection is the language acquisition 'bottleneck' through which successful grammatical forms must pass repeatedly with each generation of new language learners. Under this view, the core evolutionary concepts of (random) variation, (adaptive) selection and (differential) inheritance are being used in their technical 'universal Darwinist' sense (e.g. Dawkins, 1983; Cziko, 1995) and not restricted to evolution of biological organisms.

To study linguistic evolution, it is necessary to move from the study of individual (idealized) language learners and users, endowed with a LAD and acquiring an idiolect, to the study of *populations* of such generative language learners and users, parsing, learning and generating a set of idiolects constituting the language of a speech community. Once this step is taken, then the dynamic nature of languages emerges more or less inevitably. Misconvergence on the part of language learners can introduce variation into a previously homogeneous linguistic environment. And fluctuations in the proportion of learners to adults, or migrations of different language users into the population can alter the distribution and nature of the primary linguistic data significantly enough to affect grammatical acquisition. Once variation is present, then properties of the LAD become critical in determining which grammatical forms will be differentially selected for and maintained in the language, with language acquisition across the generations of users as the primary form of linguistic inheritance.

9.2 The language acquisition device

A model of the LAD incorporates a theory of UG with an associated finite set of finite-valued parameters defining the space of possible grammars, a parser for these grammars, and an algorithm for updating initial parameter settings on parse failure during acquisition (e.g. Clark, 1992). It must also specify the starting point for acquisition; that is, the initial state of the learner in terms of the default or unset values of each parameter of variation (e.g. Gibson and Wexler, 1994).

9.2.1 The (universal) grammar

Classical (AB) categorial grammar uses one rule of application which combines a functor category (containing a slash) with an argument category to form a derived category (with one less slashed argument category). Grammatical constraints of order and agreement are captured by only allowing directed application to adjacent matching categories. Generalized categorial grammars (GCGs) extend the AB system with further rule schemata (e.g. Wood, 1993). Each such rule is paired with a corresponding determinate semantic operation, shown here in terms of the lambda calculus, which compositionally builds a logical form from the basic meanings associated with lexical items. The rules of forward application (FA), backward application (BA), generalized weak permutation (P) and forward and backward composition (FC, BC) are given in figure 9.1 (where X, Y and Z are category variables, | is a variable over slash and backslash, and ... denotes zero or more further functor arguments). Generalized weak permutation enables cyclical permutation of argument categories, but not modification of their directionality. Once permutation is included, several semantically equivalent derivations for simple clauses such as *Kim loves Sandy* become available. Figure 9.2 shows the non-conventional left-branching one. Composition also makes alternative non-conventional semantically-equivalent (more left-branching) derivations available (see, e.g. Steedman, 1996, 2000).

This set of GCG rule schemata represents a plausible kernel of UG; Hoffman (1995, 1996) explores the descriptive power of a very similar system, in which P is not required because functor arguments are interpreted as multisets. She demonstrates that this system can handle (long-distance) scrambling elegantly and generate some mildly context-sensitive languages (e.g. languages with cross-serial dependencies such as $a^n b^n c^n$, though not some MIX languages with arbitrarily intersecting dependencies, e.g. Joshi *et al*, 1991). The majority of language-particular grammatical differences are specified in terms of the category set, though it is also possible to parameterize the rule schemata by, for example, parameterizing the availability of P, FC or BC or whether P can apply solely to categories in the lexicon or to derived categories as well.

The relationship between GCG as a theory of UG (GCUG) and as a specification of a particular grammar is captured by defining the category set and rule schemata as a default inheritance network characterizing a set of (typed) feature structures. The network describes the

Forward Application:
X/Y Y $\Rightarrow$ X λ y [X(y)] (y) $\Rightarrow$ X(y)
Backward Application:
Y X\Y $\Rightarrow$ X λ y [X(y)] (y) $\Rightarrow$ X(y)
Forward Composition:
X/Y Y/Z $\Rightarrow$ X/Z λ y [X(y)] λ z [Y(z)] $\Rightarrow$ λ z [X(Y(z))]
Backward Composition:
Y\Z X\Y $\Rightarrow$ X\Z λ z [Y(z)] λ y [X(y)] $\Rightarrow$ λ z [X(Y(z))]
(Generalized Weak) Permutation:
$(X\|Y_1)\ldots\|Y_n \Rightarrow (X\|Y_n)\|Y_1\ldots$ λ $y_n\ldots,y_1$ [X($y_1\ldots,y_n$)] $\Rightarrow$ $\lambda\ldots$ y_1,y_n [X($y_1\ldots,y_n$)]

figure 9.1. GCG Rule Schemata

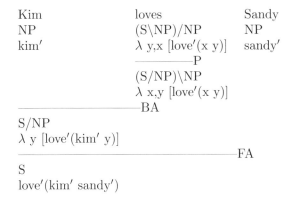

figure 9.2. GCG Derivation for *Kim loves Sandy*

set of possible categories, each represented as a feature structure, via
type declarations on network nodes. It also defines the rule schemata in
terms of constraints on the unification of feature structures representing the categories. Type declarations $CON(Type, \subseteq)$ consist of path
value specifications ($PVSs$). An inheritance chain of (super)type declarations (i.e. a set of $PVSs$) defines the feature structure associated
with any given (sub)type (see Lascarides *et al.*, 1995; Lascarides and
Copestake, 1999, for further details of the grammatical representation

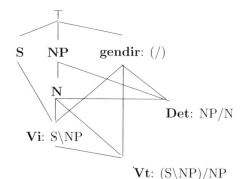

figure 9.3. Simplified Fragment of an Inheritance Semi-Lattice

language, and Bouma and van Noord (1994) for the representation of a categorial grammar as a constraint logic grammar).[1] Figure 9.3 is a diagram of a fragment of one possible network for English categories in which *PVS*s on types are abbreviated informally, ⊤ denotes the most general type, and meets display the (sub)type / (default) inheritance relations. **Vi** inherits a specification of each atomic category from which the functor intransitive verb category is constituted and the directionality of the subject argument (hereafter **subjdir**) by default from a type **gendir**. For English, **gendir** is default 'rightward' (/) but the *PVS* in **Vi** specifying the directionality of subject arguments, overrides this to 'leftward', reflecting the fact that English is predominantly right-branching, though subjects appear to the left of the verb. Transitive verbs, **Vt**, inherit structure from **Vi** and an extra NP argument with default directionality specified by **gendir**. Nevertheless, an explicit *PVS* in the type constraints for **Vt** could override this inherited specification. We will refer to this *PVS* as **objdir** and the equivalent specification of the determiner category's argument as **ndir** below. A network allows a succinct definition of a set of categories to the extent that the set exhibits (sub)regularities. Villavicencio (1999) provides a more detailed description of the encoding of categories for English verbs in the default inheritance network.

The parameter setting procedure utilizes a function *P-setting*(*UG*) which encodes the range of potential variation defining $g \in UG$ where

---

[1] In fact, the representation of P as a constraint may be problematic. Instead it may be better represented as a unary rule which generates further categories. See Briscoe and Copestake (1997) for a discussion of lexical and other unary rules in the nonmonotonic representation language assumed here.

NP	gendir	subjdir	objdir	ndir
A 1/T	D 0/R	D 1/L	? ?	? ?

figure 9.4. A P-setting Encoding for the Category Fragment

UG is an invariant underspecified description of a GCUG and *P-setting-* (*UG*) encodes information about the *PVS*s which can be varied. For the experiments below a GUCG covering typological variation in constituent order (e.g. Greenberg, 1966; Hawkins, 1994) was developed, containing 20 binary-valued unset or default-valued potential parameters corresponding to specific *PVS*s on types which are represented as a ternary sequential encoding (A = Absolute (principle), D = Default, ? = unset, 0 = Rightward / False, 1 = Leftward / True, ? = unset) where position encodes the specific *PVS* and its (partial) specificity. Figure 9.4 shows a p-setting encoding of part of the network in figure 9.3, where the **S** and **N** categories are the only definitely invariant principles of GCUG, though this p-setting also encodes **NP** as an absolute specification and, therefore, effectively a principle of GCUG. This encoding reflects the fact that *PVS*s specifying directionality for the object of a transitive verb or argument of a determiner are redundant as directionality follows from **gendir**. *CON*(*Type*, ⊆) defines a partial ordering on *PVS*s, which is exploited in the acquisition procedure. For example, **gendir** is a *PVS* on a more general type than **subjdir** and thus has more global (default) consequences in the specification of the category set, but **subjdir** will inherit its specification from **gendir** in the absence of an explicit *PVS* for **Vt**.

The eight basic language families in UG are defined in terms of the unmarked, canonical order of verb (V), subject (S) and objects (O). Languages within families further specify the order of modifiers and specifiers in phrases, the order of adpositions, and further phrasal-level ordering parameters. In this paper, familiar attested configurations of parameters are abbreviated as 'German' (SOVv2, predominantly right-branching phrasal syntax, prepositions, etc), and so forth. Not all of the resulting 300 or so languages are (stringset) distinct and some are proper subsets of other languages. 'English' without P results in a stringset-identical language, but the grammar assigns different derivations to some strings, though their associated logical forms are identical.

There are 3 parameters which determine the availability of application, composition and permutation, 5 which determine the availability of specific categories (S, N, NP, Prep, Compl), and one, **argorder**, whose marked value allows a subject argument to combine first with a verbal functor for 'true' VOS or OSV languages.[2] The remaining 11 parameters determine canonical constituent order by setting the directionality of arguments in functor categories. A more detailed description of the p-setting encoding and GCUG fragment is given in Briscoe (1998, 2000a) and Villavicencio (2000).

Some p-setting configurations do not result in attested grammatical systems, others yield identical systems because of the use of default inheritance. The grammars defined generate (usually infinite) stringsets of lexical syntactic categories. These strings are sentence types since each defines a finite set of grammatical sentences (tokens), formed by selecting a lexical item consistent with each lexical syntactic category.

9.2.2 The parser

The parser uses a deterministic, bounded-context shift-reduce algorithm. It represents a simple and natural approach to parsing with GCGs which involves no grammar transformation or precompilation operations, and which directly applies the rule schemata to the categories defined by a GCG. The parser operates with two data structures, an input buffer (queue), and an analysis stack (push down store). Lexical categories are shifted from the input buffer to the analysis stack where reductions are carried out on the categories in the top two cells of the stack, if possible. When no reductions are possible, a further lexical item is shifted onto the stack. When all possible shift and reduce operations have been tried, the parser terminates either with a single 'S' category in the top cell, or with one or more non-sentential categories indicating parse failure. The algorithm for the parser working with a GCG which includes all

---

[2] The p-setting encoding of the non-ordering parameters does not correspond to a single PVS in the grammatical representation language. We make the assumption for the parameter setting model that the definitions of rule schemata and of complex categories are predefined in UG as sets of PVSs but that a single element must be switched 'on' for them to become accessible. This could correspond to the PVS that links these definitions to the rest of the inheritance network by, for example, specifying that **application** is a subtype of **binary-rule**. However, this is a simplification in the case of complex categories since these will typically inherit subcomponents from several places in the part of the network defining the category set. These assumptions speed up learning but do not alter fundamental results concerning convergence, provided that a more direct encoding retained a finite number of such finite-valued 'parameters'.

1. THE REDUCE STEP: if the top 2 cells of the stack are occupied,
   then try
   a) Application (FA/BA), if match, then apply and go to 1), else b),
   b) Composition (FC/BC), if match then apply and go to 1), else c),
   c) Permutation (P), if match then apply and go to 1), else go to 2)
2. THE SHIFT STEP: if the first cell of the Input Buffer is occupied,
   then pop it and move it onto the Stack together with its associated
   lexical syntactic category and go to 1),
   else go to 3)
3. THE HALT STEP: if only the top cell of the Stack is occupied by a
   constituent of category S,
   then return Success,
   else return Fail

THE MATCH AND APPLY OPERATION: if a binary rule schema matches
the categories of the top 2 cells of the Stack, then they are popped from
the Stack and the new category formed by applying the rule schema is
pushed onto the Stack.

THE PERMUTATION OPERATION: each time step 1c) is visited during the
Reduce step, permutation is applied to one of the categories in the top
2 cells of the Stack (until all possible permutations of the 2 categories
have been tried in conjunction with the binary rules). The number of
possible permutation operations is finite and bounded by the maximum
number of arguments of any functor category in the grammar.

figure 9.5. The parsing algorithm

the rule schemata defined in section 9.2.1 is given in figure 9.5. This
algorithm finds the most left-branching derivation for a sentence type
because Reduce is ordered before Shift. The algorithm also finds the
derivation involving the least number of parsing operations because only
one round of permutation occurs each time application and composition
fail. The category sequences representing the sentence types in the data
for the entire grammar set are unambiguous relative to this 'greedy,
least effort' algorithm, so it will always assign the correct logical form to
each potential trigger given an appropriate sequence of lexical syntactic
categories. Briscoe (1998, 2000a) describes the parser in more detail.

9.2.3 Parameter setting

The parameter setting algorithm used here is a statistical extension of an
n-local partially-ordered error-driven parameter setting algorithm uti-

lizing limited memory. Briscoe (1997, 1998) discusses related proposals
(e.g. Gibson and Wexler, 1994; Niyogi and Berwick, 1997) and Briscoe
(1999, 2000b) motivates the statistical approach to parameter setting).
The algorithm only adjusts parameters when trigger input leads to parse
failure given the learner's current grammar. If flipping the settings of n
parameters results in a successful parse, then these settings receive further support and, after a few such consistent observations, the learner's
parameters will be more permanently updated, though there is nothing
to stop subsequent triggers reversing the settings. The setting of parameters is partially-ordered in the sense that the partial order on $PVSs$ corresponding to particular parameters defined by the inheritance network
determines the manner in which updating and resetting proceeds. More
general supertype parameters acquire their settings (and probabilistic
support) from their more specific subtype parameters. A p-setting not
only encodes the current settings of parameters but also the degree of
evidence supporting that setting, as a probability, and this determines
how easily a setting can be updated. The statistical approach adopted
is Bayesian in the sense that initial p-settings encode a prior probability
for each possible parameter value and posterior probabilities for settings
are computed incrementally in accordance with Bayes' theorem.

Bayes' theorem, given in (9.1), adapted to the grammar learning problem states that the posterior probability of a grammar, $g \in UG$, where
UG defines the space of possible grammars, is determined by its likelihood given the triggering input, t_n, multiplied by its prior probability:

$$P(g \in UG \mid t_n) = \frac{P(g)P(t_n \mid g)}{P(t_n)} \qquad (9.1)$$

The probability of an arbitrary sequence of n triggers, t_n, is usually
defined as:

$$P(t_n) = \sum_{g \in UG} P(t_n \mid g) \, P(g) \qquad (9.2)$$

Since we are interested in finding the most probable grammar in the
hypothesis space, UG, given the triggering data, this constant factor
can be ignored and learning can be defined as:

$$g = argmax_{g \in UG} \, P(g) \, P(t_n \mid g) \qquad (9.3)$$

A trigger is a pairing of a surface form (SF), defined as an ordered
sequence of words, and a logical form (LF) representing (at least) the

correct predicate-argument structure for the surface form in some context: $t_i = \{< w_1, w_2, ...w_n >, LF_i\}$.[3] A valid category assignment to a trigger ($VCA(t)$) is defined as a pairing of a lexical syntactic category with each word in the SF of t, $< w_1 : c_1, w_2 : c_2, ...w_n : c_n >$ such that the parse derivation, d, for this sequence of categories yields the same LF as that of t.[4]

We augment the account of GCG from section 9.2.1 with probabilities associated with (parametric) path value specifications ($PVSs$) in type declarations on nodes in the default inheritance network, $CON(Type, \subseteq)$. (The probability of a PVS with an absolute value is simply taken to be 1 for the purposes of the experiments reported below.) A parametric PVS which plays a role in differentiating the class of grammars $g \in UG$ and is encoded in a p-setting will be binary-valued so we must ensure $P(PVS_i = 0) + P(PVS_i = 1) = 1$. An initially unset PVS will therefore have a probability $P(PVS_i = 0) = P(PVS_i = 1) = 0.5$. The probability of each parametric PVS is taken to be independent. A subtype PVS, which is encoded in a p-setting but which inherits its setting from a supertype PVS, is assigned a probability of 1 because such $PVSs$ are not genuinely parametric (or independent) in this configuration of $P\text{-}setting(UG)$. However, if $P\text{-}setting(UG)$ is reconfigured so that the inheritance chain between the supertype and subtype is broken and the subtype PVS acquires a conflicting value, then the probability of this value must be recorded and used to assess the probability of the resulting grammar.[5] The prior probability of a grammar, g is the product of

---

[3] The definition of a LF is not critical to what follows. However, we assume that a logical form is a (possibly underspecified) formula of a well-defined logic representing at least the predicate-argument structure of the sentence (see e.g. Alshawi, 1996). It is possible that the definition of a trigger could be further relaxed to allow underdetermined predicate-argument structure(s) to be associated with a SF (Villavicencio, 2000).

[4] We assume that the parse recovered will be that yielded by the parser of section 9.2.2; namely, the 'least effort', most left-branching derivation. Strict equivalence of LFs could be relaxed to a consistency/subsumption relation, but this would not affect the experiments described below.

[5] The assumption of independence rests on the semantics of the representation language in which a feature structure is a conjunction of atomic path values each specified by a single PVS. As with any such model assumption though, one can question whether the phenomenon modeled justifies it. In this case, the model is cognitive so a demonstration that in language there are dependencies between phenomena treated by distinct $PVSs$ is at best only very indirect evidence against the psychological claim that this is the appropriate cognitive model. For further discussion of probabilistic interpretation of similar representation languages see Abney (1997).

the probabilities of all its (parametric) PVSs:

$$P(g) = \prod_{PVS \in CON(Type, \subseteq)} P(PVS) \tag{9.4}$$

This defines a prior distribution over G which prefers succinctly describable and, therefore, maximally-regular and minimally-sized category sets.[6]

The prior probability of a category is defined as the product of the probabilities of the PVSs in the type declarations which define it normalized with respect to the entire category set in UG:

$$P(c) = \frac{\prod_{PVS \in CON(c, \subseteq)} P(PVS)}{\sum_{c \in CON(Type, \subseteq)} \prod_{PVS \in CON(c, \subseteq)} P(PVS)} \tag{9.5}$$

The prior probability of a category from a particular grammar can be defined similarly by restricting the normalization to specific grammars:

$$P(c \mid g) = \frac{\prod_{PVS \in CON(c, \subseteq)} P(PVS)}{\sum_{c \in g} \prod_{PVS \in CON(c, \subseteq)} P(PVS)} \tag{9.6}$$

The likelihood, $P(t_n \mid g)$, is defined as the product of the probabilities of each trigger:

$$P(t_n \mid g) = \prod_{t \in t_n} P(t \mid g) \tag{9.7}$$

Where the probability of a trigger is itself the product of the probabilities of each lexical syntactic category in the valid category assignment for that trigger, $VCA(t)$:

$$P(t \mid g) = \prod_{c \in VCA(t)} P(c \mid g) \tag{9.8}$$

This is sufficient to define a likelihood measure, however, it should be clear that it yields a deficient language model (e.g. Abney, 1997) in which the total probability mass assigned to sentences generated by g

---

[6] Because the parameters of variation are a set of binary-valued PVSs, the product of these PVSs effectively defines an informative prior on G consistent with the minimum description length principle/stochastic complexity (e.g. Rissanen, 1989). A more sophisticated encoding of the grammar would be required to achieve this if the parameters of variation differed structurally.

will be less than one and some of the probability mass will be assigned to non-sentences (i.e. sequences of lexical syntactic categories which will not have a derivation (or VCA) given g).[7]

9.2.4 Implementation

The Bayesian account of parameter setting has been implemented as an on-line, incremental grammar acquisition procedure which updates probabilities associated with the subset of PVSs which define parameters as each trigger is parsed. Though acquisition is restricted to the space defined by P-$setting(UG)$, the preference for the most succinct descriptions within this space requires that settings on more general types are updated to reflect the bulk of the probability mass of subtypes which inherit settings from them. The resulting learner finds the locally maximally probable grammar given the specific sequence of triggers, t_n, seen so far:

$$g = locmax_{g \in UG} \ P(g) \ P(t_n \mid g) \tag{9.9}$$

Each PVS in a p-setting is associated with a prior probability, a posterior probability and a current setting, as shown in table 9.1 for the different types of possible initial p-setting (before exposure to data). The current setting is 1 if the posterior probability associated with the parameter is >0.5, 0 if it is <0.5. Probabilities are stored as fractions so that incremental updates based on new observations can be expressed as additions to denominators and/or numerators, and larger denominators can be used to represent stronger priors. In the experiments reported below the values shown in table 9.1 are used to initialize simulations, but values of numerators and denominators in priors can be modified

---

[7] The use of such a deficient model amounts to the (psychological) claim that learners are sensitive to the probabilities of lexical (sub)categories (see e.g. Merlo 1994) but not the derived probabilities of phrases or clauses. Given the equivalence of probabilistic and compression perspectives exploited in minimum description length approaches (e.g. Rissanen, 1989), 'likelihood' is being defined in terms of the degree of compression of the data achieved by grammar, g. These definitions can be straightforwardly extended to define a 'lexically-stochastic' GCG in which the probability of a trigger is conditioned on the lexical items, w which occur in the trigger $P(w \mid c)$. However, we do not do so here since in the experiments which follow we assume that valid category assignments, $VCA(t)$, are given, and thus abstract away from the lexicon and lexical probabilities. Extending the model in this fashion would be critical if we wanted to deal with (probabilistic) selection between valid category assignments in order to resolve ambiguity.

Table 9.1. *Probabilities of Parameter Types*

P-setting Type	Prior	Posterior	Setting
Default Parameter	$\frac{1}{5}$	$\frac{1}{5}$	0
	$\frac{4}{5}$	$\frac{4}{5}$	1
Unset Parameter	$\frac{1}{2}$	$\frac{1}{2}$	?

by mutation and crossover operators during the reproduction of new language agents (see section 9.4 below).

The Bayesian approach to incrementally updating the posterior probability of each parameter is approximated by incrementally computing the maximum likelihood estimate for each parameter after each trigger input, but smoothing this estimate with the prior probability.[8] Firstly, the posterior probability is initialized to the (inherited) prior probability and these values are used to compute the parameter settings which define the starting point for learning. Then, as the learner successfully parses triggers, the posterior probability of each parameter expressed in the potential trigger is updated, reinforcing the probabilities of the parameter settings required to assign them the correct LF. The posterior becomes the new prior for the next step of incremental updating as the next potential trigger is input.

When a trigger cannot be successfully parsed, the acquisition procedure flips the settings of n parameters in a p-setting, and, if this results in a successful parse, updates posterior probabilities according to these revised settings. The effect of this acquisition procedure is that a trigger does not usually cause an immediate switch to a different grammar. Rather the learner is more conservative and waits for enough evidence

---

[8] Strictly smoothing the maximum likelihood estimate with the prior does not conform to Bayes theorem in the limit because, given (9.9), if the likelihood is zero then the prior has no effect. Very similar and strictly Bayesian results could be had in the implementation by using a Laplace-corrected estimate of the likelihood (that never goes to 1 or 0), corresponding to the assumption that in incremental updating of likelihood probabilities the data observed so far may not constitute a representative sample. The simpler and perhaps more psychologically-plausible (Cosmides and Tooby, 1996) approximation used here only differs in assigning more weight to the prior than would be achieved by multiplying the prior by a Laplace-corrected likelihood.

to shift a posterior probability through the $P = 0.5$ threshold before changing a setting more permanently. For example, suppose parameter i has a prior and initial posterior probability of $1/5$, and thus a default value of 0. A single successful parse of a trigger expressing i as 0 will cause the denominator of the posterior probability to be incremented by 1, yielding a new posterior of $1/6$. A single observation of a trigger expressing i as 1 which gets a successful parse when n parameter settings are flipped, including that for i, will cause the numerator and denominator to be incremented by 1, yielding a new posterior probability of $2/6$. Thus, it will take at least 4 such observations to take the posterior past $P = 0.5$ and cause the learner to change the parameter setting. For unset parameters at the beginning of the learning period, a single trigger, t, will suffice to set the parameter appropriately for $VCA(t)$, but incorrect default parameters will require a few more consistent observations, as will initially unset parameters which become inappropriately set as a result of noise or miscategorization.

Categorized triggers, $VCA(t)$, are encoded in terms of the most specific parameters required to parse them successfully. However, each time posterior probabilities of most specific parameters are updated, it is necessary to examine the probabilities of their supertypes, and the pattern of default inheritance from them to subtypes, in order to determine the most probable grammar $P(g \in \text{P-setting}(UG))$ for these settings. The probability of a supertype PVS is defined as the sum of the probabilities of those subtypes which inherit that PVS. Since inheritance is default, not all subtypes will necessarily inherit a given PVS from a supertype, they may instead override it with an explicit specification on the subtype. Both the value of the supertype PVS and its probability are determined by the amount of evidence supporting specific values for that PVS on subtypes. For example, in the grammar fragment introduced above the PVS for **gendir** is a supertype of **subjdir**, **objdir** (subject and object argument direction for verbal functors, respectively) and of **ndir** (general direction of arguments in nominal functors). The value of the PVS for **gendir** (right/left) is determined by the values required on its subtypes and the probabilities associated with the subtype values. For example, if both **objdir** and **ndir** are 'right' (0) (i.e. their posterior probabilities are both < 0.5) but **subjdir** is 'left' (1), then the PVS for **gendir** will be set to 'right' with probability derived from that of these two inheriting subtypes. However, **subjdir** will override the supertype with an explicit PVS whose probability will not

$\forall supertype_i \in CON(Type, \subseteq)$

$\forall PVS_j \in subtypes_k \ of \ supertype_i$

if

    $\mid PVS_j = 1 \in subtypes_k \mid > \mid PVS_j = 0 \in subtypes_k \mid$

then

      $P(PVS_j = 1) \in supertype_i = \dfrac{\sum P(PVS_j=1)\in \ subtypes_k}{|PVS_j=1\in \ subtypes_k|}$

(and vice-versa)

else

    if

      $\dfrac{\sum P(PVS_j=1)\in \ subtypes_k}{|PVS_j=1\in \ subtypes_k|} > 1 - \dfrac{\sum P(PVS_j=0)\in \ subtypes_k}{|PVS_j=0\in \ subtypes_k|}$

    then

      $P(PVS_j = 1) \in supertype_i = \dfrac{\sum P(PVS_j=1)\in \ subtypes_k}{|PVS_j=1\in \ subtypes_k|}$

    (and vice-versa)

    else

      $P(PVS_j) \in supertype_i \ is \ 0.5$

figure 9.6. Computing posterior probabilities of supertypes

affect that of the supertype since the inheritance chain has been broken. This will ensure that the resulting grammar has the minimal number of explicit genuinely parametric PVSs on types required to specify a grammar consistent with the data observed (so far), and thus that this is the most probable grammar. If subsequent evidence favors a 'left' setting for **ndir** or **objdir** then the PVS for **gendir** will be revised to 'left' and the remaining rightward subtype will become the one requiring an explicit PVS to override the default. Similarly, if **subjdir** in the above example was unset, then the setting of **gendir** rightward on the basis of the evidence from **ndir** and **objdir** would cause the learner to adopt a default rightward setting for **subjdir** too.

Figure 9.6 summarizes the algorithm used to find the most probable grammar compatible with the evidence for PVSs on the most specific types, where PVS_j denotes a path value specification in a potential inheritance chain of type declarations which may or may not need to be explicitly specified to override inheritance.

The complete learning algorithm is summarized in figure 9.7. Potential triggers, t from g^t are encoded in terms of p-setting schemata inducing $VCA(t)$, following Clark (1992). This obviates the need for on-line parsing of triggers during computational simulations. It also means that flip can be encoded deterministically by examining the parameter

Data: $\{S_1, S_2, \ldots S_n\}$

if
   $VCA(S_j) \in$ *P-setting$_i$*(UG)
then
   P-setting$_j$ $(UG) = \mathrm{Update}($*P-setting$_i$*$(UG))$
else
   P-setting$_j$ $(UG) = \mathrm{Flip}($*P-setting$_i$*$(UG))(VCA(S_j))$
   if
   $VCA(S_j) \in$ *P-setting$_j$*(UG)
   then
      $\mathrm{RETURN}\ \mathrm{Update}($*P-setting$_j$*$(UG))$
   else
      $\mathrm{RETURN}\ $*P-setting$_i$*$(UG)$

Flip:
Flip or set the values of the first n default or unset most specific parameter(s) via a left-to-right search of the p-schemata representation of $VCA(t)$.

Update:
Adjust the posterior probabilities of the n successfully flipped parameters and of all their supertypes so that they represent the most probable grammar given the data so far (see figure 9.6 etc.).

figure 9.7. The new parameter setting algorithm

settings expressed by a trigger and computing whether any resetting of n parameters will yield a successful parse. If so, then these parameters are deemed to have been flipped and posterior probabilities are updated. The use of a deterministic flip speeds up convergence considerably and amounts to the strong assumption that learners are always able to determine an appropriate $VCA(t)$ for a trigger outside their current grammar, if it is reachable with n parameter changes. However, as there are a finite number of finite-valued parameters, relaxing this assumption and, for example, making random guesses without examining the trigger encoding would still guarantee (eventual) convergence.

9.3 Feasible and effective grammatical acquisition

Two learners were defined on the basis of the grammar acquisition procedure described in section 9.2. Both learners can flip up to 4 parameters

Table 9.2. *Convergence times for two learners*

Lrner	Languages							
	SVO	SVOv1	VOS	VSO	SOV	SOVv2	OVS	OSV
U-n4	33	32	34	32	34	32	32	32
D-n4	19	32	21	39	20	21	22	23

per trigger and differ only in terms of their initial p-setting. The unset learner was initialized with a p-setting consistent with a minimal inherited GCUG consisting of application (FA, BA) with the **NP** and **S** categories already present. The unset learner was initialized with the remaining PVSs in the p-setting unset, while the default learner had default settings for **argorder, gendir, subjdir, v1** and **v2** which specify a minimal SVO right-branching grammar.

Each variant learner was tested against a source grammar generating one of seven full languages in the grammar set (section 9.2.1) which are close to an attested language; namely, 'English' (SVO, predominantly right-branching), 'Welsh' (SVOv1, mixed order), 'Malagasy' (VOS, right-branching), 'Tagalog' (VSO, right-branching), 'Japanese' (SOV, left-branching), 'German' (SOVv2, mixed branching), 'Hixkaryana' (OVS, mixed branching), and a hypothetical OSV language with left-branching phrasal syntax. In these tests, a single learner parsed and, if necessary, updated parameters from a randomly drawn sequence of unembedded or singly embedded (potential) triggers, t from $L(g^t)$ with $VCA(t)$ preassigned.

The predefined proper subset of triggers used constituted a uniformly-distributed fair sample capable of distinguishing each $g \in UG$ (e.g. Niyogi and Berwick, 1996). Table 9.2 shows the mean number of potential triggers required by the learners to converge on each of the eight languages. These figures are each calculated from 1000 trials and rounded to the nearest integer. Presentation of 150 sentence types for each trial ensured convergence with $P \geq 0.99$ on all languages tested for both learners. As can be seen, the unset learner (U-n4) converges equally effectively on all eight languages, however, the preferences incorporated into the default learner's (D-n4) initial p-setting make languages compatible (e.g. SVO) or partially compatible (e.g. VOS, SOV, etc) with these settings around 30% faster to learn, and ones largely incompatible with them (e.g. VSO) somewhat slower than for the unset learner. Thus, the initial configuration of a learner's p-setting (i.e. the prior probabilities) can alter the relative learnability of different languages.

Many experiments of this kind with these and other predefined variant learners demonstrate experimentally that convergence is possible, under these assumptions, for the 70 full and over 200 subset languages defined in *P-setting(UG)* (see Briscoe, 1997, 1998, 1999, 2000a).

The mean number of potential triggers required for convergence may seem unrealistically low. However, this figure is quite arbitrary, as it is effectively dictated by the number of n flippable parameters, the distribution and size of the trigger set, t, preassignment of $VCA(t)$ and the deterministic flipping of parameters. The more fundamental requirement for convergence is that their be a specific trigger sequence which allows the (re)setting of all parameters for g^t in n-local steps from the predefined starting point for learning. For this the trigger set must constitute a fair sample capable of uniquely identifying $g^t \in UG$ and the specific sequence of triggers supporting a n-local algorithm must be observed frequently enough during the learning period to support the n parameter updating steps at each stage. The number of triggers required will depend, primarily, on the proportion of triggers for which $VCA(t)$ can be recovered by the learner.

A wider demonstration of the feasibility of the algorithm depends on replacing the optimal and strong assumptions above with more empirically motivated ones. Such modifications would be unlikely to alter the relative learnability results of table 9.2, though they might increase the mean number of potential triggers required for convergence by several orders of magnitude (see e.g. Niyogi and Berwick, 1996 for further discussion). Here we focus on exploring the consequences of allowing some miscategorizations of trigger input and of allowing 'spurious' triggers not drawn from g^t in the learner's input.

The results of table 9.2 are computed on the basis that the learner is always able to assign the appropriate lexical syntactic categories to a trigger (i.e. that $VCA(t)$ is always given). However, this is an unrealistic assumption. Even if we allow that a learner will only alter parameter settings given a trigger, that is, a determinate SF:LF pairing, there will still be indeterminacy of parameter expression. For example, Clark (1992) discusses the example of a learner acquiring German (SOVv2) in which triggers such as S-V, S-V-O, S-V-O_1-O_2, S-Aux-V will occur. These triggers are all compatible with a SVO grammar, though if German is the target language, then SVO triggers such as Aux-S-V-O will not occur, while other non-SVO ones such as O-V-S, S-Aux-O-V, O-Aux-S-V, and so forth will (eventually) occur. That is, neither SVO or SOVv2 is a subset of the other, but they share a proper subset of triggers. Thus, for a trigger like S-V-0 there is indeterminacy over the setting of the **objdir** parameter: it might be 'right' in which case VO grammars will be hypothesised, or 'left' with **v2** 'true' in which case OVv2 grammars will be hypothesised, and under either hypothesis the correct LF will be recovered. So, depending on the precise order in which specific triggers are seen by a learner, a deterministic learner may converge to an incorrect target grammar.

In the Bayesian framework parameters can, in principle, be repeatedly reset during the critical period for learning. And their setting is conservative, based on observing a consistent though possibly non-contiguous *set* of triggers supporting a specific setting. The robustness of the acquisition procedure in the face of examples of such indeterminacies of parameter expression can be explored by exposing a learner not only to triggers from SOVv2 but also from the proper subset of SVO triggers which overlap with SOVv2 (with $VCA(t)$ predefined). This simulates the effect of a learner miscategorizing a proportion of the triggers compatible with SVO (i.e. assigning a $VCA(t)$ valid given the current state of the learner, but incorrect with respect to g^t). In these circumstances, the Bayesian parameter setting procedure should converge reliably to SOVv2 provided that the proportion of miscategorized triggers (to their correctly categorized counterparts) does not cause any particular parameter to be expressed incorrectly in around 50% of all relevant triggers. The precise proportion will depend, of course, on whether the initial value is unset or default-valued and, if the latter, the relative strength of the prior. For a default-valued parameter with a strong prior probability whose correct value is marked, it is possible that quite a low proportion of miscategorized triggers could prevent its resetting within the learning period.

The two learners were tested on a mixture of 150 triggers randomly drawn from SVO-N-PERM-COMP and SOVv2 or SVOv1 in various proportions. SVO-N-PERM-COMP is the language corresponding to the proper subset of ambiguous triggers between 'English' and 'German' and also to a proper subset of ambiguous triggers between SVO-N-PERM-COMP and 'Welsh' (SVOv1).[9] In each case, SVO-N-PERM-COMP

---

[9] Subset languages are denoted by mnemonic names, where -F indicates that property F is missing, so -N indicates no multiword NPs, and -PERM and -COMP that permutation and composition are not available in derivations.

Table 9.3. *Percentage Convergence to SOVv2 / SVOv1*
with SVO Miscategorizations

Lner/$L(g^t)$	Trigger Proportions				
SVO-N/$L(g^t)$	15/85	30/70	40/60	50/50	60/40
SOVv2					
Unset (n4)	100	97.7	86.8	50.8	22.6
Default (n4)	100	97.6	87.9	62.2	28.8
SVOv1					
Unset (n4)	100	97.7	89.9	57.2	23.8
Default (n4)	100	96.6	90.1	59	25.1

triggers conflict with SOVv2 and SVOv1 in two parameters: **objdir** and **v2**, and **argorder** and **v1**, respectively. The percentage convergence to the 'target' SOVv2 or SVOv1 grammars over 1000 trials is given in table 9.3. The first column gives percentage convergence when a miscategorized trigger was randomly drawn 15% of the time, the second 30% of the time, and so on until the proportion of miscategorized triggers exceeds that of the target grammar 60%/40%. By this stage, most trials for both learners are converging to a SVO subset language, usually with some features determined by the full source grammar.

The percentages given in table 9.3 include cases where the learner initially converged to the target grammar and then switched to SVO. These accounted for from 4% up to 50% of the overall convergence rate, increasing as the proportion of SVO miscategorized triggers increased.[10] These experiments suggest that the Bayesian approach to parameter setting, in principle, provides a robust and general solution to the indeterminacy of parameter expression. However, contingent details such as the frequency and order of specific (mis)categorized triggers, the weighting of priors, and so forth will determine the detailed behavior and effectiveness of such a learner, in practice. The differences between the unset and de-

---

[10] One could posit that the proportion of miscategorized triggers would decrease or cease over the learning period. Or that the n updatable parameters per trigger over the learning period decrements; that is, the learner becomes more conservative towards the end of the learning period. Or that the learner knows when every parameter has been (re)set or 'reinforced' and then terminates learning. In each case, similar exploratory experiments indicate that the incidence of such 'postconvergence' to a different language, not actually exemplified in the source can be drastically reduced or eliminated.

fault learners are minor in the results in table 9.3 and only emerge, as expected, when the data has least influence on the initial settings; that is, when the proportion of miscategorized subset triggers to correctly categorized full language triggers is higher, so though two of the parameters receive more incorrect support, the majority are simply observed less frequently. Therefore, on balance, prior probabilities have a greater effect on posterior probabilities because the likelihood probabilities are less informative overall. Then the default learner converges slightly more successfully to either target grammar because, provided that the learner sees enough correctly categorized triggers to reset the two conflicting parameters with respect to each target, the rest of the directional parameter settings for each target grammar are correctly set by **gendir**'s default 'right' value, so these need less exemplification. Nevertheless, the probability that the two conflicting parameters will be correctly set for either target declines more for the default learner than the unset learner, as their initial default values also conflict with that required by each target. Therefore, increasing the prior weight of all the default valued parameters, or just of the two conflicting parameters, and rerunning the experiment would probably yield a worse convergence rate for the default learner.

The non-statistical acquisition procedures of Briscoe (1997, 1998), as well as those of Gibson and Wexler (1994) and Niyogi and Berwick (1996), are excessively sensitive to miscategorizations of triggers or to other forms of noise in triggering input. If the learner is exposed to an extragrammatical or miscategorized trigger given the target grammar at a critical point, this can be enough to prevent convergence to the correct grammar. For example, given the deterministic parameter setting procedure of Briscoe (1997, 1998), a learner who has converged to a SVO grammar with right-branching phrasal syntax will, by default, assume the target grammar utilizes postnominal relative clauses. However, at this point exposure to a single trigger (mis)categorizable as containing a prenominal relative clause will be enough to override the default assumption of rightward looking nominal functors and, for the specific case of nominal functors taking relative clauses, permanently define these to be prenominal. On the other hand, a memoryless parameter setting procedure like the Trigger Learning Algorithm (Gibson and Wexler, 1994) will continue to switch between grammars, as mutually inconsistent sequences of triggers are observed, until the learning period ends. So effectively the final trigger and its (mis)categorization will determine the grammar selected (e.g. Niyogi, this volume). Clearly, the problem here is a special case of that of the indeterminacy of parameter expression. In the Bayesian framework, small proportions of noisy triggers encountered at any point in the learning period will not suffice to permanently set a parameter incorrectly. More systematic miscategorizations based on the indeterminacy of parameter expression will only result in misconvergence if the distribution of the triggering data allows the learner to miscategorize a high proportion of all triggers expressing a given parameter.

9.4 Populations of language agents

A language agent (LAgt) is minimally defined as a language learner, generator and parser endowed with the model of the LAD described above and a simple generation algorithm. The latter outputs a sentence type generated by the LAgt's current grammar (if any) drawn randomly according to a uniform distribution. In addition, LAgts have an age, which is used to determine the length of the learning period, and a fitness which can be used to determine their reproductive success and time of death.

A population of LAgts participates in a sequence of interaction cycles consisting of a predetermined number of random linguistic interactions between its members. A linguistic interaction consists of a randomly chosen generating LAgt emitting a sentence type to a randomly chosen distinct parsing agent. The interaction is successful if their p-settings are compatible. Compatibility is defined in terms of the ability to map from a given SF to the same LF, rather than in terms of the sharing of an identical grammar. Populations are sometimes initialized with LAgts speaking a specific full language. Linguistic heterogeneity can then be introduced and maintained by regular migrations of further adult speakers with identical initial p-settings, but speaking a distinct full language. Alternatively, populations can be initialized to speak a variety of languages so that the range of variation can be controlled directly.

A LAgt's age is defined in terms of interaction cycles. LAgts can learn from age one to four; that is, during the first four interaction cycles. If a LAgt is a learner and cannot parse a sentence type during a linguistic interaction, then it is treated as a potential trigger and the LAgt applies the parameter setting procedure to its current p-setting. LAgts are removed from the population, usually at age ten. Two LAgts can reproduce a new LAgt at the end of an interaction cycle, if they are both aged four or over, by single point crossover and single point mutation of their *initial* inherited p-setting encodings. The crossover and mutation operators are designed to allow variant *initial* p-settings to be explored by the population. For example, they can with equal probability flip the initial 'genetically-specified' value of a default parameter, make a parameter into a principle or vice versa, and so forth, by altering the prior probabilities inherited by a new LAgt. LAgts either reproduce randomly or in proportion to their fitness. The fitness of a LAgt is defined by its communicative success; that is, the ratio of its successful interactions over all its interactions for the previous interaction cycle. The rate of reproduction is controlled so that a population always consists of >60% adult LAgts.

The simulation model and typical values for its variables are outlined in figure 9.8. The mean number of interactions per LAgt per cycle are fixed so that acquisition of the target grammar in a linguistically homogeneous population is reliable ($P > 0.99$) for either of the predefined learners. The simulation can be used to study the process of learning and consequent linguistic selection for grammatical variants, or the interaction of linguistic selection with natural selection for more effective learners defined in terms of variant initial p-settings. Further details and motivation are given in Briscoe (2000b).

9.5 Linguistic selection experiments

Linguistic selection can be seen as a population level, and therefore dynamic, counterpart to the individual learner's problem of the indeterminacy of parameter expression. For example, if we initialize a population of LAgts so that some speak the SVO-N-PERM-COMP subset language, corresponding to the proper subset of triggers which overlap with 'German' (SOVv2), and the remainder speak 'German', then learners should reliably converge to 'German', even when exposed to triggers from all the population, provided that SVO-N-PERM-COMP triggers do not much exceed 15% of all triggers (see the results of section 9.3). On the other hand, if the initial proportion of SVO-N-PERM-COMP speakers is higher, but still below 50%, then we would expect a minority of learners to converge to SVO subset languages or mixtures of the two sources. However, as the simulation run continues, SVO (subset) speakers will disappear because the relative frequency of SOVv2 speak-

LAgt: <P-setting(UG),Parser,Generator,Age,Fitness>

POP_n: {$LAgt_1$, $LAgt_2$, ... $LAgt_n$}

INT: ($LAgt_i$,$LAgt_j$), $i \neq j$, Gen($LAgt_i$, t_k),Parse($LAgt_j$, t_k)

SUCC-INT: Gen($LAgt_i$, t_k) $\mapsto$ LF_k $\wedge$ Parse($LAgt_j$, t_k) $\mapsto$ LF_k

REPRO: ($LAgt_i$,$LAgt_j$) $\mapsto$ $LAgt_k$, $i \neq j \neq k$,
  Create-LAgt(Mutate(Crossover
  (Reset(P-setting($LAgt_i$))),(Reset(P-setting($LAgt_j$)))))

LAgt Fitness:

1. Generate cost: 1 (GC)
2. Parse cost: 1 (PC)
3. Success benefit: 1 (SI)
4. Fitness function: $\frac{SI}{GC+PC}$

LAgt Death: Age 10

Variables	Typical Values	
POP_n	Initially	32
Interaction Cycle	Mn. Ints/LAgt	65
Simulation Length	Int. Cycles	1k
Crossover Probability		0.9
Mutation Probability		0

figure 9.8. The evolutionary simulation

ers will increase with each new batch of learners, and as the original
SVO-N-PERM-COMP adults die out.

A series of simulations was run to test these predictions, in which an
initial population of either 32 default or 32 unset learner LAgts reproduced randomly and the number of SVO-N-PERM-COMP, SOVv2 and
SOVv2 subset language speakers was tracked through interaction cycles.
In these simulations there is no variation amongst LAgts, and so no evolution at the 'genetic' (initial p-setting) level – all learners are either
default or unset n4 learners as defined in section 9.3. However, there
is linguistic selection between the languages, where the ultimate units
of selection/inheritance are competing parameter values. The selection

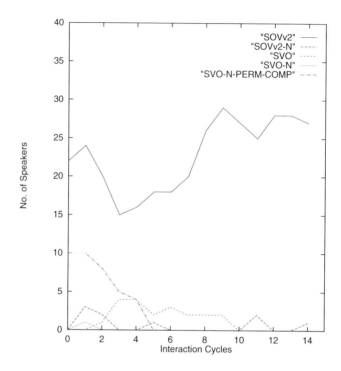

figure 9.9. Linguistic selection between languages

pressure comes from two conflicting sources: learnability and relative frequency. SVO-N-PERM-COMP is easier to learn than SOVv2 because it requires the setting of fewer parameters, but it may be less frequently exemplified in the primary linguistic data than SOVv2, depending on the proportions of speakers in the initial population.

Figure 9.9 plots the languages spoken across interaction cycles for a population of default learners initialized with 10 SVO-N-PERM-COMP and 22 SOVv2 adult LAgts with ages varying randomly from 5–9; so the first generation of learners will be exposed, on average, to 30% SVO-N-PERM-COMP triggers. This plot is typical: the SVO-N-PERM-COMP speakers dwindle rapidly, though a few SVO (superset) language learners emerge briefly, until cycle 10 when only SOVv2 speakers and SOVv2-N learners remain. In 19 out of 20 such runs, the population fixated on SOVv2 in a mean 9.8 interaction cycles; that is, within two and a half full generations of LAgts.[11]   After the first interaction cycle in which learners were present, no subsequent learner converged to a SVO (subset) language in any of these runs. However, in the one other run, the population fixated on a full SVO language after 11 interaction cycles, and in around half the other runs, a few learners briefly spoke the full SVO language. In runs with a lower proportion of initial SVO-N-PERM-COMP speakers, linguistic selection for SOVv2 was 100%. In the runs initialized with unset learners, the results were similar except that there was much less tendency for learners to visit the full SVO language on the path to SOVv2. Finally, in an otherwise identical series of runs initialized with 16 SVO-N-PERM-COMP and 16 SOVv2 speakers, an equally clear opposing result was obtained: populations nearly always fixated on SVO-N-PERM-COMP within 15 interaction cycles. Here ease of learnability swayed the balance in favor of the subset language when each was exemplified equally in the learners' data, regardless of whether the population comprised default or unset learners.

These experiments examine the interplay of the relative frequency with which linguistic variants are exemplified and the relative learnability of languages in determining what learners acquire. They are sufficient to demonstrate that linguistic selection is a viable approach to accounting for some types of language change. In Briscoe (1997, 1998, 2000a) more experiments are reported which look at the role of parsability and expressiveness in linguistic selection and also at the potential impact of natural selection for LAgts on this process. Whenever there is linguistic heterogeneity in a speech community, a learner is likely to be exposed to sentence types deriving from more than one source grammar. In reality this is the norm rather than the exception during language acquisition. Learners are typically exposed to many speakers, none of whose idiolects will be entirely identical, some of them may themselves be learners with an imperfect command of the grammar of their speech community, and some may come from outside this speech community and speak a different dialect/language. The Bayesian approach to parameter setting predicts that learners will track the frequency of competing variants in terms of the posterior probabilities of the parameters associated with the variation. This accords with the empirical behavior of learners in such

---

[11] I use fixation here and below to denote the point at which every adult LAgt in the population has converged to the same grammar. It is not possible for fixation to occur in less than 6 interaction cycles in these experiments unless no initial SVO-N-PERM-COMP adult is aged 5.

situations (e.g. Kroch, 1989; Kroch and Taylor, 1997; Lightfoot, 1997). They appear to acquire both variants and choose which to produce on broadly sociolinguistic grounds in some cases, and to converge preferentially to one variant in others. This behavior could be modeled, to a first approximation in the current framework, by assigning varying weights to prior default-values and postulating that parameters are set permanently if their posterior probabilities reach a suitable threshold value. In this case, parameters which never reached threshold might be accessible for sociolinguistically motivated register variation, while those which did reach threshold within the learning period would not.[12]

9.6 Coevolution of the LAD and of language

The acquisition experiments of section 9.3 demonstrated the effectiveness of the Bayesian parameter setting procedure with several initial p-settings on some full languages, even in the presence of noise and indeterminacy of parameter expression. The simulations of populations of LAgts of section 9.5 demonstrated linguistic selection on the basis of learnability and the relative frequency of conflicting triggers without any variation at the 'genetic', initial p-setting level. Introducing variation in the initial p-settings of LAgts, allows for the possibility of natural selection for better initial settings, at the same time as languages, or their associated grammars, are themselves being linguistically selected.

Variation amongst LAgts can be introduced in two ways. Firstly, by initializing the population with LAgts with variant p-settings, and using a crossover operator during LAgt reproduction to explore the space defined by this initial variation. And secondly, by also using a mutation operator during reproduction which can introduce variation during a simulation run, with reproduction via crossover propagating successful mutations through the population. Single point crossover with a prespecified probability of 0.9 is utilized on a flat list of the numerators and denominators representing the prior probabilities of each p-setting. The mutation operator can modify a single p-setting during reproduction with a prespecified probability (usually $P = 0.05$). Mutation alters

---

[12] A modification of this type might also form the basis of a less stipulative version of the critical period for learning in which LAgts simply ceased to track posterior probabilities of parameters once they reached threshold; see, e.g. Hurford and Kirby, 1997 for discussion and putative explanations of the critical period for language acquisition.

an element of a p-setting, with equal probability, from its existing type (absolute principle, default or unset parameter) and initial setting (1, 0, ?) to a new type and/or initial setting. Thus, no evolutionary bias is introduced at this level, but mutation can alter the definition of UG by making a principle a parameter or vice-versa, and alter the starting point for learning by altering the prior probabilities of parameters.

Briscoe (1998, 2000a) argues in detail that, under the assumption that communicative success confers an increase in fitness, we should expect the learning period to be attenuated by selection for more effective acquisition procedures in the space which can be explored by the population; that is, we should expect genetic assimilation (e.g. Waddington, 1942, Pinker and Bloom, 1990). In the context of the Bayesian acquisition procedure, genetic assimilation corresponds to the evolution of the prior probabilities which define the starting point for learning to more accurately reflect properties of the environment (during the period of adaptation). Staddon (1988) and Cosmides and Tooby (1996) independently argue that many aspects of animal and human learning behavior can be accounted for under the assumption that learning is Bayesian, priors evolve, and this general learning mechanism can be recruited for specific problems with domain-specific representational and inferential components. Nevertheless, the selection for better language acquisition procedures will be relative to the dominant language(s) in the environment of adaptation (i.e. the period before the genetic specification of the LAD has gone to (virtual) fixation in the population). And these languages will themselves be subject to changing selective pressures as their relative learnability is affected by the evolving LAD, creating reciprocal evolutionary pressures, or *coevolution*. However, the selective pressure favoring genetic assimilation, and its subsequent maintenance and refinement, is only coherent given a coevolutionary scenario in which (proto)language(s) supporting successful communication within a population had already itself evolved on a historical timescale (e.g. Hurford, 1987; Kirby, 1998), probably with many of the constraints and biases subsequently assimilated already present in the (proto)language(s) as a consequence of *linguistic* selection, perhaps initially driven by quite general cognitive constraints such as working memory limitations (e.g. Deacon, 1997).

Here we report the results of a series of simulation experiments designed to demonstrate that the LAD evolves towards a more specific UG (more principles) with more informative initial parameter settings (more default-values) consistent with the dominant language(s) in the environment of adaptation, even in the face of the maximum rate of language change consistent with maintenance of a speech community (defined as mean 90% adult LAgt communicative success throughout a simulation run). Populations of LAgts were initialized to be unset learners all speaking one of the seven attested languages introduced in section 9.3. Simulation runs lasted for 2000 interaction cycles (about 500 generations of LAgts) and each condition was run ten times. Reproduction was proportional to communicative success and was by crossover and mutation of the initial p-settings of the 'parent' LAgts. Constant linguistic heterogeneity was ensured by migrations of adult LAgts speaking a distinct full language with 1–3 different parameter settings at any point where the dominant (full) language utilized by the population accounted for over 90% of interactions in the preceding interaction cycle. Migrating adults accounted for approximately one-third of the adult population and were initialized to have initial p-settings consistent with the dominant settings already extant in the population; that is, migrations are designed to introduce linguistic, not genetic, variation. Populations typically sampled about 100 languages with the dominant language changing about 40 times during a run.

The mean increase in the proportion of default parameters in all such runs was 46.7%. The mean increase in principles was 3.8%. These accounted for an overall mean decrease of 50.6% in the proportion of unset parameters in the initial p-settings of LAgts. Figure 9.10 shows the relative proportions of default parameters, unset parameters and principles for one such typical run with the population initialized to unset n4 learners. It also shows the mean fitness of LAgts over the same run; overall this increases as the learning period gets shorter, though there are fluctuations caused by migrations or by an increased proportion of learners. These results, which have been replicated for different languages, different learners, and so forth (see Briscoe, 1997, 1998, 1999, 2000a) suggest that a minimal LAD, incorporating a Bayesian learning procedure, could evolve the prior probabilities and UG configuration which define the starting point for learning in order to attenuate the acquisition process by making it more canalized and robust. On average, a shorter learning period will result in increased communicative success because learners will be able to parse the full range of sentence types from the dominant language by an earlier age.

In these experiments, linguistic change (defined as the number of in-

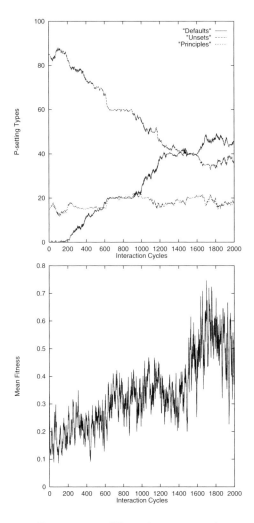

figure 9.10. Proportions of P-setting types and mean fitness

teraction cycles taken for a new parameter setting to go to fixation in the population) is about an order of magnitude faster than the speed with which a genetic change (new initial p-setting) can go to fixation. Typically, 2–3 grammatical changes occur during the time taken for a principle or default parameter setting to go to fixation. Genetic assimilation remains likely, however, because the space of grammatical variation (even in the simulation) is great enough that typically the population is only sampling about 5% of possible variation in the time taken for a single p-setting variant to go to fixation, or in other words, 95% of the selection pressure is constant during this period (see Briscoe, 2000a for further details and discussion).

Though many contingent details of the simulation are arbitrary and unverifiable, such as the size of the evolving population, size of the set of grammars, UG, and relative speed at which both can change, it seems likely that the simulation model massively *underestimates* the size of the potential space of grammatical possibilities. Few linguists would baulk at 30 independent parameters of variation, defining a space of billions of grammars, for an adequate characterization of a parameter setting model of the LAD, while even fewer would argue that the space of possibilities could be finitely characterized at all prior to the emergence of a LAD (e.g. Pullum, 1983). Thus, although there is a limit to the rate at which genetic evolution can track environmental change (e.g. Worden, 1995a, this volume), while the speed limit to major grammatical change before effective communication is compromised will be many orders of magnitude higher, it is very likely that 95% of this space would *not* be sampled in the time taken for fixation of any one parameter of variation in the LAD, given plausible ancestor population sizes (e.g. Dunbar, 1993). Nevertheless, there is a limit to genetic assimilation in the face of ongoing linguistic change. In simulation runs with LAgts initialized with all default parameters, populations evolve away from such 'fully-assimilated' LADs (e.g. Briscoe, 1998) when linguistic variation is maintained.

9.7 Creolization

The abrupt transition from pidgin to creole, which Bickerton (1981, 1984, 1988) argues occurs in one generation, constitutes one of the most dramatic and radical attested examples of language change. In more recent work, Roberts (1998), using a large database of Hawaiian pidgin and creole utterances, has revised Bickerton's original claim slightly, by arguing that some aspects of the transition in Hawaii took two generations. Nevertheless, this careful empirical work by-and-large confirms Bickerton's original claims that the creole emerges very abruptly and embodies a much richer grammatical system than the pidgin, whose properties are not directly exemplified in the super- or sub-stratum languages to which learners might be exposed, and are very similar to the properties of other creoles which emerged at geographically and historically unrelated points. Bickerton (1984:173) has described the process by which learners acquire a creole grammar as one of invention in terms of an innate bioprogram.

Creolization represents a potential challenge for the account of language learning and language change presented here. Though we argue that language learning may be partially innate and that many of the constraints and biases incorporated into the LAD may have evolved via genetic assimilation, the parameter setting algorithm is purely selectionist and largely data-driven, and the associated account of change is thus also selectionist. Confronted with variation, a language learner will preferentially acquire variants which are more learnable or more robustly exemplified in the primary linguistic data.[13] If there is an element of 'invention' in creolization how could this arise? The account that we will pursue here is that in some respects the primary linguistic data that creole learners are exposed to is so uninformative that they retain their prior default-valued parameter settings as a direct consequence of the Bayesian parameter setting procedure. However, this is not enough to ensure that a rich and full grammatical system will emerge if the data never exemplifies, however indirectly, a particular grammatical phenomenon. When exposed exclusively to a subset language, the Bayesian parameter setting procedure reliably acquires that subset language and does not go 'beyond the evidence' to predict a full language 'extension' of the subset language learners have been exposed to. Critically, although the p-setting encoding adopted assumes that a supertype parameter, **gendir**, determines ordering of arguments to all functors by default, the use of 5 category parameters (see section 9.2.1, means that complex categories, such as those associated with a complementizer or nominal modifier, are only accessible to a learner if expressed in a trigger. Without such category parameters, learners would not obey the subset principle and would routinely converge to superset grammars on exposure to proper subsets of triggers (Berwick, 1985).

Plantation creoles arise as a result of unusual and radical demographic conditions (Baker and Corne, 1982; Bickerton, 1988). In the initial preparatory phase of plantation colonization, the speech community consists of European managers and technicians and some native laborers. At this stage, the laborers may learn the European language with rea-

---

[13] In addition, parsability and expressiveness may also play a role either by affecting learnability or by influencing speakers' choice of sentence types in order to optimize communicative success; see Briscoe (1998, 2000a) for further discussion.

sonable proficiency on the basis of frequent contact with the Europeans. However, in the second exploitative stage, when the plantation is up and running, the (indentured or slave) labor population increases five to tenfold within a single generation as successive waves of immigrants are brought in from diverse parts of the world to increase the labor force and to compensate for the typically high mortality. These new immigrants do not share a native language and have much reduced exposure to the European superstratum language, as the proportion of colonialists to laborers decreases radically and the original native population or earlier arrivals take on much of the day-to-day management of the plantation. In these circumstances, the *lingua franca* of the laboring community rapidly develops into an extremely impoverished pidgin language, consisting of a limited vocabulary, learnt indirectly via the original native population from the European superstratum language, and virtually no grammatical system (see Bickerton, 1990:122f for a summary of the properties of pidgins). Children born to laborers during the third stage of the community are predominantly exposed to the pidgin language – contact with the Europeans is limited, many parents are of mixed descent and do not share a native language, and the children are mostly cared for by a few older women in large groups, while all able-bodied men and women labor for long hours in the fields (Bickerton, 1984:215). The birthrate in most plantation communities was not particularly high, with under twelves typically accounting for no more than 25% of the population, except in Hawaii where the birthrate was higher (Bickerton, personal communication). The mixture and composition of substratum native languages spoken by the laborers varied widely between communities. Nevertheless, in the third stage when native creole speakers emerge, remarkably similar grammatical extensions of the impoverished pidgins, which provide the bulk of the learners' primary linguistic data, have been documented (see Roberts, 1998 for recent discussion and argument that such similarities cannot be the result of substratum language influences).

Bickerton (1984:179) describes the prototypical creole grammar, based on Saramaccan, as a minimal SVO right-branching grammar with distinct syntactic categories for determiners, adjectives, numerals, nouns, verbs, auxiliaries and complementizers.[14] The predefined default learner

---

[14] Many similarities, such as the tense-modality-aspect morphosyntactic systems of creoles or choices for lexicalization of specific grammatical properties, are not modeled in the set of grammars used in the current simulation so cannot be

of section 9.3 incorporates prior probabilities favoring a SVO right-branching grammar consistent with a Saramaccan-like grammar, but underdetermining all the properties of the creole language. The questions that we will attempt to answer experimentally in the remainder of this section are: What distributions of primary linguistic data would cause learners hypothetically endowed with this initial p-setting via co-evolution (see section 9.6) to converge to a Saramaccan-like grammar? And how well do these distributions accord with the known demographic conditions governing the emergence of creoles? We will make no attempt to model the emergence of an impoverished pidgin language but concentrate entirely on the third stage pidgin–creole transition in which learners exposed to predominantly pidgin data rapidly converge to a creole language.

In all the experiments which follow, the initial population contains 64 LAgts, who live for 20 interaction cycles and reproduce randomly without mutation. LAgts are all default learners in the initial population, and thus all new LAgts reproduced during these runs are also default learners. The birth rate is set to six new LAgts per interaction cycle which grows quickly to a stable population of around 115 LAgts always containing 18 learners. The highest proportion of learners to adults occurs around the sixth interaction cycle, before the adult population has peaked, when learners constitute about 28% of the total population.[15] We do not model high mortality rates or influxes of new immigrants directly but rather keep the original adult population constant over the first twelve interaction cycles. This represents the assumption that the

---

investigated directly here. Nevertheless, the main points about the acquisition process made below should carry over to these phenomena too.

[15] The estimate of 28% learners is extrapolated conservatively from census figures for Hawaii from 1890, 1900 and 1910 kindly supplied by Derek Bickerton. These are incomplete in some areas but indicate an under 15 population of at least 20% by 1900 and 35% by 1910, assuming a similarly high birthrate amongst Hawaiians as amongst Portuguese immigrants (44% by 1910). (This assumption is in turn supported by school attendance records of 5–14 year olds.) Bickerton suggests that creoles emerge when the proportion of under twelves is between 15% and 25%. The speed of spread of the creole through the learner and total population will both be increased if the proportion of learners is greater and the increase in this proportion is steeper. Therefore, it is possible that (features of) Hawaiian creole spread more rapidly (within two generations, according to Roberts, 1998) because the birthrate was higher. Only further demographic and linguistic work on other pidgin–creole transitions will tell, but the model predicts such speed differences.

pidgin and sub-/super-stratum trigger distribution heard by learners remains constant over the first three generations from the onset of the third stage. However, the fact that new learners are added at the end of each interaction cycle means that the first learners reach the end of the learning period in the fourth interaction cycle, and that the proportion of learners to adults grows over the first few cycles. Thus, the overall linguistic distribution of triggers does change, as learners and new adults begin to form a significant proportion of the population and participate in interactions; and therefore, the degree to which early learners converge consistently to a specific language significantly affects the probability that later learners will follow suit by skewing the distribution of triggers in favor of this language.

We model a pidgin as a subset language without embedded clauses or multiword NPs in which a wide variety of constituent orders is possible, perhaps partly influenced by the substratum native languages of the individual speakers and/or by pragmatic factors. In a first series of experiments, populations of adult LAgts were initialized to speak such subset languages with between three and five of the six basic word orders available (SVO, SOV, VSO, VOS, OSV, OVS) in equal proportions (as before, all conditions were run 10 times). Thus learners were exclusively exposed to subset language input, either exemplifying SVO order or not, with a variety of other orders also present. This corresponds to the hypothesis that learners are exclusively exposed to pidgin triggers and either do not hear sub-/super-stratum utterances or do not treat them as triggering data. When SVO subset triggers are present, even if these only constitute one fifth of the triggering experience of learners on average, default learners reliably converge to the SVO subset language. By the fourth interaction cycle – the end of the first generation – a mean 95% of learners are speaking a SVO subset language. From that point, new learners all converge to SVO subset grammars.[16] When SVO triggers are not present learners converge to non-SVO subset languages.

The picture that emerges, then, is largely expected given the Bayesian learning model. The great majority of default learners, faced with con-

---

[16] The results for similar runs with unset learners show a similar overall preference for SVO subset grammars, but a lower proportion of learners speak SVO in the early cycles and in a minority of runs the learner population still contains non-SVO subset language speakers beyond the third generation. The tendency for unset learners to converge to SVO subset grammars, though weaker, was not expected and must be a consequence of the 'topology' of the hypothesis space created by the encoding of *P-setting(UG)*.

flicting triggering input, converge to SVO order because the prior probabilities of their inherited p-settings tend to dominate over the likelihood probabilities acquired during learning, as these are inconsistent
and broadly 'uninformative'. Nevertheless, if SVO is never exemplified in
the data, learners never converge to it, though they frequently converge
to 'close' right-branching grammars. Default learners do not overgeneralize and converge to a full language as the triggering data does not
express parameters for complex nominal categories, and so forth. Thus,
no process of creolization occurred.

In further experiments, populations were initialized with adult LAgts
speaking a variety of languages exemplifying five of the six basic constituent orders, but also some sub-/super-stratum language utterances.
In a first series of runs one fifth of the LAgts were full SVO right-
branching speakers and the remaining four fifths spoke four non-SVO
subset languages. Thus the average trigger distribution for initial learners consisted of 80% non-SVO pidgin utterances, 7% SVO pidgin or
superstratum language utterances, and 13% SVO superstratum utterances. Corresponding to the hypothesis that creole learners are exposed
to a small minority of 'English' superstratum language triggers. In these
runs, populations of default learners converged rapidly to a full SVO
language. By the second interaction cycle when twelve learners were
present, ten or more were speaking a SVO subset language with the
remainder, if any, currently speaking a subset language with VOS or
SOV order. By the end of the fourth interaction cycle, most of the
earliest learners had converged to 'English' with the minority speaking
SVO subset languages compatible with it. After this point, all subsequent learners converged to 'English'.[17] These runs demonstrate that
the default learner predicts that creolization (that is, 100% convergence
by learners and consequent fixation by new adults on a SVO superset
language) will occur essentially within a generation with minimal exposure to a superstratum language which is compatible with the acquired
creole grammar.

The previous experiments ignored the role, if any, of the substratum

---

[17] Similar runs with unset learners also mostly converged to 'English' by the third
generation, but in about 40% of cases a non-SVO subset language was also being
spoken by a significant proportion of the new population. Furthermore, in the
crucial early interaction cycles a higher proportion of learners converged to non-
SVO subset languages. On average, by the end of the first interaction cycle only
one learner had converged to 'English'.

languages. In a further otherwise identical series of runs, populations were initialized with SVO, two non-SVO subset languages, and two non-SVO languages with randomly-defined full language extensions in equal proportions. This meant that initial learners were exposed, on average, to 54% pidgin-like triggers with four equally-frequent non-SVO orders, 26% non-SVO richer triggers further exemplifying two of these non-SVO orders but otherwise randomly exemplifying more complex syntax, 7% SVO subset pidgin or superstratum triggers, and 13% richer 'English' superstratum triggers. The non-SVO extensions are intended to model the rich and often conflicting variety of fragments of substratum languages that creole learners might hear uttered amongst the adult laboring population (e.g. Bickerton, 1984:182f). The broad effect of adding this degree of substratum data (or interference) is to very slightly slow down learners' convergence to SVO. By the fourth interaction cycle half the earliest learners have converged to 'English' and a mean 91.3% of all learners present are speaking a SVO (subset) language. By the twelfth interaction cycle a full SVO language is spoken by virtually all the new population, with 'English' predominant (though in some runs a second full SVO language with some substratum influences is also present at this stage).[18] These experiments suggest that positing substratum interference does not affect the basic conclusion that creolization will occur rapidly with default learners.

Though creoles display SVO right-branching syntax, it is not the case that the superstratum language is always English or even SVO. It seems reasonable to assume that SVO order will always be exemplified to some extent in the pidgin data to which learners are exposed, but the account we have developed so far relies on initial learners' exposure to 13% of richer 'English' superstratum triggers. While this might be plausible for Hawaii it is not for Berbice where Dutch, with a SOVv2 grammar, was the superstratum language. In a final series of experiments otherwise identical to those above, SOVv2 was substituted for the superstratum language, though SVO order remained one pidgin language variant order. The initial trigger distribution was 89% pidgin-like subset languages with 4% random non-SVO substratum extensions and 7% SOVv2

---

[18] With the unset learners, only a mean 60% of new adults and learners are speaking a SVO subset language by the sixth interaction cycle. By the twelfth interaction cycle the new population typically speaks a mixture of SVO languages, with 'English' dominant but other full SVO language and some adult SVO subset language speakers present.

superstratum extensions. 28% of the pidgin-like triggers had SVO order. The early dynamics of these runs are almost identical to those described above: learners predominantly speak SVO (subset) languages from the beginning and do so exclusively after the first two or three interaction cycles. By the end of the twelfth interaction cycle, the new population was speaking the SVO pidgin-like subset language in a mean 68% of cases, 28% was speaking SVO-PERM and the rest 'English'. Given that 18 of those speaking the SVO pidgin-like subset were still learners and that SVO-PERM was the best represented full language by the twelfth interaction cycle, we would expect most if not all of these learners to converge to this language. In 80% of these runs, the new population had converged to SVO-PERM (and in one case 'English') by the twentieth interaction cycle. Runs with a slightly lower proportion of initial SVO pidgin-like triggers resulted in slower convergence to SVO languages. These results suggest a slower learner convergence rate to a SVO creole superset language when the superstratum language is SOVv2. Nevertheless, SVO-PERM ('English' without permutation) is the closest grammar to Saramaccan available in the set UG used in the experiments.

The experiments suggest, then, that creolization could result as a consequence of a Bayesian parameter setting learner having default settings for some parameters, acquired via genetic assimilation as outlined in section 9.6. Prior probabilities, and thus initial parameter settings, will play a bigger role in the acquired grammar whenever the data the learner is exposed to are inconclusive. It seems plausible that pidgin data are inconclusive about constituent order because pidgin speakers order constituents in inconsistent or primarily pragmatically-driven ways. Nevertheless, order is necessarily expressed in pidgin data, so the learner defaults to SVO order, and also predicts, by default, that right-branching, head-first order will extend to more complex categories. The encoding of *P-setting(UG)* and predefined definition of the default learner we utilize does not allow the learner to hallucinate or invent more complex categories for nominal modification, complementizers, and so forth. However, if such categories are reliably expressed somewhere in the triggering data for each learner, even with inconsistent ordering, then the default learner will 'switch on' a generic unordered form of these categories, and predict their ordering behavior by default via supertype directional parameters (see section 9.2.3). This account does not require that the superstratum language be SVO, or that substratum languages consistently exemplify properties of the creole; merely, that richer triggers expressing parameters for more complex categories be present in the primary linguistic data. Thus, the learning procedure is different from that outlined by Bickerton (1984): there is no invention or other special mechanism at work, rather the grammar acquired is a consequence of the distribution of triggers and the prior probabilities of the Bayesian learner.

The timing of creolization for the simulation runs initialized with default learners with SVO superstratum input is remarkably consistent with the timecourse documented by Roberts (1998), especially given that the prior probabilities of the default learner were not modified at all for these experiments. The Bayesian parameter setting framework and the population model are quite capable of simulating variant accounts in which, for example, prior probabilities are stronger and the data exemplifies some parameters less, or the proportion and growth rate of learners during the third stage of plantation communities is different. To refine the account developed here will require both a better understanding of the language learning procedure and a more precise and detailed account of demographic change and speed of creolization in different plantation communities. For instance, Bickerton (1984:178) suggests that sub-/super-stratum influence cannot be important because some communities of pidgin speakers were 'marooned' and learners did not have access to any speakers of either. If this is accurate, then 'invention', or at least a propensity to acquire superset grammars with default parameter settings on the basis of no triggering evidence, will need to be reconsidered. However, such a model would conflict with prevailing assumptions derived from learnability criteria, like the subset principle (Berwick, 1985), that predict that learners are conservative and do not overgeneralize to superset grammars because no parse failure could force subsequent convergence to the target grammar. Moreover, the data concerning such marooned communities is very sparse, so it is difficult to know whether learners did completely lack sub-/super-stratum input.

9.8 Conclusions

The experimental results reported above suggest that a robust and effective account of parameter setting, broadly consistent with Chomsky's (1981) original proposals, can be developed by integrating generalized categorial grammars, embedded in a default inheritance network, with a

Bayesian learning framework. In particular, such an account seems, experimentally, to be compatible with local exploration of the search space and robust convergence to a target grammar given feasible amounts of partly noisy or indeterminate input. It extends recent work in parameter setting by integrating the learning procedure more closely with a fully-specified grammatical representation language, by using a Bayesian statistical approach to resolve indeterminacies of parameter expression, and by demonstrating convergence for a more substantial language fragment containing around 300 grammars/languages. Villavicencio (1999, 2000) demonstrates that essentially the same model can account for acquisition of constituent order and argument structure from documented caretaker utterances to a single child.

Human language learners, in certain circumstances, converge to grammars different from that of the preceding generation. Linguistic selection for more learnable variant constructions during language acquisition offers a promising formal framework to account for this type of language change. Creolization represents a particularly radical version of such change which is potentially challenging for a selectionist and essentially data-driven account. However, given assumptions about the starting point for learning, the initial distribution of triggers, and the changing constitution of the plantation community, the model of the language acquisition device developed here predicts that creolization will occur within the timeframe identified by Roberts (1998) for SVO superstratum languages. The highly-biased nature of language learning is a consequence of the coevolutionary scenario outlined in section 9.6 in which there is reciprocal interaction between natural selection for more efficient language learners and linguistic selection for more learnable grammars. The range of distributions of triggers to creole learners is compatible with the known linguistic and demographic data for the better studied cases, though it does require that creole learners are influenced, albeit somewhat indirectly, by sub-/super-stratum language triggers. The growth of the native learner and adult population during the third stage of plantation communities partly determines the speed of creolization and thus ideally requires more detailed examination.

Gold's (1967) negative 'learnability in the limit' results have been very influential in linguistic theory, accounting for much of the attraction of the parameter setting framework and for much of its perceived inadequacy (e.g. Clark, 1992; Niyogi and Berwick, 1996; Gibson and Wexler, 1994; Muggleton, 1996). Within the framework explored here, even a much weaker result, such as that of Horning (1969), that stochastic context-free grammars are learnable from positive finite evidence is only of heuristic relevance, since all such results rest crucially on the assumption that the input comes from a single stationary source (i.e. a static and given probability distribution over a target (stochastic) language). However, from the current evolutionary perspective, contingent robustness or local optimization in an irreducibly historical manner is the most that can be expected. The coevolutionary account suggests that the apparent success of language learning stems more from the power of our limited and biased learning abilities to select against possible but less easily learnable grammatical systems, than from the omnipotence of the learning procedure itself (Deacon, 1997). Given this perspective, there is little reason to retain the parameter setting framework. Instead, learners might extend a specification of universal grammar in this model by adding path value specifications to the default inheritance network to create new grammatical categories when triggering data warranted it. An implementation of this aspect of the model is a priority since it would also allow such innovations to be incorporated into universal grammar via genetic assimilation, and this in turn would underpin a better evolutionary account of the development and refinement of the language acquisition device.

The model of a language agent assumes the existence of a minimal language acquisition device, since agents come equipped with a universal grammar, associated learning procedure, and parser. Simulation runs demonstrate that an effective, robust but biased variant learning procedures specialized for/on specific grammars could emerge by genetic assimilation or coevolution. However, they do not directly address the question of how such an embryonic language acquisition device might emerge. Evolutionary theory often provides more definitive answers to questions concerning the subsequent maintenance and refinement of a trait than to ones concerning its emergence (e.g. Ridley, 1990). However, other work suggests that the emergence of a minimal language acquisition device might have required only minor reconfiguration of cognitive capacities available in the hominid line. Worden (1998) and Bickerton (1998) argue that social reasoning skills in primates provide the basis for a conceptual representation and reasoning capacity. In terms of the model presented here, this amounts to claiming that the categorial logic underlying the semantic component of a generalized categorial grammar was already in place (see also Steedman, 1996:94fn3). Encoding aspects of this representation (i.e. logical form) in an 'external' transmittable language would only involve the comparatively minor step of linearizing this representation by introducing directionality into functor types. Parsing here is, similarly, a linearized variant of logical deduction with a preference for more economical proofs or derivations.

Staddon (1988), Cosmides and Tooby (1996) and others have argued that many animals, including primates and homo sapiens, exhibit reasoning and learning skills in conditions of uncertainty which can be modeled as forms of Bayesian learning. Worden (1995b) argues that Bayesian learning is the optimal approach to many tasks animals face, and therefore the approach most likely to have been adopted by evolution. If we assume that hominids inherited such a capacity for Bayesian learning, then evolution could construct a minimal language acquisition device by applying this capacity to learning grammar, conceived itself as linearization of a pre-existing language of thought. Given this scenario, much of the domain-specific nature of language acquisition, particularly grammatical acquisition, would follow not from the special nature of the learning procedure *per se*, as from the specialized nature of the morphosyntactic rules of realization for the language of thought.

Acknowledgements

I would like to thank Jim Hurford and Simon Kirby for helpful comments on an earlier draft of this paper. All remaining errors are my responsibility.

References

Abney, S. (1997). Stochastic attribute-value grammars, *Computational Linguistics, vol.23.4,* 597–618.

Alshawi, H. (1996). Underspecified first-order logics. In K. van Deemter, and S. Peters, (eds.), *Semantic Ambiguity and Underspecification,* University of Chicago Press, Chicago, pp. 145–158.

Baker, P. and Corne, C. (1982). *Isle-de-France Creole,* Karoma, Ann Arbor.

Berwick, R. (1985). *The Acquisition of Syntactic Knowledge,* MIT Press, Cambridge, MA.

Berwick, R. (1998). Language evolution and the minimalist program: the origins of syntax. In J. Hurford, M. Studdert-Kennedy, and C. Knight, (eds.), *Approaches to the Evolution of Language,* Cambridge University Press, Cambridge, pp. 320–340.

Bickerton, D. (1981). *Roots of Language,* Karoma, Ann Arbor.

Bickerton, D. (1984). The language bioprogram hypothesis, *The Behavioral and Brain Sciences, vol.7.2,* 173–222.

Bickerton, D. (1990). *Language and Species,* University of Chicago Press, Chicago.

Bickerton, D. (1998). Catastrophic evolution: the case for a single step from protolanguage to full human language. In J. Hurford, M. Studdert-Kennedy, and C. Knight, (eds.), *Approaches to the Evolution of Language,* Cambridge University Press, Cambridge, pp. 341–358.

Bouma, G. and G. van Noord, (1994). Constraint-based categorial grammar, *Proceedings of the 32nd Assoc. for Computational Linguistics,* Morgan Kaufmann, Palo Alto, CA, pp. 147–154.

Brent, M. (1996). Advances in the computational study of language acquisition, *Cognition, vol.61,* 1–38.

Briscoe, E. J. (1997). Co-evolution of language and of the language acquisition device, *Proceedings of the 35th Assoc. for Computational Linguistics,* Morgan Kaufmann, Palo Alto, CA, pp. 418–427.

Briscoe, E. J. (1998). Language as a complex adaptive system: co-evolution of language and of the language acquisition device, *Proceedings of the 8th Meeting of Computational Linguistics in the Netherlands,* Rodopi, Amsterdam, pp. 3–40.

Briscoe, E. J. (1999). The acquisition of grammar in an evolving population of language agents, *Electronic Trans. of Art. Intelligence (Special Issue: Machine Intelligence, 16. (ed) Muggleton, S., vol.Vol 3(B), www.etaij.org,* 44–77.

Briscoe, E. J. (2000a). Grammatical Acquisition: Co-evolution of Language and the Language Acquisition Device, *Language, vol.76.2,* 245–296.

Briscoe, E. J. (2000b). Evolutionary perspectives on diachronic syntax. In S. Pintzuk, G. Tsoulas, and A. Warner, (eds.), *Diachronic Syntax: Models and Mechanisms,* Oxford University Press, Oxford, pp. 75–108.

Briscoe, E. J. and A. A. Copestake (1999). Lexical Rules in Constraint-based Grammars, *Computational Linguistics, vol.25.4,* 487–526.

Chomsky, N. (1957). *Syntactic Structures,* Mouton, The Hague.

Chomsky, N. (1981). *Government and Binding,* Foris, Dordrecht.

Clark, R. (1992). The selection of syntactic knowledge, *Language Acquisition, vol.2.2,* 83–149.

Clark, R. and Roberts, I. (1993). A computational model of language learnability and language change, *Linguistic Inquiry, vol.24.2,* 299–345.

Cosmides, L. and Tooby, J. (1996). Are humans good intuitive statisticians after all? Rethinking some conclusions from the literature on judgement under uncertainty, *Cognition, vol.58,* 1–73.

Cziko, G. (1995). *Without Miracles: Universal Selection Theory and the Second Darwinian Revolution,* MIT Press, Cambridge, Ma..

Dawkins, R. (1983). Universal Darwinism. In D. S. Bendall (eds.), *Evolution: From Molecules to Men,* Cambridge University Press, Cambridge, pp. 403-425.

Dunbar, R. (1993). Coevolution of neocortical size, group size and language in humans, *Behavioral and Brain Sciences, vol.16,* 681–735.

Gibson, E. and K. Wexler, (1994). Triggers, *Linguistic Inquiry, vol.25.3,* 407–454.

Gold, E. M. (1967). Language identification in the limit, *Information and Control, vol.10,* 447–474.

Goodman, J. (1997). Probabilistic feature grammars, *Proceedings of the 5th Int. Workshop on Parsing Technologies,* Morgan Kaufmann, Palo Alto,

Ca., pp. 89–100.

Greenberg, J. (1966). Some universals of grammar with particular reference to the order of meaningful elements. In J. Greenberg (eds.), *Universals of Grammar*, MIT Press, Cambridge, MA., pp. 73–113.

Hawkins, J. A. (1994). *A Performance Theory of Order and Constituency*, Cambridge University Press, Cambridge.

Hoffman, B. (1995). *The Computational Analysis of the Syntax and Interpretation of Free Word Order in Turkish*, Ph.D. dissertation, University of Pennsylvania.

Hoffman, B. (1996). The formal properties of synchronous CCGs, *Proceedings of the ESSLLI Formal Grammar Conference*, Prague.

Horning, J. (1969). *A study of grammatical inference*, Ph.D., Computer Science Dept., Stanford University.

Hurford, J. (1987). *Language and Number*, Blackwell, Oxford.

Hurford, J. (1998). Introduction: the emergence of syntax. In J. Hurford, M. Studdert-Kennedy, and C. Knight, (eds.), *Approaches to the Evolution of Language*, Cambridge University Press, Cambridge, pp. 299–304.

Hurford, J. and S. Kirby, (1997). *The evolution of incremental learning: language, development and critical periods*, Edinburgh Occasional Papers in Linguistics, 97-2.

Hyams, N. (1986). *Language acquisition and the theory of parameters*, Reidel, Dordrecht.

Joshi, A., K. Vijay-Shanker, and D. Weir, (1991). The convergence of mildly context-sensitive grammar formalisms. In P. Sells, S. Shieber, and T. Wasow, (eds.), *Foundational Issues in Natural Language Processing*, MIT Press, pp. 31–82.

Keller, R. (1994). *On Language Change: The Invisible Hand in Language*, Routledge, London.

Kirby, S. (1998). Fitness and the selective adaptation of language. In J. Hurford, M. Studdert-Kennedy, and C. Knight, (eds.), *Approaches to the Evolution of Language*, Cambridge University Press, Cambridge, pp. 359–383.

Kroch, A. (1991). Reflexes of grammar in patterns of language change, *Language Variation and Change, vol.1*, 199–244.

Kroch, A. and Taylor, A. (1997). Verb movement in Old and Middle English: dialect variation and language contact. In A. van Kemenade, and N. Vincent (eds.), *Parameters of Morphosyntactic Change*, Cambridge University Press, pp. 297–325.

Lascarides, A., E. J. Briscoe, A. A. Copestake and N. Asher (1995). Order-independent and persistent default unification, *Linguistics and Philosophy, vol.19.1*, 1–89.

Lascarides, A. and Copestake A. A. (1999, in press). 'Order-independent typed default unification', *Computational Linguistics,*

Lightfoot, D. (1992). *How to Set Parameters: Arguments from language Change*, MIT Press, Cambridge, Ma..

Lightfoot, D. (1997). Shifting triggers and diachronic reanalyses. In A. van Kemenade, and N. Vincent (eds.), *Parameters of Morphosyntactic Change*, Cambridge University Press, pp. 253–272.

Merlo, P. (1994). A corpus-based analysis of verb continuation frequencies, *Journal of Psycholinguistic Research, vol.23.6*, 435–457.

Muggleton, S. (1996). Learning from positive data, *Proceedings of the 6th Inductive Logic Programming Workshop*, Stockholm.

Niyogi, P. and R. C. Berwick, (1996). A language learning model for finite parameter spaces, *Cognition, vol.61,* 161–193.

Osborne, M. and E. J. Briscoe (1997). Learning stochastic categorial grammars, *Proceedings of the Assoc. for Computational Linguistics, Comp. Nat. Lg. Learning (CoNLL97) Workshop,* Morgan Kaufmann, Palo Alto, Ca., pp. 80–87.

Pinker, S. and P. Bloom, (1990). Natural language and natural selection, *Behavioral and Brain Sciences, vol.13,* 707–784.

Pullum, G. K. (1983). How many possible human languages are there?, *Linguistic Inquiry, vol.14.3,* 447-467.

Ridley, M. (1990). Reply to Pinker and Bloom, *Behavioral and Brain Sciences, vol.13,* 756.

Rissanen, J. (1989). *Stochastic Complexity in Statistical Inquiry,* World Scientific, Singapore.

Roberts, S. (1998). The role of diffusion in the genesis of Hawaiian creole, *Language, vol.74.1,* 1–39.

Sanfilippo, A. (1994). LKB encoding of lexical knowledge. In E.J., Briscoe, A.A. Copestake and V. de Paiva (eds.), *Defaults, Inheritance and the Lexicon,* Cambridge University Press, 190–222.

Staddon, J. E. R. (1988). 'Learning as inference' in R. Bolles, and M. Beecher, (ed.), *Evolution and Learning,* Lawrence Erlbaum, Hillside NJ.

Steedman, M. (1996). *Surface Structure and Interpretation,* MIT Press, Cambridge, Ma.

Steedman, M. (2000). *The Syntactic Process,* MIT Press, Cambridge, Ma..

Villavicencio, A. (1999). Representing a System of Lexical Types Using Default Unification, *Proceedings of the Eur. Assoc. for Computational Linguistics,* Morgan Kaufmann, Palo Alto, Ca., pp. 261-264.

Villavicencio, A. (2000). The acquisition of a unification-based generalized categorial grammar, *Proceedings of the 3rd Computational Linguistics in the UK (CLUK3),* ITRI, Brighton.

Waddington, C. (1942). Canalization of development and the inheritance of acquired characters, *Nature, vol.150,* 563–565.

Wexler, K. and Manzini, R. (1987). Parameters and learnability in binding theory in T. Roeper and E. Williams (eds.), *Parameter Setting,* Reidel, Dordrecht, pp. 41–76.

Wood, M. M. (1993). *Categorial Grammars,* Routledge, London.

Worden, R. P. (1995a). A speed limit for evolution, *J. Theor. Biology, vol.176,* 137–152.

Worden, R. P. (1995b). *An optimal yardstick for cognition,* Psycoloquy (electronic journal).

Worden, R. P. (1998). The evolution of language from social intelligence. In J. Hurford, M. Studdert-Kennedy, and C. Knight, (eds.), *Approaches to the Evolution of Language,* Cambridge University Press, Cambridge, pp. 148–168.

10

Expression/induction models of language evolution: dimensions and issues

James R. Hurford
Language Evolution and Computation
Research Unit, Linguistics Department,
University of Edinburgh

10.1 Introduction

Evolutionary modeling is moving into the challenging field of the evolution of syntactic systems. In this chapter, five recent models will be compared. The following abbreviations will be used in referring to them.

Batali (1998)	JB1
Batali (this volume)	JB2[1]
Hurford (2000)	JH
Kirby (2000)	SK1
Kirby (this volume)	SK2

Other related work will be mentioned where relevant[2]. The goals of the comparison will be to highlight shared and different assumptions and consequent shared and different outcomes.

The models of the evolution of syntax that have been constructed so far fall short of the kind of syntactic complexity found in real languages. In this work, idealization and simplification are immediately obvious. So far, the emergent language systems are, by the standards of extant languages, very simple. The models surveyed here all claim to present examples of the evolution from situations with no language to established syntactic systems. The evolved systems are admittedly simple, but this

---

[1] The discussion of JB2 here is based largely based on a slightly earlier version than that published in this volume. Nothing significant turns on this.

[2] Steels (1998) outlines a model very similar in spirit to those compared here, but gives no details of any language-like system that is its outcome. For this reason, and for lack of space, it is discussed in less detail here.

can be seen as a strength, rather than a weakness of these models, which abstract away from peripheral and incidental features of language, to focus on core properties such as compositionality, recursion and word order. As human syntactic ability has for long been held (by linguists) to be at the core of the innate language faculty, any claim to have simulated the evolution of some syntax needs to be evaluated with care. Questions that arise include:

- In what sense, and to what degree, do the evolved systems actually exhibit true syntax? This requires a theory-neutral definition of the term 'syntax'.

- If some syntax is present in the evolved systems, to what extent is this syntax truly emergent, that is, neither simply programmed in nor an obvious consequence of the definitions of the central mechanisms (production and learning) or of the predefined semantic structures?

- In what ways do the evolved systems resemble natural languages?

After this introductory section, successive subsections will address these, and related, questions.

10.1.1 Characteristics of expression/induction models

'Expression/Induction', henceforth E/I, is a natural mnemonic for a class of computational models of language. In such E/I models, a language is treated as a dynamical system in which information is constantly re-cycled, over time, between two sorts of phase in the language's life. In such a model, a language persists historically through successive instantiations in two quite different media: (1) mental grammars of individuals, and (2) public behavior in the form of utterances (possibly affected by noise) paired with manifestations of their meanings (also possibly incomplete). In the history of a language, grammars in the heads of individuals do not give rise directly to grammars in the heads of other individuals; rather, grammars are the basis for an individual's performance, and it is this overt behavior from which other individuals induce their own mentally represented grammars.

There is nothing new in this view of language constantly spiraling between induced mental representations of its system (Chomskyan I-Language), and expressions of the system in behavior (Chomskyan E-Language); it is essentially the picture presented by Andersen (1973), and assumed in many generative historical linguistic studies (e.g. Lightfoot, 1999). The term 'E/I' is deliberately reminiscent of the E-language/I-language distinction. However, the class of models I shall discuss under the rubric of 'E/I models' have certain further common features, listed in outline below.

Computational implementation: These models are fully implemented in computer simulations. They thus benefit from the clarity and rigor which computer implementation forces, while incurring the high degree of idealization and simplification typical of computer simulations. Obviously, the authors of these models, while admitting to the idealization and simplification, feel that the compensations of clarity and rigor yield some worthwhile conclusions.

Populations of agents: In these simulations, there are populations of individuals, each of whom is endowed with two essential capacities, given in the next two paragraphs below. During the course of a simulation, these agents are variously and alternately designated as speakers/teachers and hearers/learners. In a typical setup, every simulated individual has a chance of talking or listening to every other at some stage. In most models, the population changes regularly, with some individuals being removed ('dying') and new ones being introduced ('being born').

Expression/invention capacity: This is the capacity to produce an utterance, on being prompted with a given meaning. The utterance produced may be defined by a grammar already possessed by the individual, or be entirely generated by a process of 'invention' by random selection from the set of possible utterances, or else be formed partly by existing rules and partly by random invention. Where the individual's grammar defines several possible utterances corresponding to a meaning, the individual's production capacity may be biased toward one of these utterances, contributing to a 'bottleneck' effect (see below).

Grammar induction capacity: This is the capacity to acquire, from a finite set of examples, an internal representation of a (possibly infinite) language system. A language system is a mapping between meanings and forms, equally amenable for use in both production and perception. The set of possible internalized grammars is constrained by the individual's acquisition algorithm. Furthermore, the individual's acquisition algorithm may bias it statistically toward one type of grammar in preference to a grammar of another type. Where the individual's acquisition device is a neural net, one may still speak of an internalized grammar, envisaged as the mapping between meanings and utterances reflected in the input/output behaviour of the trained net.

Starting from no language: These models focus on the question of how incipient languages could possibly emerge from situations in which language is absent. At the start of a simulation, the members of the initial population have no internalized representations of a particular language. The simulations nevertheless usually end with populations whose members all have substantial (near-)identical mental representations of some language, and all produce utterances conforming to a standard applying to the whole community. These models are thus not primarily models of historical language change in relatively mature and complex languages, although the methodology of these simulations, extended and refined, would be very suitable for models in historical linguistics. (Examples of such applications to historical language change, from quite contrasting theoretical backgrounds, are Hare and Elman (1995) and Niyogi and Berwick (1997)).

No biological evolution: In these models, there are no differences between individuals at the point when they are introduced into the population. They all have identical capacities for responding to their environment, either in the production of utterances or in the acquisition of an internal language system triggered by exposure to the utterances of others. Thus these are models of the cultural evolution of learned signaling systems, a quite special case of historical language change, as noted above. These models are not models of the rise of innate signaling systems.

No effect of communication: These models are clearly inspired by situations in which humans communicate meanings to each other. It is in fact possible in these models to measure the degree to which the emergent systems allow successful communication between agents (JB2, in particular, emphasizes this). And the states on which the models converge would typically allow efficient communication. But raw communicative success is not a driving force in these models. That is, there is no instance in which a simulated speaker attempts to communicate a meaning, using a particular form, and then, noting how successful the attempt is, modifies its basis for future behavior accordingly. The basic driving force is the learning of behavior patterns by observation of the behavior of others. The fact that the behavior concerned can be interpreted as communicative, and that communication may happen to be beneficial to a group, is not what makes these models work. These are models of the process by which patterns of behavior (which, quite incidentally, happen to be communicative) emerge among agents who acquire mental representations determining their own future behavior as a result of observing the behavior of others. The undoubtedly interesting and significant fact that such patterns of behavior may convey selective advantage on individuals or populations that possess them is no part of these models.

Lack of noise Unrealistically, all the models surveyed here are noise-free. That is, every utterance produced by a speaker is assumed to be perfectly observed by a learner. Similarly, learners are assumed to have perfect access to the meanings expressed by their 'teachers'. Thus these models do not deal with an obvious and potent source of language change. Nevertheless, leaving noise out of the equation, at least temporarily, serves a useful purpose, in that it allows us to see the evolutionary effects of other factors, such as bottlenecks (see below), all the more clearly. Perfect access to primary linguistic data is a basic assumption of classic work in language learnability theory and related theory of language change (e.g. Clark & Roberts (1993); Gibson & Wexler (1994); Niyogi & Berwick (1997)) . It is not a problematic assumption, because it is clear that it could be relaxed to partial access all of the time, or perfect access some of the time (or both), so long as such access is sufficient.

Pre-defined meanings: The extant models all take as given some set of pre-defined meaning representations. Such representations can be seen as thoughts, ideas or concepts, which the pre-linguistic agents can entertain, but not express. In the course of a given simulation, the set of available meanings does not change, although their expressibility in utterances changes, typically from 0% to 100% . The pre-defined meanings are always structured and somewhat complex. The contribution of such semantic structure to the emergent language systems will be discussed in detail later.

Pre-defined 'phonetic' alphabets: The extant models all assume some unchanging finite vocabulary of atomic symbols from which utterances are constructed, by concatenation. The size of this vocabulary relative to the meaning space is an important factor.

Emergence: All such models aim to show how certain features of language emerge from the conditions set up. A major goal is to demonstrate the emergence of features which are not obviously built in to the simulations. This presupposes that the essential dynamic of an E/I model itself produces certain kinds of language structure as a highly likely outcome. The interaction of assumptions produces non-obvious outcomes explored by simulation. Actual models differ in the extent to which various structural properties of the resulting language system can be said to be built in to the definitions of the crucial processes in the simulation cycle.

'Bottlenecks': An individual's acquired grammar may be recursive, and define an infinite set of meaning–form pairs, or, if not recursive, it may nevertheless define a very large set of meaning–form pairs. The set of example utterances which form the basis for the acquisition of an internal representation of language in an individual is necessarily finite (as is life). A bottleneck exists in an E/I model when the meaning–form pairs defined by an individual's grammar are not presented in full as data to learners. A subset of examples from the infinite (or very large) range of the internalized grammars of one set of speakers is fed through a finite bottleneck to constitute the acquisition data of a set of learners. The simulation may, by design, prompt individual speakers with only a (random) subset of the available meanings, so that the data given to an acquirer lacks examples of the expression of some meanings. I will label this a **'semantic bottleneck'**. With a semantic bottleneck, learners only observe expressions for a fraction of all possible meanings. Even where all individuals are systematically prompted to express all available meanings (possible only where the set of meanings is finite), the individual speakers' production mechanisms may be designed to produce only a subset of the possible utterances for those meanings as defined by their grammars. We will label this a **'production bottleneck'**. Note that it would in fact be unrealistic **not** to implement a production bottleneck. Communication in real societies involves singular speech events, in which a speaker finds a single way of expressing a particular meaning. There is no natural communicative situation in which a speaker rehearses **all** her forms for a given meaning. It is the kind of metalinguistic exercise that might be part of fireside word games, or perhaps be used in a second language classroom, but nowhere else.

10.1.2 Simple examples: evolution of vocabulary

To outline the basic shape of an E/I model, and to demonstrate the potential effects of bottlenecks in simple cases, we will start with the case of the evolution of a simple vocabulary. A number of earlier studies (Oliphant, 1997; Steels, 1996a, 1996b, 1996c, 1997; Vogt, 1998) model the emergence of simple vocabularies. Some of these vocabulary models technically satisfy the criteria listed above for E/I bottleneck models, and in doing so, illustrate some basic effects of the dynamics of these models. It is characteristic of models of vocabulary evolution that they assume a finite set of unrelated, atomic meanings. The lack of structured relationships between and inside vocabulary items ensures that each meaning–form pair must be acquired individually, and the whole lexicon is memorized as an unstructured list, over which no generalizations are possible. (The following informal examples are composed for this paper and representative of the literature, though not drawn wholly from any single publication.)

Learned vocabulary transmission without bottlenecks

Take a population of, say P individuals, each with access to a finite set of concepts, say C in number, and none, as yet, with any known means of expressing these concepts. Let each individual now try to express every concept to every other individual, uttering a syllable drawn from a large set. At first, no individual has any acquired means of expressing any concept (no mental lexicon), and so each resorts to invention by random selection from the large set of syllables. Let us say that the set of syllables is so large that, over the whole population, there are likely to be few chance repetitions of the same syllable for the same meaning. The typical experience of an individual hearer/learner will be to hear p ($p < P$) different syllables for each of the C concepts, and he will thus acquire a large lexicon consisting of $p \times C$ meaning–form pairs. Across the whole population, there will be a great variety of such lexicons, overlapping with each other to some small degree. Now 'kill off' a fraction of the population; this reduces the linguistic diversity somewhat, but not much. Introduce a corresponding number of new individuals as learners, to whom all the surviving individuals will express **all** the available concepts, and, moreover, using **all** the syllables they have acquired for each of those meanings. Thus, the newly introduced learners are in fact exposed to the **whole** language, which they will acquire *in toto*, and in due course pass on *in toto* to the next generation. After the random inventions of the initial generation, there will be no further change, either in the internalized lexicons of successive members of this hypothetical community, or in its public language, for the rest of its history.

This is a situation with no bottleneck. A community which transmits its language without bottlenecks preserves an aboriginal set of meaning–form pairs down through the ages with comparable fidelity (but not by the same mechanism) as a community with an innate signaling system. After the invention of the original meaning–form pairs, there is no evolution in such a system.

Vocabulary transmission with only a production bottleneck

Let us now modify the scenario, and introduce a production bottleneck, but not, at this stage, a semantic bottleneck. A production bottleneck exists when a speaker has learned several forms for a given meaning, and selects among them when prompted with that meaning, with the result that some acquired forms are never uttered for this meaning by this speaker. We assume that all agents in a simulation apply the same selection method in implementing a production bottleneck. Some possible production bottleneck selection methods are:

- for a given meaning, use the form that was most frequently used for that meaning in your learning experience,
- for a given meaning, use the form that was first acquired for that meaning,
- use the shortest form in your vocabulary for the given meaning,
- use the form that is cheapest, according to some well defined metric,
- pick a random form from your vocabulary for the given meaning.

The last (random) method here has a special status as it assumes a uniform distribution; it is the weakest assumption about sampling, and all the others will set up some kind of positive feedback between learning and production, so that an explanation of emergent properties is no longer totally in terms of the learning algorithm. A selection method can also be probabilistic, not necessarily, but still possibly, eliminating the use of some dispreferred form. With a non-random production bottleneck implemented, each speaker is consistent over time in his method of choice of expressions for particular meanings.

It is apparent that, whatever selection method is used, the effect will be, over the course of many simulation cycles, to narrow down the set of forms used for a given meaning, until eventually there is only one form for a given meaning used across the whole community. Even if the selection of forms by agents is genuinely random, there will still occasionally be chance instances of some learner not acquiring some particular form–meaning pair, because this particular form happened not to have been used by any of the speakers from whom he learned; and such a form will be rarer in the E-Language of the next generation. If the population is a genuine single population, rather than several subpopulations completely isolated from contact with each other, then over time the number of forms for a given meaning will approach, and finally reach, 1. Even with a large population, if the production behavior of an agent at one time may in principle historically affect, through the constant cycle of expression/induction/expression/induction, the learning of any agent at a much later time, then the population is guaranteed to converge, sooner or later, onto a common vocabulary, with just one form for each meaning. That is, the E/I model, with a production bottleneck, but no semantic bottleneck, leads inevitably to the elimination of synonyms in a language system. There is no corresponding tendency or mechanism for the elimination of homonyms. This is because, with no semantic bottleneck, the system is driven by meanings; it is a requirement of this condition that all the meanings be expressed to each learner each generation.

Vocabulary transmission with only a semantic bottleneck

Although the absence of a production bottleneck is unnatural, we will briefly consider the converse situation, in which an E/I model contains a semantic bottleneck, but no production bottleneck. In such a situation, the meanings that are expressed by speakers each generation are a subset of the available meanings. In a given generation, some meanings will be picked for expression which were not picked in the previous generation, or vice-versa. Some meanings may be passed over for a period long enough to lead to expressions for them being lost from the grammars of all speakers (although all speakers are still capable of conceiving of the meanings). In this event, the first speaker called upon to express a particular meaning for which he has acquired no paired form will randomly invent a new form, which will then enter the language and be transmitted to subsequent generations. If several speakers in the same generation invent new forms for a given meaning, they will almost certainly invent different forms, and a case of synonymy is created. If the semantic bottleneck is especially fierce, with frequent omission of meanings, such re-invention will be constant, leading to an unstable language system with multiple synonymy evident at all stages.

It can be seen that, at the level of vocabulary, the two kinds of bottleneck are in tension with each other with regard to the phenomenon of synonymy. A semantic bottleneck tends to increase synonymy, by frequently triggering (re-)invention of forms; a production bottleneck tends to reduce synonymy, by guided selection of forms. We shall later see some echoes of these effects in the evolution of syntax, but with a crucial difference, in that the availability of general syntactic rules can preempt an appeal to random (re-)invention of forms.

Frequency effects

A model may have a near no-semantic-bottleneck condition, even without an explicit stipulation in the code that every meaning be expressed to every learner. This can happen if the selection of meanings to be expressed is random, but the number of available meanings is small in relation to the number of 'speech-events' typically experienced by each learner. In such a case, the probability of a meaning being omitted at some stage in the cycle is small, but real, and one can expect some occasional instability to result, with some form–meaning pairs disappearing from the system and being replaced by newly invented ones.

If we manipulate the frequency with which meanings are chosen to be expressed, so that some meanings are expressed so seldom that whole generations can pass without these meanings being expressed, there will be greater instability in the form–meaning pairings for these less used meanings, with frequent re-invention of new forms. On the other hand, meanings that are expressed with high frequency (i.e. at least once to each learner every generation) will preserve their ancestral forms without change. Thus, in general, conservative form–meaning pairings are correlated with high frequency of use.

The principles underlying the evolution of vocabularies in situations with cyclic production and learning are now fairly clear. The phenom-

ena encountered in this section on the emergence of simple vocabularies
foreshadow, *mutatis mutandis*, phenomena found in the emergence of
syntactic systems in E/I models. The introduction of syntactic capability brings new, and more interesting, features to language systems
transmitted by E/I dynamics.

10.2 Modeling the emergence of syntax

10.2.1 Does true syntax emerge in E/I models?

A syntactic system is here defined to be any system in which strings
of concatenated symbols are paired with somewhat complex meanings,
by any systematic means other than exhaustive listing of the one-to-one
meaning–form pairs. The mere fact that the forms are strings and that
the meanings are complex is not sufficient to define a system as 'syntactic'. With a truly syntactic system, what is important is that the
structure of the expressions is part of what conveys meaning. Clearly,
finite sets of meaning–form pairings involving symbol strings and complex meanings **could** evolve, and persist in a community, in exactly the
same way as was outlined above for vocabularies with atomic meanings
and forms. It will be seen, however, that, even with agents who are
able (and sometimes even prefer), to rote-memorize individual correspondences between strings and complex meanings, there are pressures
inherent in E/I bottleneck models which lead to the emergence of syntactic systems in the sense defined.

With symbolic (as opposed to connectionist) models (i.e. SK1, JH,
SK2, JB2) there is a relatively direct method of diagnosing whether a
system emerging from an E/I simulation is truly syntactic. This direct
method is by inspection of the internalized grammars of the simulated
agents, given an understanding of how these grammars are used to produce forms for target meanings. As a general working principle, if the
number of separate statements in a grammar is less than the total number of meaning–form correspondences defined by the grammar, then
some degree of syntactic generalization is present in the system. This
principle relies on an intuitive grasp of what should be counted as a separate statement in a grammar. In SK1, SK2 and JH, separately stored
rules are clearly identifiable; in JB2, each stored exemplar is a separate
statement of the grammar. Table 10.1 shows that, by this criterion, all
the models surveyed have evolved syntactic means of expressing their
meanings.

Table 10.1. *Comparing language size to grammar size in emergent E/I systems.*

Model	Language size		Grammar size		
	Actual	Principled	Lexical	Phrasal	Total
SK1	100	100	10	1	11
SK2a	100	100	10	1	11
SK2b	65,000	infinite	15	2	17
JHa	4,137	infinite	16	3	19
JB2	23 trillion	infinite	35	305	340

Key: SK2a = 1st experiment in SK2; SK2b = 2nd experiment in SK2; JHa = 1st experiment in JH; Language size (Actual) = Number of meaning–form correspondences defined within practical size limit imposed on simulation; Language size (Principled) = Number of meaning–form correspondences defined in principle; Grammar size (Lexical) = Number of atomic meaning–form statements in grammar; Grammar size (Phrasal) = Number of rules or exemplars in grammar; Grammar size (Total) = Total number of statements in grammar. Figures for JB2 are approximate and from an early version of his paper.

In the case of the relatively orthodox phrase structure grammars of SK1 and SK2, if an agent has acquired any rule which, by including one or more variables, generalizes over more than one meaning–form pair, then that agent has at least some syntax. Agents may possess syntax to varying degrees, as shown by the intermediate phases of many of the simulation runs surveyed here, in which agents have some 'partially syntactic rules'. A partially syntactic rule contains one or more variables which generalize over parts of a sentence, but also contains constant elements of both meaning and form, which are thus correlated only by the fact of their co-occurring in this rule, as in a lexical entry. An example of such a partially syntactic rule, from SK2, is reproduced below:

$$S/\text{loves}(\text{john},x) \rightarrow \texttt{johnloves} \ N/x$$
$$N/\text{mary} \rightarrow \texttt{mary}$$
$$N/\text{jane} \rightarrow \texttt{jane}$$

In the first of these three rules, the variables N and x generalize over the forms and meanings, respectively, seen in the other two (lexical) rules. At least two such other rules are necessary in the grammar for the generalization in the first rule to have any generalizing effect. Given such a combination, one may legitimately claim that the system containing them is at least incipiently syntactic in nature[3].

Note that the presence, in an agent's internal grammar, of some apparently rote-learnt correspondences between complex meanings and strings of symbols, with no generalizing variables, does not imply that some of those correspondences are not also the subject of generalization by rules also present in the grammar. The internal grammars of agents may be redundant, specifying the same facts about the emergent language system in more than one way. This is true, for example, of the system emerging from the third experiment described in JH, in which the capacity of learners to internalize generalizations was deliberately somewhat (but not totally) impaired.

10.2.2 Phases in the emergence of syntax

SK1 and JB2 both present graphs of typical runs which reveal three distinct phases in the emergence of syntactic systems. The first phase could be termed a 'holistic' phase. It is described by the modelers as follows:

The grammars at this stage are basically vocabulary lists, with each complex meaning being expressed as an arbitrary unanalysed string of symbols. ...there is no consistent way in which the meanings are related to the strings.

SK1

Each utterance is analysed as a token, and such tokens are worthless for expressing anything but the exact meaning they contain.

JB2

The second phase could be termed 'uncoordinated transitional'. It is described as follows:

The number of meanings covered increases dramatically, as does the size of the grammar. ...the grammars at this stage are far more complex and byzantine than the earlier ones.

SK1

---

[3] The reservation implicit here arises from the fact that, in the example given, only two sentences are generated by three statements; adding further lexical items to fill the N slot does not help, as there will still always be one more statement in the grammar than there are sentences generated.

...the agents begin to acquire and use complex phrase exemplars. This is followed by rapid accumulation of exemplars ...

JB2

The third phase could be termed 'stable economical'. It is described as follows:

The transition [to stage 3] is marked by a sudden increase in the number of meanings that can be produced to the maximum value and a drop in the size of grammars

SK1

The average number of token exemplars, which by round 8000 almost all contain a single formula as their meaning, decreases from its peak of 220 to 35 by round 25000.[4]

JB2

The similarities between the typical runs of SK1 and JB2, despite the markedly different structures and assumptions of the models, are suggestive. Further work needs to be done to see whether these three phases are in any sense necessary to the emergence of syntax. SK2 does not report such distinct phases, which may be a consequence of using the minimal 2-agent (1 'teacher', 1 learner) population, thus eliminating the factor of coordination of grammars within a population. The runs in JH converge on syntactic systems so rapidly that it is not possible to discern any middle or transitional phase. The final version of JB2 (in this volume) actually distinguishes four phases, with the third 'stable economical' phase above split into two. See Batali (this volume) for discussion.

10.2.3 Agents' representations of syntax

It is useful to mention that for a system to be called 'syntactic' it is neither necessary nor sufficient that the internalized grammars of agents contain symbols that are interpreted as autonomous of both meaning and form. One of the central claims of generative grammar is that syntax is autonomous, that is, the terms used to characterize the syntactic system of a language are neither purely semantic nor purely phonetic, but are

---

[4] This is quoted from an early version of Batali's paper. The figures for the final model described in this volume are somewhat different, but nothing significant turns on this.

to some degree independent of both meaning and form. The thesis of the autonomy of syntax is an empirical claim, subject to falsification by analysis of actual languages. Thus, it cannot be a matter of definition that syntax is autonomous of form and meaning. We should define 'syntax' independently of the notion of autonomy. Having done so, we can then judge whether the systems evolved in E/I models do exhibit syntax. And, if they do, we can then ask whether, and in what sense, these evolved syntactic systems are autonomous of form and meaning.

It is of course possible, though not desirable, to write very complex phrase structure grammars, with a wealth of different syntactic categories, for very simple finite data, for which an intuitively better account would be provided by a list. If a simulation in an E/I model, through some quirk of its expression and induction algorithms, happened to culminate in a situation where agents had internalized complex grammars with such unjustified 'syntactic' structuring, we should not conclude that true syntax had emerged in this model, despite the grammars containing what look like syntactic category symbols.

The models of SK1 and SK2 contrast with those of JH and JB1 and JB2 in the degree to which learners postulate autonomous syntactic structure. The agents in SK1 and SK2 models induce context-free phrase structure grammars with symbols representing autonomous syntactic categories. Apart from one specially designated symbol, S, for 'sentence', these syntactic category symbols are simply integers, generated as needed by the induction algorithm (and translated in the examples of SK2 as italic capital letters, A, B, C, ...). The agents thus have the facility to represent generalizations over classes of atomic forms ('words') and over classes of strings of atomic forms ('phrases'), on the basis of their distribution in sentences, and of the systematic mapping of such classes to semantic terms. But the mere existence in an agent's grammar of an apparently autonomous syntactic symbol, such as S, does not imply that the agent has acquired a syntactic system. The early grammars induced by the agents in SK1 and SK2 are essentially lexicons, in which the symbol S is present, but does no work. But the grammars which emerge later are clearly syntactic, by our criterion.

In the JH model, agents acquire grammars in which the rules have no syntactic category symbols. There are dictionary statements, relating atomic meanings to atomic forms, that is translating predicates and individual constants into words, for example:

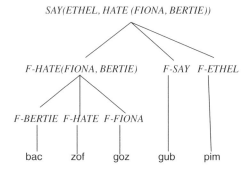

figure 10.1. Example derivation.

$$SING \rightarrow \texttt{vag}$$
$$FIONA \rightarrow \texttt{goz}$$

Such lexical statements contain no variables. In addition, there are rules defining the order in which the components of a proposition are expressed, for example:

$$\{PRED,\ ARG1,\ ARG2\} \rightarrow \text{F-ARG2 F-PRED F-ARG1}$$

Here, 'F-' is an operator meaning 'form of' (as defined by other rules, including lexical rules); all the other terms are variables; the left hand side of the rule depicts an unordered set of the identifiable parts of a proposition; and the right hand side of the rule states the linear order in which the defined forms occur. Such grammars contain no syntactic category symbols. But, by the definition of syntax followed here, the emergent systems are clearly syntactic, achieving a high degree of generalization over meaning–form correspondences. Figure 10.1 shows a tree diagram of the derivation in this grammar of a string expressing a complex meaning.

Such a tree structure contains no nodes labelled with specifically syntactic categories.

In JB2, as the table above shows, the emergent systems also achieve a high degree of generalization over meaning–form correspondences, and thus satisfy our criterion for having evolved some syntax. In this model the representations induced by agents are not rules of any familiar kind, but 'exemplars'. An exemplar, in JB2, is a more or less simple bit of tree structure whose terminal nodes are the syllable strings of the emergent language, and all of whose preterminal nodes are parts of semantic

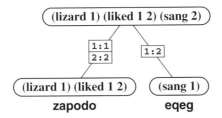

figure 10.2. JB2 exemplar.

representations. An example is given in figure 10.2. In the absence
of autonomous syntactic categories, such tree structures resemble the
previous one, derived in the JH model. The two structure types also,
of course, resemble each other, and the tree structures derived in SK1
and SK2 in their progressive decomposition of a complex semantic representation, as one descends the tree, but this compositionality is to be
expected of any truly syntactic system.

More important are the differences between SK1, SK2, JH, on the one
hand, and JB2. In SK1, SK2 and JH, tree structures are not represented
in an agent's grammar, although they can be constructed by an analyst
from the agent's rules, whereas the JB2 exemplars are actually what
the agents' grammars consist of; in JB2, agents do not store rules.

The power of a grammar to define a large set of meaning–form correspondences in a few statements resides either in the grammar itself or
outside the grammar, in the processing conventions or algorithms used
to 'read' the grammar when producing forms for target meanings. This
difference echoes the debate, in the early days of generative grammar,
on the rival merits of **rules** and **analogies**.

Linguists have had their share in perpetuating the myth that linguistic behavior is 'habitual' and that a fixed stock of 'patterns' is acquired through
practice and used as a basis for 'analogy'. These views could be maintained
only as long as grammatical description was sufficiently vague and imprecise.

Chomsky (1971/1965:154)

Analogy, multiplied over and over, is the process by which a grammatical
rule is formed.

Bolinger, 1968:114

The agents in JB2's evolved systems, have acquired a fixed stock of
patterns (exemplars) and use them as a basis for analogy in producing
new forms. They do not progress to the stage described by Bolinger in
actually forming general grammatical rules. The term 'exemplar' itself

implies that the agents' stored representations are illustrative rather
than generative. Variables are the explicit instruments of generalization.
The exemplars of JB2 actually contain variables, the numbers 1 and 2,
which are the arguments of predicates. However, the use which is made
of these variables is not to characterize classes of expressions, but rather
to define possible transformations of individual exemplars. The main
generative power of the emergent systems in JB2 does not reside in the
variables in the agents' grammars. The JB2 model fits very closely with
the 'instance-based' style of learning algorithm characterized by Langley
as follows:

> ... *instance-based* or *case-based* learning represents knowledge in terms of spe-
> cific cases or experiences and relies on flexible matching methods to retrieve
> these cases and apply them to new situations. One common approach simply
> finds the stored case nearest (according to some distance metric) to the current
> situation, then uses it for classification or prediction. The typical case-based
> learning method simply stores training instances in memory; generalization
> occurs at retrieval time, with the power residing in the indexing scheme, the
> similarity metric used to identify relevant cases, and the method for adapting
> cases to new situations.
>
> *Langley (1996:21)*

JB2's evolved agents end up with an average of about 340 exemplars,
of which about 35 are lexical, or 'tokens' stating the atomic meaning–
form correspondences. This means that the remaining roughly 300 exemplars are complex or phrasal, and it is clear that many such stored
phrasal exemplars are quite similar to each other. There is likely to
be, for example, a whole set of separate exemplars along the lines of
the three shown on the next page. In the classical parlance of generative grammar, a grammar which contained a set of such similar forms
is 'missing a generalization'. The obvious generalization could be captured by using variables over predicates. It is not necessarily a criticism
of the JB2 model that its agents fail to capture a generalization. What
is interesting, and more important, is that the population of agents has
converged on a set of representations **over which a generalization is
possible**. It is a notable general property of E/I models that they converge on systems over which generalization is possible, even where the
agents themselves do not represent such generalizations internally. The
third experiment of JH also involves agents who represent their emergent
language in a redundant, non-general way, but whose behavior nevertheless has converged on a system over which strong generalizations are
possible.

The intellectual background of the JB2 model is a view of language which is less Chomskyan than those of SK1, SK2 and JH, in its emphasis on exemplars, rather than generative rules. Here is not the place to discuss the empirical psycholinguistic issue of the degree to which humans store exemplars rather than rules. Certainly, the issue is not as cut-and-dried as many generativists perhaps believe.

> ... there have always been pockets within linguistics, sociolinguistics, and applied linguistics which have suggested that ready-made chunks of unanalysed language are as important as productive rules (Bolinger 1976; Coulmas 1979, 1981; VanLancker 1975; Widdowson 1984, 1990; Yorio 1980). Peters (1983) and more recently Nattinger and DeCarrico (1992) suggest that the role of ready-made chunks of language in L1 and L2 development may be underestimated.
>
> *Weinert, 1995:180*

The issue is that of the 'formulaicity' of language organization in the brain, and is closely related to the issue of holistic utterances in language evolution, discussed by Wray (1998, 2000). The issue of rules versus whole stored chunks also arises in computational parsing theory (e.g. Bod, 1998). The fact that computational models with such contrasting assumptions about generativity have succeeded in getting some degree of simple syntactic organization to evolve in a dynamical system shows (a) that both approaches (rules and stored chunks) are compatible with some of the most basic facts of language organization, and (b) that computational evolutionary models have a long way to go in complexity before they can begin to shed light on such issues.

In the model of JB1, the agents are implemented as trainable recurrent neural nets, in which configurations in the output layer are taken to be vectors representing meanings, and the input layer is used for coding successive 'phonetic' characters of utterances. One might, perhaps, argue that the rest of the apparatus, the configurations in the hidden and context layers and the weights of all the connections, can then be interpreted as neither semantic nor phonetic, and hence must be 'syntactic' in nature. This would be a spurious, even silly, argument.

Syntax in the sense defined involves **compositionality**, the principle that the meaning of a string of symbols is a function of the meanings of the constituent symbols. The evolved systems on which the models discussed here converge all exhibit compositionality. This is achieved in more or less stipulative ways. To introduce the ways in which this compositional relationship between strings and complex meanings emerges, we need first to look at the ways in which these models represent complex meanings.

10.2.4 Representation and mapping of meanings

Computers can only manipulate symbols; the human users of computer programs interpret their inputs and outputs semantically, assigning the symbols significance outside the symbolic system. The models of language evolution discussed here adopt sets of symbolic representations which are designated 'semantic' or 'meanings'. These representations are typically structured according to very simple wellformedness rules borrowed (uncritically) from such sources as classical predicate logic and various versions of generative grammar. Thus the semantic representations incorporated into the evolutionary models already have a syntax, in the sense of having different classes of terms and strict rules governing the combination and distribution of these terms.

The emergent language systems in these works all have sets of strings which can be analyzed into meaningful substrings, where the meanings of the substrings combine to yield an appropriate meaning for the whole string. To what extent do the emergent syntaxes of the stringsets on which these models converge echo the pre-specified syntaxes of the given sets of meanings? In this respect, again, the SK1, SK2 and JH models contrast as a group with the JB2 model; JB1 is similar to SK1, SK2, JH, but has some interesting characteristics deriving from its neural net implementation.

In SK1, SK2 and JH, in general, where the pre-specified meaning representations contain N classes of term (e.g. 'predicates' and 'referents'), the stringsets of the emergent languages will also contain N distributional classes of term (which one can choose to interpret as, for example, 'verbs' and 'nouns'); and the emergent mapping between semantic classes and surface syntactic classes is typically one-to-one. These models assume standard predicate–argument relations in their semantic representations.

SK1 has semantic representations such as [**ag-john, pt-mary, pr-love**], for which a handy mnemonic is the English, *John loves Mary*. Each such representation is a triple of attribute–value pairs, in which exactly one attribute (or slot) is always **pr**, suggesting 'Predicate', another is always **ag**, suggesting 'Agent', and the third is always **pt**, suggesting 'Patient'. The Predicate slot is always filled by a term drawn from one set (the set of 'actions'), and the Agent and Patient slots are always filled by terms from a second, distinct set (the set of 'objects'). Again, this model contains a semantic component into which pre-specified regular and structured representations are built. The emergent grammar groups the arbitrary syllables of the 'phonetic' level of the language into two syntactic classes, one for the syllables expressing the 'actions' and the other for the syllables expressing the 'objects'. SK2 and JH similarly converge on grammars in which the distributional classes of the 'phonetic' elements directly mirror distributional classes of terms in the semantic representations. Furthermore, in SK2 and JH, in which recursive embedding of propositions as arguments of predicates is allowed, the structures of the emergent languages all directly reflect this embedding in what can be interpreted as grammatical clause-subordination. Thus, these models converge on ways of topographically mapping semantic form in strings of 'phonetic' symbols, taking advantage of the availability of the generalizing facilities inherent in their specified grammatical formalisms. In a quite clear sense, the emergent languages in JH and SK2 simply mirror pre-specified hierarchical semantic structure.

The emergent languages in SK2 and JB2, while relating to semantic structure in quite different ways, have a feature in common, namely that they, unlike SK1 and JH, contain meaningless substrings. In SK2, for example, a language emerges from one run in which the string `stlwrkazqpfd` means *Pete knows that John loves Mary*. Glossing this string in the way familiar to linguists, one can see that only some parts of this string have any semantic interpretation.

stlw	r	k	a	z		gp	f	d
	love	Mary	John	know			Pete	

Here, the substrings `stlw`, `gp`, and `d` are not lexical items in the language, i.e. they are not interpreted as any semantic term. These substrings are simply specified as constants in the relevant grammatical rules; they are obligatory grammatical parts of phrasal or sentential structures in the emergent language, without any obvious function. To the extent that they contain such non-lexical items, the emergent syntaxes in SK2 diverge from the prespecified syntax of the semantic representations.

In JB2, there are also empty strings. An example from an emergent language in this model can be glossed as follows.

da	iwa	ke	noz	sa	pay	ke
flee	snake		bite	rat	wave	

The whole string `da iwa ke noz sa pay ke` could be translated into English as something like *A fleeing snake bit a waving rat*. The substring `ke` has no interpretation as any of the predicates in the semantic representation, and is thus contentless. `ke` is never used by itself. Its use in an exemplar is what makes a phrase containing it be interpreted correctly. Batali suggests that this `ke` might serve some function in the language as a marker of a phrasal boundary. If such suggestions can be sustained, it would be an important step toward accounting for the rise in natural languages of function words, such as determiners and complementizers (as opposed to content words like nouns, verbs and adjectives).

Another example of an empty word in JB2 is seen in a case where the emergent language has alternative word orders for the same meaning, reminding one of an active/passive alternation. A parallel quasi-English example would be *Cat dog chase* versus *Dog foo cat chase*, both meaning that the cat chased the dog, and where *foo* might be interpreted as a passive marker. One wonders whether, in a long run of JB2's model, such alternative ways of expressing the same meaning would survive, as there seems to be no reason why one form should not eventually oust the other, just as lexical synonyms tend to be eliminated.

In JB2, the structure of the emergent languages does not mirror the pre-specified semantic representations as obviously as in SK1, JH and SK2. JB2's semantic representations are 'flat' unordered sets of elementary propositions, such as

(waved x) (rat x) (fled y) (snake y) (bit x y)

The x and y are treated as variables, not constants. The structures assigned to strings expressing such meanings have two properties absent from the semantic representations, linear ordering and (binary) hierarchical structure. The imposition of linear ordering was also a feature of SK1, JH and SK2, but the emergence of semantically unmotivated binary hierarchical structure over strings is specific to JB2 and the fourth experiment in JH; I will focus on JB2. This binary structure arises from JB2's learning and production algorithms, which build in the principle that complex exemplars have binary structure, and can be plugged into each other to form new structures.

The deep binary hierarchical structures which emerge in JB2 tend to have a linguistically interesting property which Batali calls 'partitioning'. There is a tendency for all words denoting 1-place predicates with a common argument to form a continuous substring, thus beginning to resemble slightly complex noun phrases in natural languages. These phrases are often separated by a word denoting a 2-place predicate, with the result that a string of up to 8 words can sometimes easily be assigned an SVO or OVS phrasal structure. Whereas in JH, SK1 and SK2, the arguments of predicates, which semantically are individual constants, come to be expressed as one-word proper names, in JB2's semantics there are no individual constants, and so no proper names emerge. But the emergence of structures in which 1-place predicate words are grouped together suggests the beginnings of a class of phrasal structures resembling natural noun phrases. At present, JB2's emergent groupings of words lack some essential features of natural noun phrases. In particular, they do not have a distinctive head word which denotes an object, rather than a state or action, i.e. they have no clear head noun.

The actual implementation of semantic representations is not necessarily directly symbolic. In particular, the neural net representation of JB1 contrasts with the overtly symbolic representations of SK1, SK2, JH and JB2. This potentially makes for an interesting difference in the kinds of emergent language one gets from these models, as I will explain.

In JB1, the agents are implemented as neural nets whose output layers encode semantic representations as bit patterns. The output layer of each net is a set of nodes, partitioned into two subsets. Batali interprets one subset as corresponding to 1-place predicates, and the other subset as corresponding to arguments ('referents'). For illustrative purposes, Batali assigns labels such as *happy, sad, ...* to the 'predicates' and pronoun-like labels such as *me, you, ...* to the 'arguments'. Thus a particular setting of the output layer might be interpreted as the predicate-logic-like formula *HAPPY(YOU)*. Batali is careful to point out that this is merely a suggestive interpretation.

In a given setting of the output layer of one of JB1's neural net agents, exactly three of the six designated 'predicate' nodes are set to 1, with the rest set to 0. The four nodes encoding 'referent' information are each a binary digit encoding the presence or absence of some feature, such as **plural** or **inclusion of speaker**. Within each designated subset of nodes, certain combinations do not occur, but there are are no restrictions on the distribution of **1**s and **0**s between these subsets. The system thus contains a level into which controlled representations have been built. It is this severely constrained regularity in one component of the model to which the emergent patterning of the other layer of the neural net agents adapts. Essentially, JB1's evolving population of neural nets finds a set of strings (from a pre-specified vocabulary, also coded as a bit pattern in the opposite layer of a net) which maps naturally onto the semantic representations.

The production algorithm of JB1 emits one character at a time, at each step building a string that gets progressively closer to the whole intended meaning. As this meaning is distributed across a vector of 10 bits, it is possible that the first couple of characters emitted will get sufficiently close to the 'predicate' part of the whole meaning, so that the choice of the next character is more effectively directed at beginning to approach the 'argument' part of the meaning. In this case, one will get discontinuous substrings denoting predicates. And in fact, some such 'discontinuous words' do appear in the emergent language of JB1.

Without going into details, I also suggest that the production algorithm of JB1, combined with its distributed representations of meaning, is likely (a) to correlate shorter strings with more distinctive meanings, and (b) to produce a kind of sound-symbolism, in which parts of strings are correlated with classes of similar meanings.

The symbolic models, SK1, SK2, JH and JB2 have an advantage in semantic representation over the JB1 neural net model. Representing a meaning as a triple of three symbolic slots, of which two can be filled by terms from the same set enables one to represent the same entity (e.g. John) as playing either the Agent or the Patient role in a meaning. This is not possible in a neural net encoding such as JB1's. A model such as JB1's cannot 'recognize' that a configuration of 1s and 0s in one partition of its output layer is to be accorded the same 'value' as an identical configuration in another partition of the layer. If one attempted to extend the coverage of JB1 from intransitive to transitive verbs, the model could at best converge on a system in which there was one set of words allocated to Agents and another set of words allocated to Patients, with no recognition of the fact that the same entities could fulfil either role. That is, the inbuilt patterning which leads the actual JB1 model to evolve a set of Predicate words and a distinct set of Referent words would also lead a model extended to 2-place predicates to evolve a set of Agent-Referent words and a distinct set of Patient-Referent words, with nothing corresponding to any recognition of the intended co-referentiality of these words.

10.2.5 Invention and production algorithms

One focus of E/I models is the question of how language systems can arise from nothing. A child born with a fully modern language acquisition device into an environment in which no language behavior exists will not develop a full language. But creolization studies (e.g. Kegl, Senghas & Coppola, 1998; Senghas, 1997) show that children can invent new forms which go beyond any data they observe, and a complex language system can emerge in a community in a relatively short time. A degree of inventiveness must be part of the picture of the rise of language. 'Invention' here should not be construed in the same way as the modern invention, by extraordinary individuals, of complex devices which many other people cannot understand. The invention involved in E/I models is something which it is assumed all individuals are capable of, but which is typically only invoked when an individual 'needs' to express some meaning for which it has not acquired a form. Invention is treated by all E/I models as an essentially random process, constrained by the in-built assumptions. The way in which invention is modeled, in particular the degree to which the invention is guided by built-in principles of language structure, has an important effect on the speed of convergence on a generalizable, coordinated language system, and, of course, on the eventual shape of the emergent system itself.

In all the models surveyed here, the act of invention is closely linked with the act of producing an utterance. In the neural net model JB1, in fact, the processes of invention and normal utterance production cannot be separated. JB1's agents are recurrent neural nets, whose inputs are strings of characters and whose outputs encode meanings. Such feedforward networks are unidirectional — they cannot be reversed to model language production with meanings as input and strings of characters as output. Batali resorts to an ingenious way of modeling the production of utterances, by testing each character in the given alphabet[5] to see which character would move the speaker's own neural net, given its current weightings, closest to the desired meaning. As the input of any arbitrary character will always have some effect on the net, there is, in the JB1 model, no concept of a speaker simply not having a way of expressing a particular meaning. Thus, a separate mechanism of invention, as distinct from the normal production of utterances on the basis of acquired internal representations, is not postulated in JB1.

---

[5] This is only practicable because the given alphabet is so small — just 4 characters.

The element of randomness in invention in JB1 is present in the initial random settings of the connection weights of the agents. Although no clear distinction can be made in JB1 between invention and normal production, it is reasonable to interpret the utterances of agents early in a simulation, before they have been trained to any extent by observing the character-input/meaning-output pairings of other agents, as being more like the outcomes of invention, and the utterances produced later in a simulation, after a good deal of learning has happened, as being less inventive and more like the normal production of an agent guided by an acquired system.

In all the symbolic models (SK1, SK2, JH, JB2) a clear distinction is implemented between invention and normal production. The important dimension here, which has a significant effect on the emergent systems, is the relationship between invention of forms for atomic meanings and that for complex meanings. An issue arises concerning the extent to which compositionality is built into the system via the invention algorithm (inter alia), as opposed to emerging, unprogrammed, from the dynamics inherent in an E/I model. In this respect, there are several clear differences between the SK models and JH. An assumption of compositionality of meaning is clearly built into JH, whereas it is built into the SK models to a much lesser degree, and arguably not at all. I will briefly contrast SK2 and JH in this respect.

Agents, regardless of whether they have any 'linguistic' knowledge, are prompted to express meanings. A factor which affects at least the speed, and possibly the converged-upon outcomes of simulations, is the nature of the semantic units which can serve as prompting meanings. In SK1 and SK2, only whole propositions are used as prompting meanings. In SK1, there are no complex propositions, and so all prompting meanings are simple propositions of the *LOVE(JOHN,MARY)* variety. In SK2, the prompting meanings are sometimes simple, and sometimes complex propositions, as in *SAY(MARY,LOVE(JOHN,FIONA))*. In JH, by contrast, the prompting meanings may also be any proper part of a proposition, such as a single predicate or a single individual constant. (It is thus assumed that there may be acts of pure reference, with no predication, and also acts of predication with unexpressed arguments.) This has the effect that learners may be exposed to, and learn from, atomic meaning–form pairs. In the SK models, on the other hand, learners are not exposed to atomic meaning–form pairs. This makes for a difference in the ways in which the emergent language is gradually built up during a simulation. In JH, the lexical items tend to emerge early, and the forms for more complex meanings are later constructed synthetically from them. In the SK simulations, initially unanalyzable invented strings for complex meanings are only later analyzed by language inducers into substrings to which simpler meanings are assigned.

(The JH and SK models can be taken to imply quite different evolutionary routes from a single-word stage of language, like a Bickertonian protolanguage, to multi-word systems. The route implied by JH is synthetic, with the early, primitive forms bearing simple meanings and becoming the atoms of the later more complex system. The route implied by SK is analytic, with the early, primitive forms bearing complex meanings, and being subsequently broken down into smaller parts which become the atoms of the later more complex system.)

In the symbolic models, given a full grammar, an agent follows the grammar to produce a form for the prompting meaning. Given no grammar at all, the agent invents a form. Given a partial grammar, an agent produces a string for the prompting meaning that is partly generated by the grammar and partly invented. In JH, the agents invent new forms for hitherto inexpressible meanings and induce rules from observed behavior in ways which quite directly follow the given semantic structure. For example, if an agent in JH knows words for the argument term *FIONA* and the predicate term *SING*, but, as yet, no grammatical rule for combining these words, then if prompted to express the proposition *SING(FIONA)*, the agent is 'intelligent' enough to know that the required expression should contain the words for *FIONA* and *SING*; what it will not know, and therefore have to invent, is the order in which these words are to be arranged. JH's agents, then, are credited with knowing that expressions for complex meanings should be composed of parts which express the simpler components of those meanings; in a sense, compositionality is built into the model. The emergent languages, not surprisingly, have words for each semantic term, and impose a linear ordering on these terms within propositions. In SK2, as in SK1, the invention and induction algorithms are less 'intelligent' than in JH and do not obviously build in a principle of compositionality. In fact, Kirby claims that compositionality **emerges** in this model without being deliberately coded in.

In both JH and SK2, at intermediate stages in a run, utterances are produced which are partly rule-generated and partly invented. But there is a difference which may be crucial. In JH, an invented form is always a form invented to express the form for some well-defined constituent of the hierarchical semantic representation, and such a form also ends up as a proper constituent of the complex forms in the evolved language. In SK2, an invented form also corresponds to a well-defined constituent of the hierarchical semantic representation (often, especially in the early phase, the whole proposition to be expressed). But the invented strings in SK2 do not necessarily end up (though they may) as proper constituents of complex forms in the evolved language.

In SK2, the invented parts of an utterance are unstructured sequences of characters, which may later be 'made sense of' by the induction algorithm of other agents. Furthermore, in JH, the invention process can be called recursively, so that invented strings can contain invented substrings; and the relation of an invented substring to a larger invented string mirrors exactly the hierarchical structure of the semantic representation. Clearly, JH attributes to its agents more 'awareness' of the structure of semantic representations than the SK models do. This may or may not reflect a plausible assumption about human-like creatures. What is notable is that the SK models converge on stringsets which are systematically mapped onto pre-existing semantic structures without such explicit direction from the invention algorithm.

The branching structures of the emergent languages in SK1 and SK2 can differ significantly from those in JH. The branching structure of the emergent language in JH is constrained to be exactly the same as that of the pre-defined semantic representations, because the invention algorithm follows the semantic tree structures. All that the JH model does, in effect, is invent lexical forms for the semantic atoms and impose an invented linear order on them, within the pre-defined hierarchical structure. Consequently, in JH, if the semantic structure is binary branching, its emergent linguistic form will also be binary branching; if the semantic structure is three-way branching, its emergent linguistic form will also be three-way branching, and so on[6].

In SK1 and SK2, on the other hand, since the invention algorithm is not guided to invent chunks exactly corresponding to proper constituents of the hierarchical semantic structure, the emergent phrase structures are often many-ways branching (sometimes because of the inclusion of 'meaningless' elements, as discussed above). It is possible, in the SK

---

[6] All the generalizations about JH in this paragraph are subject to the reservation "except for the fourth experiment".

models, for example, to get emergent VP structures bracketing together the forms for a predicate and just one of its arguments. The branching structures defined by the emergent grammars in the SK models can be quite heterogeneous.

In JB2, the production algorithm imposes a binary branching structure on the building blocks (the exemplars) of the emergent language. All emergent complex structures over strings are, by definition, binary branching. It is this binary branching structure, rather than any structure in the semantic representations (which are flat), which guides JB2's invention procedure. In JB2, when a new string is invented, it is either a form for a whole meaning or for a proper subpart of an existing binary branching structure. The invention algorithm in JB2, then, like that in JH, also builds in to the model an assumption of compositionality.

10.2.6 Induction algorithms

Grammar-induction was implemented in strikingly different ways in these models. But all models had some features in common. The common ground exists in their treatment of new examples early in simulations at stages when agents have relatively little stored linguistic knowledge. At early stages in all models, the mode of learning was what Langley would classify as 'incremental'.

> A ... distinction holds for learning algorithms, which can either process many training instances at once, in a *nonincremental* manner, or handle them one at a time, in an *incremental* fashion.
>
> *Langley (1996:19)*

Given a newly presented meaning–form pair, as yet unanalyzable by any of the agent's rules or exemplars, all symbolic models simply store this meaning–form pair. This happens even if the meaning is quite complex, with the result that agents early in a simulation tend to have vocabularies of holistic expressions idiosyncratically linked to a random range of meanings.

For later stages in a simulation, by which time agents typically have internalized large sets of rules or exemplars, one can differentiate the models along a scale according to how much internal rearrangement of an agent's previously stored information takes place. On this scale, JH and JB2 are at one end, and the SK models are at the other. Learners in JH and JB2 respond to a presented meaning–form pair by attempting a parsing or analysis of it in terms of their existing grammars. In JH and

JB2 the minimum addition necessary to enable a grammar to analyze the given meaning–form pair is made to the grammar. In JH and JB2, the reorganization of an agent's grammar specifically in response to a given observation can result in the addition of a new piece of grammatical information, but never in the deletion of an existing rule or in any change to the substance of an existing rule; existing rules may, however, be 'demoted' in various ways, so that they become less likely to be used in later learning and production. The SK models, on the other hand, after each presentation of a meaning–form pair, firstly take in this meaning–form pair 'raw', without analysis, but then undertake an exercise of rationalization of **the whole existing grammar** (including the new example), with a view to seeking coincidental similarities between rules, and collapsing them where generalizations over them are possible. This collapsing of rules involves introducing variables where there were previously constants. SK's inducer is like an obsessively tidy librarian, who at every opportunity (e.g. after each book is returned) tries to rearrange the items in his whole storeplace in the most economical and general way. The JH and JB2 models, by contrast, take a less global approach to the maintenance of agents' grammars.

This dimension, on which SK differs from JH and JB2, is not exactly the dimension of incremental versus nonincremental learning as characterized by Langley (1996). All the models are strictly incremental, in that they process one datum at a time. In SK, strictly speaking, no revisiting of previous data actually happens, but there is substantial revisiting and reprocessing of the internal representations directly caused by the earlier data.

On another dimension, the induction mechanisms of the JH and SK models fall together, with JB2 differing. This is in the degree of generalization which an inducer does. As mentioned earlier, in the section on syntactic representation, JB2 essentially does not make generalizations, by inducing rules containing variables, but rather stores whole exemplars, which may have much in common, but are not explicitly generalized over. In JB2, the work done by a generalizing inducer is in a sense done by the production algorithm in finding the least costly way of combining stored exemplars. SK and JH induce general rules, while JB2 does not.

Although both SK and JH induce general rules, their methods are radically different. In SK, the generalization is done by a search involving comparison of all pairs of rules. In JH, the inducer can infer a new lexical rule or general constituent-ordering rule simply by exposure to a single example. JH thus implements one-exposure learning, an extreme form of generalization. In principle, this is no different from accumulating a larger set of examples with some property in common, and then making the appropriate generalization when the number of examples reaches some critical number; in JH this critical number is simply 1. A constraint on this one-exposure learning in JH was that only one new rule could be acquired from any given example.

The topics of invention and induction are linked by the question of whether agents learn from their own inventions. In SK1 and SK2, an agent learns from its own inventions/productions. In JH and JB2, this is not the case. Learning from ones own inventions speeds up the social coordination of the acquired system, as this makes a particular agent's productions more self-consistent. In JH and JB2, where agents do not learn from their own productions, successive invented forms for the same meaning are not constrained to be the same; the inventor/speaker does not listen to itself. The feature of 'self-teaching' is, at least in some models, dispensable without any effect on whether the model eventually converges. Whether self-teaching is actually dispensable in all models in not clear.

Finally, the assumed relationship between production/invention and reception/induction appears to differ in the models surveyed, along a dimension that might be glossed as 'explicit guidance by *a priori* unifying principles'. In JH and JB2, on the one hand, the algorithms for production and learning are explicitly constructed around assumed common principles defining the possible mappings between meanings and strings. The production and the reception algorithms are both informed by a knowledge of the same pre-defined possibility space of meaning–form mappings, and are both essentially, *mutatis mutandis*, searches of this space. In JH and JB2, there is a clear sense in which the response of a learner to a particular example (by acquiring some rule(s) or exemplar(s)) can retrace, in reverse, and given enough shared linguistic knowledge between speaker and hearer, a similar route to that by which the example was produced. In the SK models, on the other hand, the production/invention and induction algorithms are defined independently of each other, and emphasis is not laid on their being built around a search of the same space of meaning–form mappings.

But this difference between models is more apparent than real. In all E/I models, the workings of production/invention and reception/

induction mesh with each other. In SK, both production and induction algorithms are based on the assumption that the linguistic knowledge of a speaker is represented as a semantically augmented context free phrase structure grammar, which in fact, along with the semantic and 'phonetic' representations, does define the space of possible meaning-form mappings. It would be possible, although it is not done in the models surveyed here, to define production/invention and reception/induction in terms of different assumptions about the space of possible mappings between form and meaning. That is, sometimes a speaker might invent a form according to a type of generalization that is actually unlearnable by a hearer/learner; and conversely there might be some learnable generalizations of which examples cannot be systematically produced by any speaker. In such a case, one might expect an emergent language to fall in the intersection of the two spaces.

10.2.7 Bottlenecks

Of the models surveyed here, JB1 alone implemented a very weak semantic bottleneck (90% of meanings), and this factor probably influenced the outcome. This follows from the conflation, in JB1, of production and invention, which in turn follows from the neural net implementation. A neural net, trained or untrained, will always respond to some input by giving some output. There is no distinction, in the neural net implementation, between meanings which an agent knows how to express, and those which it doesn't know how to express. Given any meaning, the JB1 algorithm will find the best (often, rather, the least bad) form to express it. A trained net will tend often to converge on a number of distinct attractor states that is no greater than the number of meaning–form pairs presented to it in training. Thus if any meaning–form pair is omitted from training, the net will sometimes respond to the form by conflating its meaning with that of some other which it 'knows'. Applying a semantic bottleneck, that is withholding some meanings from the training schedules, can result in under-differentiation of the meaning-space. How strong a semantic bottleneck a neural net model such as JB1 can 'tolerate', while still leading to an emergent system distinguishing all possible meanings is an open question.

All the other models, with symbolic (rather than neural net) architectures and dynamics, did implement a semantic bottleneck, and this, paradoxically, was vital to their outcomes. In a model with a semantic bottleneck, an agent is always likely to be prompted to express some particular complex meaning which did not form part of its learning experience. In this situation, one of two things may happen. The agent may have generalized from the meaning–form pairs which comprised its learning experience some rule which does cover the prompting meaning, and it will then apply this general rule to produce the required form. Any such general rule will use one or more variables ranging over subparts of the complex meaning and their possible forms, and an appropriate form is produced. The other possibility is that the agent will not have acquired an appropriate general rule, and will thus resort to inventing a novel form for this particular complex meaning. Thus the omission of particular meanings from the learning experience of one agent causes in its subsequent production behavior either the invention of idiosyncratic forms for these meanings or the application of general rules to produce forms similar in shape to forms with related meanings. A general rule acquired by one agent covering N different form–meaning pairs will be N times more likely to be represented in the learning experience of some other agent learning from it than a one-off idiosyncratic form–meaning pair. Thus, models will converge on behavior conforming to general rules. This mechanism is at the heart of symbolic E/I models.

If a symbolic E/I model did not implement a semantic bottleneck (which is only possible with a finite semantic space), then no agent would ever be forced to generalize beyond its learning experience, and the aboriginal first-invented forms for each meaning would simply be re-used and relearned by each generation.

As mentioned earlier, all the models, very naturally, implemented a production bottleneck, so that, when prompted with a particular meaning, an agent acting as speaker would only ever use a subset of its possible forms for that meaning. Both JH and JB2 implement mechanisms which promote the use of commonly experienced meaning–form pairings, thus creating a positive feedback loop. JB2's mechanism is quite complex, involving searching through exemplars related to a given meaning–form pair in the agent's existing grammar, and adjusting their cost. JH's mechanism is brutally simple; acquired rules are stored in order of acquisition, and earlier stored rules are always favored in use over later acquired rules. As earlier acquired rules tend to be those more commonly used by other agents in the examples presented to the learner. Rules at the bottom of an agent's list may in fact never be used, and thus do not give rise to examples from which other agents can learn.

SK1 kept a numerical count of the examples used to induce particular rules, and given a choice in the production task between two rules, used the rule with the highest empirical justification. The obvious effect of these devices is to reduce synonymy.

A further kind of bottleneck is also, but less often, as it happens, directly implemented in the models surveyed here. In language acquisition, one should distinguish between input and intake. That is, not all the meaning–utterance pairs presented to a child as data may actually be taken in and used in language acquisition. The child's 'trigger experience' can be a subset of the primary linguistic data to which she is exposed. This could be modeled by placing a selective filter (alias bottleneck) on the language acquisition device. This could be labeled an '**intake bottleneck**'. (See Kirby (1999) for extensive discussion of the effects of intake bottlenecks on diachronic language drift.) The SK models had a kind of intake bottleneck. The SK induction algorithms simply ignored any meaning–form pair for which the agent's rules already assigned some meaning to the presented form, regardless of whether the presented meaning was the one its existing grammar assigned to the presented form. In effect, this prevents homonymy from arising in the emergent system.

Models without any kind of bottleneck produce no interesting kind of linguistic evolution. It is also clear that, in the actual transmission of human languages across generations, there are huge bottleneck effects. This is simply to reiterate the axiom that the grammar of a language is massively underdetermined by the observed data.

The size of the bottleneck is an important variable. The size of a bottleneck determines how much data a learner is exposed to during its learning period. If the bottleneck is too small, the learner is simply not given enough data from which to generalize, and no interesting syntactic system can emerge. If the size of the bottleneck is too large, the learner is given ample opportunity to internalize a set of non-general statements giving somewhat adequate coverage of the whole language as defined by the internalized grammars of the previous generation, whose behavior it has observed; in such a case, internalized general rules are slow to emerge. Where a language is in principle infinite, through recursion, no finite amount of data can exhaustively exemplify the whole language, and there is thus pressure on general syntactic rules to emerge in any case, but E/I simulations in which the bottleneck is set rather large are known to take longer to converge on syntactic systems than the experimenter has time for, running for perhaps millions of simulated generations without convergence. (The idea of the 'size' of a semantic bottleneck is in fact only applicable to 'multi-generational' models — see next subsection.)

10.2.8 Population dynamics

In the models surveyed here, the agents in the simulated populations interact in rather different ways. We can distinguish two broad types, which I will label **multi-generational** and **uni-generational**. Within these types there are also some differences between models.

JH, SK1 and SK2 are multi-generational models. In such models, agents are periodically removed from the population, and their grammars die with them. Only the effect that their behavior has on a cohort of learners lives on. When an agent dies, it is replaced with a 'newborn' agent without any internalized grammar, but only the innate capacity to induce a grammar from observed behavior. In the multi-generational models discussed here, the number of agents in the population at any given time is kept constant.

(Conceivably, simulations could permit the population size to expand and contract historically, with correspondingly varying proportions of learners and adult performers. In a period of population expansion after a period of contraction, the proportion of young people in the population increases. In more sophisticated models than these, such details might give rise to some phenomena of theoretical interest, with periods of linguistic simplification correlating with periods with a high proportion of learners in the population. See Johansson (1997) for some detailed work along these lines of thought.)

SK1 reports a simulation with a population of 10, in which the single most recently introduced individual is designated as the learner. In SK1, there is the added complication of some simulated spatial organization of the population. The individuals each occupy a location in a notional two-dimensional space, so that it is possible to identify an individual's neighbors. The learner only observes, and learns from, the behavior of two of its immediate neighbors in the population. None of the other models discussed here implemented spatial organization, and while it may have had some accelatory effect on the outcomes in SK1, spatial organization does not seem to be vital to the emergence of syntax in such models. (See Di Paolo (1999, 1998, 1997); Oliphant(1997, 1996) for other related work on the effects of spatial organization in the evolution of language.) In fact, the typical size of a population in these simulations is so small as to make spatial differentiation unrealistic. The JH model used a fixed population size of 5, including one designated learner, with no spatial organization.

The minimum population size which will allow for an essential feature of E/I models, namely the acquisition of a grammar by an agent on the basis of observation of at least one other agent, is 2. SK2 works with this minimum population size: at any one time, there is just one speaker whose behavior is being observed, and just one learner. After a certain time, the 'adult' disappears, the former learner becomes a speaker, and a new learner is introduced. There is no overlap of generations in this version of the model.

A population size of just 2, with no overlap of generations, as in SK2, may seem an overly drastic simplification. But in fact it usefully eliminates one factor from the evolutionary scene. In all the reported work, except SK2, at least part of what is going on in a simulation is the social coordination of individuals. Given an adult population of more than 1, there will be, especially at the beginning of a run, when invention of forms is still in full swing, a variety of different forms for the same meaning. Part of what happens in these simulations is simply standardization of usage between individuals. But this is not the real focus of these studies. The more interesting phenomenon is the evolutionary transition into syntax, which is not a matter of coordination among individuals, but a matter of how successive single individuals organize their mental representations of their language. A simulation with only one individual learner and one individual transmitter per generation simply avoids the work of having to get the population coordinated, as well as developing syntax.

Simulations in the multi-generational models needed to run for varying numbers of generations before interesting results emerged. A run reported in SK1 ran for 500 turnovers of the whole population of 10, i.e. for 5000 births. A simulation reported in SK2 took almost 8000 births before converging on an elegant syntax; Kirby (personal communication) tells me that other runs of the SK2 model converged much faster, sometimes in as little as 30 births. The simulations in JH typically achieved results very quickly, usually less than 100 births; this speedy convergence is due to the unrealistically great generalizing power attributed to learners and inventors in JH. In fact, the issue of 'time' to convergence is difficult, if not impossible, to interpret in any empirically enlightening way, given the high degree of idealization and simplification of human communities and minds found in all these models.

The JB1 and JB2 models are uni-generational. In such simulations, the population comprises the same set of individuals for the whole of a run. Changes take place within these agents, as they learn from the behavior of their companions, internalizing grammars. These are models of stable populations in which all individuals learn by listening to the others. As the agents acquire more and more knowledge of the community language (as the language itself simultaneously begins to form), they change. Just as a real person can be, in some sense, a different person from the one he was a few decades earlier in life (for example by having experienced more, or forgotten some of what he knew before), so these simulated agents 'become different people'. But they are not different people in the radical sense of having been 'biologically' conceived and introduced with zero knowledge into the population, as in multi-generational models.

The question arises whether uni-generational models such as JB1 and JB2 incorporate a bottleneck in the same sense as multi-generational models. With uni-generational models, one may perhaps say that the metaphor of a bottleneck is less appropriate, as representations of the language are not passed from one generation to the next via a small set of examples. But nevertheless, a kind of bottleneck effect is present, as we have defined it, because learners' internal representations are induced from limited numbers of examples of the behavior of other agents. Two further factors are characteristic of the JB1 and JB2 models; these are **decay of unused internal representations** and a **cost metric on internal representations**. These factors may contribute to the result of convergence on syntactic systems, compensating for the lack of the specific kind of bottleneck found in multi-generational models.

JB1 implements agents as neural nets. The agents 'talk to each other' and thereby train each other in the emerging community language. As this training goes on and on, the weights in the nets are constantly being readjusted in response to the most recent training data, and any residual effect of data presented earlier, to the extent that it is incompatible with later data, is superseded.

The JB2 model is implemented symbolically (not in neural nets), and there is an explicit pruning procedure by which any internalized statements that have not been used for a certain number of episodes are deleted from an agent's memory. Clearly, one could set up a uni-generational simulation with this kind of grammar decay in such a way that it was effectively a notational variant of a multi-generational model. One could, for example, partition the population into two halves, and decree that every even hundred episodes (i.e. at 200, 400, 600, ... episodes), one half of the population forgets everything it has learnt, and starts to learn anew by listening to individuals from the other half of the population; this other half of the population would similarly lose all its knowledge of the language every odd hundred episodes (at 100, 300, 500, ... episodes). Forgetting everything is like being born again. Partial forgetting, as in JB1 and JB2, is partially like being born again, and to this extent, there is some effect similar to the intergenerational bottleneck effect seen in SK1, SK2 and JH.

Pruning of rules is not exactly equivalent to killing off agents. When JB2's exemplars are pruned, it is because they are not part of the agent's active repertoire. But when an agent dies, **all** of its exemplars (or rules) are eliminated. If similar rules or exemplars are possessed by surviving members of the population, the disruption to the continuous evolution and transmission of the community's language might be negligible.

Here a provocative question arises. Would a unigenerational model with a bare minimum of one agent learning from itself, with forgetting of infrequently used rules, converge, like the models surveyed here, on a system with some incipient syntax? The experiment remains to be tried. Obviously, it would not model an actual human historico-cultural process so closely as the models surveyed here. But if it did produce an emergent system of similar interest, this would reveal a new lower bound on the conditions under which an E/I model could produce language emergence. Even such a bare model would still have the essential ingredients of an E/I model, namely the constant cycling of information through agent-internal representations and external behavior.

Postscript: John Batali (personal communication) tells me that he has conducted single-agent simulations just as described here, mostly with rapidly converging results. And Timm Euler, in a dissertation at Edinburgh University, has implemented a single-agent, 'talking-to-onself' version of SK2, with decay of little-used rules. Euler's model also produces evolutionary convergence on syntactic systems, with some interesting differences from SK2.

10.3 Methodology: What IS a language?

The workings of the models surveyed here raise a fundamental question about any model of the dynamic historical interaction between individuals' mental lexicons/grammars and their production behavior. The overt speaking behavior of any agent at many stages in a simulation will not give a faithful picture of the totality of its acquired meaning–form pairings. The expressions actually used will be a subset of those internally represented. The spirit of this research paradigm is that a language is neither just I-Language nor just E-Language, but their dynamic interaction. The conclusion truest to this spirit is that the language over any given time period (say a generation) is a pair, consisting of both the (perhaps heterogeneous) internalized lexicons/grammars of the individuals in the population and the totality of their behavior. Defining a language in this way is hardly elegant, but (a) it recognizes the essential interdependence of the two phases of language, I-Language and E-Language, and (b) it avoids an arbitrary privileging of one phase over another.

Symbolic computational modelers enjoy a luxury unavailable to empirical grammarians, in that they can directly inspect the grammars of their simulated agents[7]. For generative grammarians, the principal method of accessing speakers' grammars is by asking for their intuitions of the well-formedness of presented examples. In questioning native speakers' grammatical intuitions, typically no distinction is made between what can be called 'active wellformedness' and 'passive wellformedness'. The metatheory of generative grammar holds that a grammar is neutral with respect to production and reception. In fact, however, human speakers will often to respond to presented examples with statements such as "Well, I can understand what it means, and I suppose you would call it grammatical, but I wouldn't put it that way myself', or "It's not actually **un**grammatical, but I'd say it differently myself". Such responses indicate that a speaker's productive language behavior reflects only a subset of the meaning–form correspondences that her internalized grammar can recognize. In the simulations surveyed here, it is very common for an agent's grammar to specify some meaning–form correspondences which the agent would never actually use in production. A definition of the language system of such agents would in some sense be wrong if based solely on their production behavior; and a

---

[7] Modelers working with agents implemented as neural nets are denied this luxury.

definition based only on the form–meaning correspondences characterized by their internal grammars would miss an important difference in
the actual **realizability** of these correspondences in the agents' production behavior. The existence of a production bottleneck in the usual
life-cycle of a language obliges us to take a view of a whole dynamical language system in terms of both E-language (the productions) and
I-language (the internalized grammars).

10.4 Conclusions

Factors which facilitate the emergence of recursive, compositional syntactic systems in E/I models are:

- Pre-defined hierarchical semantic representations. These are present
  in SK1, SK2 and JH, but not in JB2, which has flat semantic structures.

- An invention (and/or production) algorithm disposed, to a greater
  or lesser extent, to construct new expressions in conformity with the
  principle of compositionality. In this respect, the invention algorithm
  of JH most strongly builds in compositionality, followed closely by the
  invention/production algorithm of JB2. The invention algorithms in
  SK1 and SK2 are least biased toward invented forms that automatically conform to the compositionality principle.

- A learning algorithm disposed, to a greater or lesser extent, to internalize rules generalizing over form–meaning mappings in a compositional way. In this respect, the learning procedures of JB2 are
  least biased to internalize such rules; JB2's agents do not internalize rules at all. JH's learning procedure, except when it is partially
  disabled, as in the third experiment of JH, is strongly biased to internalize compositional rules wherever possible. The rule-collapsing
  procedures of the SK learners are also disposed to arrive at general
  rules incorporating compositionality wherever possible.

- A strong semantic bottleneck effect, by which the information in the
  evolving system is recycled very frequently through the alternating
  phases of representation as internal rules (I-Language) and exemplification in utterances (E-Language), and learning takes place on the
  basis of examples covering a very small subset of the available semantic space. This effect is strongest in the multi-generation models,
  SK1, SK2 and JH, and least strong in JB2, a uni-generational model.

- A production bottleneck effect, by which certain rules are preferred over others in the production process. All the models discussed incorporate such a production bottleneck, based explicitly or implicitly on the frequency of examples in the learning experience, thus effectively providing a feedback loop favoring rules of greater generality.

It is tempting to imagine a 'minimal hybrid model', eclectically put together out of those components of the various models which are the least disposing to the emergence of a recursive compositional system. But it seems clear that an extreme minimal hybrid model would not yield an emergent recursive compositional syntactic language system. In particular, an opportunity (but not a compulsion) for compositional rules to arise must be present in either the invention/production algorithm (as in JB2) or in the induction algorithm (as in SK1 and SK2). Given that either the invention/production component or the induction component of a model must allow for compositional rules to arise, the availability of such rules can nevertheless be impaired or restricted, as in the third experiment of JH.

I end, then, with a bold speculation that a hybrid model stripped down to the following components would yield an emergent recursive compositional syntactic system.

- Flat semantic structures as in JB2.
- An invention algorithm with no bias toward compositional structures, as in the SK models.
- A learning algorithm, such as JH's, SK1's or SK2's, which may, but does not only, induce general rules incorporating a principle of compositionality; the disposition of such a learner to form general compositional rules could be experimentally disabled to various extents, to determine a minimum level necessary for a syntactic system to emerge.
- Uni-generational population dynamics, as in JB2, but with only a single agent, talking to, and learning from, itself, plus some experimentally varied decay and forgetting of rules, giving a weak semantic bottleneck effect.
- The feedback effect of a production bottleneck experimentally weakened by allowing various degrees of randomness in the selection of the rules by which utterances are produced.

Now there's a set of experiments crying out to be done!

Acknowledgements

This general kind of work was significantly stimulated by a workshop in computational evolutionary syntax sponsored by the Collegium Budapest Institute for Advanced Study in 1997. The particular work of this paper was substantially helped by a UK ESRC research grant, No. R000 237551. I thank Simon Kirby, John Batali, Ted Briscoe and Mike Oliphant for helpful comments, but I take sole responsibility for what is said here.

References

Andersen, H. (1973). Abductive and deductive change. *Language 40*, 765–793.

Batali, John, (1998). Computational simulations of the emergence of grammar. In James R. Hurford, Michael Studdert-Kennedy and Chris Knight (eds.), *Approaches to the Evolution of Language: Social and cognitive bases*, Cambridge University Press, Cambridge, pp. 405–426.

Bod, Rens, (1998). *Beyond Grammar: an experience-based theory of language.* University of Chicago Press, Chicago.

Bolinger, Dwight (1968). *Aspects of Language.* Harcourt, Brace and World, New York.

Bolinger, Dwight (1976). Meaning and Memory. *Forum Linguisticum 1*, 1–14.

Chomsky, Noam (1971/1965). Paper read at the Northeast Conference on the Teaching of Foreign Languages, 1965. Reprinted in J. P. B. Allen and Paul van Buren (eds.), *Chomsky: Selected Readings*, Oxford University Press, Oxford.

Clark, R., and I. Roberts (1993). A computational model of language learnability and language change. *Linguistic Inquiry 24.2*, 299–345.

Coulmas, Florian (1979). On the sociolinguistic relevance of routine formulae. *Journal of Pragmatics 3*, 239–266.

Coulmas, Florian (1981) (ed.), *Conversational Routine.* Mouton, The Hague.

Di Paolo, Ezequiel (1999). *On the Evolutionary and Behavioral Dynamics of Social Coordination: Models and Theoretical Aspects.* D. Phil Thesis, University of Sussex.

Di Paolo, Ezequiel (1997). Social coordination and spatial organization: Steps towards the evolution of communication. In Phil Husbands and Inman Harvey (eds.), *Proceedings of the 4th European Conference on Artificial Life, ECAL97.* MIT Press, Cambridge, MA.

Di Paolo, Ezequiel (1998). An investigation into the evolution of communication. *Adaptive Behavior 6.2*, 285–324.

Gibson, E., and Kenneth, Wexler (1994). Triggers. *Linguistic Inquiry 25.4*, 407–454.

Hare, M., and Jeff Elman (1995). Learning and morphological change. *Cognition 56*, 61–98.

Hurford, James R., (2000). Social transmission favours linguistic generalization. In Chris Knight, Michael Studdert-Kennedy and James R Hurford (eds.), *Approaches to the evolution of language: The emergence of phonology and syntax.* Cambridge University Press, Cambridge, pp. 324–352.

Johansson, Christer (1997). *A View from Language: Growth of language in individuals and populations*. Lund University Press.

Kegl, Judy, Anne Senghas, and M. Coppola (1998). Creation through contact: sign language emergence and sign language change in Nicaragua. In M. DeGraff (ed.), *Language Creation and Change: creolization, diachrony and development*, MIT Press, Cambridge, MA.

Kirby, Simon (1999). *Function, Selection, and Innateness: The emergence of language universals*. Oxford University Press, Oxford.

Kirby, Simon, (2000). Syntax without natural selection: How compositionality emerges from vocabulary in a population of learners. In Chris Knight, Michael Studdert-Kennedy and James R Hurford (eds.), *Approaches to the evolution of language: The emergence of phonology and syntax*. Cambridge University Press, Cambridge, pp. 303–323.

Langley, Pat (1996). *Elements of Machine Learning*. Morgan Kaufmann, San Mateo, CA.

Lightfoot, David (1999). *The Development of Language: Acquisition, change and evolution*. Blackwell, Oxford.

Nattinger, J. R. and J. S. DeCarrico (1992). *Lexical Phrases and Language Teaching*. Oxford University Press, Oxford.

Niyogi, Partha, and Robert Berwick (1997). Evolutionary consequences of language learning. *Linguistics and Philosophy 20*, 697–719.

Oliphant, M. (1997). *Formal Approaches to Innate and Learned Communication: Laying the foundation for language*. Doctoral dissertation, Department of Cognitive Science, University of California, San Diego.

Oliphant, M. (1996). The dilemma of Saussurean communication. *BioSystems 37.1-2*, 31–38.

Peters, Ann (1983). *The Units of Language Acquisition*. Cambridge University Press, Cambridge.

Senghas, Anne (1997). *Children's Contribution to the Birth of Nicaraguan Sign Language*. Ph. D dissertation, MIT.

Steels, Luc, (1996). Self-organizing vocabularies. In Chris Langton (ed.), *Proceedings of Alife V*, Nara, Japan.

Steels, Luc, (1996). A self-organizing spatial vocabulary. *Artificial Life Journal 2(3)*.

Steels, Luc, (1996). Emergent Adaptive Lexicons. In Pattie Maes (ed.), *Proceedings of the Simulation of Adaptive Behavior Conference*. MIT Press, Cambridge MA.

Steels, Luc, (1997). The Spontaneous Self-organization of an Adaptive Language. In S. Muggleton (ed.), *Machine Intelligence 15*. Oxford University Press, Oxford.

Steels, Luc, (1998). The origin of linguistic categories. Report, SONY Computational Research Laboratory, Paris.

VanLancker, D., (1975) Heterogeneity in Speech. *UCLA Working Papers in Phonetics*, 29.

Vogt, Paul (1998). The evolution of a lexicon and meaning in robotic agents through self-organization. In Han, La Poutri and Jaap van den Herik (eds.), *Proceedings of the Netherlands/Belgium Conference on Artificial Intelligence*. Amsterdam: Centrum voor Wiskunde en Informatica, 7–22.

Widdowson, Henry, (1984). Comments on the implication of interlanguage for language teaching. In A. Davies, C. Criper and A. P. R. Howatt (eds.), *Interlanguage*. Edinburgh University Press, Edinburgh.

Widdowson, Henry, (1990). *Aspects of Language Teaching*. Oxford University

Press, Oxford.

Weinert, Regina, (1995). The role of formulaic language in second language acquisition: A review. *Applied Linguistics 16.2*, 180–204.

Wray, Alison, (1998). Protolanguage as a holistic system for social interaction. *Language and Communication 18*, 47–67.

Wray, Alison, (2000). Holistic utterances in protolanguage: the link from primates to humans. To appear in Chris Knight, Michael Studdert-Kennedy and James R Hurford (eds.), *Approaches to the Evolution of Language: the emergence of phonology and syntax*. Cambridge University Press, Cambridge, 285–302.

Yorio, C. (1989). Idiomaticity as an indicator of second language proficiency. In K. Hyltenstam and L. Obler (eds.), *Bilingualism Across the Lifespan: Aspects of acquisition, maturity and loss*. Cambridge University Press, Cambridge.

Index